Library of
Davidson College

Although Parliament is the principal source of authority in the British political system, it is the Cabinet which stands at the pinnacle of government. Yet what actually happens at Cabinet meetings? How are decisions made, particularly in the arena of foreign policy? Such questions have hitherto been largely overlooked by both historians and political scientists. In this book, Dr Christopher Hill breaks new ground in presenting a detailed case-study of the British government and foreign policy.

Dr Hill takes the dramatic period from the Munich Conference of 1938 to the German invasion of the Soviet Union three years later and analyses the patterns of argument and influence within the British Cabinet. By using extensive archival material, he examines how far the strong personalities of Neville Chamberlain and Winston Churchill were really able to dominate their Cabinets in an area of policy where Prime Ministers have traditionally been supposed to exercise considerable freedom. This analysis concentrates on six decisions of key importance in committing Britain to the war which began in September 1939 but which changed so sharply in character in June 1940 with the fall of France.

This book is an original study of foreign policy-making at the highest level. It will be widely read by international relations specialists while historians will welcome the close-textured account of key episodes of this period. The study will also reinvigorate debates among political scientists on the nature of Cabinet government.

Cabinet decisions on foreign policy

LSE MONOGRAPHS IN
INTERNATIONAL STUDIES

Published for The Centre for
International Studies, London School of
Economics and Political Science

Editorial Board
Michael Leifer (*Chairman*)
Rosalind Higgins   Anthony Polonsky
Dominic Lieven   Donald Watt
James Mayall   Peter Wiles
Ian Nish   Philip Windsor

The Centre for International Studies at the London School of Economics and Political Science was established in 1967. Its aim is to promote research on a multi-disciplinary basis in the general field of international studies.

To this end the Centre offers visiting fellowships, sponsors research projects and seminars and endeavours to secure the publication of manuscripts arising out of them.

Whilst the Editorial Board accepts responsibility for recommending the inclusion of a volume in the series, the author is alone responsible for views and opinions expressed.

LSE MONOGRAPHS IN INTERNATIONAL STUDIES

CHRISTOPHER HILL
Cabinet decisions on foreign policy
The British experience October 1938–June 1941
BEATRICE LEUNG
Sino-Vatican relations: Problems in conflicting authority 1976–1986
URI BIALER
Between East and West: Israel's foreign policy orientation 1948–1956
SELIM DERINGIL
Turkish foreign policy during the Second World War
An active neutrality
INGRID DETTER DE LUPIS
The law of war
CHO OON KHONG
The politics of oil in Indonesia: Foreign company–host government relations
JOO-HONG NAM
America's commitment to South Korea
The first decade of the Nixon doctrine
B. J. C. MCKERCHER
The second Baldwin government and the United States, 1924–1929
Attitudes and diplomacy
ROBERT S. LITWAK
Detente and the Nixon doctrine
American foreign policy and the pursuit of stability, 1969–1976
PROCOPIS PAPASTRATIS
British policy towards Greece during the Second World War 1941–1944
PAUL BUTEUX
The politics of nuclear consultation in NATO 1965–1980
ROGER BUCKLEY
Occupation diplomacy
Britain, the United States and Japan 1945–1952
IAN NISH (editor)
Anglo-Japanese alienation 1919–1952
Papers of the Anglo-Japanese conference on the history of the Second World War
JAMES MAYALL and CORNELIA NAVARI (editors)
The end of the post-war era
Documents on Great-Power relations, 1968–1975
MARTIN SELIGER
The Marxist conception of ideology
A critical essay
YITZHAK SHICHOR
The Middle East in China's foreign policy, 1949–1977
KENNETH J. CALDER
Britain and the origins of the New Europe 1914–1918

For a list of titles out of print please see back of book.

Cabinet decisions on foreign policy

The British experience October 1938–June 1941

CHRISTOPHER HILL
London School of Economics and Political Science

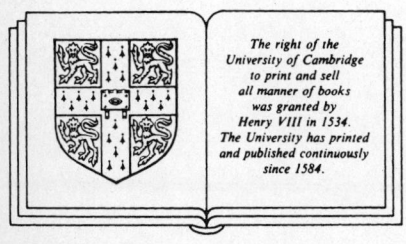

CAMBRIDGE UNIVERSITY PRESS
Cambridge
New York   Port Chester   Melbourne   Sydney

Published by the Press Syndicate of the University of Cambridge
The Pitt Building, Trumpington Street, Cambridge CB2 1RP
40 West 20th Street, New York, NY 10011–4211, USA
10 Stamford Road, Oakleigh, Melbourne 3166, Australia

© Cambridge University Press 1991

First published 1991

Printed in Great Britain at the University Press, Cambridge

British Library cataloguing in publication data
Hill, Christopher *1948–*
Cabinet decisions on foreign policy: the British
experience October 1938–June 1941 – (LSE monographs in
international studies).
1. Great Britain. Foreign relations. Policies of
government, history
I. Title II. Series
327.41

Library of Congress cataloguing in publication data
Hill, Christopher, 1948–
Cabinet decisions on foreign policy: the British experience
October 1938–June 1941 / Christopher Hill.
     p.   cm. – (LSE monographs in international studies)
Includes bibliographical references and index.
ISBN 0-521-39195-4
1. Great Britain – Foreign relations – 1936–1945. 2. Cabinet
system – Great Britain – History – 20th century. I. Title.
II. Series.
DA586.H48 1991
327.41 – dc20 90–41804 CIP

ISBN 0 521 39195 4 hardback

WD

To the memory of Peter Hill

CONTENTS

List of figures		*page* x
List of tables		xi
Acknowledgements		xiii
Preface		xvii
1	Cabinets, foreign policies and case-studies	1
2	Constructing the Polish Guarantee, 15–31 March 1939	18
3	The Soviet question, April–August 1939	48
4	Entry into war, 1–3 September 1939	85
5	Reacting to the 'peace offensive', October 1939	100
6	To continue alone? May–July 1940	146
7	The longer term: War Aims and other committees, October 1940–June 1941	188
8	Decision-making in Cabinet	224
Appendix 1	The Chamberlain Cabinet, 31 October 1938–3 September 1939	248
Appendix 2	Attendance at the Foreign Policy Committee of the Cabinet, 14 November 1938–25 August 1939	250
Appendix 3	Neville Chamberlain's statement in the House of Commons, 12 October 1939	252
Appendix 4	Lord Halifax's paper for the War Aims Committee, October 1940	256
Appendix 5	Anthony Eden's speech at the Mansion House, 29 May 1941 (extract)	258
Notes		263
Bibliography		338
Index		353

FIGURE

1 Level of ministerial and official attendance at meetings of the Foreign Policy Committee of the Cabinet, 14 November 1938–1 September 1939 *page* 74

TABLES

1. Six cases of Cabinet decisions on the issue of what kind of war to fight, October 1938–June 1941   *page* 13
2. Attendance of individual ministers at meetings of the Foreign Policy Committee of the Cabinet, 14 November 1938–25 August 1939   80
3. The War Cabinet, 3 September 1939–5 January 1940   105
4. Attendance at the War Cabinet by ministers of Cabinet rank but not full members of the War Cabinet, 1–31 October 1939   132
5. Contacts between the British government and Mr Birger Dahlerus, 3 September–31 December 1939   140
6. Membership of the War Cabinet in the Coalition Government, 11 May 1940–22 June 1941   148
7. Membership of the War Cabinet, and of the War Aims Committee, October–December 1940   198
8. Meetings of the War Aims Committee, October–December 1940   203
9. Initial membership of the Reconstruction Problems Committee of the War Cabinet, March 1941   219

ACKNOWLEDGEMENTS

In one way or another much of my life has been taken up with this book, not always intentionally. Ever since I can remember, politics in general and the onset of the Second World War in particular have been a stimulus to argument and imagination. My first coherent thoughts on the subject revolved around the puzzle of how it was that Britain became embroiled in another devastating conflict so soon after the blood-letting of 1914–1918, and on such difficult terms. This interest has broadened over the years into a concern with how foreign policy is made in liberal democracies and with the nature of the difficult trade-offs between domestic and international preoccupations.

I should like to thank the people who have helped me along the way to develop my ideas. At Merton College, Oxford, John Roberts was the most stimulating and generous of tutors, while the different demands of postgraduate work were enlivened by the Students and Fellows of Nuffield College. I benefited in particular from the shrewd advice of Keith Banting and the late Sir Norman Chester, the latter of whom also demonstrated to my great relief that political science and association football could be mutually supportive interests. I am also grateful to Lords Beloff and Bullock for their knowledge and assistance as supervisors of the D.Phil. thesis in which the argument of this book was first tried out. The Social Science Research Council, as it then was, provided the grants without which I should have had, like so many of my current students, to leave the world of reflection and study for that apparently more real world of action and money. Its successor, the Economic and Social Research Council, has recently supported me during the two terms of leave I needed from the London School of Economics and Political Science to bring the book to completion (Award number R 000 23 1444). I am very grateful to both institutions, and to those in Britain who have continued to make the case for social science research in an adverse political climate.

At the LSE, I am grateful to the one-time trustees of the Noel Buxton Fund for awarding me the Scholarship which enabled me to discover how my interests gelled with those of foreign policy analysis, which I had barely come across at Oxford. Since joining the Department of International Relations at LSE, I have been kept on the *qui vive* by both students and colleagues. In particular Geoffrey Goodwin has, from our very first meeting, been positive and sympathetic about my work, and I owe him a considerable debt of gratitude for many acts of kindness over a long period. He and the late Fred Northedge, from rather different standpoints, sharpened my understanding of the nature of foreign policy and confirmed my view that foreign policy analysis needs both theory and history. Christopher Coker, James Mayall, Nicholas Sims, Paul Taylor and Michael Yahuda have also provided advice about various aspects of the work presented here, while Mark Hoffman and Finn Laursen taught me word-processing. I am grateful to them all.

The same applies to Ian Nish and to Michael Leifer who, as successive Chairmen of the Centre for International Studies at LSE, have helped me to bring this work to publication, despite delays arising from my misguided efforts to tackle several major projects at the same time. I have also benefited from Fred Halliday's encouragement, Donald Cameron Watt's great knowledge of the inter-war years and Pamela Beshoff's immaculate research assistance. Neither William Wallace nor John Vincent have ever flagged in their interest and support. These and others too numerous to name have shown that academic expertise is not yet just another branch of paid consultancy.

Several people have provided invaluable practical assistance. Trevor Gunn has kindly helped with a translation from Swedish. Chris Holcroft and Jane Pugh of the LSE's Drawing Office provided artwork for Figure 1 and Table 2. Gus Stewart was very efficient with research grant applications, and Hilary Parker endlessly helpful with almost everything in the Department of International Relations. My copyeditor at Cambridge University Press, Maureen Street, has been calm and expert throughout.

I should also like to acknowledge the help provided by various libraries and holders of copyright. For permissions to use the private papers in their care as well as in many cases indispensable professional help, I should like to thank the University of Birmingham (in particular Dr Benedict S. Benedikz, Sub Librarian, Special Collections); the British Library of Political and Economic Science; the Syndics of the University Library, Cambridge; the Master, Fellows and Scholars of Churchill College in the University of Cambridge; the Executors of the late Sir Alexander Cadogan; Lord Caldecote; Sir John Cripps; Mrs Elizabeth Crookshank; the English-Speaking Union; Lady Evison; Lady Greenwood; the Earl of Halifax; the Marquess of Lothian; the Trustees of the National Maritime Museum; Mrs Davina Howell; and Viscount Simon. For assistance in finding and using sources I am also indebted to Dr Joseph Fewster and Mrs Christine Woodland, and to the staffs of the Bodleian Library, Oxford; the Borthwick Historical Institute, York; the Mass Observation Archive at the University of Sussex; Northallerton County Record Office; Nuffield College, Oxford; the Public Record Office; the Royal Institute of International Affairs; the Scottish Public Record Office; *The Times* newspaper; and the Library of the University of Newcastle.

Any major piece of work relies on the assistance of an unseen inner circle of family and friends. My mother, Dawn Hill, has always been the staunchest of supporters and I am deeply grateful to her. My wife, Maria McKay, has helped at every level. Her companionship has been even more important than her good historical judgement. Our children, Alice and Dominic, have encouraged me enthusiastically. All of them will understand my saying, however, that the single most important influence on this book has been my father. Peter Hill was a scholar and outstanding schoolteacher whose love of history made an impact on hundreds of pupils and friends in the Welwyn Garden City area. I had free access to his deep knowledge, his feeling for the English language, and his passionate concerns with the Second World War. It is a matter of great sadness to me that I could not finish this book before his premature death in 1988. He and I are both in this book, despite (more probably because of) the fact that we disagreed on almost every point of political argument. As a political scientist, however, I know that influence and responsibility are very different things, and the latter is mine alone.

PREFACE

Parliament is the principal source of authority in the British political system, but it is the Cabinet which stands at the pinnacle of government and focuses our attention onto the strategies and internal divisions of our leaders. Yet the Cabinet has been neglected in terms of detailed studies of what actually happens inside its institutional walls. Historians have sometimes drawn back the veil on proceedings, *en route* to other destinations, but political scientists, whose professional concern it is to dissect patterns of influence and the exercise of power, have generally preferred the eclectic overview to the close-textured case-study. In particular, foreign policy has almost always been left to one side; it is as if the Cabinet's decisions on international relations are either unimportant or uncontroversial. Yet nothing could be further from the truth, as a moment's reflection on the Hoare–Laval pact, the Suez crisis or recent arguments about the European Community makes clear. What the Cabinet does and does not do in the area of foreign policy can have dramatic consequences inside and outside the state, and it is certainly not, in a still secretive political culture, an open book.

But there is no lack of materials for those prepared to venture back beyond 1960. The archives teem with relevant sources, both in the great store of public records and the private papers of innumerable former Cabinet ministers. The evolution of policy can often be studied on a day-by-day, even an hour-by-hour, basis. This book takes this invaluable data-base as its starting-point, and analyses the behaviour of the Cabinet on key foreign policy decisions relating to war and peace during the three years following the Munich Conference at the end of September 1938. This is a period not only of irresistible fascination in itself, but also of a transition – from British primacy to the world of nascent superpowers – that placed foreign policy at the centre of political life in Britain.

Research has its own unpredictable logic, and in this case it gradually became clear that the established debate about the Cabinet, centred on the seeming competition for power between the Prime Minister and his senior colleagues, did not fit the realities of foreign policy-making. Furthermore, commonly held views about the supremacy enjoyed during these years by two strong personalities, Chamberlain and Churchill, turned out to be no more convincing. The pattern of influence was clearly more varied and complex than either of these perspectives tended to allow, while it was also apparent that the issues considered in Cabinet had their own dynamics, and could not be subordinated analytically to the problem of the location of internal power.

The main conclusion presented in what follows is that the Cabinet operated on the basis of neither prime ministerial domination nor systematic collective control. In the first instance, foreign policy (perhaps more than any other issue-area) was supervised on a daily basis by the departmental minister (in this case the Foreign Secretary) and the Prime Minister working together. This team can be termed the 'foreign policy executive'. It was subject to its own internal tensions and was imbalanced by the power of one side to hire and fire the other, but in general it represented the element of political leadership in the process of making foreign policy. The Prime Minister was not, therefore, alone inside the Cabinet.

The foreign policy executive did at times dominate on major issues as well as on the often significant discretionary issues arising from routine management. On other occasions, however, the Cabinet as a group was able to participate to surprising effect. Such variability requires explanation, and it is not enough simply to split the difference and argue that power is shared in a form of structural compromise between the Prime Minister and the Cabinet.

In fact the variability, for example between Chamberlain's steamrollering through of the Policy Guarantee and his humiliating climbdown two months later over the possibility of a Soviet alliance, was neither random nor at the mercy of exogenous factors such as personality or domestic politics. Certain key factors seem to have determined when and how far the foreign policy executive could dominate. First among these was the nature of the options facing the government. If the relevant alternatives were clear and limited in number, right from the point at which a problem rose to the level of Cabinet consideration, then the ability of non-specialist ministers to understand and become embroiled in the issue was significantly increased. Cabinet committees became vehicles for detailed investigation rather than the diversionary tactics they could sometimes fall prey to. This could be true despite prime ministerial opposition. On the other hand, if policy options were cloudy and open-ended, opportunities arose for the Prime Minister and Foreign Secretary to take the initiative and produce the new proposals, even new definitions of the problem, which the situation required. Creativity tended to be beyond the resources of the Cabinet as a group.

The clarity of the options before the Cabinet was itself partly determined by a second factor, namely the extent to which a problem disturbed the settled images of foreign policy held by ministers. Where the continuity of expectations about the events in which Britain was immersed was ruptured, as when the Maginot Line proved no barrier to the Panzer divisions in 1940, it created a vacuum – both psychological and procedural – into which the foreign policy executive was usually able to step. Conversely, where a problem fitted in well with what ministers in general had expected to occur, they were in a better position to insist, if they so wished, on the executive staying closer to the conventions of collective responsibility.

The years from Munich to the Soviet Union's entry into the war, phoney peace followed by twilight war and only then by the shattering trauma of French disintegration, inflicted regular crises on decision-makers. Panic and emotionalism sometimes held sway, as in the dramatic exchanges between Churchill and Halifax over a compromise peace as France staggered to defeat. Policy in such circumstances tended towards haste, inconsistency and disequilibrium.

Nonetheless, crisis as such did not dictate the pattern of Cabinet behaviour. In the crisis over Poland which finally brought Britain to war with Germany, ministers behaved with great collective determination in forcing their foreign policy executive to hurry on with the issuing of an ultimatum. Conversely, Churchill was able to use the relative lull after the Battle of Britain to derail his Foreign Secretary and temporarily divert the Cabinet's attention from the issue of war aims. Crisis is only part of the story.

In general, both the Cabinet and the executive in this period observed limits on power-maximising behaviour whether in or out of crisis. Indeed consensus was a major priority, particularly once disagreement had surfaced. There were no settled inner groups excluding the majority, and little by way of factionalism within the Cabinet.

This was partly because the members of the government saw themselves as a team (even in a multi-party national government), and tended to share certain basic outlooks or values. On certain key issues they would always make concessions, or at least not raise problems, so as to prevent differences from sharpening beyond a certain point.

Where real disagreement was evident, there were definite attempts to build a consensus and to reconcile divisions before action was initiated. The Cabinet had its own preventive diplomacy. The unity of the government was always a foremost consideration, as the rarity of threats of resignation suggests; the instinct for political survival, and the psychological tendency to rationalise their own actions as inevitable and/or desirable, had a bonding effect on both leaders and led inside the Cabinet. Styles of policy-making varied with the type of issue, but whatever the particular decisional unit, the outcomes always had to be capable of attracting the overall agreement of the Cabinet, even if on occasions that meant fudging or delaying decisions. To this extent the focus on competitive relations between the Prime Minister and his fellow barons is beside the point.

Essentially, this book is built on the key assumption of foreign policy analysis, that there will always be a two-way flow between process and policy; each affects the other. The theme of Cabinet government demonstrates how foreign policy decisions are subject to internal political argument, just as the pattern of influence within the Cabinet is partly shaped by the demands made by external events. At this highest level of responsibility, foreign policy-making is made up of a set of moving relationships, played out within the limits laid down by institutions, precedents, personalities and the structure of the issue of the moment. Dynamic equilibrium is the condition generally sought by the Cabinet and its members, in the sense that they seek to preserve major values in various arenas simultaneously, but the complexity of the interplay involved means that it cannot always be sustained. The compelling hold which politics can exert derives from our knowledge that human beings can both rise above and fall beneath the structures which normally contain them. When this happens at the level of the Cabinet and foreign policy, whole societies feel the effects.

1. CABINETS, FOREIGN POLICIES AND CASE-STUDIES

A great deal has been written about both the British Cabinet and British foreign policy, but hardly anyone has tried to put the two together systematically. Work on Cabinet government has alluded to foreign policy examples in passing, and Patrick Gordon Walker provided a short case-study of a foreign policy decision in his 'imaginary' accounts of discussions around the Cabinet table.[1] Historians have more often written about particular Prime Ministers and the foreign policies they pursued in conjunction with their Cabinet colleagues. The books produced in recent years on the Labour government of 1945–51 and on the second Churchill administration are cases in point.[2] But the neglect of foreign policy by British political science as much as the natural preoccupation of historians with chronology and doing justice to the wealth of archive material has meant that there is a striking gap in the literature, namely the absence of any full-length discussion of how the British Cabinet behaves in the realm of foreign policy. It is this gap which the present book, through the case-study method, seeks to fill.

The approach is cross-disciplinary, dealing with the three closely related academic areas of political science, International Relations (the capital letters are to distinguish this from real-world international relations) and international history. There is an inevitable risk of falling between stools when attempting to straddle three well-established specialisms, each with its voluminous literature, but it is a risk well worth taking. If a real contribution is to be made to our understanding of top-level foreign policy-making in Britain, there is no escaping the need to draw on the work already done on the Cabinet from the viewpoints of constitutional theory and domestic policy, on foreign policy decisions from the International Relations perspective of decision-making theory and the character of international system and on the peculiarities of context explained by experts in a particular period. It is worth saying a little more about the three levels of analysis.

In the area of political science (or what is often called in the United Kingdom 'the study of government'[3]), it has been assumed for many years that the Cabinet and its anthropology is a suitable, indeed crucial subject for research, given its standing at the apex of the political system. Although in recent decades a degree of scepticism has grown up among some scholars about the worth of investigating superstructural phenomena like institutions, leading to the belief that the Cabinet should be accorded rather less importance than the political and social systems which condition its membership and constrain its choices,[4] there is undoubtedly a well-established tradition – reflected in higher education courses throughout the country – of writing about the powers and interactions of the ministers of the Crown inside that citadel known as the Cabinet.

This writing has covered the last 150 years of British history, and encompassed the whole range of government business. Part of the work has concentrated on the history of the constitutional and administrative problems of the Cabinet and its associated bodies.[5] Much of the controversy in the field, however, has been engendered by a dispute over the degree to which the twentieth-century Cabinet has become one of Bagehot's 'dignified' institutions, its authority supplanted by 'Prime Ministerial' government.[6] Protagonists have sought to identify the basic pattern of central policy-making.

Broadly speaking, although those involved have often been more subtle than they have been given credit for, the debate has mainly been conducted in terms of the techniques by which Prime Minister or Cabinet may respectively monopolise the finite powers at stake, and the sanctions which each may exert to protect their own position. Analysis has thus been based on the shared assumptions that it is possible to discover the general locus or tendency of 'power' and that, to some extent at least, all actors compete between themselves over participation in policy-making – most ministers through their collective role in Cabinet and the Prime Minister by either by-passing or dominating the Cabinet.[7] Academic work in this field has tended to conceive of the powers of Prime Minister and Cabinet as subject to a zero-sum game between separate entities, and has concentrated on trying to mark out the boundaries between them.

There are, despite the thousands of pages generated on the Cabinet since Bagehot, certain *lacunae* in the literature. Of these one is clearly foreign policy,[8] but another important need is for detailed case-study treatment of *any* area of policy. The generalising instincts of political scientists, whether of traditional, behaviouralist or structuralist inclinations, has led them to range widely over the history of British government without stopping long enough to use the available public records on Cabinet discussions for a close-textured analysis. Where writers have focused on the Cabinet in particular periods, it has usually been through the device of the political biography, which has produced some interesting but also inherently incomplete versions of life in Cabinet.[9] A detailed study of how the Cabinet made foreign policy decisions should, therefore, go some way towards adding two extra elements to the study of Cabinet government.

In the area of International Relations, the pertinent sub-field is foreign policy analysis, which deals with the actions and motivations of the actors in the international system, principally states. Over the last thirty years this subject has developed to the position where it is now an orthodox, indeed major, component in most university degrees in International Relations, and it has spawned much comparative and theoretical research. By definition a large proportion of this work has been on the conduct of foreign policy by such elite institutions as the American National Security Council and the Soviet Politburo. There have been various excellent case-studies produced, in the accessible form denoted 'structured empiricism' by Michael Brecher,[10] such as those by Graham Allison on the Cuban Missile-Crisis and by Karen Dawisha on the Soviet invasion of Czechoslovakia.[11] The subject is like its sibling 'policy analysis' in political science in that it tends to question the truth of accounts of policy-making which focus only on institutions and the relative powers of formal office-holders. Its working assumption is that decisions are subject to far more complex processes than constitutional theory and institutional description generally allow.

Although a 'British school' of foreign policy analysis has developed strongly in recent years, and more attention has been focused on specifically British foreign policy after a hiatus since 1974,[12] there have been no structured case-studies and surprisingly little work on the foreign policy-making process in Britain. In the 1960s the growth of American foreign policy analysis led to the first introductory surveys of British foreign policy-making, culminating in what is still the standard book on the subject, by William Wallace.[13] As for the

Cabinet and foreign policy, treatment has been extremely patchy. Donald Bishop has written briefly about the pressures of maintaining Cabinet cohesion in the face of modern foreign policy developments, and a group of scholars at Reading University have produced a useful survey of relations between post-war Prime Ministers and Foreign Secretaries, but other references have only been made in passing.[14] Moreover the terms of reference of the discussion of Cabinet government in the context of foreign policy have been largely carried over from the mainstream debate; that is to say, they are still preoccupied with the administrative functions of the Cabinet and the institutional location of power within it. What has not been done is to apply some of the interesting work done in the areas of political psychology and group dynamics to the analysis of top-level policy formulation in Britain, as writers such as May and Janis have done for the United States.[15]

An equally striking omission (with one notable exception[16]) is the fertile area of crisis studies. This is the section of foreign policy analysis which has produced the biggest and probably the best co-ordinated research effort, under the leadership of Michael Brecher.[17] Apart, however, from observations in the comparative surveys of such writers as Bell, Williams and Lebow,[18] this literature has hardly been picked up by those writing about British foreign policy, let alone about the institution of the Cabinet. Although it is not a primary aim of the current study to test the hypotheses of the crisis and political psychology areas of foreign policy analysis, an awareness of their preoccupations has informed the research on which it is based and has, as will become clear, shaped some of its conclusions. The basic intention is to create a dialogue between the discussion of policy-making from a traditional institutional perspective and that from the post-behaviouralist angle of foreign policy analysis.[19] Some of the central questions at stake will be set out towards the end of this chapter.

The third level of analysis is the historical or, to be more exact, the international-historical, since there is now a flourishing sub-discipline in existence known as international history, which has superseded the old specialism of diplomatic history by paying far more attention to the non-governmental forces which cross boundaries and in many respects shape the crucial domestic environment of foreign policy.[20] But historians of all kinds are defined by their interests in periods, and that chosen here is one of the most magnetic of all, the years from the Munich Conference in September 1938 to the German invasion of the USSR on 22 June 1941. These thirty-three months have been chosen out of personal interest as well as for their intrinsic importance, but they also provide excellent material for a case-study of the foreign policy operations of the Cabinet.

The need for a case-study approach as such seemed evident from the deficiencies of the existing literature. Whether traditionalist or behaviouralist, comparative works on foreign policy devoted too little space to the Cabinet, while studies of the Cabinet barely touched upon foreign policy. Moreover, in Jim Bulpitt's words, 'British political science . . . has always professed an interest in the general subject of government, but it has been markedly reluctant to develop any enthusiasm for the study of particular governments. That task has usually been hived off to historians or memoir-mongers'.[21] Equally, when detailed studies of particular governments or individuals have emerged, they have tended to concentrate on domestic policy, and/or to neglect the interplay of Cabinet ministers in the particular dynamic context of a Cabinet meeting regularly over a period of months and years. Only by examining in sequence the events of a limited period can we get to grips with theories about the existence or otherwise of settled patterns of influence within a group like the Cabinet, which is at once both an intimate, continuous, club and an ever-changing forum for the meeting of diverse interests and ideas. This is particularly true for Britain, where a close observation of internal governmental behaviour is possible through access to the immense public archive of the Public Record Office. Cabinet minutes and memoranda, which have been put to extensive use already by modern historians, are crying out for exploitation by political scientists interested in the interaction between process and policy, and in the testing of their theories about the sources of power, influence and change.

There are, of course, contrary arguments about the value of case-studies, from those who believe on the one side that the case-approach does little more than dress up history, without transcending the limits of all phenotypical work, in producing non-commensurable results, and on the other that cases inevitably miss the deeper, more impersonal forces of long duration which shape choice without always being revealed at the point of surface decision.[22] In some ways this debate is akin to that between the elitists and the pluralists which enlivened much of the world of political science in the 1960s and 1970s.[23] For reasons already stated, however, there is little choice but to follow the case-study path if one wishes to advance the study of the British Cabinet beyond the illumination of a limited historical period (important as that is), but lacks faith in the ability of broad surveys to generate further insights than the field of Cabinet studies have already produced. The present enterprise is, therefore, a case-study in the sense that it focuses closely on a period of just under three years, but its mode of discussion is constantly geared to the preoccupations of those who think analytically and theoretically about the nature of the foreign policy process *per se*. It should at least be possible to conduct the investigation in such a way as to make comparisons possible, even if an end-result of substantial generalisation cannot be guaranteed.

If a case-study is desirable, however, the reasons for the suitability of this particular period still need detailing. At one level it is enough to argue that the origins of the Second World War, and Britain's part in it, remain one of the great issues of our times and of the academic subject of International Relations (one of whose classical texts, incidentally, was sparked by its onset[24]). Yet a huge literature now exists on this subject, and a historical debate has grown to maturity.[25] What is the justification for extending it?

One reason is the very richness of the historical literature, which enables a political scientist to be more confident in basing analysis on secondary sources than would have been possible twenty years ago, when the public records had only just become available and political controversy over appeasement was still the order of the day. While there is still no substitute for direct work in the primary sources, it is possible to plot something approaching a professional consensus on many issues among those who have devoted their careers to studying the late 1930s or early 1940s, and this makes the task of the would-be discipline-crosser somewhat more manageable.

A second reason for choosing the years from Munich to Barbarossa is that these dates encompass a period of some considerable unity. It is now a truism that the Second World War only became truly global in 1941, when the USSR, the United States and Japan entered the conflict. This is not to downplay the sombre significance of the Franco-British declarations of war on 3 September 1939, or to overlook the shattering impact of the fall of France in 1940. But the first twenty-one months of the conflict, and particularly those of the 'Phoney War', have at least as much in common with the European crisis of 1938–9, as with what followed.[26] The pattern of tension punctuated by German *putsche* characterises nearly every year from 1935 onwards, if with increasing severity. On the other hand Munich was clearly the apogee of the attempt to accommodate rather than resist Hitler's demands, and the prospects for a lasting peace receded soon afterwards. There are therefore quite natural breaks at both ends of our period. In any case, the controversies over Munich and the Second Front, which lie respectively just beyond each terminal date, are large subjects in their own right and would require more than passing attention if included here.

Thirdly, the coming together of war and peace in such a close conjunction – an intermittent war of peace, to paraphrase Alistair Horne's subsequent description of the Algerian conflict[27] – provides us with interesting opportunities for comparisons. Does decision-making alter significantly under conditions of war, or is crisis the most significant variable, in both war and peace? What difference did the institution of the War Cabinet make to relations between the Prime Minister and his colleagues, both inside and outside that small body? Does foreign policy itself become attenuated in conditions of war? Or does Churchill's view apply, following Clausewitz, that 'It is not possible in a major war to divide military from political affairs. At the summit they are one . . . the word "politics" has been confused, and even tarnished, by its association with party politics'?[28] What pattern of leadership in the Cabinet on external policy matters can be found before and after war is declared? Is it justifiable to talk of a 'foreign policy executive' within the Cabinet, as the team of Prime Minister and Foreign Secretary might be termed? Does the pre-eminence of military events in wartime diminish the role of the Foreign Secretary, or is personality a crucial factor?

Certainly what happens at the highest level of the government of Britain, in terms of the making of foreign policy, matters to the ordinary citizens of the country, whose lives are ultimately at stake. At no time was this more evident than in 1938–41, when the agonies of the Great War were fresh in the mind, and a new age of democratic activism on foreign policy issues had produced constraints of which politicians were only too aware.[29] This is why the decisions about whether or not to fight, and afterwards to what ends and for how long, were so agonising for Chamberlain and his colleagues. They were sobered by an awareness of the consequences of what they were doing in domestic as well as foreign terms, in contrast to many of their predecessors, and the moral claims of each realm could not, in the end, have been more sharply posed.[30] Moreover this was just as true for the first year of the war, when the impact of Chamberlain and Halifax was still to be felt, as it was for 1938 and 1939.

This brings us to the fourth reason for choosing 1938–41, namely that these years are not in fact as unrepresentative of modern British history as they might seem. To the criticism that the years 1938–41 are not 'typical', and that we should be better served by studying more routine decisions, the rejoinder is clear: these were *crucial* times, but in important respects not unique. Crises happen frequently enough (and often when least expected) to warn us that we need to understand them and be prepared for the time when – if in different forms – their stresses recur. The handling of foreign policy at Cabinet level needs more exposure and dissection for the benefit of both practitioners and society at large.

What period, indeed, is to be regarded as 'typical' of British foreign policy in the twentieth century? Britain's recent history has been that of a major power directly involved in the ordering and re-ordering of international relations. The onset of the Second World War, although clearly unique in what it unleashed, did not make wholly unfamiliar demands of British politicians, who even today are used to international affairs coming to dominate their agenda. It is true that Hitler was an unmanageable phenomenon for almost all his contemporaries, but Chamberlain and his colleagues were not otherwise ill at ease at having to spend so much time on foreign policy and the settlement of Europe's problems. After the withdrawal of the United States from 1919 onward Britain had remained the main supervisor of world affairs, if with steadily waning power. If the Polish crisis of 1939 had not resulted in war it would soon have joined the canon of those events in British history which are seen as important but not climacteric, such as Schleswig-Holstein, Fashoda, Chanak, Manchuria and (after 1945) Suez, Rhodesia and the Falklands. The few years after Munich are untypical of British foreign policy in that not all crises lead to world wars,[31] but they posed similar dilemmas about the boundaries of Britain's vital interests and the interpretation of leaders' motives to those present in many of the other difficult periods studding Britain's twentieth-century experience.

The last reason why it is worth focusing on Britain's entry into the Second World War is because there has not yet been much systematic analysis of the decision-making process in that period. Although we have long since left the 'guilty men' era of highly coloured judgemental history, and professional use of the public archives has revised many aspects of our thinking about appeasement, the dominant approach to causation and explanation has remained that of chronology.[32] This has meant that we now have a very good idea of how thinking changed over time on the content of policy, and why and how the war came when it did. We also have the benefit of a considerable range of historical studies of particular elements in the evolving story of appeasement. Moving beyond the tradition of writing about bilateral relations,[33] studies have appeared of the impact of the Dominions and the United States on British policy and, institutionally, on that of the Treasury, the military, the Intelligence services and the press.[34] These are indispensable, and of course often highly analytical. Yet they almost all operate from within the distinctive historical paradigm of being fundamentally concerned with the linear movement of events over time. Only Peden and Wark show much interest in the political scientists' preoccupations with the functioning of institutions and systems on the one hand and the relevance of theory on the other. The sheer weight of work to be done on the archives of the period has imposed strict priorities, quite apart from methodological preferences and convictions. Reflections on the *nature* of civil–military relations or the good use of intelligence, for example, have only occurred in passing. Even Donald Cameron Watt, who was one of the first historians to see the potential common ground with decision-making theory which has subsequently attracted figures such as Samuel Williamson and Ernest May in the United States, has not been tempted down the paths of abstraction or generalisation.[35] In general the fertile continental tradition of placing history and theory in close proximity has not infected the sceptical brand of empiricism dominant in Britain.[36]

What is perhaps more surprising than the fact that the historians have stuck to their last is how little interest political scientists have shown in mining the vast source-material now available for the years before 1960 and exploiting the more settled perspective offered by hindsight. The siren song of contemporary politics almost always proves irresistible. This is particularly true with respect to the higher estates. Although the political parties have been well-served, Parliament, the Cabinet and most great offices of state have not received the in-depth case-studies they deserve – the Foreign Office, for example, still awaits the kind of specialised monographs that have appeared in the context of nineteenth-century history. J. M. Lee's account of 'the Churchill coalition' is in this respect something of a pioneer, but it has to cover a lot of ground in a short span.[37]

Beyond the discussion of institutions, moreover, there is a need for a more direct discussion of causation than has yet occurred. Always implicit, but no more than that, in the historical accounts is the dichotomy between the two fundamentally opposed theories of political choice: voluntarism and determinism. Few people subscribe fully – or even consciously – to either of these positions, but they act as useful yardsticks of belief. The voluntarist position sees decisions as the product of free minds applying themselves rationally to the problems confronting them, and therefore tends to concentrate on rehearsing the arguments used by those involved in making the policies in question. Different conclusions may be reached, but the main focus is still on the intellectual dimension, rather than on the organisational, psychological or historical contexts in which decisions were made. Politicians are to be regarded as fundamentally in control of their own actions. In the case of 1938–9 this leads to an analysis of the reasons which the Chamberlain government had for acting as they did, and whether they were justified.

The alternative, determinist, view holds that foreign (or any other) policies are essentially the outcrops of deeply rooted interests, circumstances or patterns. The important factors to analyse from the viewpoint of explaining international relations are those of basic structure – whether this be human nature, civilisation type, the domestic regime, balances of power or the character of economic relationships. Calvinists, Marxists, anti-Communists and neo-Malthusians may all take this line.[38] In the case of our period British policy may be ascribed, along such lines, to the compelling constraints of insufficient resources or of domestic pacificism.[39]

Both voluntarists and determinists regard the ways in which decisions are made as having only a marginal impact on the ebb and flow of history. More profound reasons are sought to explain great events, although voluntarists often find room for 'chance'. Any position between these two extremes, however, must accept to some degree that how men and women deliberate about their actions, whom they consult and whom they do not, what prejudices they display and how thoroughly they examine their information will affect what they do. Decisions are not merely the superstructural product of ratiocination or impersonal forces; they are part of a complex process of causation in which change results from interaction between many different actors, inside organisational and intellectual settings that are continually reinterpreted with the passage of time.[40] At the level of states operating within international relations, action is the result of individuals, organisations and groups competing for influence within a distinctive political culture, whose institutions and procedures may be decisive for the future course of events.

A decision-making approach, therefore, whether on a comparative basis or to a particular historical set of events, should enable us to weigh the roles of different factors against each other, and to use counterfactual analysis to consider more directly the contribution of particular variables – that is to say, would events have differed greatly if Sir Robert Vansittart had continued as Permanent Under-Secretary at the Foreign Office instead of Sir Alexander Cadogan or, more pertinently for us, if Halifax had accepted the offer of the premiership on 10 May 1940? Such speculative questions may seem lacking in rigour, but in fact it is a delusion to believe that the 'why' questions are ever answered without reference to 'what if' suppositions, and it is essential to address them explicitly.[41] It is certainly not fanciful to suggest that the balance between the decisions actually taken and other possibilities was a fine one, in (say) late March 1939 or June 1940. Some might also suggest that a more positive British attitude towards the negotiations with Moscow in the spring and summer of 1939 might have averted the Nazi-Soviet Pact, or that France would not have taken much encouraging from Britain to have reneged on Poland in September.[42] Even where historians eschew an explicitly counter-factual methodology, they do not necessarily shrink from value-judgements on particular questions of this kind, and these contain within them implicit speculations about alternative possibilities.

Ultimately, direct attention to the decision-making level of analysis also makes progress possible on one of the key questions of the study of politics, that of responsibility. Because of the moral undertones of all history, and our urge to empathise with figures from the past, we are naturally concerned with who precisely was responsible for what, and whether there were alternative actions available which might have had 'better' consequences. This is so even if we restrict ourselves to the premises of those acting at the time, and exclude our own preferences. It applies equally to the condition of slaves in the young United States, the revolution which overthrew the Tsar in 1917 and responses to the rise to power of Hitler.

In the case of the British Cabinet we come directly to the issue, for the Cabinet operates on the basis of the doctrine of collective responsibility. In the sphere of foreign policy, this means that the members of the Cabinet were all answerable for foreign policies conducted overtly by the Prime Minister and Foreign Secretary. This tells us about subsequent pressures for solidarity, but does not say very much about policy-formation. Were the Cabinet led willy-nilly through the intricacies of diplomacy by the forceful character of Chamberlain, ultimately being willing to defer to his judgement and intellect? Or were they a group of like-minded men, responding collectively to the painful dilemmas imposed by Hitler's revisionism? What divisions existed within this body of senior politicians? Were Foreign Secretary and Prime Minister fundamentally at one? The history of the varying relationships between the two office-holders means that consensus cannot be taken for granted.[43]

The answers to these questions will go a good way towards telling us who, among the elected representatives constitutionally responsible to the British people for protecting their security, actually exerted most influence over the crucial decisions of 1938–41, and whether either the constitutional theory of collective responsibility or the popular picture of Chamberlain's dominance over his Cabinet is accurate.

Beneath the whole attempt of decision-making analysis to build on historical work while asking different questions is an assumption that some historians, but perhaps not many scholars in other areas of International Relations, would instinctively share: that is, the belief that the nature and practice of decision-making procedures may themselves significantly affect the outcome of events. At the simplest level this is just the truism that an inefficient secretariat or intelligence service makes realistic decisions difficult. Less obviously, it points towards the distortion of rational policy-making that can result from such phenomena as intra-bureaucratic competition or cognitive dissonance, and from the very nature of choice and decision itself.[44]

Working from such a starting-point, the aim here is twofold: first, to use the case-study to illuminate the practice of Cabinet government on foreign policy, and thereby to further our knowledge of top-

Table 1. *Six cases of Cabinet decisions on the issue of what kind of war to fight, October 1938–June 1941*

1 The Polish Guarantee, March 1939
2 The prospect of a Soviet alliance, April–August 1939
3 Entry into war, 1–3 September 1939
4 Hitler's 'peace offensive', October 1939
5 The crisis over fighting on alone, May–June 1940
6 Thinking about long-term war aims, August 1940–June 1941.

level group dynamics; second, to contribute to our understanding of an important period in recent British history, partly by a closer and more textual examination of Cabinet discussions than has yet taken place, despite existing treatments in print, and partly by the mining of new material in certain sections of the book.

The particular format employed involves, within the case-study of the years 1938–41, the analysis in detail of six mini-cases (see Table 1). The six share two important common features. First they are all examples of important decisions which had ultimately to be decided at the highest political level, and would therefore ultimately have to come to the Cabinet in some form. They were not decisions to be taken by permanent officials within the confines of a policy already laid down, or even decisions of the type where officials might feel free to use their discretion and to make new policy on the run. Secondly, they all deal with a unifying problem, that of how to cope with the central issue of war and peace, whether in the guise of the prospect of war and when to initiate it, or the reality of war and on what terms to prolong or conclude it. The phrase 'war aims' can usually be used as a shorthand for both. The interplay between the two themes, of Cabinet government and of war aims, is intended to serve each, so that the discussion of policy-making does not take place in a vacuum, while that of policy content is informed by an analysis of the impact of process.

The six mini-cases vary within their commonality, partly through the nature of changing events, and partly by deliberate choice on the part of the author so that Cabinet behaviour can be examined in a range of different conditions within those generally imposed by the stresses of imminent or actual war. The Polish Guarantee represents a situation where a new foreign policy, even a revolutionary change was initiated within the relatively short period of two weeks. The crisis of the summer of 1940 is similar, in that it was reactive to unexpected and unwelcome events, but unique in the severity of the challenge it posed to the entire government of Britain. By contrast the debate over a Soviet alliance was perceived as being a process which would necessarily take up months rather than days, and would not always rank first on the policy agenda. Indeed its importance dawned only gradually on ministers. The September crisis and the response to Hitler's peace offer of 6 October 1939 both raised problems for the Cabinet of short-term implementation more than initiation, although both had the potential for divisions and the latter imposed the necessity of thinking about the future in the sense of the criteria to be used in judging when the war should end. The last short case deals with this same issue in a much longer time-frame, the year between losing France and gaining the Soviet Union. The war aims debate was also the result of internally generated needs as much as external stimuli.

Between them, these six cases should give us a fairly full picture of how the Cabinet handled foreign policy issues, even allowing for the fact that this soon became a period of maximum danger. In some ways the functioning of an institution, like a machine, becomes clearer when it is tested most strenuously. However it would be foolish to claim that generalisations can be based firmly on a single case, and that other circumstances would not produce different patterns of action. More realistically, the suggestion is simply that our understanding of how the Cabinet and perhaps top-level decision-making groups in other states handle foreign policy will be furthered by looking in depth, and systematically, at a period for which detailed archives are available and a period, furthermore, when the fundamental issues at stake in external relations were more starkly apparent than at almost any other time. The wartime cases will be treated at slightly greater length as they are covered rather less well in the existing historical literature than those from the last year of peace.

It is also important to stress briefly what this study is *not* attempting to do, so that it can be judged by its actual objectives rather than those which might easily be attributed in error to a cross-disciplinary venture. It is not attempting to provide a full explanation of why British foreign policy followed the course that it did, or even a full picture of the British foreign policy process at the time. To do this would be redundant in the first case and a massive undertaking in the second.[45] Thus the relations between officials and politicians are only studied as they directly touch on the deliberations in Cabinet; there is no attempt made to follow a policy through from source to completion and thus to provide a picture of where ideas come from or the extent to which politicians are in the hands of the permanent civil service. These are related but analytically separate questions. The focus is rather on the variable of the Cabinet, meaning the nature of the debates and struggles which take place *once an issue comes to Cabinet attention*, and how it feeds back into the direction of policy. That means to an extent taking as given the stages of policy formulation which may have already taken place. Naturally it is important to use the archives of the Foreign Office, of the Chiefs of Staff and so on to learn more about the nature of the arguments taking place in Cabinet, and in particular about the activities of what has been termed here 'the foreign policy executive', consisting of the team of Prime Minister and Foreign Secretary.[46] But the process is necessarily top-down, rather than (as Foreign Office minutes were written) bottom-up, starting from the desk officer's first thoughts and ending with the decision whether or not to bother ministers with the matter.

Nor is this a study of the process of diplomacy between states, on either a bilateral or multilateral basis. Thus although at times it has proved important to look at published French, German and American sources, the requirements of space and of intellectual control mean that the delights and complexities of, say, Anglo-Soviet discussions during 1939 or Anglo-American conversations about the future during 1940–1 have largely been left to other scholars – who have in many cases already provided reliable monographs on which the foreign policy analyst can lean. At the same time, there is a recognition that the Cabinet discussions cannot be treated *in vacuo*, as if they were purely the product of internal British politics. As in most things, it is a matter of balance, here between doing justice to the dynamics of Cabinet politics and retaining a sense of the wider context in which that politics took place. The aim is to relate the decisions under scrutiny to the outside forces of press, public opinion and Parliament at home, and allies, neutrals and antagonists abroad, but without losing sight of the central thrust of the investigation.

The principle of parsimony does not mean that primary sources are neglected. The study makes full use of the Cabinet records, and indeed would be infeasible without them. As indicated above, other classes of official documents, such as Foreign Office minutes and correspondence, material from the wartime Ministry of Information and the minutes and papers of the Chiefs of Staff meetings, have been used selectively but still extensively. As important as the Cabinet Conclusions themselves have been the records in CAB 21 of the Cabinet Office and in PREM of the Prime Minister's office. Away from Kew, the now-numerous collections of private papers available for the period have also been consulted at length, in order to provide a depth of scholarship on the Cabinet and its individual members. On the other hand memoirs have been treated with extreme caution, on the assumption that the frailties of even the best human memories are compounded by considerations of vanity, rationalisation and profit, when it comes to remembering the past in print. However *bona fide* contemporary diaries, left in their original condition despite the temptations of hindsight, have proved invaluable.

This brings us finally to the particular issues addressed in the case-studies that follow. Although the methodology is not so structured as to pose definite hypotheses which are then 'tested' (because of doubts about the scientific approach that implies, and a desire not to cramp detail and subtlety into a skimpy straitjacket), the general concerns deriving from the three different academic disciplines outlined above do translate into specific questions, of three separate types.

First, in terms of the concern, deriving from political science, with Cabinet government and foreign policy:

- Were the Cabinets of this period dominated by their Prime Ministers, or did they approximate more to a process of genuine collective decision-making? To adapt Robert Dahl, who governed, in Cabinet?
- What special problems did foreign policy pose for the Cabinet as a whole?

Secondly, in terms of foreign policy analysis and International Relations literature:

- What does the activity of the British Cabinet tell us about the relationship between democracy and foreign policy? Did the principles of liberal democracy restrict prime ministerial leader-

ship, or did the demands of international diplomacy tend to override questions of democratic responsibility, whether applying to relations within the Cabinet or between the Cabinet and the broader political system?
– Building on the work of Janis and Allison, what were the characteristics of the Cabinet as a decision-making *group*? Did they display the symptoms of 'groupthink', or did they tend to be more riven by differences of personality, belief and departmental interest?
– How do the various crises endured by the British government in this period fit in with the findings of the other crisis case-studies now proliferating? In particular, did Cabinet unity increase or decrease, and was performance (insofar as the quality of decisions is susceptible to objective analysis) enhanced or degraded, according to the stress crisis imposes?

Last, in terms of international history:

– Were the Chamberlain and Churchill governments able to pursue consistent policies on the crucial foreign policy decisions which faced them, or did internal divisions lead to uncertainty and erratic behaviour? How as a group did they interpret and reinterpret the balance to be struck between peace and the other fundamental values, such as security, honour and prestige, for which they stood? How far were they collectively willing to think through the long-term implications of the decisions for war or peace which they were continually called upon to make, and how far overwhelmed by the pressures of the moment?

This is a large menu to cope with, even if the various courses are designed to complement each other. But the operations of the Cabinet and the dilemmas of British foreign policy are each fascinating themes in their own right, and together they represent a subject which is of importance not only to both academic and politician, but ultimately and most significantly to the citizen as well.

2. CONSTRUCTING THE POLISH GUARANTEE, 15–31 MARCH 1939

The first of our case-studies concerns reactions in the British government to the destruction of Czechoslovakia on 15 March 1939, an event which was a new departure for Hitler in that it went beyond his concerns with German national self-determination and laid bare a wider preoccupation with the strategic dominance of central Europe. It can also be seen as a turning-point in British foreign policy, in terms of both stripping the scales from Chamberlain's eyes and producing the obligation – in the shape of the Guarantee to Poland – which not only was to determine British involvement in the Second World War, but also ushered in that period of firm continental commitments which survives today, and which contrasts so sharply with the preceding centuries of British policy towards Europe.

The interpretation of the events of March 1939 is of course a matter of sharper historical controversy than this brief summary suggests. One school of thought tends to emphasise the elements of continuity between the new, pro-Polish, policy and previous British attempts, particularly after Munich, to pursue a policy of containment of Germany by trying to build up the economic and political strength of the small states to the east.[1] The other principal approach stresses the abrupt nature of the change in British policy, and focuses on the practical as well as symbolic importance of implementing a commitment to Poland.[2] Both schools naturally contain various refinements on the central theme, and each is cut across by divisions on the separate issues of the desirability and effects of the Polish Guarantee. What can be said with confidence, however, whatever the context into which the Guarantee fitted, is that it was not an option which had been rehearsed at the highest levels of the British government as the possible next step in the event of Hitler renewing his acts of aggression. The two weeks following on from the German move into Bohemia were a period of hectic activity and relentless ingenuity in Whitehall as a result of the lack of any off-the-shelf contingency plan which could be brought into play.

It was not that the German move was a total surprise to the Cabinet. On 4 October 1938 the Chiefs of Staff had advised the Cabinet that no military action by Britain and France short of 'a prolonged struggle' would be able to prevent any German absorption of Bohemia and Moravia.[3] And Halifax and some of his advisers even became for a short time inured to the prospect that 'henceforth we must count with German predominance in Central Europe'.[4] Thus when intelligence reports in February 1939 started to list Czechoslovakia among the possible targets for what seemed an increasingly likely new strike by Hitler, the emptiness of Munich was simply being spelt out with brutal clarity.[5] Nonetheless, despite what seems with hindsight the ample need for advance planning, at the highest levels there seems to have been no particular forethought as to what direction British policy should take if the worst case actually occurred. It is an interesting comment on the style of British foreign policy-making in this period that although such a major event as the tearing up of the Munich settlement had been foreseen (if not fully expected) in the abstract, little had been done to cater for the eventuality. In passing, indeed, we may note that this case provides a classic illustration of the effects of 'cognitive dissonance', the well-documented psychological state that leads to the suppression of information which does not fit in with existing hopes or beliefs.[6] Chamberlain, in particular, ignored the reports passed on by Sir Robert Vansittart from his German contacts, and preferred to believe that Hitler 'is searching round for some means of approaching us without the danger of a snub ... all the information I get seems to point in the direction of peace'.[7] This was partly because the reports tended to come from the same sources as had produced an abortive war scare in January, and because the optimistic Henderson had returned to Berlin on 13 February after four months' sick leave. But the challenge of intelligence assessment is precisely that of knowing how to sift information independently of the past performance of its sources.[8]

FIRST REACTIONS

The very decision that a new policy would be necessary in these unpleasant new circumstances emerged slowly and was in large part the result of an executive lead.[9] The first Cabinet meeting after the news of the invasion shows no feeling of a watershed in Anglo-German relations. Ministers allowed Chamberlain and Halifax to monopolise the discussion, and confined themselves to factual questions about, for example, the role of Hungary in the affair or the treatment of the Czechoslovak representatives. They were surprisingly low-key, and seemed to feel no need to analyse the new environment or to suggest shifts in policy, with the exception of one isolated suggestion from Leslie Hore-Belisha, to the effect that Britain should now encourage the closest relations with Turkey, Roumania and Hungary. This drew no response from his colleagues, who seemed as inclined to think of the night's events in terms of the spontaneous combustion of Czechoslovakia as to condemn its subordination by Germany.[10] Perhaps Chamberlain's formal presentation of the issues influenced the tone of the meeting. He said that the Cabinet had to decide: (1) whether Oliver Stanley (President of the Board of Trade) should still visit Germany; (2) what the Government should say in the Commons about the now defunct guarantee to Czechoslovakia; (3) the future of the loan to Czechoslovakia; and (4) whether to recall Nevile Henderson, British Ambassador in Germany. All these questions related either to Czechoslovakia or to issues of purely short-term significance. All were retrospective, and not concerned with the evolution of future policy. The government as a whole were wriggling with embarrassment at the prospect of being called to account for their failure to act on the guarantee given to Czechoslovakia as a result of Munich.

Although this post-invasion Cabinet met at 11 a.m. on 15 March, and so had little time in which to assimilate the events still being played out, the condition applied no less to the Foreign Secretary, who did display the beginnings of a positive reaction. He stressed that Germany had made a deliberate choice to use force rather than negotiation, and that the occasion was significant, as for the first time Hitler had achieved the subjugation of non-Germans. He advocated the use of language which would warn Germany that she was now on a dangerous path.[11]

Further indications that a new policy might be in the making continued to come from the executive. On 17 March, after the scares about an economic ultimatum to Roumania, which the Roumanian diplomat Virgil Tilea had relayed to Sir Orme Sargent, Assistant Under-Secretary at the Foreign Office and to Lord Halifax, the latter dispatched telegrams to Britain's representatives in Poland, Russia, Turkey, Greece and Yugoslavia, asking about the attitude which the governments of these countries would take in the event of Germany attacking Roumania – this information being a precondition of the formulation of any British attitude.[12] And on the same evening the Prime Minister made his famous speech at Birmingham, where he spelt out the serious implications of the conquest of Czechoslovakia, and indicated both that Britain had interests in south-east Europe and that she would resist 'an attempt to dominate the world by force'.[13] The fear was that another *coup de théâtre* was imminent.

All the available evidence suggests that the telegrams and the 'landmark' speech in Birmingham were the product of independent activity by Chamberlain and Halifax (and Foreign Office officials), as opposed to other ministers, although all policy-makers were operating in the newly uneasy domestic environment caused by the invasion and the government's flat response to it in the Commons on 15 March.[14] The Cabinet did not meet until the 18th at 5 p.m., nor did the Foreign Policy Committee meet until 27 March. Both Oliver Harvey, Private Secretary to Lord Halifax in the Foreign Office, and the Permanent Under-Secretary Sir Alexander Cadogan described in their diaries the way in which the idea of a British-backed front against aggression in Eastern Europe was rapidly put into diplomatic circulation by the executive acting alone. They noted Tilea's visit to Halifax on the 17th, and continued respectively: 'As a result of this visit telegrams were sent off . . . ' and 'On that, S. of S., O.S., and I drafted telegram to threatened states . . . '[15]

There was, indeed, hardly sufficient time for much consultation outside the Foreign Office. Tilea probably arrived at 5 p.m. and stayed for some time.[16] (He had been trying to gain British attention over the previous few days, and had been enlisting other prominent Roumanians to spread his rumours.[17]) The resulting telegrams left Whitehall at 10 p.m.[18] Halifax told the Roumanian Minister that while an ultimate decision on any guarantee would have to be the Cabinet's, he 'anticipated' that his colleagues would want the various countries later contacted to know about the issue and to give their opinion on the proposal for a guarantee system. In setting in motion this diplomacy the Foreign Secretary was merely using his departmental powers to the full. He had even anticipated the Prime Minister's views, since the latter could only be caught briefly on the telephone before his speech at Birmingham and convinced of the need to insert a remark about south-east Europe. However, when at 5 p.m. on the next day the Cabinet considered the proposed approach to eastern Europe, Halifax showed a surprising ignorance of the actions he had authorised. He told ministers that 'he was not certain whether the telegrams had all been dispatched', when in fact they had left nineteen hours previously. Halifax's uncertainty conveniently obscured the fact that he had acted without consulting the Cabinet.[19]

As for the important speech by Chamberlain that evening, collective policy-making seems to have gone little further than consultation with Halifax. On 16 March Harvey recorded: 'Prime Minister is speaking in Birmingham tomorrow and Halifax had previously talked to him about it.'[20] A day later Halifax displayed advance knowledge of the content and importance of the speech to both Tilea and the American Ambassador, Joseph Kennedy. He told the former that the Prime Minister was about to deliver to those who might wish to dominate Europe 'a very unmistakable warning'.[21] To Kennedy he added that the speech would indicate how deeply British political thinking had been affected by recent events, in the direction of leading 'many people' to reconsider 'the advantages of general cooperation' as a means of guaranteeing security.[22] The Foreign Secretary clearly identified himself with the new position expressed in the Prime Minister's speech, which he had indeed helped to rewrite away from its original domestic orientation.

But while Halifax and Chamberlain played the prime roles in producing the speech, it is still just possible that other members of the Cabinet were also influential. Cadogan's cryptic reference to the Prime Minister can be read in this way: 'He speaking again at Birmingham tomorrow night. Think he's been binged up to be a bit firmer.'[23] However the Prime Minister's ignorance in Cabinet on 18 March of his colleagues' opinions of the speech suggests that the number of ministers who had the opportunity to 'firm' him up was limited, and confirms the picture of influence coming from the Foreign Office more than political colleagues.[24] He asked 'whether the Cabinet agreed generally with the change of policy which he had outlined'. Chamberlain went on to describe how the invasion of Czechoslovakia had disillusioned him of the idea that Germany had limited and negotiable aims: 'He had now come definitely to the conclusion that Herr Hitler's attitude made it impossible to continue to negotiate on the old basis with the Nazi regime.' He indicated that the formation of this important opinion had probably preceded any consultation: 'it was on the basis of this conclusion, and after consultation with the Foreign Secretary and others of his colleagues *who were immediately available,* that he had made his speech in Birmingham'.[25] None of the available sources specifies which individual politicians (or perhaps officials) might have pressed Chamberlain into a more resolute attitude. It may well be that Cadogan was referring to the effect of public criticism on the Prime Minister, as Keith Feiling's account suggests.[26] If any of his colleagues did influence Chamberlain here, they were certainly a very small group.

Even so it is not suggested that Chamberlain and Halifax initiated these major developments in British foreign policy behind the back of a Cabinet which held different views. In fact, ministers applauded Chamberlain's speech when they met on the following day. The argument is rather that while the British government was very likely to respond to the Prague coup with hostility, the actual form of that response was by no means pre-determined. The fact of Nazi aggression had made an Anglo-German conflict more probable, but it was still an open question as to when, where and how war might break out. It was hardly obvious that Britain would break away from her traditional mode of waiting on events and pledge herself to a new system of guarantees in eastern Europe. The burden of the entire history of modern British foreign policy was that advance commitments would not be made by British governments, for compelling strategic and constitutional reasons. Indeed, when the March crisis began, ministers still assumed that Britain's vital continental interests went no further than the defence of western Europe and the Mediterranean. Therefore while most ministers probably felt that a new scepticism and resolution would inform future policy towards Germany, it was not a necessary consequence of that feeling for them to expect and demand the guarantees to Poland, Roumania, Greece and Turkey which eventually followed.

On the contrary, ministers were generally thrown into a certain confusion by the crisis.[27] The apparent urgency over a reformulation of policy made it difficult for the informal processes of collective deliberation to get under way, particularly since there were no obvious or limited courses of action to consider. In June 1940, again under traumatic circumstances, the important choices facing the Cabinet were crude, concrete and unmistakable – those of war or peace. In March 1939, the options for a new policy were relatively open-ended. Various degrees of hostile inaction, a multilateral European pact, an alliance with the USSR were all notional possibilities. In terms of their participation in policy-making, therefore, a premium was placed on the clarity with which ministers could perceive the issues, and on the conviction with which they could advocate a positive line of action during the first period of uncertainty. But its very size meant that the Cabinet as a whole was unlikely to forge a clear and strongly felt new attitude very quickly. By contrast, their immersion in daily diplomacy encouraged the Prime Minister and Foreign Secretary to arrive at definite (but not necessarily well-judged) opinions without delay. In effect, the guarantees were the product of energetic activity by Chamberlain, Halifax and their officials, for whose advice they were responsible to the Cabinet, in constructing a definite course of action out of the confusion caused by the lack of contingency planning. They originated and developed a new and specific policy, obtaining Cabinet approval rather than participation, and secured its implementation before alternative lines of policy could be fully explored and measured as serious options against the guarantee to Poland.

The Cabinet that met on 18 March, for example, showed enthusiasm for the sentiments publicly expressed by the Prime Minister the night before, but their approval was perforce retrospective. Although Chamberlain made it clear that he regarded his speech 'as a challenge to Germany on the issue of whether or not Germany intended to dominate Europe by force', and therefore as an embodiment of major policy, his request for contributions from other ministers was slightly disingenuous. While no specific commitment had yet been made, the 'change in policy which he had outlined' had already been made public in a major speech, specially reworked to counter criticism of the 'briefest and most objective statement' which he had made in the Commons on 15 March in the immediate aftermath of the invasion.[28] If the Cabinet had disagreed they would have had to contemplate asking the Prime Minister to go back on this important public pronouncement – an inhibiting if not impossible prospect.

As it was, ministers showed a collective desire for Britain thenceforward to take the lead in warning Germany generally that aggression in Roumania or elsewhere would not go unchecked. Sir John Simon and Malcolm MacDonald simply acquiesced passively with the Prime Minister's view. Most other ministers, however, made positive contributions – and in all at least sixteen of the twenty-two present spoke on the subject. The import of their remarks was that a broad-based combination should be formed of all those states which might resist subsequent German aggression; the more countries that could be involved in this declaration of mutual support, the more obvious would be Britain's new determination, and the greater would be the chances of containing Germany should war actually break out. Sir Thomas Inskip, for instance, thought that Britain could do little immediately: 'if, however, it was possible to organise an effective combination among the states in South Eastern Europe, the position would be greatly changed and improved'. Lord Chatfield also subscribed to this view, and Lord Stanhope told the Cabinet that the Chiefs of Staff believed that war would at once be less likely and more winnable if a Second Front could be ensured. Stanley added that any guarantees should thus be 'joint and several', as the attack might fall elsewhere than on Roumania. W. S. Morrison pointed out that if such 'opposition to German aggression' were to be co-ordinated, then only Britain was in a position to organise it. The Marquess of Zetland took a similar line. Hore-Belisha was more specific; he 'was in favour of reconsidering our policy and contracting frank and open alliances with countries such as Poland and Russia' so as to help define the point at which 'we should make our stand'. Thus the Cabinet approved generally 'the new line of policy proposed by the Prime Minister, namely that we should make approaches to Russia, Poland, Yugoslavia, Turkey, Greece and Roumania with a view to obtaining assurances from them that they would join with us in resisting any act of German aggression aimed at obtaining domination in South East Europe'.

As we have seen, this policy had already been set in motion on 17 March by Halifax and Chamberlain. However, even as the Cabinet were brought into the discussion, and were showing their preference for a generally co-ordinated front against Germany, the Prime Minister and Foreign Secretary were on the verge of a second stage of policy, involving a narrowing of the scope of Britain's initiative and the establishing of implicit priorities among the states with whom agreement was desirable. By the end of this same meeting Chamberlain was indicating his partiality for a more specific solution than 'amateur collective security', as a member of the Foreign Office described the proposals for multilateral consultations which had inspired the Cabinet's enthusiasm:[29] 'He thought that Poland was very likely the key to the situation, and he suggested that our communications to Poland should probably be to go somewhat further than our communications to other countries.' In other words Poland should be asked not only for her attitude, but also directly for a promise of resistance.[30]

Although the Cabinet neither responded to this suggestion, nor embodied it in their conclusions, it was to be the main principle on which Chamberlain acted in the course of the fast-developing diplomacy of the next fortnight – despite the generally expressed ministerial desire for a system of co-operation with and between as many states as possible in eastern Europe. The concentration on Poland also went against the concern of some ministers for special co-operation with the USSR. Hore-Belisha, in advocating a net of alliances, had specified both Poland and Russia as key members. He was not alone. Chatfield had argued the Chiefs of Staff view, that the joint adhesion of Poland and Russia would make feasible British resistance to German aggression in Roumania. Without it, the only practicable policy would be to obtain the support of Turkey and Greece. The Minister of Health, Walter Elliot, twice urged the importance of the USSR. Elliot thought that 'it was most important to get in touch with Russia, since Russia's attitude would have a very considerable effect upon the smaller powers'.[31] There were even two ministers who voiced qualified doubts about the intrinsic wisdom of increasing the risk of war, by whatever means. Both Lord Maugham and Kingsley Wood accepted that Britain and Germany were converging towards war, but thought 'the right moment' should be chosen; if that moment could be delayed, say until the end of 1939, Britain's position would be stronger. Morrison also urged caution, lest Germany retaliate against 'encirclement'.

DECISIVE INITIATIVES

It will be apparent that the actual development of British foreign policy during the ensuing two weeks did not conform very closely to these concerns of the Cabinet on 18 March. On the 19th the group of four[32] which the Cabinet had delegated to supervise the multiple 'approaches' to south-east Europe, met twice, and was confronted with the first replies to the telegrams of 17 March. Unsurprisingly, these acknowledgements contained no firm reactions of any kind, since the governments of Poland, Greece, Turkey, Yugoslavia and the USSR were themselves still formulating reactions to the rumours about Roumania; they in their turn enquired about British intentions.[33] Chamberlain, however, saw this as a reason for altering the whole direction of the British *démarche*. Now, thinking that 'the F.O. were as usual pretty barren of suggestions', he proposed a declaration of interest in opposing aggression by Britain, France, Poland and Russia alone. Chamberlain characterised this as a 'pretty bold and startling' idea.[34] This was quickly agreed and drafted. The Foreign Secretary told the Cabinet next day that his small group had decided that Britain ought not to attempt too much too quickly: 'The essential point was to secure the early consent of France, Russia and Poland.'[35] Consequently, to reassure Poland, it had changed the designation of the area to be protected from 'South East Europe' to the vaguer 'European States'.[36] In other words, as it became clear that Roumania after all was not immediately threatened (the Prime Minister had actually said in the last Cabinet meeting that he did not think that an immediate attack was likely), the creation of a broadly based peace front was soon abandoned by the executive group,[37] under Chamberlain's inspiration, in favour of a declaration which at once involved fewer states and sought to keep promises of support at a high level of generality.[38] The formula 'left it open what would constitute a "threat" and what steps we should take in the events of a "threat"', since the main purpose of the new four-power declaration was simply to act as an earnest of Britain's determination to stop Germany if the latter continued to show signs 'that she intended to proceed with her march for world domination'.

Thus the Cabinet found themselves, suddenly and without detailed justification, expected to accept a proposal which explicitly rejected the main planks of their own suggestions at the previous Cabinet meeting. Simon and Stanley had been present at the Meetings of Ministers, but the former was having to back-pedal on the caution he had shown in the Commons on 15 March, and the latter was very much a junior member of the informal committee, as the very full record of the meetings bears out. Where on 18 March the discussion had centred on ensuring future co-operation between France, Britain and the majority of eastern European states – which several ministers hoped would develop into a net of firm alliances or guarantees – on 20 March Halifax presented a draft declaration which was to apply to only two countries east of Berlin (and to none in the Balkan peninsula), and which deliberately eschewed formal engagements. It is perhaps a measure of both the built-in expectations of ministers about the role of the Prime Minister in such situations and their objective difficulties in forming clear collective opinions during this crisis, that the Cabinet hardly demurred at the switch in policy for which its executive now asked approval. Lord Zetland did suggest that Turkey might be invited to join the declaration, but Halifax and Chamberlain were quick to reply that this could antagonise both Greece and Italy. It was difficult for the average Cabinet member to prevail against such positive and concerted disagreement, arguing as he was only from a general appreciation of the situation and from the special viewpoint of his own department.[39] Zetland received no support, and his suggestion was consigned to oblivion. This ability of the foreign policy executive to predominate purely by virtue of initiating action which had then to be proven positively undesirable was further instanced during the same Cabinet meeting. During the discussion of various terminological amendments to the draft declaration, it was suggested that in the phrase 'European peace and security may be affected by any action which constitutes a threat to the political independence of any European state', the word 'must' should be substituted for the word 'may'. This was not a trivial matter, but merely by showing strenuous personal opposition and without needing to appeal for general support from his colleagues, Chamberlain succeeded in squashing the idea.[40]

Chatfield at least made an attempt to contribute to this new stage in policy-formulation. He argued for more precision in Britain's commitments, lest the government be forced to admit that they 'were prepared to guarantee the independence of practically every state in Europe'. The minutes then record that the Prime Minister suggested an alternative draft, which was discussed 'in considerable detail, and various alterations were from time to time suggested'. It is here that we come up against the intrinsic limitations of the Cabinet documents as source material, with their frequent use of the passive tense and their unpredictable lacunae. There is no hard evidence for the degree of influence exerted by the Cabinet as a whole during the discussion of the final form of the declaration. By inference, however, we can be fairly sure that the contributions made by ministers outside the small group which had initiated the four-power proposal were relatively superficial. Not only did they accept quite meekly the departure from the path they themselves had approved and developed only two days before, but the declaration as dispatched shows no divergence either from the two principles announced by Halifax at the beginning of the meeting or from Cadogan's description of it the day before as a four–power declaration of 'non-désintéressement'.[41] The Foreign Secretary had argued for the limitation of the declaration to France, Britain, Poland and Russia, and said that the draft 'aimed at avoiding specific commitments'. The draft as eventually approved by the Cabinet accepted the concept of four-power co-operation, and merely pledged the prospective signatories, on the basis of their concern for the 'security and political independence of European States', 'immediately to consult together in the event of any action being taken which appears to constitute a threat to the security or independence of any of them'.[42] The only 'specific commitment' in this was that to 'consult', consultation being in any case the normal diplomatic response to an imminent crisis.[43] In practice the Cabinet had added nothing to the scheme which had been brought before them, and Chatfield had failed in his attempt to bring more 'precision' to the declaration. As Cadogan noted on the evening of the 20th: 'Saw H. at 12.45 . . . Told me Cabinet had approved draft telegram [subject] to certain amendments . . . We propose to publish a declaration that, *in the event of a further outrage*, we will consult. Point: c'est tout.'[44]

Moreover, by this move Halifax and Chamberlain came yet closer to that focusing on Poland which was to be the final outcome of the March deliberations, in preference to a wider security pact or an agreement with the USSR. Chamberlain now saw Poland as one of 'the three big powers' and considered that a joint declaration involving her would be 'a bold step and a considerable advance on any action we had previously taken'.[45] As the triumvirate phraseology suggested, Russia was not in the foreground of the picture of events held by Chamberlain and Halifax. The day before, Halifax had peremptorily discounted the USSR's proposal for a five-power conference, perhaps in Bucharest, 'to discuss possibilities of common action'.[46] The suggestion had first reached the Foreign Office at 9.30 a.m. on 19 March. At 11.30 a.m. the group of four ministers (Chamberlain, Halifax, Stanley and Simon) had met for the first of that day's two meetings in which the four-power declaration was forged. In the afternoon, before the second of these, Halifax saw

Ivan Maisky, the Soviet Ambassador. He told Maisky that the British government was in the midst of formulating a plan of their own; he thought that the idea of a conference should be laid on one side for the present (that is, in deference to the forthcoming British suggestion), for two reasons: because 'we could hardly in present circumstances manage to send a responsible Minister to take part in the conference', and because the holding of a conference without an advance certainty of its success would be 'dangerous'.[47] Thus Halifax, possibly after a brief consultation with the Prime Minister and two other colleagues, rejected the Soviet proposal for vague and unconvincing reasons, only six hours after it had arrived in London. The rest of the Cabinet was not informed until the 22nd, by which time the rejection was a *fait accompli*. Halifax then reported that the Soviet Commissar for Foreign Affairs, Maxim Litvinov, 'seemed to be somewhat perturbed that we had not been more enthusiastic over his proposals for a conference'. The Foreign Secretary added that Britain might see whether she could get closer to the Soviet point of view.[48]

THE CRUCIAL CHOICE

During the next five days, however, the policy which in fact took shape was that of an Anglo-French-Polish mutual guarantee, with the four-power declaration itself abandoned and the USSR largely excluded from proceedings, as Litvinov complained bitterly on 1 April after the announcement of the Polish Guarantee.[49] This was the third stage of policy-making after the Prague coup. Moreover, while this key new development took place, from 22 to 27 March, neither the Cabinet nor its Foreign Policy Committee (one of the intermittently important Cabinet committees that had proliferated since 1936 to cope with increased work loads;[50] for a list of its regular attenders, see Appendix 1, below) met. Halifax and Chamberlain determined the intellectual direction of policy, by concentrating their attention on Poland and subsequently presenting the Cabinet with proposals which dealt exclusively with that country. They also took steps to implement their preferences, by ceasing to pursue the four-power declaration, and by treating the Polish government with particular solicitude.

The first stage in the process came on 22 March, with the second round of Anglo-French talks in London.[51] Even on the 21st the germ of the final policy had been present in Halifax's initial conversation with Georges Bonnet, the French Foreign Minister, when the two men had 'entirely agreed' that securing Poland's co-operation against German aggression, particularly with regard to Roumania, was the highest priority. Halifax had further introduced the idea that Poland might be willing to promise France and Britain aid in the event of the attack coming in the west.[52]

Thus emerged for the first time the idea of the Polish Guarantee, in other words, the notion that the best response to the destruction of Czechoslovakia would be that of a special arrangement with a single major power – if that power were Poland.[53] At the meeting on 22 March, with Chamberlain and the British Ambassador to France Charles Corbin additionally present, the seed of this understanding began to germinate. The Foreign Secretary described how Poland's reactions to the proposal for a quadrilateral declaration had been hostile because of its dislike of association with the Soviet Union. Although Halifax said he disliked the possibility of the USSR feeling excluded, he did not suggest exerting further pressure on the Poles, or treating them as of secondary importance. On the contrary, in summing up the meeting's views he argued that the essential precondition of western European help to Roumania – the issue which had sparked off the whole consideration of collaboration with eastern Europe – was the participation of Poland, to the extent that 'Great Britain and France would have to give Poland a private undertaking that, if Poland came in, they would both come in also.'[54] Chamberlain was also concerned above all for the Poles. He said that if Poland's reply to the suggested four-power declaration was 'as was to be expected ... negative or evasive, the intention would not be to press them any further, but to try the new procedure now proposed'. That was to get Poland to join Britain and France in promising assistance to Roumania if attacked, by undertaking to provide the same aid to Poland herself.[55]

There was no examination, or even exposition, of why Roumania and Poland were of such overriding importance that the normal methods of diplomatic pressure could not be applied to 'press' them to adhere to the same declaration as the Soviet Union – even if, ultimately, the conclusion reached might have been the same. The problem of Polish-Soviet relations, like most of the other inconvenient aspects of the emerging British infatuation with Poland, was essentially being skirted.[56] Equally, given that a choice between

Poland and Russia was in practice being made, there was no attempt to weigh up directly the relative advantages of each as a potential source of co-operation. The basic assumption was that Polish fears of association with the USSR were ineradicable, even understandable, and accordingly that any plan which sought to incorporate both powers was automatically out of court. Moreover there could be no question of ignoring Polish concerns in favour of the wider strategy of an alliance with the Soviet Union, on balance of power grounds, to achieve a serious and generalised deterrent against German aggression. That option – like the notion of the balance of power itself – does not seem to have been considered at this point in the evolution of British policy.

The reasons behind this bias are complicated and mostly irrelevant to a study of the relations between executive and Cabinet.[57] The essential point as far as the making of policy is concerned is that Halifax and Chamberlain shaped a new programme for the British government almost immediately after the Cabinet had accepted a different plan, itself originated by the executive. By representing the government in the talks with Bonnet, which centred almost entirely on guarantees to Poland and Roumania at the expense of a four-power declaration, the Prime Minister and Foreign Secretary began to commit Britain to liaison with Poland but detachment from the USSR. For not only did the two men determine the general frame of ideas in which discussion took place; they also began to lead Poland to believe that the current deliberations in British government circles would result in the offer of a direct guarantee. Already on 21 March Halifax had told Count Raczynski, the Polish Ambassador, that if the German-Polish quarrel over Danzig 'should develop in such a way as to threaten Polish independence, then I thought that His Majesty's Government would have to treat it as a question which was of the gravest concern to themselves'.[58] This probably expressed correctly the general Cabinet feeling about how Britain would react in the contingency of a Polish crisis. But because Halifax revealed its existence to the Polish Ambassador it was also a definite hint that Britain might be about to enter into an advance commitment to Poland and, at that stage, a disincentive to the latter to make the best of her anxieties about the USSR and join in a four-power declaration.[59] The Prime Minister was certainly sensitive and sympathetic to the Polish antipathy to the Soviet Union. He wrote, 'As soon as I appreciated this position fully,

I saw that it was unlikely that we should get their signature [to a four-power declaration]. Was it worthwhile to go in with Russia in that case?'[60]

Subsequent Polish actions suggest that the Poles were keen to court Britain at this stage, even if it is unlikely that they were particularly strengthened in their attitude towards Germany by British encouragement. On 24 March, in the course of a long conversation, Raczynski developed a proposal his Foreign Minister Josef Beck had made two days before, for a secret understanding between the two countries in which Britain would promise Poland help if the latter were threatened over Danzig, while Poland would promise to consult in the event of a German attack in the west. Halifax took up this idea, and slightly reformulated it so as to assure Britain of greater reciprocity. Although he implied that the question would need to be considered further, the Foreign Secretary raised no objections to the plan, and appeared mainly concerned to clarify its provisions.[61] He seems not to have concerned himself with the fact that this would amount to a complete turnaround in both the letter and spirit of Anglo-Polish relations over the previous six months, which had been characterised by mutual distrust and even hostility.[62]

By accepting these terms of reference Halifax must therefore have given Beck, via his Ambassador, the impression that Polish policy could thenceforward be based on the assumption that Britain was near to a bilateral agreement, and had abandoned her pressure for a four-power declaration.[63] In its turn Polish enthusiasm for the British initiative fed back to reinforce Chamberlain's and Halifax's concentration on the Polish connection.

Halifax's personal diplomacy was also important for what it omitted. Britain did not inform the Soviet Union of the abandonment of the plan for a four-power declaration until 29 March[64] although, as we have seen, Halifax and Chamberlain were aware on 22 March, when they met the French, that Poland's reply was likely to be 'negative or evasive' about the proposal.[65] Certainly by the 24th Halifax knew that Poland had definitely refused to participate in the public declaration. In the Raczynski–Halifax conversation noted above, the Polish Ambassador had told the Foreign Secretary explicitly of his country's fear of any link with Russia.[66]

The propensity of Chamberlain, Halifax and to some extent Cadogan to distrust the Soviets, strengthened by Ambassador Maisky's preference for Opposition circles in Britain, had not been dispelled by Moscow's perceived failure to respond to tentative British overtures in the first few months of 1939, and by reports of the Soviet Union's military weakness.[67] This is the background to Cadogan's failure to give more than an oblique hint to Maisky that the proposal for a joint declaration was likely to fall through when he saw the Soviet Ambassador on 23 March, despite the fact that the USSR had informed Britain on the 22nd of her willingness to participate. In fact the Under-Secretary came near to dissimulation, as he told Maisky that while Poland was hesitating about joining a bloc which included the Soviet Union she had made no final answer and was still considering a reply. Britain 'would of course keep closely in touch with M. Maisky'. When the latter asked about procedure after the declaration had been made, Cadogan did not mention the emerging inclination of Halifax and Chamberlain, in the talks with Bonnet, to replace the four-sided scheme with a bilateral Anglo-Polish agreement. Instead he replied that the declaration would be followed (in other words, not replaced) by a general exchange of views, and possibly by some specific arrangements 'with certain countries who appeared to be more directly in the road of German advance and who were already organised in some treaty arrangements'. This clearly pointed to Poland, but the impression given by Cadogan was that of the construction of special mottes following on from the completion of a general bailey, and not, as actually happened, the total exclusion of the Soviet Union from the important stages in anti-German diplomacy. Cadogan's private note reads: 'Saw Maisky and had to stall him.'[68]

The policy of the Polish Guarantee was probably finalised during the weekend of 25–6 March, although the data for these two days is limited. By 'finalised' is meant that Halifax and Chamberlain came to commit themselves completely to this course of action, and by doing so inevitably narrowed the scope of policy-making for their colleagues, since the choice they presented for ultimate Cabinet decision consisted only in accepting or rejecting the option of the Guarantee. Because the executive's deliberations and diplomacy focused predominantly on Poland, by the time the Cabinet and its Foreign Policy Committee came to examine the situation, ministers were faced with two virtual *faits accomplis*: the abortion of the previous schemes which they had approved and to some extent participated in, and the pressure to accept the executive's new proposal, because a rejection would leave the government without a policy, or even a plan for a policy, at a time when most ministers felt as a main priority the need for a response to the Prague 'outrage' which would be both dramatic and prophylactic. Moreover the attitudes and expectations of Poland and the USSR towards Britain had been deeply affected by the activities of Halifax and Chamberlain, so that if the Cabinet had wished to alter the direction of policy, it would have had to reckon with two considerable difficulties. Once Britain had indicated an intention to conclude the Guarantee, Poland would not easily have co-operated in anything less. Equally, the failure to take the USSR into British confidence could not be conveniently erased from the memory of Soviet policy-makers.

It is evident that during the weekend of 25–6 March Chamberlain and, particularly, Halifax completed the detailed construction of the Guarantee policy in some haste, with the result that a finished product was presented for the rapid approval of the Cabinet. On the 26th itself the Prime Minister wrote, 'the declaration is dead and I am now exploring another possibility'.[69]

The general requirement of urgency had acquired added impetus through the signing of the German-Roumanian Trade Treaty on 23 March. Cadogan noted, and complained at, the frenetic pact of policy-making at the time: 'There are neither week-ends, nor nights nor days.'[70] His diary also simply notes a meeting held at noon on 25 March in the Foreign Office, which he attended with Halifax, Sir Robert Vansittart, Sargent, Sir William Malkin and William Strang,[71] to work out the next steps. Harvey was also there, and recorded an extended meeting in which Halifax advocated at some length a definite mutual-guarantee agreement with Poland and Roumania above any arrangement which included Russia. Because of what he saw as Poland's crucial ability to provide a Second Front, the Foreign Secretary thought 'we cannot have Russia in the forefront of the picture'. Polish hostility plus the need not to alienate Italy, which he still hoped to wean from Hitler, were the justifications for this treatment. The USSR would be useful, Halifax apparently concluded, but only in the secondary sense that it could act as an 'arsenal' in any conflict, and might be encouraged to develop the existing Franco-Soviet Pact into a direct defensive alliance.[72]

It was on the basis of these attitudes towards Poland and Russia, which had quickly hardened into constants in the minds of Halifax and Chamberlain as deliberation progressed, that Strang prepared a draft summary of the discussions. This was brought to Chamberlain by Halifax, together with his Parliamentary Under-Secretary R. A. Butler and Cadogan, for a further reading at 9.30 p.m. on 26 March.[73] The Prime Minister gave his approval to the proposals, which thus solidified into a ready-made programme for Cabinet consideration; unless ministers rejected the proposals *in toto*, their only means of participation was through amending the details of the scheme. If they were inhibited by the prospect of rejecting the executive's careful preparations, then the creative stage of policy formulation was over without their ever having fully participated. Cadogan certainly thought that the meeting on the 26th finalised matters. He described his work on the next day: 'In afternoon busy on draft telegrams giving effect to our decisions of last night.'[74] His only qualification was that he expected certain 'objections' in the Foreign Policy Committee, which he was subsequently surprised not to find. But it is revealing that Cadogan considered the decisions effectively to have been taken even before the Cabinet had met: objections or not, the thought of a refusal did not occur to him.

CABINET REACTIONS: A NEGATIVE CONSENSUS

Thus the Cabinet were not drawn into the consideration of the new policy until the executive had discarded alternative lines of action and were strongly committed to a concrete set of proposals. Eventually the Foreign Policy Committee met at 5 p.m. on 27 March for the first time in nearly seven weeks. It is difficult to know why it was called at this particular time. The need to take the burden of some business from the full Cabinet cannot have been a major consideration since, as we have seen, the work of policy-construction had already been completed, while the telegrams of implementation had been drafted that afternoon. Moreover the Cabinet itself met two days later, substantially to duplicate the Committee's approval.[75] One may therefore surmise that Chamberlain called the Committee to test the response of other ministers, and possibly to mobilise support in advance of any opposition which might be encountered in the larger and less intimate Cabinet. There is no direct evidence for this theory, which is inferred mainly from the apparent lack of real function for the meeting, and from Cadogan's expectation of some ministerial criticism of the Polish Guarantee. Yet it seems a convincing explanation when we look at the Prime Minister's remarks in the Com-

Constructing the Polish Guarantee, March 1939   37

mittee itself. Chamberlain reported that 'He had not thought it expedient to summon an emergency meeting of the Cabinet to consider the new proposals, as this might have caused publicity.'[76]

This accounts for the calling of the Committee simply in terms of a desire for secret diplomacy. But closer examination leads us to suspect the importance attached to avoiding publicity. If a full Cabinet had been called on 27 March, instead of the Foreign Policy Committee, it would have been the first for five days. Normally the Cabinet met once a week, so that in this period of obvious turmoil it would not have attracted too much attention to advance the meeting by two days – especially since the regular Cabinet meeting of 15 March had been followed by three more in the four days from 18 to 22 March. The precedents for emergency Cabinet meetings had been well and truly set by the 27th. Indeed, it would almost have attracted more attention if the Cabinet had not met irregularly. Furthermore, unless the Foreign Policy Committee's meeting could be kept completely secret (unlikely in the light of the interpenetration of government and press circles and the many private contacts between people like Hore-Belisha and Liddell-Hart, and Liddell-Hart and Maisky),[77] it would have seemed more extraordinary to the outside observer that the Cabinet Committee should have a special meeting after such a long hiatus than that the Cabinet itself should meet a mere two days early. Probably Chamberlain wanted partly to keep the possibility of leaks to a minimum and partly to manage events by making it difficult for the full Cabinet to oppose his new initiative. The two explanations are, of course, compatible, given that leaks are one of the main instruments open to ministers seeking to derail a prime ministerial bandwagon.

The minutes of this meeting of the Committee illustrate well the way in which the Guarantee policy had gathered a nearly unstoppable momentum by the time that other ministers became involved. Chamberlain related the fate of the schemes that the Cabinet had approved at its last meeting, and then seemed to present the Committee with a choice between two options, as if they were equally free to choose either:

It looked therefore, as if a failure to associate with Soviet Russia would give rise to suspicion and difficulty with the Left Wing both in this country and in France, while on the other hand insistence to associate with Soviet Russia would destroy any chance of building up a solid and united front against German aggression.[78]

The Prime Minister was still concerned that Roumania, as the next likely victim, should be assisted, but he now saw Poland as the key in such a scheme. In practice he had limited the options by beginning from the assumption that a *démarche* which included both Poland and the Soviet Union was simply not practicable or politic (a hypothesis which, although in some respects borne out by events,[79] had not been subject to very rigorous testing, either in argument or diplomatic action). The problem was presented as an inescapable choice between the two powers, with no other possibilities. It was also fairly clear from the language of the antithesis which option Chamberlain intended the Committee to accept. He opposed the destruction of 'a solid and united front against German aggression' (by which he now meant 'agreement with Poland') only with the disadvantage of left-wing antagonism – a plague which his government had suffered and survived many times previously.

Given the consensus of ministers in the Cabinet meetings since Prague that Hitler had now to be confronted with some kind of defiant gesture, it was hardly likely that the Cabinet Committee of a predominantly Conservative government would rank the guarantee with Poland below good relations with the 'Left Wing', which probably meant both the Labour movement and some of the Prime Minister's Conservative critics.[80] It was particularly improbable because Chamberlain did not raise the question of the long-term strategic hazards which failure to join forces with the USSR might involve, or conversely the strategic advantages that might accrue from co-operation. Indeed, in terms of the broad geo-political issues (which partly supported their position in that Poland, not Russia, bordered on Germany, and partly called it into question, in that Poland could hardly constitute the second front they sought), Halifax and Chamberlain emphasised the value of Poland as the second front,[81] and implied that the countries which also opposed Russian involvement, such as Finland, Spain, Portugal, Yugoslavia and Italy, were also important components of it.

Although other members were, of course, free to bring up such questions, Chamberlain's narrow presentation of the issue, with one option cast as obviously the more attractive, constituted a firm lead that could only have been negated by radical questioning of the course of diplomacy from the very beginning of the crisis, as well as of the basic assumptions on which the executive had operated.[82] For those who had been excluded from the intricate daily manoeuvres of foreign policy, and who now possessed far less information than Halifax and Chamberlain, the task of undoing work to which the executive was fully committed would therefore have been formidable, even if there had been no urgency in the situation. Simon made a gesture in the direction of further investigation – 'JS sent for copies of last night's telegram. Is he getting cold feet?' – but nothing more.[83]

As it was, Chamberlain rapidly exerted positive pressure in favour of the proposed Guarantee. He made explicit his own preference by setting out the 'two fronts' argument as proof of the key importance of Poland, and the 'offence to third parties' argument as the compelling reason against inviting the Soviet Union to take part in the plan to guarantee Roumania and Poland. He stressed the need for urgency, and hoped that if the Foreign Policy Committee approved the proposals before it, the draft telegrams could be dispatched that evening. The general tone of Chamberlain's introduction made it plain that he required ratification from the Committee, not inputs. In this he was reinforcing his initial remark to ministers that they were to be 'informed of certain conclusions which had been provisionally reached on the previous day'.[84]

In the event the executive achieved the requisite authorisation, although after conspicuous dissent in the Committee. Yet their very ability to override this disagreement is further evidence of the strength of the position enjoyed by Halifax and Chamberlain in a crisis atmosphere in which the essential requirement was that of the rapid and creative construction of a new policy to fit a new environment. For the opposition was persistent and fairly outspoken, in the circumstances a striking indication of the critical stage which British foreign policy had reached; ministers in home departments were trying, however forlornly, to keep up with the arguments and pace of affairs.

Sir Samuel Hoare in particular emphasised throughout the discussion that it would be counter-productive to leave Russia out of any arrangement. In his opinion there should be further efforts to organise 'some kind of parallel action, vis-à-vis Russia' so as to bring her 'in to the common front'. He was afraid that, without this, Britain's policy would be seen 'in many quarters' as having suffered 'a considerable defeat'. Even more important would be the loss of the USSR's military value: 'Russia constituted the greatest deterrent in the East against German aggression. All experience showed that

Russia was undefeatable and he was apprehensive of the possible consequences that might result if at this juncture the enmity of Soviet Russia towards this country was increased.' Hoare's advocacy of this view may have been lent extra force by his insistence that he had no 'predilections' in favour of the Soviet Union, although it was probably already clear to those present that there was little moral enthusiasm for the USSR in the National Government. If a senior minister did therefore argue the case for close foreign relations with Stalin's government, he must at the least have commanded serious attention – although Hoare clearly had personal reasons for wanting to salvage his reputation for far-sightedness after his ill-timed 'golden age' speech exuding optimism, on 10 March.[85] Moreover, in this committee of eight, Hoare was supported fully by Oliver Stanley, who also feared 'serious consequences' unless a form of declaration could be found which could accommodate Russia without raising the difficulties outlined by Chamberlain. This combination was an important challenge to the argument which the executive sought to present to the Committee about the inevitability of having to choose between Poland and Russia (although they suffered by arguing on this middle ground, and by not advocating clearly that the USSR should be the first priority).

The pressures against dissent in the making of this policy left Hoare and Stanley alone in their outspokenness. But other ministers were by no means fully convinced by the executive argument. Rather they seem to have been slightly bemused by the change of events. Of the eight ministerial members, Halifax, Chamberlain and (insofar as we can decipher their preferences from two relatively marginal comments) Simon and Inskip, argued actively in favour of the proposals brought to the meeting.[86] The remaining two, Chatfield and Morrison, were non-committal. Morrison pointed out that the newness of the latest proposals lay in their willingness to envisage action and not just consultation. But he neither drew any conclusion from this observation nor crossed swords with the Prime Minister when the latter replied by saying that the original proposals for consultation had always been 'with a view to determining the nature of any action that might be taken'. Later in the proceedings Morrison did predict that Russia would 'sulk', but went no further. Morrison was insufficiently sure of his opinions and his information either to enthuse or complain over Halifax's plan.[87]

Lord Chatfield contributed far more to the discussion, but he too adopted an ambivalent position on the main issue. On the one hand he feared the dangers of involvement with Russia to the extent of risking hostilities with Japan, and in any case he believed that 'On the whole Poland was, from the military point of view, probably the best of potential eastern allies.' But he could see the other side of the argument: 'he thought Soviet Russia would act as a greater deterrent so far as Germany was concerned'. In taking this even-handed line, Chatfield was obscuring the impact of the Chiefs of Staff appreciation of 18 March, which – hedged about with qualifications as it was – had replied to direct questions about the relative military values of Poland and the Soviet Union with the view that the latter was at least capable of causing Germany some real difficulties.[88] This was personal weakness approaching the dereliction of duty, given the importance of ventilating all the relevant arguments before such a crucial decision as that of formulating a deterrent against Germany. Chatfield further criticised the proposals before the Committee, by observing that Roumania was no longer worth her place as a prospective ally, now that she was dependent on Germany for military equipment after the signature of the Commercial Treaty on 23 March. In this he was abandoning the view he had expressed on behalf of the military on 18 March, namely that Roumania's value would be dependent on an agreement with Turkey and possibly Greece.[89]

Thus Halifax and Chamberlain were faced with a Committee in which two ministers gave them tepid support, two were relatively neutral and two were actively critical of their proposals. Yet the telegrams as broadly approved by the Foreign Policy Committee, and dispatched that evening, contained the plan which they had formulated and introduced to their colleagues, with no substantial alteration.[90] The text of the telegrams corresponds closely to the guarantee scheme which Harvey describes as having been finalised between 25 and 26 March.[91] It accepted the exclusion of Russia and the demise of the four-power declaration, and provided for Anglo-French help to Roumania and Poland should they resist attack and Poland undertake to aid both Roumania and the Allies in the event of the first German attack falling there. Various pieties were expressed as to the need to avoid Soviet isolationism, but the consideration of any action to involve the USSR was postponed until an unspecified date. Halifax conceded that in the event of war, there would be 'good reasons' for trying to ensure at least the 'benevolent neutrality' of the USSR: he would consider 'in due course' how best to secure this.[92]

Why did the executive carry the Committee with them so successfully, despite the lack of strong support from a majority of members? The answer seems to lie mainly in the holding of the initiative by Halifax and Chamberlain, and in the inability of the opposition to challenge the justifications which the executive made from a position of authority but which were in fact as much assertions as those made by non-specialist ministers. The guarantee plan may not have commanded the wholehearted support of the Committee, but equally it did not provoke confident or detailed criticism, for reasons we have outlined earlier.[93] Halifax and the Prime Minister were faced by only two ministers who called strongly for structural modifications to the scheme. In this numerically balanced dispute, with Simon and Inskip mildly sympathetic to the original proposals,[94] there was no way in which Hoare and Stanley could impose their view over that of the ministers constitutionally responsible for foreign policy, who were also the authors of diplomacy during the crisis thus far.

Although mutual criticism was perhaps easier in the small group than in an imposing full Cabinet,[95] the executive still had crucial advantages when it came to a stalemate: they possessed ready-made proposals, an air of special authority with which to make judgements on the arcane questions of high diplomacy and a physical involvement in detailed day-to-day developments. The combination of these qualities made it possible for Chamberlain to pay obeisance to the views of Hoare and Stanley, without conceding the substance of the argument. He agreed to examine Stanley's suggestion for a form of declaration which could incorporate the USSR, but insisted that no decision could be taken on the issue until Poland had replied to the proposed telegram. In other words, the guarantee proposals were to be accepted as they stood, and made to Poland and Roumania on the existing basis of the exclusion of the Soviet Union, whose role could be re-examined later. But in practice it was highly improbable that Poland would accept any subsequent reformulation of the plan to include Russia once she had been offered the guarantee alone, a fact which Chamberlain must have realised from the breakdown of the declaration proposals. As the future was to confirm, the likely outcome was that events would gather their own momentum once the proposal had been made, that the agreement would be concluded without Soviet participation and that the options for British foreign policy would narrow as a result. Essentially the Prime Minister had ignored the opposition in the Committee.

In this imperviousness he followed Halifax's blunter lead. Replying to Hoare's first remarks in the Foreign Policy Committee about the importance of the USSR to Britain, the Foreign Secretary had merely asserted without explanation that 'if we had to make a choice between Poland and Soviet Russia, it seemed clear that Poland would give the greater value'. He had also quoted very selectively from military advice about the relative values of Poland and Russia. He had referred to comments made by the British Ambassador in Moscow and from the Military Attaché in Berlin, neither of which went to show directly that Poland was the better potential ally, and yet he too had failed to mention the Chiefs of Staff conclusion of 18 March that Poland was not only incapable of containing a German attack, but that 'If the USSR were on our side and Poland neutral, the position would alter in our favour.'[96] Finally, Halifax had felt it necessary to make only the most cursory responses when Hoare had returned to the charge. On the second of these occasions the Foreign Secretary simply replied that France was not very sympathetic to the Soviet Union at that time. (This was broadly true, but since France had not been consulted about the sudden development of British policy, it was not the frankest of answers[97]). To the last attempt he did not respond at all, but instead raised the different question of Danzig.

Thus Halifax and Chamberlain side-stepped the opposition of two important ministers, by refusing to join argument. Had the debate become more rigorous and more specific, others might have been drawn in, and basic premises might have been more critically examined. As it was, the executive repeatedly asserted the rightness of their policy, and capitalised on the general desire to avoid delay. Throughout they treated the guarantee proposal as if it were already adopted policy, open only to amendment. Such confidence forced dissentients into negative criticism of the executive's programme and away from the construction of alternative policies which might have attracted support from the uncommitted. With such diffuse opinions elsewhere, Halifax and Chamberlain were able to confine the argument to their own terms of reference.[98]

The submission of the draft telegrams to the full Cabinet witnessed a repetition of the events in Committee, if in a minor key. Halifax and Chamberlain repeated their previous arguments and assertions. Once again Poland was represented as 'the key to the situation'.[99]

Chamberlain continued to adduce assumptions as facts. He thought 'that it was of the utmost importance to obtain the support of Poland and that it was impossible to secure this if Russia was brought into the declaration'. The two statements in that sentence expressed principles on which the guarantee policy was based; but they were principles which had still not been exposed to full questioning and debate, either in Cabinet or within the executive itself. When a further attempt was made on this occasion to put right the relegation of the Soviet Union which these assumptions implied, and had ensured in practice, Halifax circumvented the issue once more by paying lip-service to the general importance of Russian help, while effectively ignoring the suggestion for specific action. Although the Minister of Health, Walter Elliott, again urged the importance of the Soviet Union and supported the proposal made by Hoare at the Foreign Policy Committee for a definite reciprocal agreement, Halifax reiterated both Bonnet's mistrust of Stalin's regime (misleadingly) and the importance of Poland.[100] In the face of such criticism his strategy was that of immovability. Soon afterwards the discussion petered out, and the draft telegrams were approved, with the vague references in Paragraph 6 to obtaining future Soviet support for the guarantees scheme as the only gesture towards the Cabinet critics.[101]

For those ministers who favoured a closer liaison with the Soviet Union crucially lacked a definite proposal to place against the telegrams already drafted by the executive. This in its turn was the result of the defensive posture constantly imposed on them by Chamberlain's and Halifax's fast-changing initiatives. The vigorous executive lead in discussion therefore led them to accept the compromise of a promised approach to Russia at a later date – an approach which was to consist only in requests for unilateral Soviet help to Poland and Roumania. As events were to prove, the delay and the half-heartedness in approaching Stalin were always likely to end in alienating the Soviet government and thus making any agreement much more difficult, if not impossible.[102] Thus the compromise won by Hoare and Stanley was chimerical, and thinly disguised a practical decision to court Polish support at almost any cost.

By 29 March the formulation of the guarantee policy had been completed. During the next two days important decisions were taken about the timing and presentation of the policy, but no major alterations of substance ensued. Indeed on the evening of 29 March the

Constructing the Polish Guarantee, March 1939

Prime Minister felt able to fulfil his commitment to entertain the King and Queen at 10 Downing Street, in relaxed style.[103] The Cabinet were then suddenly called to a meeting on the evening of 30 March for Halifax to relate the new information from various sources about the possibility of an immediate German move against Poland.[104]

Once again dramatic but unreliable intelligence sources (in this case from the US Ambassador in Warsaw, the young journalist and Secret Service contact Ian Colvin and seemingly detailed local information[105]) were being allowed to stampede British foreign policy into actions of the most serious kind. Halifax now proposed that Britain should announce her guarantee in the very near future, rather than wait for both her own and Germany's negotiations with Poland to run their natural course. The reasons for such action would be precisely those which had governed the formation of the policy in the first instance; the only variable which had changed was the perception of a new and imminent German aggression. The *raison d'être* of the new policy was to deter Hitler from further aggressions, and in particular from attacking Poland. It was also to ensure the existence of a Second Front if he should fail to be deterred. Thus if an attack was being contemplated at that very moment, the guarantee plan was in danger of becoming superfluous unless it were announced immediately.

On the other hand, it is possible, as Simon Newman suggests, that Halifax and his officials were using these sources to force the pace, and that behind them figures from the intelligence world such as Colonel Mason-MacFarlane, the British Military Attaché in Berlin, were themselves trying to hurry on a British commitment.[106] The thinking behind such moves would have been a mixture of concern to signal resistance to Germany and thus initiate deterrence – the German takeover of the port of Memel had followed Prague on 23 March and events seemed to be getting so out of hand that on the 28th Chamberlain was panicked into agreeing to double the Territorial Army overnight – and increasing anxiety to secure an arrangement with Poland.[107]

The Cabinet therefore were asked to approve immediate action, but in effect they were only duplicating their ratification of the previous day. Even here, the definition of the situation as sufficiently serious to require a sudden announcement, which would mean going ahead without full reciprocity or a guarantee for Roumania, was made by Halifax and Chamberlain. In such a fluid and unpredictable environment, they gave impetus, direction and cohesion to an otherwise disconcerted government. Once again the Chiefs of Staff warnings about the importance of the USSR were overlooked, despite being repeated in the draft paper which Chatfield had asked for 'as a matter of great urgency' on 28 March but which did not go to Cabinet ministers until 3 April, and then in a revised version much more sympathetic to the Polish Guarantee than the original drafted by the experts in the Joint Planning Sub-Committee of the Chiefs of Staff. Chatfield said that the Chiefs had come 'to the fairly definite conclusion' that if Britain had to fight Germany over Poland it would be better to do so with Poland as an ally – an apparently innocuous assessment but one full of meaning for those *au fait* with the argument over the Soviet Union, and also at odds with the truth.[108] Chatfield's personal ambivalence[109] had made him into a follower rather than a leader, and it may have been uneasy memories of this episode that eventually led him into advocating a Soviet alliance, to the Prime Minister's displeasure, in mid-May.[110]

Despite some disquiet in Cabinet about the risks of precipitate action, the guarantee to Poland was British policy, and it was announced in the Commons at 3 p.m. on 31 March, to be greeted by Arthur Greenwood, the Deputy Leader of the Labour Party, as being potentially 'as momentous a statement as has been made in this House for a quarter of a century'.[111]

The evidence from the case of the guarantee to Poland demonstrates a particular type of policy-making, and one in which the Cabinet as a whole took only a peripheral part, displaying little collective unity or purpose. It has been argued that this style correlates strongly with the nature of the problem which was under consideration at the time. The crisis of March 1939 was of major importance. It dissolved many of the hopes and views which decision-makers had previously held about Germany and the likelihood of maintaining a viable peace in Europe. On the accepted premise that Britain was vitally interested in the maintenance of European stability, it required a fundamental reformulation of strategic images and possibly a specific new act of policy. It affected foreign policy in a most basic and total way. No area of the British national interest could be unaltered by the decisions it demanded about war and peace. It was also felt by those involved that the situation was one of great urgency.

The combination of all these demands seems to have favoured a pyramidal form of policy-making in the government, with the foreign policy executive's creative initiatives and control of the channels of advice acting upon the confused and malleable opinions of their colleagues. The power of origination devolved upon the Prime Minister and Foreign Secretary, who exercised it with enthusiasm, even impulsiveness, after a brief initial hesitation. The consensus finally reached in Cabinet was essentially negative, deriving from the lack of any clear alternatives to falling in with the lead coming from the chair. Despite clear signs of unease from certain ministers, and full if rather shapeless discussions over two weeks, a new policy had been conceived, designed, changed three times and then implemented by a Prime Minister and Foreign Secretary who were only too keen to fill the policy vacuum.

3. THE SOVIET QUESTION, APRIL–AUGUST 1939

The problem of Anglo-Soviet relations in the later spring and summer of 1939 usefully provides both a parallel and a contrast to that of the Polish Guarantee. It was of equally vital importance to British foreign policy, both objectively and increasingly in terms of the way it was perceived by participants. Its outcomes, whatever they might be, would inevitably affect the military and political balance in Europe, since it involved the consideration of advance commitments to go to war. It was also seen as a pressing issue, although slightly less so than the events of March. Ministers rapidly recognised in April that continued German expansionism meant that relations between Britain and the USSR could no longer remain ill-defined. An immediate attempt to reach some kind of agreement had to be made. However, in contrast to the guarantee to Poland, the salience of this problem did not deeply disturb the central notions of British policy-makers about European politics. For it arose gradually out of the deliberations about Poland, and it was not a new or sudden trauma of itself. Indeed to some extent it was left-over business from those last two hectic weeks of March. Once the invasion of Prague had been assimilated, and the guarantee issued to Poland, the idea of concluding a full alliance with the USSR was not so radical as it would have seemed even six months previously. Moreover the proposals that emerged were formal, detailed and multifaceted. Both procedurally and substantively the contrasts and similarities between the March crisis and the Soviet negotiations throw interesting light on the relationship between policy-making and the problems with which it deals.

From the policy-making viewpoint, the important questions raised in the case of Anglo-Soviet relations centre on the influences in the British Cabinet which led to:

The Soviet question, April–August 1939   49

1 The initiation of negotiations in April
2 The rejection of the Litvinov proposals of 18 April for a full alliance
3 The decision after all on 24 May to accept the proposals
4 The various British bargaining positions during the prolonged negotiations for the alliance from May to August 1939.

A DEBT OWED TO CABINET

Without embarking upon a daily history of British diplomacy in April 1939, it is necessary to sketch the details of how negotiations with the USSR began.[1] Halifax had assured the Cabinet on 29 March that Britain would approach the Soviet Union about the latter's possible contribution to a 'Peace Front', once the guarantee agreement with Poland had been concluded.[2] After the declaration of 31 March, therefore, the Foreign Secretary dispatched to Moscow on 14 April the ingenuous proposal that the USSR should make a unilateral declaration of support to any of her European neighbours which might require and desire it.[3]

The responsibility for this *démarche* cannot be attributed to enthusiasm on the part of the executive. Chamberlain at least was still profoundly sceptical of the value of Soviet help. He told the Cabinet on 5 April that 'he had very considerable distrust of Russia, and had no confidence that we should obtain active and constant support from that country', while, if R. S. Hudson's recent first-hand observations about Russia's lack of an offensive military capacity were correct, he continued, 'if an arrangement which included Russia would be likely to cause an explosion, the question of making any arrangement with Russia was obviously one which required a great deal of further consideration'.[4] 'Consideration' in this context clearly meant postponement, and the unrealistic request to Moscow for open-ended declarations of support was hardly more serious in its intent. But if Soviet support could be obtained at little cost, then Chamberlain, and certainly Halifax, were now ready to envisage it.

There were various reasons for this. Some were substantive, such as the Italian attack on Albania, a desire to soothe growing public criticism, and his own genuine acceptance of the value – if it could be relied upon – of Soviet military aid to Poland.[5] But equally important must have been the knowledge that there was a vocal body of opinion within his Cabinet which favoured Anglo-Soviet co-operation at this time, and which had only been contained with difficulty in March despite the great advantages enjoyed by the executive during that crisis. As a result Halifax had made a formal commitment to take steps which would ensure some Soviet support in the event of war, once the Polish Guarantee had been concluded. It had been a condition of pacifying Hoare and Stanley, and keeping the Cabinet united in a period of extreme international instability. The price of unity was that Halifax and Chamberlain were left with a sense of obligation to take some action at least towards the Soviet Union, after their previous evasions, and also the creation of a general expectation among other ministers of an imminent approach. R.J. Minney gives us the Secretary of State for War's record of this expectation: 'Hore-Belisha's notes at this time indicate that the Government was anxious to include Russia in their efforts and negotiations to secure a common front against aggression.'[6] C. Hendricks, Secretary in the Privy Council Office, wrote to his chief Walter Runciman, who was touring the Dominions, that the main difficulty facing British policy was now Russia.[7] Even Leslie Burgin, who was inclined at first to stress the difficulties facing an Anglo-Soviet arrangement, and whom Hugh Dalton described privately as 'a Simonite of the worst type', told the Labour front-bencher that it would be very useful if Britain could take steps to ensure the USSR's neutrality in a future war.[8]

Despite the fact, therefore, that Chamberlain might have been personally willing to allow the question of co-operation to sink slowly from the centre of policy-making debate, the compromise over the Polish Guarantee left him in debt to a section of his Cabinet, in a way that he had not been during March, when the executive had been able to sketch out policy upon a blank sheet. It was an obligation which Chamberlain could only ignore at the risk of damaging both his own credibility and possibly the internal harmony of the government. Moreover the Prime Minister could not rely on Halifax's continued opposition to some closer relationship with the Soviet Union. The debates in Cabinet in March had led Halifax to feel that moves should be made at least to involve the USSR in the new diplomacy.[9] In the first two weeks of April the Foreign Secretary showed himself fairly anxious not to appear unreasonable. In Cabinet on 5 April he commented that 'he thought it might be desirable for him to see the Russian Ambassador rather more frequently than in the past, so as to avoid any suspicion that we were cold shouldering Russia'.[10] Indeed the Foreign Secretary called Maisky to the Foreign Office on 6 and

11 April, first to inform him of the general lines of the talks with Beck, and then 'in order that I might keep him in touch with recent developments'.[11] Another meeting was held three days later, at Maisky's request.[12] These three meetings in nine days bear out Harvey's contemporary comments that 'H. is anxious to find a way round the Russian difficulty and is working on the idea of proposing to Stalin that he should make a unilateral declaration of support against aggression on much the same lines as we have.'[13] In some situations the collective discussions of Cabinet government inevitably detached the two major foreign policy ministers from each other, with the result that any pressure from other groups of ministers had a greater chance than usual of becoming policy. In early April 1939 the recruitment of Halifax to a more open-minded attitude about moderate co-operation with the USSR at least ruled out any united executive attempt to evade an approach to that country.

As a result Chamberlain informed his colleagues on 13 April that he was thinking of telling the Soviet Union frankly to stop talking in general terms, and to make a unilateral declaration of support for any state which might be attacked. The abrasive tone of his remarks suggests that on this occasion the Prime Minister was catching up with the general sense of his Cabinet, not initiating a course for them to follow. Ministers showed no surprise at the proposals and made little comment.[14]

THE SOVIET INITIATIVE

The second major stage in the development of Anglo-Soviet relations in 1939 began with the sudden Litvinov proposals of 17 April for a full military pact with France and Britain. This was to involve a 'five- to ten-year' period in which the three parties would render each other and all eastern European states 'situated between Baltic and Black Seas and bordering on USSR . . . all manner of assistance including that of a military nature'. They should operate a no separate peace agreement if war were to break, and London would be expected to explain that the guarantee to Poland applied only in the event of German aggression.[15] The British government rejected this plan on 6 May and repeated their appeal to the Soviet Union for a unilateral declaration of support to those countries which might request it.[16] How was this important decision made?

The full Cabinet was informed by Halifax of the Soviet proposal the day after its arrival in the Foreign Office.[17] They agreed that a reply should be formulated in the Foreign Policy Committee. On this occasion the issue was sufficiently complicated to require fairly detailed consideration; it also invited real ministerial participation. The problem was not urgent, in the very short term and, more importantly, it did not demand the wholesale formulation of a positive and original course of action to replace an outmoded strategy – as in March. For although the Litvinov proposals were a complete surprise to the Cabinet, in that, as the Foreign Office memorandum reminded the Committee, 'we have taken the attitude that the Soviet preach us sermons on "collective security" but make no practical proposals. They have now made such . . . ',[18] they were only proposals, not actions which could physically compel a reorientation of views. At a deeper level they overturned none of the strategic or political realities on which governmental attitudes were based, as the fall of France was to do. They did not destroy any key images of the European situation, as the Nazi–Soviet Pact ought to have done. Their effect was rather the opposite; to bring the Cabinet at last to consider in depth their attitude towards co-operation with the USSR against Germany – an issue which had been latent for at least six months. The question had been on the verge of resolution during both the Munich crisis and that of March 1939. Moreover the suggestion for a full alliance did not reverse British conceptions of Soviet interests. It merely made clear what had previously been a reasonable supposition: that the USSR was sufficiently concerned about the threat posed by Hitler to venture out into very new diplomatic pastures.[19] It could, moreover, be easily rationalised away as a further sign of Soviet unreliability, by those of a suspicious cast of mind.

The Litvinov proposals were thus surprising but not shocking. They demanded no sudden reformulation of basic attitudes. Consequently the Cabinet were not dependent on creative leadership for their understanding of the problem at hand. Ministers' general picture of the USSR in European politics remained intact, to equip them with at least a basic confidence in their opinions for the discussion which was to follow. The continuity of the views expressed by Hoare and Stanley in both March and May testifies to this. The nature of the issue did not for once militate against dissent in Cabinet. Together with the executive's foreknowledge of the existing divisions among ministers over the Soviet question, still to be reconciled, this factor lessened the likelihood of Halifax and Chamberlain being able to monopolise the vital initiatives and harness the Cabinet to their own views. In the event, the way that the debate developed through April and May increasingly imposed positive pressures on the executive to allow the Cabinet (in the form of the Foreign Policy Committee) to operate in a much more participatory spirit.

The Foreign Policy Committee met on the afternoon of the same day on which the Cabinet had delegated discussion of the Litvinov proposals to them.[20] Halifax was absent, but approved of a paper prepared by the Foreign Office and read out by Cadogan which set out the arguments on both sides and then came down clearly against acceptance of a triple alliance. The proposal was extremely inconvenient:

> we are trying to build a 'Peace Front' in Europe, and it seems, on balance, better to refuse an offer that may alienate our friends and reinforce the propaganda of our enemies without bringing in exchange any real material contribution to the strength of our Front.[21]

The Prime Minister added his opinion in support of the Foreign Office, giving various sources for the view that 'the Russian fighting services were at present of little military value for offensive purposes', and still ignoring the Chiefs of Staff conclusion of 18 March, repeated to this meeting of the Foreign Policy Committee, that 'if the USSR were on our side and Poland neutral the position would alter in our favour' – although with the caveat that 'the USSR is militarily today an uncertain quantity'. It seems clear that the information coming through Foreign Office channels about Soviet military capacity now being largely defensive was being eagerly seized upon to neutralise Chiefs of Staff arguments – here again represented in the most muted terms by Chatfield – that a Russian alliance might make Germany's position more difficult in the Baltic and might deter Japan from joining in any war.[22] Chatfield, only a minister since January, and possibly deaf into the bargain, seems to have been too diffident to stand up against Chamberlain's confident presumptions.[23]

Hoare expressed unhappiness about the situation in eastern Europe, on the grounds that Poland was militarily impotent and only the USSR could furnish her with adequate supplies of munitions. But he could still suggest no positive alternative to the current policy, and the Committee drifted unimpeded into acceptance of the Foreign Office view. Chatfield ended the meeting on a note of resentment, accepting that the Committee took the view that political arguments against an alliance were 'irresistible, and such as to outweigh any military advantages'. He thus asked for strictly limited terms of reference for the paper which the Chiefs of Staff were now being asked to provide on Russian capacity. This covered his position but compounded his failure to grasp the nettle of relating military and political considerations closely to each other.

Inskip and Morrison had both professed doubts as to Soviet sincerity in making the offer of an alliance, whereupon Chamberlain had rapidly proceeded to 'collect the voices' in classic style: 'THE PRIME MINISTER said that if this were our view we had to consider how to frame our reply.'[24] By thus seizing the initiative in rather prematurely summarising the collective opinion of the Committee, the Prime Minister had made it difficult for the doubts of Hoare and Stanley (the latter's were noted by Cadogan in his diary)[25] to grow into fully fledged arguments through the process of further discussion. Chamberlain informed the Committee of their own basic conclusion before it had been fully articulated. Nevertheless, it is fairly certain that the majority of ministers present at this stage did share the view that Britain should not enter into an alliance with the Soviet Union. Those who spoke aligned themselves with Chamberlain, apart from Stanley and Hoare. Of the seven ministerial members of the Committee present apart from the Prime Minister, Inskip and Morrison had taken the view which Chatfield was eventually to summarise as representing an 'irresistible' political case against a triple alliance. Cadogan, representing Halifax, had set the example for such a conclusion, and in doing so had been supported by R. A. Butler;[26] Simon and MacDonald seem to have made no contribution.

Thus there was a clear majority actively opposed to the Soviet proposals. This was the more easily translated into a formal decision by the fact that the doubts of Hoare and Stanley did not lead them any more than their colleagues into an enthusiasm for the full alliance now in question. They feared for the consequences of alienating the Soviet Union, but preferred some intermediate arrangement whose form they could not see clearly. Even for those ministers sympathetic to association with the USSR, the suggestion of a major alliance came too soon and too boldly. Having failed to win the argument in March on more modest proposals, they did not now welcome having to advocate a radical version of their case. Thus as Cadogan recorded, 'there was general approval' of his advice to refuse the proffered liaison.[27]

In this way the Foreign Policy Committee had at least played a full part in the making of the decision. The issue had immediately been placed before it, there had been quite an extensive discussion and the conclusion reached represented the general will of the Committee, although partly by default. On the other side of the coin, the executive had yet again forcefully argued in favour of one side of the case – as, indeed, they were probably expected to do. Yet the Committee soon had another opportunity to influence the handling of the problem, at a meeting on 25 April to discuss the latest French response, which substantially accepted the desirability of a general, tripartite, agreement.[28] Halifax and Chamberlain once more made plain their view that this would gravely disrupt the construction of a 'Peace Front' with the other eastern European countries without obtaining any significant military advantages. The Committee was inclined to agree, although not without some ambivalence. The Chiefs of Staff paper on 'the military value of Russia' was now before the Committee, and Chatfield could not help admitting that, despite Russian weaknesses, her help in war would be of considerable help to the allies. Nonetheless he once again misrepresented the broad thrust of military advice. While the paper talked of the value of the Russians in the Baltic, as a deterrent to Japan and in particular as a source of food and raw materials which it would be vital to deny to Germany (it drew attention to the 'very grave military dangers inherent in the possibility of any agreement between Germany and Russia'), Chatfield concluded that 'the assistance which Russia could bring to bear was not nearly as great as certain quarters represented it to be'. This was true but far from the whole truth.

Other signs of uncertainty were also evident. Inskip stressed South Africa's hostility to the proposal, but also now pointed out that the Soviet Union might be a potential help to the British position in the Far East, by restraining Japan.[29] MacDonald went further, saying that it would be better to have the USSR on Britain's side in a war than to have her neutral, or an enemy.

Yet essentially the same consideration applied as on 19 April. While some of the Committee were by no means as convinced as the executive of the merits of a policy which was based primarily on

Poland, when as an alternative they were asked to consider the commitment of a generalised alliance with the USSR, even these ministers shared Chamberlain's misgivings. Hoare epitomised the way in which those furthest from the Prime Minister's viewpoint still approved of the conclusion which the committee arrived at, that is, to let France know that Britain viewed all proposals involving an alliance as impracticable, since they would impair the erection of 'a barrier against aggression in Eastern Europe on behalf of the States directly menaced by Germany', by impairing the confidence of those states.[30] The Home Secretary said that if the present policy were to fail the situation would have to be reconsidered, but that in the meantime he was in agreement with the critical reply to Paris. Again Cadogan pithily summarised the meeting's collective view of the Soviet proposals: 'Didn't last long – all agreed to turn them down.'[31]

Although the Foreign Policy Committee had examined the issue in some detail, their decision was submitted to the Cabinet before implementation.[32] Naturally the Cabinet 'expressed general approval of the policy vis-à-vis Soviet Russia', since the ministers who now were given their chance to keep in touch with developments were given a one-sided and necessarily compressed report by Halifax. Together with the circulated copies of selected telegrams and the paper by the Chiefs of Staff (the availability of the latter, at least, representing an advance on the events of late March), this second-hand report was the only point of access for these ministers to the main issues, and unsurprisingly it did not equip them with sufficient expertise to stimulate an interest in continuing the debate. Accordingly Halifax was able to dispatch a telegram to Sir Eric Phipps in Paris on 28 April which definitely rejected the Litvinov proposals and their later French expression.[33]

While the full Cabinet had only fulfilled the function of formal authorisation, its offspring body had fully participated in the making of this decision. And, as is explained below, as an institution the Foreign Policy Committee was far nearer to representing Cabinet participation throughout these negotiations than it was to being a vehicle for executive elitism.[34] Committees could be used in a number of ways – to keep discussion away from most ministers, as a means of resolving disputes in the full Cabinet (as happened at precisely this time over the legislative proposals for conscription[35]) or simply to allow more lengthy and specialised examination of a problem. Moreover the Prime Minister's intentions in taking a matter to a committee were not always fulfilled by the course of its discussions, as will become clearer with respect to the Foreign Policy Committee when we look at the next important stage in the evolution of attitudes towards the Soviet Union.

CONFLICT IN CABINET

Between 28 April and 24 May, in the third stage of this phase of decision-making, the British government came to accept that an alliance with the USSR might after all be necessary. This considerable volte-face (in both the short-term and the longest perspectives of British history), was only achieved by the purgative of constant internal dispute. By the time the Cabinet agreed on 24 May to authorise the conclusion of a mutual-guarantee arrangement, there had taken place the conversion of a majority of ministers in the Foreign Policy Committee and the Cabinet from opposition or ambivalence to positive agreement. Chamberlain and Halifax themselves had come from the distaste and disapproval we have already noted to a reluctant acquiescence in the negotiation of an alliance. The course of this development is in essence straightforward, and represents on the surface a classic case of rational policy-making through argument and counter-argument. In the process of regular and prolonged discussion in both Cabinet and Committee, that minority which advocated the step from the beginning gradually recruited more and more ministers to their group, with every new addition disproportionately increasing the pressure on those still unconverted to change sides, as the numerical balance of the debate was automatically altered.

But why in the first place should sufficient ministers have become converted to the desirability of a Soviet alliance, after it had twice been rejected? How was it that Chamberlain and Halifax, the last to change their minds but the weightiest ministerial combination of all, could not together prevent the drift towards an alliance or, in the final analysis, simply hold out against implementing such a reversal of their policy?[36] To some extent the reasons are clearly to be found in the changing nature of external circumstances. The refusal of the USSR to countenance anything less than a full alliance, and its consequent rejection of all Britain's compromise formulae which involved unilateral Soviet declarations or possible political and military consultations, faced the government with a direct and narrow choice between, as Cadogan noted on 19 May, 'Soviet alliance (or pact of mutual assistance) and breakdown – with all consequences'.³⁷

The 'consequences' of the failure of negotiations were outlined by Chamberlain in explaining his own last-minute change of view. They added up to various putative discouraging effects on European public opinion, at a difficult psychological moment after the conclusion of the German-Italian Pact.³⁸ The details of these factors, and the reasons why they might have combined to make ministers prefer an alliance to breakdown, are dealt with throughout what follows.³⁹ Here it is sufficient to note that in themselves they amounted to no more convincing a list of *objective* circumstances than those cited a few weeks previously for the diametrically opposite policy, of avoiding a Soviet entanglement. The reasons for a change of direction have to be sought in the interaction of external circumstances with the nature of internal debate – internal both to the Cabinet and their advisers and to the minds of the individuals concerned. This helps us to understand the paradox that, while some ministers were distinctly unenthusiastic about an alliance, none were willing in the last instance to go so far as rupturing the negotiations once they had been drawn into some move towards Moscow. They fell into the process known as 'policy drift'.⁴⁰

Another new factor to be taken into account was a heightened perception of the possibility of a Russo-German agreement. The Chiefs of Staff, in an *aide-mémoire* which Chatfield read to the Foreign Policy Committee on 16 May, stressed that a failure to reach agreement with the USSR would have serious repercussions 'in that it would have the immediate effect of encouraging Germany to further acts of aggression and of ultimately throwing the USSR into her arms'.⁴¹ Halifax took up the point when he announced his own eventual conversion: 'so far as he had been able to sift the available information, he thought that the idea of some rapprochement between Germany and Russia was not one which could be altogether disregarded'.⁴² This kind of consideration had rarely been mooted at such a high level in the consideration of the Soviet Union before May 1939.⁴³

The final changed circumstance which might have operated to convince the reluctant of the necessity of an alliance was the possibility that fewer third parties would be alienated from Britain by such a move than had previously been supposed. On 22–3 May, in response to a British enquiry, the governments of Poland and Roumania had replied in substance that they did not wish to cause difficulties for the conclusion of an alliance with the Soviet Union, at least in the slightly more limited form still envisaged by Britain on 19 May, when the enquiry was made.[44] Halifax certainly interpreted their views in this way, telling the Cabinet that the two countries did not object 'provided that such an arrangement was concluded without those Governments respectively being consulted or mentioned in the agreement'.[45] Thus any fears which there were for the effects of association with the Soviet Union on the Polish Second Front, thought of as so crucial by Chamberlain and Halifax, were here partly assuaged.

Yet by themselves these new facts of external relations fall a good deal short of being a satisfactory explanation of the British government's altered decision over a Soviet alliance. They do not seem to constitute sufficiently pressing or strongly held motives to change what was, in Chamberlain, Halifax and Morrison at least, a deep hostility to the prospect of such an unprecedented commitment. The very way in which they had engineered the prompt rejection of both Soviet and French proposals in April was an indicator of the depth of their conviction. Moreover the antipathy was based on more serious reasons than simple ideological distrust. Chamberlain had privately recorded his agreement with Beck, for example, that association with the USSR might actually provoke a German attack. The Prime Minister essentially regarded 'Russia ... as a very unreliable friend ... with an enormous irritative power on others ... I can't believe that she has the same aims or objects as we have ... the alliance would definitely be a lining up of opposing blocs'.[46] This view, that an Anglo-Soviet alliance would accelerate the formation of blocs and the coming of war, runs right through Chamberlain's argument and was probably his most serious concern.[47] W. S. Morrison thought along similar lines, and supported the Prime Minister unwaveringly. On 16 May he expressed their joint outlook concisely. Morrison preferred, he said, a more limited agreement, by which 'we should run much less risk of getting involved in an ideological war than if we entered into a formal military alliance with Russia'.[48] Halifax also subscribed to the view that the alliance would actually increase the dangers in Europe. He told the Cabinet that 'a tri-partite pact on the lines proposed, would make war inevitable'.[49] Such views were presented too consistently in private meetings to have been mere rhetoric.

Thus the executive and the ministers sympathetic to them would hardly have worked for an alliance with the USSR of their own volition. The new factors we have noted were just not plausible enough to outweigh the basic hostility shown by both Prime Minister and Foreign Secretary, or even the moderate antagonism of some other ministers. For example, the fears for the effects of the breakdown of negotiations, expressed by Chamberlain on 24 May as the reason for his change of heart, seem no more serious than those he had previously presented about the possible alienation of neutrals by an alliance.[50] On 3 May Halifax had been concerned for the 'unfortunate' effect of an alliance on Portugal, Italy, Japan and 'large numbers of people in Europe'.[51] Two days later he had argued against 'changing the whole basis of our policy and risking the alienation of our friends', a theme which Chamberlain took up on 16 May when he insisted that any military advantages of the alliance must be weighed against the political disadvantages – such as damage to Dominion sympathies for British policy.[52] It is difficult to see how these arguments could logically have been superseded by the concerns for 'public opinion in Europe' and 'a discouraging effect on France and Turkey' that Chamberlain finally cited as the factors which had convinced him not to allow the breakdown of negotiations.[53] There is no intrinsic justification in the arguments themselves for Chamberlain's transference of his concern for one amorphous group of countries and peoples to another.

Similarly, the spectre, raised for the first time in May, of a Russo-German pact was hardly taken sufficiently seriously by the opponents of a British alliance with Stalin to cause their defection to the other side of the debate. From a purely numerical point of view, they made few comments in Cabinet or Committee on the possibility or its significance. Although Hore-Belisha, Zetland and Chatfield brought up the question at various times and with varying degrees of interest,[54] the only positive response from the executive was made by Halifax on the day that the Cabinet decided to go for an alliance, and even then he would only say that a Russo-German *rapprochement* 'was not one which could be altogether disregarded'.[55] In fact neither he nor Chamberlain seems to have been convinced either that such a liaison would occur or that it would be of any great importance. On 5 May Halifax had retorted to Chatfield in the Foreign Policy Committee that Litvinov's dismissal in favour of Molotov (which took place on 3 May) might point more to a policy of closer ties with western Europe than to co-operation with Germany. The Foreign

Secretary even thought that reports of such an eventuality 'might be spread by persons who wished to drive us into making a pact with Russia'.[56] Chamberlain was also dubious. When Hore-Belisha and MacDonald had tentatively raised the 'fantastic' idea of an arrangement between Hitler and Stalin, the Prime Minister did not respond sympathetically or with any sense of urgency. He thought that 'no decision was called for at the present time'. Negotiations would continue.[57] Finally, on 24 May, the argument found no place in the Prime Minister's canon of reasons for giving way. In short, it is highly unlikely that anticipation of the Nazi-Soviet Pact was a crucial reason for the eventual switch of attitude by the more die-hard opponents of a Soviet alliance in May 1939.[58]

Towards the end of this stage of the discussion, those who were in the process of reluctant conversion began to sprinkle their argument with the point that '*having gone so far* it would be right to make an agreement rather than risk a complete breakdown'.[59] Halifax himself told Harvey that '*we had gone so far* that the little more would not make much difference in its effect on Hitler'.[60] The phrase here emphasised was perhaps the most often expressed reason for the change of policy by the participants themselves.[61] It is to be found in their arguments only from 16 May onwards since it refers to the Foreign Office draft generally approved by the Committee on that day, which sought to avoid a full alliance by proposing instead to the USSR a set of mutual declarations – this virtually equalled an alliance.[62] It was a natural debating point to make for those who had been convinced from the outset of the utility of an alliance with the Soviet Union. However, as an explanation for the retraction of those who had been implacably opposed to such a move, it was circular, begging the question of how it was that the latter had been brought 'so far' in the first place. Up to a point the absolute Soviet refusal to accept anything less than a full alliance explains this retreat from earlier positions, but it does not account for the basic inability of the British executive to take up an equally rigid bargaining position where they were undoubtedly inclined on personal grounds to do so. On the contrary, the British government continued to slide towards the point where its offer of compromise seemed even to Halifax such a large concession to the Soviet viewpoint that the last small step to complete acquiescence might be taken without further detriment.[63]

It is necessary, therefore, to look beyond the 'objective' factors of a changing external environment, beyond the logic of the issue itself, if we are to explain what was an extraordinary overturning of two formal policy decisions not to conclude a Soviet alliance. As important from the theoretical point of view, and indeed in this particular case, is the way the policy-making process itself interacts with the changing pattern of events.

The very persistence of debate for so long inside the Cabinet and the Foreign Policy Committee was a crucial factor towards altering the decision, in that otherwise the executive would have had the opportunity of not prolonging the approach to Russia immediately their own first proposal (for a unilateral Soviet declaration) had been rejected. In the event the government came to be faced with an alarming choice of extremes, between an alliance and the public breakdown of what by then had grown to be lengthy and substantial negotiations. Without the pressure from within the Cabinet, itself stimulated by outside arguments[64] and made possible by the open-ended, long-term character of the issue itself, Chamberlain and Halifax would have been much better placed to follow their own views and to resist the demands which came from the USSR, and to some extent from the French.[65] That they were finally coerced more than convinced into a possible alliance reinforces the view that the executive would probably have accepted the failure of the negotiations, if left to themselves. Instead, the combination of foreign actors and internal divisions operated to place the two ministers in a very weak bargaining position in both the international and the domestic context.

This fact found expression in two chronologically distinct phases of argument in Cabinet circles. First, with the help of the external factors we have touched on, the 'pro-Russians' in the Cabinet were able to convert to their viewpoint those ministers whose lack of strong feelings on the issue had previously led them to follow Chamberlain's lead, but who now were subject to the influence of the constant exposure, and resolute argument, which Hoare, Stanley and MacDonald, on occasions, brought to discussions of the Soviet question. Where at other times and on other issues the Cabinet might have witnessed only the monologue of an executive report, there was now more likely to be consistent advocacy by several members of a course of action which the fact of formal negotiations laid clearly before them as an option. The written proposals and counter-proposals, made within the ritualised framework of a bargaining relationship, required less transmission and explanation by the executive before the Committee could grasp their nature, and feasibility, than had other types of problem which demanded more originality and speed of agreement.[66] Whereas the crises of both September 1938 and March 1939 had involved speed of deliberation, and had been subject to a whole range of different British responses, here the type of policy decision was defined quite narrowly as a choice of some point along a scale of Anglo-Soviet agreement which reached from a rupture of negotiations at one end to a full alliance on the other. While more open-ended issues often worked against Cabinet government, the rather legalistic nature of the debate about the Soviet negotiations tended to increase the number of accessible points of reference on which ministers could form a relatively sophisticated opinion.

Indeed the Hoare faction kept up a constant pressure to alter policy. The Foreign Policy Committee meeting of 5 May witnessed a long and rigorous argument between Hoare, Stanley and MacDonald, on the one side, and Chamberlain, Halifax, Morrison and all the other contributors, on the other. No ground was given by either, and those in favour of an alliance were clearly in the minority. Nevertheless, the latter's introduction of the possibility of a tripartite 'no separate peace agreement', their refusal to allow the general argument to go by default and their willingness to prolong discussion were the key factors in bringing a sense of division, seriousness and unfinished decision to the Committee.[67] The unmistakable split which now emerged was a relatively rare characteristic of Cabinet argument, and its existence was partly the result of the lengthy policy-formulation phase, which enabled the normal cross-pressures of a period of diplomatic flux to act more consistently and effectively on the opinions of the individual members of the Committee.

Once disagreement with current policy had been seriously voiced, it seems to have had a multiplier effect, in terms of winning piecemeal concessions and thus pushing the executive ever nearer to the Soviet position and of gradually attracting support from those ministers otherwise diffident about opposing the Prime Minister, but who were potentially receptive to the case for an agreement with the USSR if it were to be given a lengthy hearing and energetic support. The first breach of a taboo always makes subsequent acts of defiance easier. For instance, the meeting of 5 May led to the Committee deciding, in deference to the views of Hoare and his allies, that if the USSR showed itself newly sympathetic to the proposal for a unilateral declaration, then Britain would be willing to reconsider the present hostility to a 'no separate peace' agreement to apply in wartime.[68] A much larger concession followed the further fundamental disputes in the Committee meeting of 16 May. It was agreed in principle that an offer of military conversations be made to the Soviet Union and that a pact be concluded whereby all three parties (that is to say, Britain, France and the Soviet Union) would promise mutual support in the event of their going to war for Poland or Roumania.[69]

By this time the accession of new supporters to the Hoare–Stanley camp had already begun, which itself exerted extra pressure on Chamberlain and Halifax to compromise. At the Cabinet meeting of 10 May, Burgin had shown signs of detachment from the executive view, by joining with MacDonald to urge that the Foreign Secretary should invite Molotov to continue negotiations at their forthcoming (coincidental) meeting in Geneva. Perhaps the import of Litvinov's dismissal was beginning to seep into ministers' minds, although there is no indication of this in the records. Nor can Seeds' account of his difficulties with Molotov have yet been reported to the Cabinet.[70] Six days later, moreover, Leslie Burgin admitted in the Foreign Policy Committee (although a new member) that if negotiations were on the point of breakdown, then he would prefer to conclude an agreement. This was advance warning to the Prime Minister of the effect the prolonged negotiations were having on ministers' willingness to envisage an alliance.[71]

A more crucial conversion was that of Chatfield and the Chiefs of Staff, again revealed on 16 May. The unresolved debate had led to the military being asked twice inside a week to produce reports at very short notice, first on the apparent choice between Spanish enmity and Soviet friendship and then on the position if Britain were to go into some kind of *entente* with Moscow (still short of a full alliance). This last led to an *aide-mémoire* being drafted in a day for the evening meeting of the Committee on 16 May. The Chiefs of Staff now concluded that 'we certainly want something better than the bare neutrality of Russia' and that fear for Spain's friendship should no longer be ranked above the military advantages of a pact with the Soviet Union during the consideration of current policy (as they had still just concluded in the paper of 10 May).[72] Chatfield proceeded to support these views vigorously. Qualitatively, the fact that the professional expertise of the military viewpoint was cast suddenly in favour of a full alliance, together with the apparent conviction with which Chatfield now advocated his new cause (seemingly spurred on by a fear that the assumption of Russian neutrality in any Anglo-German conflict might not be tenable), obviously gave considerable new impetus to the arguments which Chamberlain and Halifax were resisting. Numerically, Chatfield's turnabout completed the polarisation of the Committee. It meant that five ministers now still opposed an alliance (the executive, plus Morrison, Inskip and probably the taciturn Simon[73]), as against five who were in favour (Hoare, Stanley, MacDonald,[74] Chatfield and, in the last instance, Burgin). Moreover it was becoming plain that there was a trend among ministers to change their views on the issue. This forced Chamberlain, who was otherwise unmoved by the reasons for Chatfield's new opinion, to argue from a defensive position. His role was now that of a rearguard resistance to encroaching, positive demands from an increasingly coherent and vociferous group of ministers – the reverse of the circumstances obtaining in the formation of the Guarantee policy, where articulate, creative initiatives from the executive found the majority of ministers in a disadvantaged position of passivity, lacking the information and opportunities to form their own positive alternatives.[75]

In its turn, this loss of initiative added to the difficulties from which it sprang, for Chamberlain and Halifax. There could now be no question of suppressing the issue, or ignoring the divisions in the Committee, particularly since there was no active additional support for the Prime Minister's view in Cabinet, which might be mobilised if the Foreign Policy Committee was divided. Of those ministers in the Cabinet but not on the Committee who also had a professional interest in foreign policy, none took up an unqualified position of opposition to the alliance. Zetland was 'impressed' with the difficulties which would accrue from accepting Russian terms, but still agreed 'that we might have to go some way in order to prevent a possible agreement between Russia and Germany'.[76] Kingsley Wood advised that an alliance be of short duration, but actively supported the decision for a pact when made.[77] Hore-Belisha seems to have made no active contribution on either side, but was close enough to Churchill at this time to have been pro-alliance.[78] Finally even Earl Stanhope, who was opposed to the alliance because of its possibly adverse effects on relations with Spain and Japan, was willing to concede, with regard to what he personally saw as the unlikely event of a Nazi-Soviet agreement, that 'If however it were a real possibility, then I feel it would be an over-riding consideration.'[79] Thus these ministers also failed to display the same refusal to countenance an alliance as Chamberlain. In large part they took up a mid-way position, lacking root-and-branch feelings for either cause.

As we have noted already, by the Committee meeting of 16 May the executive was being forced to make concessions of substance. The Cabinet meeting of the following day confirmed that there was now a real degree of self-conscious participation among ministers concerned for an alliance, and a resolve to continue to exert pressure until the arguments had been fully exposed and all possible support had been marshalled. In discussion, the view was expressed that members of the Cabinet should themselves see the latest Chiefs of Staff report which Chatfield had just paraphrased, together with the minutes of the Foreign Policy Committee and the relevant draft telegrams. The opinion was also voiced that only the Cabinet should decide between a full military alliance and the breakdown of negotiations. The Cabinet were beginning to assert themselves as a factor independent of executive initiative, as at times they had done during the September crises of the previous year. In consequence Chamberlain accepted these conditions despite his resentment of the Chiefs' volte-face, having little grounds on which to refuse, and stressed that it was his intention that 'there should be full opportunity for discussion'.[80]

In this way, as the Prime Minister encountered substantial informed and self-confident opposition, his style of positive leadership, which had flourished in other circumstances, with its clear opinions and recommendations, increasingly dissolved. The next Foreign Policy Committee meeting was not opened by Halifax or Chamberlain making their usual statement of assessment and direct advocacy of the line which ministers ought to take. Instead, the Prime Minister said that he thought it necessary for the Committee to decide on the next step. Caught between his persistent distaste for an alliance and an increasing realisation that dissentient colleagues would not allow the question to be dropped, Chamberlain found himself forced to allow the debate to take its full and natural course.

It was at this meeting on 19 May that two more antagonists of the alliance policy gave indications of their increasing sympathy for the arguments of Hoare and company. Sir Thomas Inskip considered that Hitler would not be likely to draw any distinction in his reactions between an Anglo-Soviet alliance and a lesser agreement. The obvious implication was that if Hitler would be alienated by any kind of pact, then Britain might as well benefit from the security of a full alliance. Cadogan's diary confirms this change in Inskip's opinion, as the Dominions Secretary is included in the list given in the entry for 19 May of ministers in favour of a triple alliance.[81] Moreover the Committee's minutes record that while Chamberlain reacted strongly against Inskip's remark, Simon expressed agreement with it. Cadogan placed a question mark by Simon's inclusion in his list of ministers still hostile to an alliance, so that it must have been clear that the Chancellor of the Exchequer was also moving away from implacable opposition to the Hoare–Stanley view. In simple terms of the number of sympathisers, the latter now dominated the Foreign Policy Committee. They held a majority of six to three, with Simon's position uncertain. Only Morrison still shared the views of Chamberlain and Halifax, and he was no heavy-weight in Cabinet.[82] Outside the Committee the Prime Minister still had some support, as in the case of Stanhope's arguments of 19 May against any step which might alienate Spain and Japan, but here again the trend was against him.[83]

This situation precipitated the second chronological phase of debate between 19 and 24 May, a period of only five days in which the resistance of the three die-hard opponents of an alliance quickly disintegrated under the sheer pressure of having demonstrably lost their support and being placed irrevocably in the minority position. Thus this second phase consisted essentially in the coercion of the core opponents of an alliance, whereas the first had been characterised by the persuasion of the relatively uncommitted through the opening up and prolongation of the debate. The rigorous initial arguments had allowed a coherent group to form in Cabinet around an opinion that for once had not been introduced or advocated by the executive. Chamberlain perhaps tacitly admitted his loss of support on 19 May when he told the Committee that a decision must be reserved for the Cabinet. Had the Foreign Policy Committee been in agreement with him, the Prime Minister might not have been so concerned for constitutional propriety. But Halifax was the first to decide that it was no longer possible to hold out against an alliance. As late as the 19th he had expressed 'the strongest possible distaste for a policy which meant our acquiescence in Soviet blackmail and bluff'.[84] Yet this very outburst may have derived from a sense that the policy distasteful to him was now inevitable. On 18 May he had written to Chamberlain about the latest Foreign Office draft, to which he reluctantly subscribed: 'This, you will observe, gives the Russians what they want, though an attempt is made to dress it up with some appearance of conformity with the policy we have hitherto been pursuing.'[85] The following day Halifax developed the point to his Private Secretary *en route* to Geneva: 'He himself took the view that we had gone so far that the little more would not make much difference in its effect on Hitler.'[86] Cadogan also noticed Halifax's change of mind, and indeed may have helped to bring it about, as he also moved slowly towards a new position. On 19 May he had noted the Foreign Secretary's continuing opposition to a Soviet agreement. But on the 20th he recorded, apropos of an alliance: 'I am, on balance, in favour of it. So, I think is H.'[87] On the way to Geneva, Halifax had stopped in Paris to consult with the French Prime Minister Edouard Daladier, and Bonnet, and had heard them confirm the hardening French conviction (already expressed in a letter from Ambassador Charles Corbin received three days earlier), that the strong Soviet bargaining position of a triple alliance or nothing would now effectively have to be conceded. The Foreign Secretary was beginning to recognise that he was boxed in.[88]

This is the background to Halifax's announcement in Cabinet on 24 May that he had finally come to accept the necessity of an alliance. The conversion was sufficiently rapid and politically unheralded to suggest that the Foreign Secretary had suddenly faced up to the twin new realities, of narrowing diplomatic options and the steadily increasing strength of the pro-alliance group in Cabinet. The tone of his remarks did not suggest enthusiasm or a sudden appreciation of the arguments themselves.[89]

It is certainly clear that the Prime Minister was constrained into acquiescence. Halifax told Harvey that Chamberlain was 'very reluctant to agree to full tripartite alliance', and Cadogan wrote that 'P.M. hates it' and 'In his present mood PM says he will resign rather than sign alliance with Soviet.' Even on 23 May, Halifax was 'still doubtful whether the PM will agree at Cabinet tomorrow'. Yet in the event Chamberlain found it 'impossible to stand out against the conclusion of an agreement', and the Cabinet took a formal decision to pursue an alliance.[90] He and Halifax both gave various reasons of policy for their change of view. As we have seen above, however, the arguments given are not *sufficient* to provide a satisfactory explanation of this major reversal of policy. The timetable of the changing balance of argument in Cabinet and Committee makes it clear that the primary cause of the success of the 'pro-Russians' in winning over the moderates and compelling the executive to relinquish their strongly held opinions was the degree and intensity of Cabinet argument. The dynamics of the negotiations themselves, together with the changing convictions evident in both France and the House of Commons,[91] were important contributory factors, but they were only brought into play by the pre-existing, and increasingly serious, division in the Cabinet on the Soviet question.

The high level of ministerial participation in this debate, itself deriving from the nature of the problem under analysis, largely prevented the executive from transposing their own preferences into policy-outcomes. The logical merits of the case were allowed full exposure – by no means always the case in policy-making, for reasons of time, partiality, psychology and the like. This in turn made possible (but not of course, inevitable) the growth of dissent in Cabinet, which finally proved irresistible. That the reasons given by Halifax and Chamberlain for accepting an alliance were indeed rationalisations of other pressures is aptly summed up in Cadogan's description: 'PM apparently resigned to idea of Soviet alliance, but depressed.'[92] The Prime Minister admitted privately that, at the end, 'the only support I could get for my views was RAB Butler and he was not a very influential ally'.[93]

As a postscript, one may perhaps speculate on what the consequences might have been if Chamberlain had continued to hold out against an alliance and had threatened the Cabinet with the resignation which he had seemed willing to contemplate on 20 May. It is possible that such a determinedly autocratic strategy would have succeeded in preventing the change in policy, and thus accorded a degree of negative power to the Prime Minister, in that his Cabinet might have ranked their desire for a particular decision below the damaging effects to the government of such a resignation in a period of general crisis.

This hypothesis runs into two damaging ripostes. The first is that Prime Ministers are unlikely to be so completely unaffected by the solidarity of their colleagues (and the defection of their Foreign Secretary) as to wish to incur hostility and distrust for the sake of a single policy-preference or a demonstration of ultimate authority over their Cabinets (this was to be demonstrated on 2 September). Secondly, as it happened, Chamberlain was forced to concede the argument, and did not feel able to threaten the Cabinet with the blackmail of resignation. There was no occasion on which the Prime Minister boldly confronted ministers, who were after all intimate acquaintances whose goodwill was essential to the harmonious running of the vast governmental process, with considerations of rank. In any event, it is not impossible, in the crisis-atmosphere of the times, that the Cabinet might have accepted a proffered resignation. Speculation cuts both ways. Moreover if a Prime Minister gets driven to such a point by extended wrangling in Cabinet he is likely to be aware that his authority has already been sufficiently damaged to make a vote of confidence a potential source of further humiliation.

SUPERVISING THE NEGOTIATIONS: A CABINET COMMITTEE IN ACTION

The last stage of policy-making towards the Soviet Union in 1939 – the negotiations for the alliance itself, running from 24 May to 22 September 1989 – is difficult to analyse in terms of the tracing of influence and participation through the various stages of bargaining.[94] The process was so prolonged, and the issues so complicated, that it is impossible to disentangle the proposals which the Foreign Policy Committee knew about and wanted from those they did not, let alone to assess the degrees of importance of each twist and turn of the negotiations. The same questions can be approached in a much more economical way by a general and semi-statistical appreciation of the overall regularity and business of Foreign Policy Committee meetings in the months of the Soviet issues, particularly in comparison to the preceding period.

Between the date of the first Committee meeting after Munich (14 November) and the outbreak of war on 3 September 1939, the Committee's business fell, broadly speaking, into five main divisions, both of chronology and of subject-matter:

1   14 Nov.–6 Dec. 38: *three meetings* on the general state of Anglo-German relations, and the future of Czechoslovakia after Munich
2   23 Jan.–8 Feb. 39: *three meetings* to consider new information that

a German attack on the Low Countries might be imminent, and to formulate an attitude to such action
3   27–31 Mar. 39: *three meetings* near the end of the making of the Polish Guarantee policy, mainly concerned with the accelerated announcement of that policy
4   10–11 Apr. 39: *two meetings* in which a reaction to the Italian move against Albania was discussed, together with the further guarantees to Greece and Turkey
5   19 Apr.–1 Aug. 39: *eighteen meetings*, fourteen of which (interspersed with occasional meetings on such other subjects as Tientsin, the purchase of Greek tobacco and Danzig) dealt with the negotiations for a diplomatic agreement with the USSR.

Other questions than those above were discussed in the Foreign Policy Committee, but not with the same detail or continuity that characterised the five principal preoccupations.[95]

It will be seen that all of the five topics were of crucial foreign policy importance; it is meaningless to attempt to rank them in terms of the seriousness with which the Committee might have regarded each issue, and correspondingly allocated their time. A more obvious and real distinction may be made between the degrees of physical attention paid by the Committee to the various questions. While the subjects of the first four divisions all occupied two or three meetings, the Anglo-Soviet negotiations took up fourteen, or nearly half the total of thirty meetings in this whole period. This was three more than the other four issues, of equal *a priori* importance, added together. Clearly at one level this was simply due to the fact that the Anglo-Soviet negotiations took longer to conclude than policy on the previous issues, none of which in the event required long-term discussion. But this very fact begs two related questions about the reasons for certain subjects involving prolonged consideration, and not others, and about the implications of such variations for the degree of Cabinet participation in policy-making.

The primary variable is the nature of the problem. In general terms the formulation of a response to a transient rumour will inevitably take less time than the resolution of complicated negotiations. More specifically, each type tends to favour one group of policy-makers more than the others, who are subsequently dependent for the degree of their participation on the attitudes of the group initially advantaged. For example, the Cabinet and their committees have a greater chance of involvement in policy-making where the alternatives are clearly defined than where ingenuity is required, in situations of confusion and low information.

There is, however, scope for varied responses to the nature of a problem, in specific instances. While the invasion of Prague did throw the onus of activity onto the executive, it need not inevitably have led Halifax and Chamberlain to devise the form of response that they did, with its stress on immediacy and intricate diplomacy and its effective exclusion of the Cabinet. It is not implausible that, perhaps through lack of a clear personal preference, they could have decided to readjust British policy in a more long-term and drastic form, by the gradual forging of a new stance through the medium of Cabinet discussion. Similarly, although a refocusing of general attitudes without any special urgency might tend to involve the Cabinet, so as to ensure basic consensus and full knowledge of the specific implications of these attitudes (as with the war aims discussions of October 1939 and 1940–1), it is equally possible that most ministers would not have strong or informed views and would be content to follow the initiative of Prime Minister and Foreign Secretary.

In other words, while the proportion of time expended and the degree of Cabinet involvement both depend initially on the objective nature of the particular issue – its newness, amenability to discussion and degree of urgency[96] – they are also strongly affected by the ways in which the actors in the policy-making process take the opportunities for influence and involvement presented to them at the outset by the type of question under consideration. The length of a problem's continuing salience, and the level of Cabinet participation, are therefore ultimately determined by interaction between the type of issue and the views of those ministers whose activity it initially favours.

As far as the Anglo-Soviet negotiations are concerned, this means that the large number of Foreign Policy Committee discussions on the subject were the consequence of the Committee's having capitalised on the opportunity of participation which the Soviet proposals for a formal and complicated alliance presented to them. Without the positive reaction which this inspired within the Committee, and the history of Cabinet concern over the USSR in late March, it is likely that an alliance would have been ruled out completely and that the negotiations would have been cut considerably short. The fourteen meetings on Soviet relations, therefore, indicate

The Soviet question, April–August 1939   73

genuine participation in policy-making by the Committee and are not simply a measure of an inevitably prolix discussion.

Other types of evidence support this observation. Figure 1 for instance, showing the numbers of ministers present at the Committee's meetings, shows a marked contrast between the months before and after the date of 19 May 1939, when the Soviet problem first came to dominate discussion. For the meetings of the first four issue-divisions, the numbers of ministers attending was, in sequence, 8, 9, 8, 6, 9, 9, 8, 8, 8, 8, 8 – an average of 8.1 per meeting. However, for those meetings concerned with the USSR, the figures were 8, 6, 9, 9, 10, 11, 11, 10, 11, 10, 11, 10, 10, 12 – an average of 9.9 per meeting.[97] Both these sets have regular lines of figures, suggesting a definite shift in behaviour for basic reasons which operated consistently over time. Thus the statistics clearly indicate that for the period in which the Anglo-Soviet negotiations were the principal diet of the Committee, it was consistently attended by an average of nearly two more ministers than had previously participated.

Insofar as this increase can be attributed to specific new appointments to the Committee, rather than to temporary and occasional factors, it was due to the appearances of Morrison, Chatfield and Burgin, all of whom were responsible for aspects of planning for an imminent war, and whose very arrivals betokened the higher profile being taken by the Cabinet and its Foreign Policy Committee in foreign affairs. There are various factors which complicate these figures, such as the dates of the appointments of Chatfield and Morrison and the absence abroad of Walter Runciman between 27 March and 19 May. Runciman's absence (on a tour of the Dominions) reduces the numerical increase in ministerial membership of the Committee, but only by 0.1 to 1.7. The appointment of Chatfield and Morrison accounts for a further 0.8,[98] and the remainder (i.e. 0.9) has to be explained by the arrival of Burgin on 10 May.

There is no firm evidence as to why Burgin was added to the already large Foreign Policy Committee, when his already evident difference of emphasis from Chamberlain's over the USSR did not make him an obvious candidate.[99] Certainly his status as Minister of Supply-designate made it plausible that he should be in touch with discussions about the imminence of war, but much of his work was to be logistical and the Committee was already almost the size of half a Cabinet.[100] It is a plausible explanation, to put it at the lowest, that the Committee was already recognised as an important forum of debate

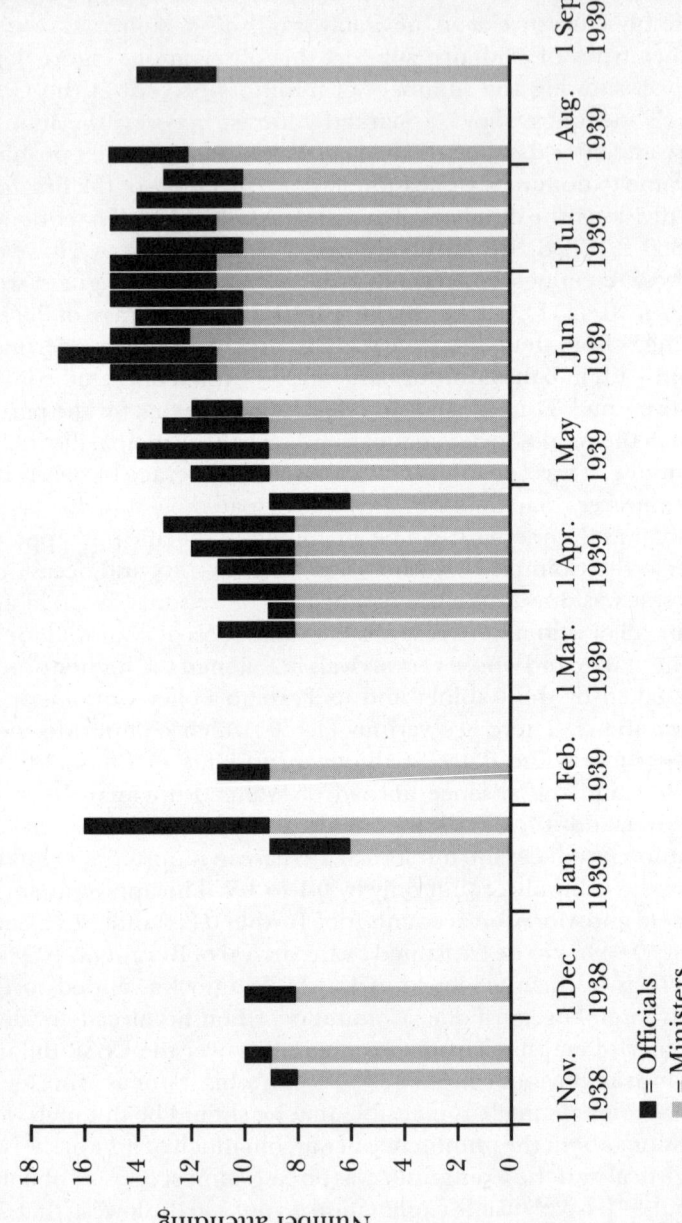

Figure 1. Level of ministerial and official attendance at meetings of the Foreign Policy Committee of the Cabinet, 14 November 1938–1 September 1939

and that the issue of the Soviet negotiations could not be dealt with without extensive ministerial participation. Certainly the rate of general absenteeism (that is, occasional non-attendance, as opposed to the overall ministerial attendance at the Committee, which has been the measure employed so far), dropped by nearly half once discussions of Soviet relations had begun, from 10.5% to 6.2%. One should not hang too much on small figures, but it is fairly clear that not only were more ministers members of the Committee for the discussions on the USSR, but also that both new and existing members showed less inclination to miss the odd meeting, for whatever reason, than before. The Committee's business came to seem a higher priority.

This in its turn seems best explained on the basis that ministers were more interested, concerned and actively involved in the debate over the Anglo-Soviet negotiations than they had been with the equally vital issues of foreign policy that had come before the Committee during the previous six months. No doubt the general level of tension about the international situation had increased, and it is impossible to disentangle concern for the Soviet question from broader anxieties about war. But the fact that on average four officials were present to service the Committee in this later period, compared with the three who attended up to 19 April 1939, is a further significant fact in favour of the hypothesis that the negotiations with Moscow themselves facilitated a strengthening of Cabinet government, since it indicates that the proceedings of the Committee were being taken with a greater seriousness and in more detail. The growing and persistent involvement of ministers in what were prolonged and highly complex negotiations meant a greater demand for the kind of specialist advice and information which officials such as Sir William Malkin could provide, as well as for more liaison with the rest of the policy-making process.[101]

Finally, the frequency with which meetings of the Committee were held once the Soviet issue became the major preoccupation also suggests that the Cabinet Committee played a particularly important role in developing British policy on the issue. If we take the terminal dates as being 14 November 1938 and 3 September 1939, we find that the average time between meetings for the two periods was as follows:

1 1 October–18 April: 11 meetings in 200 days, or one every 18.2 days

2 19 April–3 September: 19 meetings in 137 days, or one every 7.2 days.

Thus there is a striking contrast between the regularity with which meetings were held in the two periods under scrutiny. In the first the Committee met once a fortnight – in the second once a week. This is too sharp a change to be dismissed as the result of factors unconnected with the type of subject under discussion, such as administrative convenience or an increasing general desire among ministers to be in touch with foreign politics. Even the increasing importance of foreign policy in the second period is balanced by its inclusion of the summer vacation (which, perhaps surprisingly, the Prime Minister saw no need to change until it was well under way[102]). Added to previous data about attendance, it strongly suggests that, from April 1939 onwards, the Committee increased markedly the degree of its participation in policy-making, largely on the specific subject of the Soviet negotiations. It spent more time on the question than it had on others; ministers were sufficiently anxious about the outcome of the debate to attend with greater regularity; the need was felt to add formally another minister to the Committee; and lastly there were no long gaps between meetings which might have broken the continuity of the discussion or reduced the level of knowledge of ministers about the intricate daily developments of the negotiations. More importantly, and as has been argued above for the months of April and May, the evidence of the quality of the discussion inside the Committee confirms these statistical indications of the central role played by the Cabinet in formulating policy during the Soviet negotiations.

Throughout June and July, the structure of the problem at stake continued to facilitate ministerial contributions. The negotiations involved complicated choices between detailed proposals with their origins in external sources. After the first timid request to the Soviet Union for a unilateral declaration of help to eastern Europe, British policy was always essentially reactive, in the sense that it consisted largely of a series of progressive concessions – beginning with the gradual acceptance of the initial Soviet proposal for a full triple alliance and continuing with regular if reluctant decisions to acquiesce in extra demands made by the Soviet Union, as the latter either sensed British negotiating weakness, played off London against Moscow, or both.[103] These external inputs came to the Committee as already thought-out and coherent ideas requiring no strictly original action.[104] This provided a body of common and concrete information which encouraged detailed discussion. For just as committees are not ideal bodies for the forging of a collective imagination, so it is a function more suited to their operations to argue over the logical and substantial differences between various sets of formal proposals, which are clear to all members and can be dealt with section-by-section. It is here, perhaps, that Cabinet decision-making in 1939 came closest to the 'rational' procedures of selecting by argument between organised and clearly separate alternatives which writers on international relations tend to assume characterise the workings of government on foreign policy issues.[105]

The formal negotiations also maximised the participation of individual members of the Committee, since it was easier to take part by making some negative analysis of written suggestions than by advocating a particular proposal without any special expertise on foreign policy. Ministers had not been excluded from the first stage of policy-formulation (conception); neither then nor in the long-drawn-out manoeuvres of June–July were they excessively inhibited by the usual pressures against criticising or dismissing ideas brought forward solely by their own Prime Minister and Foreign Secretary. In this instance all members of the Committee, including the executive, were considering the Soviet initiatives on equal terms and at virtually the same time. There was little scope for pre-emption of the response, or for advance weightings of the issue, by Halifax and Chamberlain. Once the Committee had been introduced to the Anglo-Soviet negotiations, they quickly became intricately involved in the issue. Even if the executive found this a matter for regret, there was little they could do to reverse the process, once it had been set in motion.

To do Chamberlain and Halifax justice, however, it is quite likely that they were themselves sufficiently uncertain about the correct judgements to be made in these extremely complex and crucial negotiations to find relief in the full involvement of the Foreign Policy Committee, if only to spread the responsibility more widely. The negotiations consisted of a continuous chain of so many equal and interlocking sub-decisions, which would only amount to a major stance on foreign policy by a process of accumulation, that they militated against Chamberlain and Halifax forming any obvious single attitude which might provide a dominant lead for the

Committee and give clear pointers to the proper response to each individual proposal. A good example of this is Cadogan's remark to the Committee on 19 April that Halifax was too busy as yet to investigate the new Soviet proposals in detail, 'still less to formulate a line of policy'.[106] If the Foreign Secretary could not fashion a clear attitude to the major initiative of 18 April, it was hardly likely that he would be able to do so for the more complicated demands yet to come.

The fact that the executive had been initially forced into agreeing that negotiations should go ahead, together with the objective factor of a real confusion about the political and strategical pros and cons of a detailed agreement with the Soviet Union, must have been further factors inhibiting them against forming a confident opinion, and must therefore have worked in favour of the issue going to the Cabinet, in the form here of the Foreign Policy Committee, for the multiple decisions which arose. In the event, the Committee and the Cabinet grappled endlessly with such questions as staff talks or the definition of indirect aggression, pulled between a grudging desire for an alliance and distrust of the Soviet Union. Each small decision involved lengthy agonisings in which extensive ministerial participation and a lack of direction in overall policy unfortunately went hand in hand.

At this point it might be useful to say something about the general characteristics of the Foreign Policy Committee in 1939, for since it is commonly argued that the Committee was essentially the creature of the Prime Minister,[107] its apparent participation in policy-making might be thought to throw in even sharper relief the autocracy of Chamberlain's premiership; by taking issues out of the forum of the genuine Cabinet into a smaller group, the Prime Minister could in theory easily manipulate them. The close look we have taken at the actual proceedings of the Committee during a two-month time-span shows without doubt that on one issue at least the very reverse was the truth. An analysis of the composition of the Committee further indicates, prima facie, that it would have been very difficult to use it as a mere vehicle for prime ministerial government, and that arguments which suggest that Chamberlain altered the membership of the Committee at will to suit his particular needs for support are at best inaccurate, and derive largely from the assumption that the Prime Minister's theoretical powers were automatically extended to the full in practice.

The 'inner Cabinet' hypothesis, as the argument may be termed, certainly has little numerical basis. The Cabinet consisted of twenty-three ministers almost throughout the Munich–September 1939 period, during which time an average of 9.4 ministers attended the Foreign Policy Committee, or 40.9% of the Cabinet. Such a high figure hardly indicates that the business of the Committee was monopolised by the Prime Minister and a handful of sympathetic associates, leaving most of the Cabinet in ignorance and without access to the discussion of major foreign issues. Moreover the Committee's personnel included all the Cabinet's senior ministers, in terms of their political status and the degree of importance of their departments, as well as the great majority of those ministers likely to take a particular interest in foreign policy. The eleven regular attenders[108] were: the Prime Minister, the Foreign Secretary, the Chancellor of the Exchequer, the Home Secretary, the Secretary of State for the Dominions, the Minister for the Co-ordination of Defence, the Chancellor of the Duchy of Lancaster, the President of the Board of Trade, the Lord President of the Council, the Secretary of State for the Colonies and the Minister of Supply – of whom only the Home Secretary and the two non-departmental ministers could be thought to be outside the foreign policy process. Of these three, Hoare was a former Foreign Secretary, Runciman had recently headed the major mission to Czechoslovakia during the September crisis and Morrison had a special responsibility for defence matters.[109] Thus the members of the Committee were unlikely to act as fodder for the Prime Minister's initiatives; rather, they were virtually all ministers with important special interests in foreign policy outcomes,[110] some of them carrying sufficient weight as individual politicians (Hoare, Stanley, Simon, Runciman) to command a very serious hearing in the Committee, whether or not they agreed with the Prime Minister.

Conversely, of those ministers who took little or no part in the Committee, only the Secretary of State for India and the three Service ministers (the First Lord of the Admiralty, the Secretary of State for Air and the Secretary of State for War) had any more specialised concerns in the foreign policy issues of 1939 than those which all shared – avoiding war or damage to British security. In fact, as the Service ministers were represented on the Committee by Chatfield, something of a prototype Secretary of State for Defence, only Lord Zetland of the ministers intimately affected by its deliberations can

Table 2. *Attendance of individual ministers at meetings of the Foreign Policy Committee of the Cabinet, 14 November 1938–25 August 1939*

	Nov. 1938	Dec. 1938	Jan. 1939	Feb. 1939	Mar. 1939	Apr. 1939	May 1939	June 1939	Jul. 1939	Aug. 1939
Chamberlain	○○	○	○○	○	○	○○○○○○	○○○○○	○○○○○○○	○○	○○
Halifax	○○	○○○○	○○	○○○○○○○	○○○○	○●○○○○	○○○○○	○○○○○○○	○○	○○
Simon	○○	○○○○	●○	○○○○○○○	○○○○	○○○○○○	○○○○○	○○○○○○○	○○	○○
Hoare	○○	○○○○	●○	○○○○○○○	○○○○	○○○○○○	○○○○○	○○○○○○○	●○	○○
Inskip	○○	○○○	○○	○○○○○○○	○○○○	○○○○○○	○○○○○	○○○○○○○	○○	○○
Chatfield				○○○○○○○	○○○○	○●○○○○	○○○○○	○○○○○○○	○●○○	○○
Morrison		○○○	○○	○○○○○○○	○○○○	○○○○○○	○○○○○	○○○○○○○	○○	○○
Stanley	○○	○○○	●○	○○○○○○	○○○○	○●○○○○	●○○○○	○○○○○○○	○○	○○
Runciman	○○	●●●	●○○	●●●●●●●	●●●●	●●●●●●	●●●●●	●●●●●●●	●●	●●
MacDonald		●●●	○○○	●●●●●●●	●●●●	●●●●●●	●○○○○	●●●●●●●	●●	●●
Stanhope	●●	●●●	○○○	●●●●●●●	●●●●	●●●●●●	●●●●●	●●○●●●●	●●	●●
Kingsley Wood	●●	●●●	○○○	●●●●●●●	●●●●	●●●●●●	●●●●●	●●●●●●●	●●	●●
Hore-Belisha	●●					●●●●●●	●●●●●	●●●●●●●	●●	●●
Burgin							○○○○	○○○○○○○	○○	○○
Brown	●●	●○	●○	●○○○○○○	●○○○	●●●●●●	●●●●●	●●●●●●●	●●	●●

○ = present
● = absent.

truly be said to have been excluded from access to the Committee. Furthermore, the 'non-attenders' – encompassing both those who never attended the Committee and those who did, but infrequently – included not a single minister who enjoyed the contemporary status of being or having been at some time a holder of one of the three most prestigious offices in the Cabinet, those of Prime Minister, Foreign Secretary and Chancellor of the Exchequer. This lack of any figure of stature among the non-attenders contrasts with the total of four such personages among those who were members of the Committee.

It only remains to deal briefly with the argument that the Prime Minister both could and did alter the balance of personnel in the Committee according to the outcome he required at the time. If one looks at the attendance records over the thirty meetings which took place during this period (see Table 2), one is struck, in contrast, mainly by the regular patterns which they illustrate. Chamberlain and Inskip were ever-present; Halifax, Hoare, Simon and Stanley all missed no more than two meetings; Chatfield[111] and Morrison each missed six, but five of these were due to the fact that they were not appointed until 29 January 1939; Runciman only attended seventeen, but was absent on a tour of the Dominions for at least eleven of those he missed.[112] Anderson, the three Service ministers and Ernest Brown were all called in only to attend one or two sessions in each case to provide strictly technical information. They were not called in to bolster Chamberlain at crucial stages of argument over policy;[113] Burgin attended all the sixteen meetings held after his appointment on 10 May 1939; MacDonald, however, was absent for one-third of the meetings, of which six absences were consecutive between 8 February and 11 April, largely because he was preoccupied by the conference on Palestine taking place in London during February and most of March, but also because of a subsequent bout of influenza.[114] He returned to regular attendance precisely on the first discussion of the Soviet proposals, for which he did not disguise his full support. This was the entire total of ministers attending the Foreign Policy Committee from Munich until the outbreak of war – sixteen.[115] The clear general conclusion from looking at this data in detail has to be that Chamberlain either could not, or did not wish to, control the day-to-day balance of views and personnel in the Foreign Policy Committee.

There remains the possibility that Chamberlain organised the permanent membership of the Committee to ensure a built-in degree of sympathy for executive thinking. As ministers without departmental interests in foreign policy, Hoare and Morrison are the only possible examples of this. So far as Hoare was concerned, if this was the motive it was a severe misjudgement, since the Home Secretary in fact led the opposition to the Prime Minister over the Soviet issue to decisive effect. In any case, Hoare was a senior minister whose exclusion from this major committee after long-time membership would have been an obvious affront. Morrison therefore stands as the sole plausible example of executive nepotism, and the available evidence only hints at this being the reason for his appointment. As Sir Horace Wilson, Head of the Civil Service, and Chamberlain's chief advisor, wrote to the Secretary of the Cabinet on 3 February, 'apart from any other reason, this is an essential move in connection with his position in relation to defence'.[116]

Thus, even here, the departmental balance of the Committee was an important constraint on the Prime Minister's ability to load the balance of opinion. Although Chamberlain may well have been influenced in replacing Winterton with Morrison by the greater degree of sympathy shown by the latter to his own views, there were natural limits to the extent to which he could replace all dissentient ministers in this way, while it would have been equally absurd to pack the Committee with associates who held office largely irrelevant to foreign affairs, such as Labour or Education. The political requirements of stability and confidence among organisations and personnel meant that the abstract shuffling of appointments, which in models of competitive power-maximisation would be the natural activity of an executive, was not part of the Prime Minister's normal style of policy-making. This was partly because the routines of balanced representation and continuity of attendance in the Committee were, among others, institutionalised in the form of the Cabinet's secretariat.[117] In 1938, for example, Sir Rupert Howorth and Sir Maurice Hankey had agreed that 'there seems no good reason' for adding the Lord Privy Seal to any more Cabinet committees, let alone to the Foreign Policy Committee, which already had nine members, of which two were peers.[118] And, in the event, neither Earl De La Warr nor his successor Sir John Anderson effectively appeared on the Committee (see n. 115, this chapter). The appointment of ministers to these bodies seems to have been the joint product of organisational constraints, ministerial prerogative and the institutional norms and routines of the Cabinet Office. Chamberlain's ability to manipulate permanent membership was therefore strictly limited.

All the above findings tend to indicate that the Foreign Policy Committee was a genuine forum of Cabinet discussion. Indeed, it may have exhibited a slightly higher level of ministerial involvement than the Cabinet itself, as most of the ministers whose lack of experience and vested interest in such questions might have led them to defer to the authority, knowledge and strong leadership of the executive were not in fact members of the Committee. All the professionally interested ministers were thus brought together in a specialised environment, unfettered by the psychological constraints against dissent which may have been present in the full Cabinet through its size and the pressure on time imposed by the amount and variety of business.[119]

An example from the summer negotiations shows how the executive recognised the constraints imposed by the growing activity of ministers in the foreign policy area. For when, on 6 July, Chamberlain and Halifax wished merely to amend the procedure of British proposals to the Soviet Union on the issue of 'indirect aggression', the Foreign Secretary felt it necessary to hold back the relevant telegram until he had obtained the views of all other members of the Committee, either in person or by individual letter. He wished to give his colleagues no cause for complaint about either method or policy.[120]

Executive discretion in this context was therefore nothing like as unfettered as some writers have suggested. Indeed, the sum of qualitative evidence of actual discussions and policies and data on the patterns of attendance and composition makes irresistible the conclusion that the Foreign Policy Committee was not a means by which Chamberlain bypassed the Cabinet; rather it was effectively a scaled-down Cabinet for foreign affairs, ultimately responsible to the full Cabinet, and subject to the same kinds of strengths and weaknesses as its parent body.

The case of the Anglo-Soviet negotiations has provided a good example of collective activity in the making of high-level decisions, characterised by constant interaction within the group of ministers concerned and by a lack of leadership-domination. It has also shown that the contributions to policy-making of a Cabinet committee may in certain circumstances be seen as the means by which the full Cabinet can maximise its own participation in a particular issue. For, in the instance we have examined, the Foreign Policy Committee was far more representative of the interests of Cabinet ministers in general, with respect to international relations, than it was a channel for executive hegemony. Thus on a major issue, in a period of crisis, involving highly technical diplomacy, we find that the Cabinet was a primary forum of policy-making.

The Cabinet's role in forcing Chamberlain's change of line might have had great substantive importance, if the Soviet Union had picked up on the cue. Hindsight suggests, however, that by the time the decision was taken to go for an alliance with Moscow, developments in German-Soviet relations had already rendered it nugatory. Stalin no longer trusted Britain and France enough to take them seriously as allies against the Nazis. Yet ministers were not to know this at the time, and the political struggle which took place in the Cabinet in the late spring of 1939 was none the less real for having affected in the end little more than the internal morale of the British government.

4. ENTRY INTO WAR, 1–3 SEPTEMBER 1939

Another case in which the Cabinet enjoyed more than formal powers over a foreign policy decision was that of entry into the war itself, a choice faced directly during the two days following the German invasion of Poland on 1 September, and after weeks of anticipation and increasing tension. This climacteric has understandably attracted a good deal of attention from historians,[1] and there is no need to rehearse its details at length here. However the events of 1–3 September provide dramatic material for the student of Cabinet decision-making, particularly in conditions of crisis, for they included one of the plainest Cabinet 'diktats' in British political history.[2]

This was a very different type of decision from those which preoccupied ministers during the Soviet negotiations. Most obviously, the time-span of deliberation was very short at less than forty-eight hours. In one sense the urgency was self-imposed. Hitler had sent no ultimatum to Chamberlain or Daladier. At bottom, however, circumstances were dictating rapid action. The arrival at 7.28 a.m. on 1 September of a Reuters report of Hitler's broadcast announcing war with Poland[3] raised the question of whether the *casus foederis* of the March Guarantee had finally arrived. His Majesty's Government were confronted with an unavoidable choice between war with Germany and the abandonment of their new policy of support for the vulnerable states of eastern Europe. The middle way, of negotiations on the basis of a status quo ante, was hardly realistic. Chamberlain called for German troop withdrawals, and the issue was complicated by Mussolini's offers of mediation,[4] but there was no chance that Hitler would remove the dilemma he had created by throwing his military operation into reverse. In any case, and as the events of 2 September were to prove, a major domestic political argument was bound to be provoked by any procrastination.[5] Thus events could not have been more pressing when the Cabinet met at 11.30 a.m. on 1 September.

If we look beneath the surface of the problem, however, it is apparent that the decision facing ministers at this time was not of the same type of crisis as that confronting, say, Israeli politicians on the afternoon of 6 October 1973 as the unforeseen Egyptian attack across the Suez Canal gathered pace.[6] Michael Brecher's basic definition requires that decision makers (i) be in danger of having to engage in military action, (ii) feel their fundamental values to be threatened and (iii) have a finite time in which to act, before they can be said to be immersed in a crisis.[7] This is only partly satisfactory as a definition (as it rules out intramural crises and does not incorporate the crucial notion of a turning-point) but it does provide a yardstick for distinguishing between the various forms of pressures usually run together in the often casually employed concept of 'crisis'.

In the case of the events of 1–2 September 1939, there is no quarrel about the condition of imminent involvement in war: that was the dilemma posed by the Guarantee to Poland. By the same token, the most deeply held values of the British government were at stake, in terms of their honour and reputation over facing up to an obligation and their perception of Britain's very international position being under threat from a German drive for hegemony. Equally, there was a limited, indeed short, time in which to act. If, events proved, Chamberlain's Cabinet were to delay in responding to the German attack, it would minimise the chances of improving Polish morale and maximise the chances of provoking a domestic furore. Thus Hitler's latest move undoubtedly produced a classic foreign policy crisis for Britain.

Surprise is no longer seen by scholars as a necessary condition of crisis, but it can certainly affect the quality of decision-making in a given set of circumstances. In this case it cannot be said that British ministers were deeply shaken or surprised by the news of the German invasion. That Hitler would next turn his attention to Poland had, by definition, been foreseen since the making of the March Guarantee, while throughout the summer of 1939 there were regular scares about Danzig and the Polish Corridor.[8] In the short term, the whole of August was dominated by the 'battle of nerves' (in Cadogan's phrase)[9] as specific threats and demands began to flow from Berlin to Warsaw. Most ministers returned from holiday for a meeting on 22 August.[10] The Nazi-Soviet Pact was rumoured in the press on the same day, and the general air of imminent conflict was such that on 27 August Chamberlain felt 'like a man driving a clumsy coach over a narrow crooked road along the face of a precipice'.[11] All essential measures of mobilisation were to be complete by 31 August.[12] When Poland was actually attacked, therefore, the Cabinet were not thrown into disarray; their outlook is described more accurately as one of resignation.

Even the Nazi-Soviet Pact, such a traumatic blow for intellectuals of the left, barely rippled the waters of Cabinet discussion. Perhaps because ministers had on the whole played down the likelihood of any German-Soviet agreement,[13] they felt disinclined to regard it as important in the event. The meeting of 22 August only turned to rumours of the Pact after a long report on the now irrelevant state of Anglo-Soviet negotiations. Halifax then welcomed the news on the grounds that British relations with Spain and Japan were now likely to improve.[14] This degree of rationalisation can of course be seen as betokening deep shock and unrealism, with ministers simply not allowing themselves to face the full implications of the turn events had taken. The ramifications of a Soviet-German *rapprochement* for Britain's ability to win the war were simply too much to take on without a considerable period for adjustment, given the hopes which had come to be vested in Moscow from April onwards.

Thus, although Chamberlain's government suffered a terrible blow through Hitler's attack on Poland, they were not strictly speaking surprised or disorientated by it in the short run. Their central images of international relations and expectations of the future were not suddenly thrown over. Whereas the coup of 15 March had forced, and in a military vein the fall of Singapore in February 1942 was later to force,[15] radical reappraisals of the direction of British policy in an atmosphere of high uncertainty, actual entry into the Second World War took place amidst feelings of confirmation about the attitudes towards Germany which had been formed painfully over the previous six months.

Well before August, ministers had recognised that the structure of contemporary European politics was on the verge of disintegration, that war had become more likely than not.[16] Halifax felt in June that 'on the political side we were living in what was virtually a state of concealed war'.[17] Equally, although after 15 March Chamberlain retained for some time hopes that Hitler was still fundamentally realistic enough to avoid a conflict[18] even the Prime Minister's illusions about Hitler's personal character were ebbing fast. In May he had written, with what was even at the time dramatic insensitivity, 'I can't yet see how the detente is to come about as long as the Jews obstinately go on refusing to shoot Hitler.'[19]

The consequence of these attitudes was that, as the August crisis developed, feelings among British ministers became if anything clearer and less uncertain. The German pressure on Beck and his colleagues precipitated no major intellectual or psychological revisions in London, except in the sense of an increased resolution to act on previous decisions. The unrolling of predictable and predicted events meant that the decisions made in Cabinet in the first few days of September were more those of implementation than of formulation. The drama of those forty-eight hours should not obscure the fact that no new stance in British foreign policy was being forged. This is probably why Cadogan was able to lunch with his friends at the Ritz and then attend a wedding in St James's on the afternoon of 2 September, whereas in the intellectual turmoil of March he had felt overwhelmed by the pace of events. Similarly, Simon and Halifax found time on the 2nd to exchange friendly notes about the breakdown of peace. These were not the actions of men struggling to respond to the unexpected and to forge new responses.[20]

As an instance of policy-making, therefore, the last stages of Britain's drift towards war with Germany represented a crisis in that an explicit choice was demanded on an issue of the highest international importance and in a period of great tension. On the other hand, this was not a time of attitudinal flux for the government. The alternatives before them were relatively clear, information was at less of a premium than in March and psychologically ministers were far better prepared for at least the possibility of war than they had been a year previously, over Czechoslovakia.[21]

SIGNS OF DISTRUST

It will be argued below that these characteristics of the issue were once again an important factor in determining the pattern of Cabinet decision-making, and that in this case they again tended to facilitate broad-based Cabinet discussion at the expense of dominant leadership. However, before this argument can be made with any clarity it is important to deal with one major complication, namely the issue of whether or not the government as a whole, or certain members of it, were trying to escape from their obligations under the March Guarantee, in order yet again to avoid the horrors of war. This interpretation used to be orthodox among those for whom 'appeasement' was synonymous with betrayal and cowardice; by extension, Chamberlain was said to have embarked on the war only because compelled to do so by a parliamentary revolt on the night of 2 September.[22] It is certainly of the greatest relevance to the role of the Cabinet at this time to decide (i) whether Chamberlain and Halifax attempted to renege on the Polish Guarantee, only to be restrained by their colleagues and by parliamentary pressures, and (ii) whether the whole Cabinet was searching for a way out of their commitment to defend the independence of Poland. How, in the last analysis, were the conflicting values of peace and of resistance to German hegemony ranked or reconciled? Was peace still a serious consideration after the invasion of Poland?

Many MPs clearly thought that Chamberlain, at least, was looking for a second Munich, to judge from the uproar in the Commons after the Prime Minister's statement on 2 September. But in Cabinet on 1 September the Prime Minister had spoken as if war was already declared:

The event against which we had fought so long and so earnestly had come upon us. But our consciences were clear, and there should be *no possible question* now where our duty lay.[23]

Halifax had then reported on his remark to the Polish Ambassador, who had called for the implementation of the Guarantee, 'that provided the facts were correct, he did not suppose that we should differ from the Polish Ambassador's conclusion'. Moreover when the private intermediary Birger Dahlerus suggested that he (Dahlerus) and Sir George Ogilvie-Forbes (at that time Counsellor in the British Embassy, later Minister in Oslo) should fly back to Berlin as a last attempt to avoid catastrophe, 'After discussion, it was agreed that the reply to be sent by telephone to Mr. D. . . . should be stiff', and should stress the fact that the only way war could be avoided was via a German withdrawal from Poland: 'No hope should be held out that we should act as mediators between Germany and Poland.' The Cabinet approved the draft message to Hitler which ended: 'unless Germany immediately withdrew her troops, His Majesty's Government would, without hesitation, fulfil their obligations to Poland'.[24]

In the Cabinet Minutes there are no signs of dissent or procrastination among ministers, and the fullness of the record for the disputes between March and May means that there is no reason to suspect that embarrassing divisions were not minuted. (In any case, dissentients usually insist on their opinions being recorded, with more than one eye on their reputations and on history.[25]) The main reasons for the delay in issuing an ultimatum after the invasion seem to have been initially the need on civil defence grounds for time to complete evacuation and other last preparations against sudden air attack, and then, more importantly, the pressure from the French government, both less well organised in its preparations and more hesitant about war, against precipitate action. Britain had no wish to be seen beginning the war in disagreement with her major ally. Only a cryptic comment made by Halifax might point to any sign of a desire in a section of the Cabinet to abandon the Guarantee: in describing 'the general feeling' in the Commons on the evening of 2 September that 'the French were trying to run out of their engagement to Poland and were taking us with them', the Foreign Secretary added that 'The whole thing to my mind showed democratic assemblies at their worst, and I could not acquit some members of the Cabinet of having fed the flames of suspicion.'[26] On the strict interpretation of the text this can be taken to mean either that some ministers, anxious for an immediate ultimatum, had been talking privately to the effect that the Prime Minister and Foreign Secretary were considering a sell-out or that some ministers, themselves reluctant to send an ultimatum, had been talking in such a way as to excite the suspicion of MPs that the whole Cabinet shared this view.

In the former case, Halifax's contemporary record suggests that he at least did not consider reneging; for the suspicion of a sell-out 'there had never been the least ground. The sole reason for the French delay was General Gamelin's desire to secure further time for completing mobilisation.'[27] Halifax was undoubtedly prepared to give Germany some more time in which to reply to the British warning of 1 September,[28] and even to make one more request for the withdrawal of troops from Poland.[29] But if this were refused, or if a communication agreeing to withdraw had still not been received by at the latest 12 noon on the next day, 3 September, he and the Prime Minister proposed to issue an ultimatum.[30] Moreover when, on the morning of the 2nd, the Italian Foreign Minister telephoned London to say that he might be able to get Germany to agree to an armistice and a conference, Halifax, speaking personally, told Count Ciano that he felt that the Cabinet would require the withdrawal of German troops from Poland before any negotiations could start.[31]

It should be noted that this was all said in the Cabinet which began at 4.15 p.m., before the scenes in the Commons which pressured the Government into advancing the time of delivery of the ultimatum to 9 a.m. on 3 September. At the end of this meeting, the Prime Minister summarised the collective view: 'There should be no negotiation with Germany unless she was first prepared to give an undertaking to withdraw her troops from Poland and Danzig', and 'it was undesirable to allow Germany longer than until midnight of 2/3 September to make up her mind on these points'.[32] The first of these statements had been repeated several times during the Cabinet meeting by various ministers and was reiterated in the Commons by the Prime Minister that evening. It remains to be explained why the second, setting an earlier time-limit on Germany's reply than Halifax and the Prime Minister had originally envisaged, was made neither to Germany when the Prime Minister finally reported to the House of Commons at 7.44 p.m. As Chamberlain admitted to his Cabinet later that night, this has been 'an important departure ... from the line in which the Cabinet had approved'.[33] In his diary Cadogan recorded the reasons:

> Trouble is the French. We can't simply wait longer for a German reply. But the French don't want to present ultimatum till noon tomorrow, with 48 hours notice ... Cabinet in afternoon, who wanted ultimatum to expire at midnight tonight. But we couldn't budge the French. Awful evening, ringing up Bonnet and Daladier ... Finally Daladier agreed a statement for Prime Minister to make at 7.30, – no time limit – merely saying we were consulting French as to procedure.[34]

The fact that Cadogan had a strong personal sense of Britain's obligation to fight for Poland indicates that French procrastination, as well as the reluctance of Chamberlain and Halifax to act regardless of the French, really was the cause of the failure to issue any immediate ultimatum, rather than any intention of avoiding war. The Permanent Under-Secretary would have been quick to note any ministerial tendency to slide back on that obligation. Even on 1 September, Halifax, and probably Chamberlain as well, had authorised Cadogan to give the following message by telephone to Dahlerus (who would communicate it to Göring and Hitler):

The only way in which a world war can be stopped is:
(1) that hostilities be suspended and
(2) German troops should be immediately withdrawn from Polish territory.[35]

This evidence all suggests that Chamberlain and Halifax were not considering abandonment of the Polish Guarantee. Rather, caught between the pressures of diplomacy and accountability and assuming rather naively their colleagues' implicit support, they chose to delay implementing the Cabinet's decision. In the absence of certain news from France, the disadvantages of entering the war separately were enough to give the two men pause. They may have been encouraged to wait for agreement with France on the timing of the ulti-matum by the fact that Germany still had to reply to the warning of 1 September. Hitler had not yet directly rejected the request for the withdrawal of his forces from Poland.[36]

It is almost certain that Halifax was referring to the accusation of back-sliding against the Prime Minister and himself when he wrote of some ministers 'having fed the flames of suspicion'. John Simon, after all, had received Anderson, Burgin, Colville, De La Warr, Dorman-Smith, Elliot, Hore-Belisha, Morrison, Stanley and Wallace in his room soon after the fracas in the House. After a short discussion they proceeded to the Prime Minister, whom they told 'very forcibly' that an ultimatum must be sent to Germany immediately.[37] In a second meeting after dinner, the rebels were joined by Kingsley Wood – who had been with Chamberlain at the House when the Prime Minister had first been bearded – and by Malcolm MacDonald.

The records now available mean that we can now virtually discount the second possible interpretation of Halifax's statement, that some ministers other than the Prime Minister and himself had been mooting the possibility of not acting on the Guarantee, thus arousing the hostility of many MPs in both parties. As previously, we can only rely on the evidence of attitudes as they were *before* the violent attack on delay in the House, which made it very difficult for any minister to argue that an ultimatum should not be sent, because of the possibility in that event of the fall of the government.

In fact our information on the attitudes of the rest of the Cabinet after the 7.44 p.m. statement tallies with what we know about their views before it. The group led by Simon, in pressing the Prime Minister to send an ultimatum without further delay,[38] was consistent with the view which its members had taken in that afternoon's Cabinet, at 4.15 p.m. There, Hore-Belisha recorded, a 'unanimous decision was taken that ultimatum should end at midnight'.[39] As we have seen, the Cabinet Conclusions confirm the decision that Germany should have no longer than until midnight to 'make up her mind'. They did not mention unanimity because that is assumed to exist in the absence of recorded dissent. The doctrine of collective responsibility, which a Cabinet minister implicitly accepts by taking office,[40] meant that all those present at the meeting agreed to this decision once taken. None were on the verge of resigning over the decision for war, as Burns and Morley had done in August 1914. Moreover if we examine the views of those ministers whose attitudes would have been most influential over the eventual policy-outcome, in determining whether or not Britain would fight for Poland[41] we find that only for Sir John Anderson, the Lord Privy Seal, is there no evidence to show that he positively supported an immediate ultimatum; there is no data at all on Anderson's views before the debate in Parliament.[42]

Of the others, Simon agreed with Halifax, some time during the afternoon, that Britain could not contemplate a conference with German troops still on Polish soil, and believed it 'to be a plant to gain time and allow more ships out etc.'.[43] For the rest, the Cabinet Minutes for the meeting at 4.15 p.m. on the 2nd record their opinions. Sir Samuel Hoare thought 'there would be tremendous risks in accepting any delay which might well have considerable reactions on public opinion'. Kingsley Wood reported that 'The Chief of the Air Staff strongly opposed a further delay for 48 hours.'[44] Chatfield added 'that on military grounds he thought it was undesirable to allow Herr Hitler any longer than until midnight 2/3 September to make up his mind', while Hore-Belisha said 'that the advice given to him by the General Staff accorded with that given by the Chief of Air Staff... Public opinion here was strongly against our yielding an inch.'[45] This phrase is included in Hore-Belisha's own account, where he also reports that he told the Cabinet that, personally, he 'was strongly opposed to further delay', which he thought 'might result in breaking the unity of the country'.[46]

These are the individual statements behind the Cabinet's decision. Of the other ministers, only the Lord Chancellor, Viscount Maugham, is recorded as having spoken, and he thought that Hitler would not make any concessions even if a conference were to be held. The other fourteen members of the Cabinet[47] included men of the experience of Elliot, Inskip, Runciman and Zetland but none of them were influential in the sense that their support was vital to the Prime Minister for his survival, as was that of Simon, Halifax and Hoare. For reasons both of personality and of ministerial position, they could not hope to carry out a decision in favour of abandoning the Guarantee, against the opinions of the senior ministers of whom we have looked. To employ a previous measure, none of the fourteen had ever held any of the three most important offices in British politics, those of Prime Minister, Chancellor of the Exchequer and Foreign Secretary. Nor were any of them to do so in the future. As it happens, what we know about the general attitudes towards Germany in 1939 of men such as Stanley, Elliot, De La Warr and MacDonald suggests that many of the fourteen would themselves have been opposed to any further 'appeasement' after 1 September.[48]

Thus a detailed look at the participants in the drama of 2 September shows that none of the twenty-one other Cabinet ministers who, in the late afternoon of the 2nd, authorised Chamberlain and Halifax to settle the final terms of the 'communication' to Germany and the statements to be made in Parliament (on the lines indicated in the discussion) wanted to push Britain into abandoning her obligation under the Guarantee to help Poland resist the German attack. Quite the reverse: Halifax himself noted their unanimity in favour of a short time-limit at this meeting, and the fact that 'the Cabinet itself was in an extremely difficult mood'.[49] But nor for their part did the Prime Minister or the Foreign Secretary intend to abrogate the obligation to an invaded Poland, although if Germany had continued to prefer the aggressive diplomacy of August to the military action of 1 September this is not to say that they might not have been willing to see Poland make some concessions in a negotiated agreement. The criterion on which British policy at this stage was assessed was not so much the absolute territorial integrity of Poland, but rather whether or not Germany was bent on European hegemony. If she was prepared to use force to win gains from Poland and thus to make that country's 'independence' meaningless, then in the eyes of British policy-makers it would be, *ipso facto*, proof that Hitler was indeed seeking hegemony. Thus the hesitation shown by Britain on 1–2 September after the invasion was due to the refusal of

France to agree to a midnight deadline.[50] The indecision arose over the timing, not the fact, of the ultimatum.[51]

Of course Chamberlain may have suspected France of being on the verge of abandoning the Guarantee, and have been reluctant to go to war without her. If he had had his way in delaying an ultimatum further, and France had actually cancelled her commitment, would the Prime Minister have wanted Britain to fight alone or to relinquish the task altogether? This speculation cannot be resolved; there are plausible hypotheses for either possibility. However, all the evidence as to his (and Halifax's) actual attitudes shows a sense of the inevitability of a war over Poland if Germany had not withdrawn her forces by noon on the 3rd. There is nothing to point to any doubt in their minds as to the necessity or rightness of declaring war once Poland had been attacked – admittedly insofar as the issue can be kept separate from that of whether war against Germany was possible or desirable without the support of France.[52]

The meaning of this account for an analysis of Cabinet unity is clear: no one in the Cabinet was about to 'rat'; ministers were not at the mercy of executive whims, but neither did they chain an unwilling Chamberlain to his post. There existed a consensus of fundamental policy issues, and disagreements were therefore largely the result of understandable edginess and misperception of Chamberlain's motives, itself rooted in uneasiness about the division of responsibility for the now-evident failures of British foreign policy in 1938–9. The main effect of the distrust which then broke surface was only to accelerate the issuing of the inevitable ultimatum.[53]

REBELLION IN CABINET

Nonetheless, the fact that such serious misunderstandings occurred, and that strong words were used to remind Chamberlain of Britain's commitments, is itself evidence of the real part played by the Cabinet in the September crisis. After the group of ministers, with Simon as their spokesman, had seen the Prime Minister in his room at the House and expressed their 'strong and deep feelings' at being placed in a 'false position' by what Simon called 'so grave a variation adopted and publicly announced when the Cabinet had decided otherwise', Chamberlain changed tack and increased the pressure on France.[54] He had obviously been hurt by his colleagues' determination to make him accountable. Halifax noted that he had 'never seen the Prime Minister so disturbed'.[55] Chamberlain's own capacity for rationalisation survived, but he could not conceal his dismay:

> To crown it all a certain number of my colleagues in the Government who always behave badly when there is any trouble about, took this opportunity to declare that they were being flouted and neglected and tried to get up a sort of mutiny. Even Edward Halifax found their behaviour unbearable and declared that I had the temper of an archangel.[56]

By this time Chamberlain was clearly out of touch even with the realities of Cabinet government. The various whims and egocentricities of his past behaviour, compounded by the foreign policy failures and wrangles with colleagues since 15 March, finally came home to haunt him in circumstances in which the whole Cabinet was in a condition of maximum critical alertness.

For the rest of the evening the Prime Minister fought to retrieve the political ground he had lost, using Simon to impress on the French Ambassador the seriousness of the domestic pressure he was under. Just after 10 o'clock, Simon had been summoned to Downing Street, but the rebels had sent Anderson with him (the latter was to wait in the car outside) and he had promised not to concede any further delays without reference back to them. Halifax and Cadogan had by this time also been summoned in haste from their evening meals to Number 10.[57] The rebel group was now so disturbed that they considered following Simon *en masse* over to the Prime Minister, eventually contenting themselves with a pressurising telephone call to Simon.[58] The climax came with a forty-five minute Cabinet meeting at 11.30 p.m. at which 'a number of ministers did not arrive until a considerable time after the proceedings had started'.[59] At this meeting Chamberlain accepted the force of disquiet in the Commons and Cabinet, and agreed to an ultimatum being delivered at 9 a.m. the next day, to expire a mere two hours later.

Even had Chamberlain known what he wanted in this crisis and set out to achieve it with the same determination that he had shown in September 1938, or during the making of the Polish Guarantee, he would have been boxed in by the combination of a public commitment to Poland and a Cabinet which had become educated both to the business of foreign policy-making and to the risks of allowing too much freedom to their first minister. For as important as the brutal display of distrust on 2 September was the participation in decisions throughout the two-day period of the Cabinet as a whole. The Cabinet met three times, views were expressed freely and unanimity displayed on the central issues. When there arose anger at the Prime Minister's going beyond his brief on the evening of 2 September, the majority of ministers were both alert and active enough to mobilise within a few hours a protest that was extraordinary but not wholly out of the blue.

That the Cabinet were able to keep in the forefront of affairs was partly due to the vital need to preserve a consensus on entering a major war. It was important for the preservation of wider domestic support,[60] as well as for the image Britain presented to Germany and the neutral states, that ministers should be unanimous in their support of the ultimatum and that their collective relinquishing of office before the formation of a War Cabinet should not be complicated by prior resignations. But this is not the whole explanation. Chamberlain had been willing to risk subsequent disagreements with colleagues both in late September 1938 and in March 1939. Moreover, in the equivalent crisis of August 1914 consensus had been an important, but not fundamental, consideration. At the last, Herbert Asquith and Sir Edward Grey had preferred a divided Cabinet to the abandonment of their own policy of support for France.[61]

The factor to which we have to return as a major if not the exclusive determinant of the Cabinet's role in the decision to declare war on Germany is the character of the problem as it presented itself at the time. Non-specialist ministers were able to form and to articulate views not only because of the obviously unparalleled importance of the occasion (in September 1938 and March 1939 there had been far less mental preparedness for an imminent war), but also because of the way in which the very existence of the Polish Guarantee acted to structure policy-choices. Its breach of the time-honoured rule of 'no advance commitments' paradoxically served to involve ministers in the final decisions for war, by clarifying the issues beforehand. Although the Guarantee failed as an act of deterrence, it worked incidentally as an act of policy-planning, ensuring that the British government entered the war relatively smoothly, with less chance of decisions being made in the erratic, *ad hoc* way that had characterised some past crises of foreign policy.[62] A case in point is the letter sent by Chamberlain to Hitler on 22 August. Euan Wallace wrote, 'its excellence was due in no small measure to the collective mind of the Cabinet, and the document actually telegraphed to Berlin that evening was substantially better both in form and substance than the draft submitted to us half-way through our meeting'.[63]

Administrative and psychological (if not military) preparations had been made for a German move to absorb Poland, so that the event when it came consolidated rather than disturbed the newly revised perspectives on European affairs now held by members of the National Government. It was revealing that Churchill had been willing to join the government since 31 March 1939, and the gap between his views and those of most ministers narrowed with every week of the summer.[64] By 1 September members of the Cabinet had become sensitised to the likelihood of continuing 'outrages' from Hitler, and they were ready to deal with the specific issue of Poland when it arose.

By contrast, their equivalents in the Liberal government of 1914 had not fully prepared for the problems that were raised by 'the guns of August'. A confrontation of some kind with Wilhelmine Germany had been in sight for some time, but the inability of the anti-war faction in Asquith's Cabinet to carry the day was partly due to the distractions of the Ulster crisis over the summer, and partly to their incomplete understanding of the implications of the Anglo-French military conversations of the previous decade. The extent of Britain's commitment to France was a very strong card in Grey's hand as he sought to obtain approval for his policy over considerable discontent in Cabinet.[65] At the point of decision, Grey (the key member of the foreign policy executive of that government) was ultimately to play on ideological differences inside the Cabinet, and the wrong-footed condition of many of his colleagues, to sustain the alliance with France.

The differences between the clarity and form of the issues involved in 1914 and in 1939 (as between the different issues of 1939 itself) are, therefore, a significant part of the explanation for the contrasting powers of the Cabinet evident in the various cases. While the peculiarities of circumstance qualify all generalisations, it is always important to delineate the interactions of policy and process. The nature of a foreign policy problem will predispose towards a certain style of top-level policy-making, while the dynamics of the ever-changing relationship between the Prime Minister, the Foreign Secretary and other ministerial colleagues will in their turn help to determine which policy options seem most feasible at any given time. The broad conclusion which therefore emerges as much from the September crisis as from the two cases which have preceded it in this study is that a model of foreign policy-making in the Cabinet that pictures the Prime Minister and his colleagues as adversaries, perpetually competing for the power of decision, must be modified to take into account the contrasting contexts in which they have to work.

5. REACTING TO THE 'PEACE OFFENSIVE', OCTOBER 1939

The next of our case-studies is at once discrete from and powerfully connected to the drama we have just left. In the first half of October 1939, Chamberlain's government faced an uncomfortably new kind of problem, albeit one with echoes of Munich, namely the 'peace offensive'. This was the term, the political jargon of the time,[1] for the next stage in Hitler's strategy after the subjugation of Poland. From quite early on in September 1939, British decision-makers began to expect, even to fear, that the Führer would try to lure them once more to the conference table, with all the humiliations that now implied. This was both an acknowledgement that the Allies were not about to take the military offensive and plunge the whole of Europe into war and an indication of the fact, pointed out by Clausewitz at the end of another great war, that politics and diplomacy did not cease in wartime.

On the surface, this should not have posed a major problem. The momentous decision to fight had been made only two or three weeks before, and the political world in London was more inclined to criticise the delays of 1–2 September than the fact of being at war.[2] Moreover nothing had happened militarily or diplomatically to precipitate any rethinking – at least, in principle.

Yet reason alone is usually a poor guide to politics and in the febrile atmosphere of the first weeks of war, psychological factors played a large part in determining ministers' attitudes. The fact was that Hitler had regained the initiative in Anglo-German relations even before the end of 1938, and had thereafter continually put Chamberlain's Cabinet on the defensive. Moreover, after the invasion of Poland it was no longer contestable that appeasement had failed; the government was, therefore, in the position of having to prosecute a policy which was the very embodiment of its own previous mistakes – however honourable. Furthermore, they were apprehensive about the future and how the war could possibly be won. Hankey admitted that he had thought there was 'a real danger that we might be knocked out in the first few weeks', while Halifax said in late September that 'it is difficult to anticipate that either Germany or the Allies will now in the near future achieve a really decisive victory by direct assault on fortified lines in the West'.[3] This made it not at all surprising that a major peace proposal from the man who had begun the war should have represented a serious test of nerve for the British government. Even on the assumption that the response from London was a foregone conclusion, there remained the possibility that errors of presentation or implementation would add seriously to ministers' problems, as they had evidently done on 2 September. The Cabinet now resembled a team used to success, but shell-shocked and playing without the crucial ingredient of confidence.

This condition was not improved by the fate of Poland. By 17 September the Red Army had invaded the country in fulfilment of the secret clauses of the Ribbentrop–Molotov Pact. By the 27th, the Poles had surrendered. The speed of this disintegration was something of a surprise. As the Secretary to the Chiefs of Staff Committee later remembered about the first week of the conflict, 'The war news was catastrophic. The Polish forces were evidently much less powerful than we had supposed and were being pulverised. It was painful and humiliating to be unable to do anything to help them.'[4] But given the French unwillingness to risk their army, and the British their air force, in an attack from the west, the fact of Polish defeat was inevitable and did not itself overturn assumptions about a necessary war and a long one. Poland was not to be abandoned simply because it had been conquered. It would be restored by the ultimate victory which was now being sought over Nazism, and the removal of the latter's style of international conduct. The Prime Minister told his Cabinet on 9 September that 'it had always been foreseen that Poland would be largely overrun before we could effectively intervene'. The Cabinet subsequently agreed that a statement should be issued to the effect that 'they were making all their plans on the assumption that the duration of the war would be at least three years'.[5] On 22 September Sir Samuel Hoare, by now Lord Privy Seal with a seat in the War Cabinet, told listeners to the BBC's Home Service, after accepting that Poland would be 'ravaged' and its armies 'destroyed', 'I warn you that we are in for a long and grim struggle that will try you more than you know.'[6]

As it happened such statements, whether private or public, were somewhat misleading. The Prime Minister was guilty of rewriting history in his view of Poland, because he had devised the Guarantee back in March partly on the ground that Poland would provide a Second Front. Moreover, on other occasions he appears to have qualified his own predictions on the length of the war. At the Supreme War Council of 12 September, he told Daladier that 'Britain is preparing for a war of three years, this figure being for information only.'[7] It is also worth pointing out that the question of how the Soviet share of a partitioned Poland was to be restored was conveniently avoided. On the one hand there was no question of fighting the USSR at the same time as Germany, and on the other Stalin's action was not enough to deter London or Paris from continuing the war.[8]

In line with the psychological defensiveness mentioned above, the British elite seems to have spent as much time on wondering about Hitler's next moves as about the possibility of their own initiatives in the war. Thus the concomitant of pessimism about Poland was the view that Hitler would follow up a triumph in Warsaw with a swift peace offer, stressing that it was not worth fighting over a *fait accompli*. Harold Nicolson, a self-styled member of the 'Eden group', can be found predicting this in his diary for 6 September,[9] while two days later and from inside the Foreign Office, Oliver Harvey noted: 'General view seems to be that Germans intend to finish off Poland as quickly as possible whilst remaining strictly defensive on the West and then to make a peace offer supported by Mussolini.'[10]

Thus the politics of the first month of the war were increasingly, from the British side, concerned with the prospect of having to cope with a proposal from Hitler to end the war – a proposal that actually came in the Reichstag speech of 6 October, preoccupied the Cabinet for a full week and reverberated for much longer. At the time it was a problem of the highest salience.

The peace offer and the responses it brought forth are interesting for our purposes for a number of reasons. First, it raises the question, not to be dismissed out of hand, as to whether there were members of the Chamberlain government (not excluding the Prime Minister) who were still looking for some alternative to the fight to the finish with the Nazi regime which seemed inherent in the declaration of war. Nicholas Bethell, for example, in his detailed study of the first six weeks of the conflict, argues that in them 'Chamberlain, the man of peace, became an influence so dangerous as to threaten the civilized world with defeat and barbarism', not because he was about to revert to pure appeasement, but because he and some colleagues laboured under the illusion that Hitler could be removed and compromise reached with a successor government.[11] Certainly many accounts of British policy in this period skate too easily over the issue of attitudes to peace feelers. The official historian, for example, devotes less than one page (out of 623 dealing with British diplomacy in the first two years of war) to the 'peace offensive' of September–October, and his conclusion about Hitler's offer, that 'the only question was whether to make a reply', is an over-simplified gloss.[12] Even Hinsley's official history of intelligence contains very little either on the public diplomacy or the various clandestine contacts which were being kept in play at this time.[13]

The second reason for focusing on reactions to the October peace offer is its importance as a source for British policy-makers' views of Hitler and Hitlerism at the beginning of the struggle. A proposal to end the war could not help but catalyse attitudes which had been in a continuous state of vacillation for at least the previous twelve months. Was the German leader now beyond redemption as a man with whom one could do business? Should a distinction be made between Hitler and other Nazis? Was he a permanent fixture, or a man deeply vulnerable to internal opposition? Ministers' reactions to these issues, inchoate as they sometimes were, revealed a good deal about both their outlooks towards the war – its purpose and sustainability – and the differences of view or determination among them.

This is closely linked to the third reason for paying attention to the impact of Hitler's Reichstag speech of 6 October. When the war started, the Cabinet and their professional advisers had only the loosest idea of how to proceed, as the hesitations over whether or not to launch an offensive in the west, and the subsequent torpor of the 'sitzkrieg', demonstrated. The broad approach was to play for time, assuming that internal divisions in Germany would undermine Hitler and that the blockade would begin to bite. The United States could not be relied upon as a source of supplies, let alone as a future ally.[14] Politically, the expectation was that the Nazis would be dislodged from within and that a peace could be engineered with a successor government which would remove the constant threat of 'coercive diplomacy', as Alexander George was later to dub the rapid resort to the threat or use of force in inter-state negotiations.[15]

It was at this point, however, that vagueness set in with a vengeance. Would Poland be restored to its pre-September boundaries, or just to the point of full 'independence'? Would (after 17 September) the Soviet Union have to withdraw from eastern Poland? Was Czechoslovakia, and even Austria, to expect reconstitution? How would guarantees of Germany's good behaviour be obtained – by amputating parts of its territory, as the French increasingly seemed to want? The answers to none of these questions had been clearly thought through, and were formulated, if at all, on an incremental basis and in response to events such as Hitler's October initiative.[16] They nonetheless were of extreme practical importance, as on their answers depended the courses of action to be taken on matters as varied as the bombing of German cities and the courtship of Mussolini. The deliberations which took place in response to Hitler in the first few weeks of October 1939 did not fully resolve these key questions, but they did map out some of the intellectual terrain on which answers might be found.

These are all good historical reasons for looking at the reactions to the Reichstag peace offer. For the purpose of this book, however, it is the role of the Cabinet which is at issue. Here the central questions are: to what extent was the War Cabinet divided on the response it had to make, and whose initiatives were decisive in formulating the statement which Chamberlain made in reply to Hitler on 12 October? It is a particularly interesting case from the viewpoint of constructing a model of small-group (Cabinet) behaviour, because it demanded on the one hand creativity and long-range planning, and on the other conformity to the discipline of a major policy-commitment entered upon in a blaze of publicity only a matter of weeks before – namely the defeat of Hitlerism. Unique among our six cases, therefore, the October peace proposal provided opportunities for ministers to contribute inputs to the making of new policy, as well as to hold a watching brief for the implementation of a pre-existing policy. In short, both originality and accountability were at stake.

The body on which these demands were made, however, was considerably changed in nature from the Cabinet which existed before 3 September 1939. On the evening of the day war was declared, a new

Table 3. *The War Cabinet, 3 September 1939–5 January 1940*[a]

Neville Chamberlain	Prime Minister
Lord Halifax	Foreign Secretary
Sir Samuel Hoare	Lord Privy Seal
Sir John Simon	Chancellor of the Exchequer
Lord Chatfield	Minister for the Co-ordination of Defence
Winston Churchill	First Lord of the Admiralty
Leslie Hore-Belisha	Secretary of State for the Army
Kingsley Wood	Secretary of State for Air
Lord Hankey	Minister without Portfolio

[a] 5 January 1940 was the date of the first change in the War Cabinet, when Hore-Belisha was sacked.

Source: David Butler and Anne Sloman, *British Political Facts 1900–1979* (5th edn, London: Macmillan, 1980), pp. 22–5.

Cabinet was formed, ministers having all tendered their resignations beforehand. The subsequent reconstruction produced a nine-member War Cabinet (see Table 3), with fifteen more ministers who held Cabinet rank but were not in the War Cabinet. The latter would have been smaller, at six, had it not been for the fact that the Liberals would not join the government, and the Prime Minister then decided to bring in the three Service ministers.[17] Ministers outside the War Cabinet were still expected to accede to the principle of collective responsibility, even though they would not have participated in decisions, and indeed none subsequently resigned over this division of power from responsibility.[18] They were summoned to the War Cabinet when their departmental interests were affected, and all were circulated with memoranda and Conclusions (except Confidential Annexes, which were reserved for those affected), giving them, in theory, the opportunity to comment and thus participate in decisions.[19] In practice, things were different. On their own subjects, ministers were expected only to ask the War Cabinet for a decision once discussions had narrowed the issue to a defined point,[20] while attendance at the War Cabinet could be anti-climactic:

While we were waiting outside, Burgin rather aptly described these discussions in the War Cabinet as a kind of 'tip and run'; by the time they get down to those items on the agenda which require the attendance of other Ministers, time rarely permits of thorough discussion on any subject ... the discussion on Burgin's paper was so abbreviated that neither Oliver,

Gilmour nor I were invited to speak. Gilmour did actually put in a few words after we had been, so to speak, dismissed.[21]

The War Cabinet itself met daily at 11.30 in 10 Downing Street, while from 7 December weekly meetings were convened (by either the Prime Minister, the Foreign Secretary or the Minister for the Co-ordination of Defence) for ministers not in the War Cabinet but of Cabinet rank, to keep them in touch with developments.[22]

The total of twenty-four Cabinet-rank ministers (9 + 15) was one more than the Cabinet had been on 2 September, in peacetime. Three men had been dropped (Runciman, Maugham and Morrison) and four added – Churchill and Hankey to the War Cabinet, Eden and Lord Macmillan to the outer circle. The new post was Hankey's, that of Minister without Portfolio, but Churchill represented the only new political tendency to be added to the inner group. It will be observed that one-third of the War Cabinet sat in the House of Lords; two more peers also had Cabinet rank, making a total of five out of twenty-four. Of the nine in the War Cabinet, only four (if we include Chatfield) were without departmental responsibilities, despite Sir Edward Bridges' anxieties on considering the precedents of the First World War: 'I should feel very gravely perturbed at any War Cabinet which was not constituted as to at least half, of non-Departmental Ministers, as I think that this might expose the Prime Minister to a good deal of criticism.'[23]

The Cabinet system could not, of course, function without committees, which continued and proliferated in wartime.[24] These bridged the gap between the two groups of Cabinet ministers, as some were chaired by War Cabinet members, and then had fairly full powers, while others were chaired by 'outside' ministers, and had to report up to the senior body. Officials tended to play an increasingly important part as the pressure of business mounted.

It was in this management of the government and the war effort simultaneously that Chamberlain differed from Churchill, as it turned out. Whereas the latter was to be confident in assuming that a national coalition meant that he could concentrate on running the small War Cabinet, Chamberlain was torn between wanting to be seen to prosecute the war efficiently and wanting to maintain continuity with his traditional mode of operating. Thus he did not want 'a second Cabinet', but he was willing to allow all those who would have been in a peacetime Cabinet (that is, those 'above the line') to receive Cabinet papers. This was a recipe for confusion, and it led to the necessity for *ad hoc* decisions, such as Bridges' decision not to allow the Minister of Information to see 'papers on highly secret strategical and policy matters', even though he received some of the WP (War Cabinet Papers) series of memoranda. Similarly, only War Cabinet members were regularly circulated with the crucial Confidential Annexes to the Cabinet Minutes. The others could come to the secretariat to look at them; they were not debarred, but not encouraged.[25]

This, then, is the background to the operation of the War Cabinet under Neville Chamberlain, which considered how best to respond to Hitler's peace offer in early October 1939. What of the offer itself? What did it contain, and how did it come to dominate the attention of the British government?

HITLER'S 'PEACE OFFENSIVE'

As we have seen, some kind of renewed German peace diplomacy had been expected from the outset of the war. Either the British government thought that the fact of an Anglo-French declaration of war would shock Hitler, or (more likely) they had become accustomed to the mix of diplomatic and military shock tactics which Hitler used to disorient his opponents. Certainly they did not appear to have held an image of Nazism as immediately moving towards a total war in which to vanquish the old order or be vanquished by it. This is an interesting example of how a particular observation could be at odds with a general proposition held simultaneously, for the theoretical line taken by the British at this time was that unless Hitler fought and won his usual blitzkrieg campaign he would be bound to lose in the end, time being on the Allied side.[26]

It seems likely that Hitler was not certain in his own mind that he wanted to struggle to the death with Britain and France, although on the matter of his motives there will always be room for disagreement. There was probably a good deal of genuineness in Hitler's statements about wanting an agreement with the British Empire (at least in the medium term), which he would 'guarantee' in return for a free hand in central Europe.[27] In this context, however, it is less important to know why Hitler offered peace on 6 October, and whether he was genuine in so doing, than to understand the impact of his action on the structure of the attitudes held by the members of the British Cabinet, and on the pattern of their decision-making.

Any formal approach from Hitler could not be ignored. Despite Chamberlain's having told Daladier 'of the complete unanimity of opinion in this country in regard to the war',[28] his private view was rather different. He observed that 'there is such a wide spread desire to avoid war & it is so deeply rooted that it must surely find expression somehow', and again, 'last week 17% of my correspondence was on the theme of "stop the war"'.[29] The Prime Minister certainly knew that the people who had acclaimed his return from Munich with peace would expect him at least to consider carefully any new initiatives, even from Hitler, just as he would be under heavy fire from other sources if they suspected a return to appeasement. Chamberlain was in a cleft stick.

The particular difficulty of the Prime Minister and his close colleagues (as opposed to the new and combative presence of Churchill) was that peace offers raised the question of war aims,[30] and specifying war aims premised a commitment to trying to change what Hitler called the 'relationship of forces'[31] by engagement in combat.[32] This Chamberlain was still reluctant to do, indulging in a wishful thinking which had moved on from trust in Hitler's word to the belief that he would be brought down without serious fighting, but was self-delusory nonetheless. On 10 September he confided to Ida that he had a feeling that 'discussing peace terms' (by which he meant here the end of the war) 'won't be so very long ... what I hope for is not a military victory – I very much doubt the possibility of that – but the collapse of the German home front. For that it is necessary to convince the Germans that they cannot win.'[33] The trouble with this approach was that it required both thinking about a peace which might be imminent, if the phoniness of the war was any indication, and keeping quiet about war aims, in case talk weakened the very implacability which would encourage the German people to remove Hitler. Psychologically, moreover, thinking about war aims so soon – however logical – was bound to make it more difficult for ministers to take on the martial spirit necessary for the new conditions. Thus external pressures – the Dominions as well as Hitler were pressing to know Britain's terms at this time[34] – represented an uncomfortably precise stimulus to think about things which the government would have preferred to shelve, and (worse) to put some of them on the record. The rate of change in war is generally such that it is intensely embarrassing to be committed to many specific aims in public. This is particularly true when there might be some doubt as to whether allies share the same outlook, as was the case in London in September after French foot-dragging over the ultimatum.[35] Any peace offer was bound to be seen, *inter alia*, as an attempt to sow discord between allies.

The British government was not, of course, without war aims of a general but agreed kind. Their starting point, against which Hitler's proposals of 6 October were measured, had four main elements:

1 No system of international relations for Europe would be sustainable in future without guarantees of any agreements which might be made, and these guarantees could only be validated by German *actions*. Words were no longer enough as an earnest of good faith. At the very least, therefore, troops would have to be withdrawn from Poland.

2 Such actions would mean the removal of Hitlerism, as a method and philosophy of inter-state conduct, from the diplomatic scene. Bullying, the cavalier breaking of pacts, the notion that only the victors have the right, and the actual use of the military instrument when negotiation meant compromise would all have to be abandoned and be seen to have failed.

3 The corollary of an end to Hitlerism seemed increasingly and inexorably to be the end of Hitler himself as a political force in Germany. It was in 1939, as indeed it still is, difficult to distinguish between the personality of Hitler and the Nazi movement in terms of the main obstacle to the return of civilised values to German policy, but the man (at whom Chamberlain felt a personal bitterness) was now certainly seen by the British government as the major barrier to peace. There is no direct evidence that assassination was seriously considered (the Munich bomb attacks on the Führer in November were to be referred to even by the anti-appeaser Oliver Harvey as 'outrages'),[36] but, as we shall see, unrealistic hopes were rising of some kind of coup against the Nazis inside Germany.

4 Some restorations of national liberties in central Europe would be necessary. If a veil had to be drawn over Austria, whose adhesion to the Reich could be seen as voluntary, Poland would clearly have to be restored to pre-invasion independence. Czechoslovakia was the real problem. Britain had connived at

the loss of the Sudetenland, but had been provoked into a change of policy by the invasion of Bohemia which, as *The Times* put it, was 'notice to the world that German policy no longer seeks the protection of a moral case'.[37] Halifax stalled Eduard Beneš, the exiled Czecho-Slovak President, on this issue on 20 September, saying that His Majesty's Government had decided to adopt no war aims for the present other than the defeat of Germany,[38] but the subsequent discussions in October proved that the Czechoslovak question could not ultimately be evaded.

These constituents of an embryonic position on war aims, however faltering in their expression,[39] amounted to a disposition to reject any peace offer that Hitler might make, since the German leader was hardly likely to make *mea culpa* gestures, let alone suggest his own removal from the scene. Any conciliatory proposal by the German leader, virtually whatever its contents, raised the spectre of further humiliations for a by now smarting British government. Thus the words 'peace' and 'offensive' came together as a cherished oxymoron, Chamberlain using the term for the first time in Cabinet on 23 September, after Churchill had talked of the unlikelihood of any 'land offensive' in the coming winter.[40] By the 29th it was thought likely that the Soviet Union would join together with Germany in 'a very early peace offensive'.[41]

It was in the two weeks leading up to Hitler's speech that the pace of what one minister called the ' "peace" threat' did indeed begin to mount.[42] On 26 September a meeting of the War Cabinet took place without officials and without any record being kept.[43] This seems likely to have been for the purpose of highly confidential discussions of the latest approaches from Birger Dahlerus, who had reported to the British Minister in Sweden on 18 September that Göring was seeking to negotiate peace and to bypass Hitler.[44] Lord Halifax then instructed Sir E. Monson that he

could conceive of no peace offer likely to come from the German Government that could even be considered by His Majesty's Government or by the French Government. His Majesty's Government could not, however, define their attitude to an offer of which they did not know the nature and if Dahlerus were willing to ascertain details from Göring they would be able to examine it.[45]

Thus Britain was stranded in no man's land: horrified at the thought of peace negotiations but unable to dismiss them out of hand, forced to consider what they knew they could not ultimately entertain. Chamberlain in particular was caught in this dilemma. He regarded Chatfield's view that this was a good time to bomb German industry as 'a very dangerous argument, since Hitler would be able to claim that at the very moment when he was about to make peace we had taken action which made it impossible for him to make the offer'.[46] The Prime Minister's point, of course, only had any force if a peace offer were to be of some interest.

By the end of September it was clear both that Hitler was about to make a specific peace offer,[47] and that it would probably come in his major speech scheduled for a specially convened session of the Reichstag on 6 October. By 2 October the peace offensive was 'impending', with the 'smaller neutral countries' favouring negotiations.[48] The joint German-Soviet declaration of 28 September had said that the 'liquidation' of the present Anglo-German war was in the interests of all nations, and that they would 'direct their common efforts, if necessary in accord with other friendly Powers, in order to attain this aim as soon as possible'.[49]

The resolve of the British government was by this time being tested on a number of fronts. On the 2nd, the Cabinet was told of the peace feeler being made in Ankara by the eccentric German Ambassador, von Papen. Dutch diplomats were attempting to mediate. Ministers made little response, and Chamberlain, recalling past meetings with von Papen at Lausanne, dismissed him as 'most hysterical and unreliable'. But the sensitivity of the issue was acknowledged by Halifax's promise two days later that exceptionally secret telegrams such as this one from Ankara would be circulated directly to ministers from the Foreign Office (that is, cutting out the Cabinet Office).[50]

Dahlerus, moreover, had actually visited London on 28–9 September to communicate the results of his two days earlier in the week with Hitler and Göring. There is no reference to this in the internal Foreign Office account prepared in 1941, and the War Cabinet were not to be informed for another week. Dahlerus first saw Cadogan (at the latter's home, from 10 p.m. until after midnight) and the next day had a meeting with Cadogan, Halifax and Chamberlain, after which he dined with the Permanent Under-Secretary and his wife at the Carlton Hotel.[51] Although Dahlerus seems to have been told consistently that Hitler's good faith could now only be demonstrated by actions, the very fact of his access to and apparent intimacy with the highest levels of British decision-making, must have encouraged him (and his German interlocutors) a good deal. It was also a sign of the government's inability to rule out peace diplomacy *ab initio*. After Dahlerus' departure Chamberlain noted that Hitler wanted an end to the war but was not 'prepared to pay the price. So that there is no reasonable prospect of a peace such as we could accept.'[52]

The Swedish intermediary was sufficiently hopeful after his reception in London to return to the charge. On 3 October he telephoned from the British legation in The Hague to report further German proposals, and to request a further secret meeting, which might lead to changes in Hitler's speech of the 6th. Halifax and Chamberlain, acting as the foreign policy executive of the Cabinet, had resisted this bait, taking the view (as Halifax told the War Cabinet on 5 October) that 'a stiff attitude' to such feelers was best 'but that we should not absolutely shut the door and should leave all initiative to the other side'.[53] In fact on the day of Dahlerus' call the Prime Minister made a speech in the House as a response to the 'peace offensive'. Oliver Harvey summarised the dual approach of listening to Dahlerus and von Papen, but remaining firm:

We are keeping both these sources in play to see what they may produce, but otherwise there is no intention of contemplating a patched-up peace with Hitler. 'Hitler must go' is the slogan, and the P.M. has now said in the H. of C. that we cannot negotiate with the present German government.[54]

Hoare, Halifax and Kingsley Wood in subsequent discussions about how to handle this tricky balance all agreed that it might be worth distinguishing between Göring and Hitler (Dahlerus' main point), as 'our real object was to destroy Herr Hitler'.[55] But Churchill immediately identified a possibly fatal ambivalence in the old guard. He thought that the feelers might not be sincere, aiming simply to sow discord. But even if they were sincere, they only showed how the Nazis were unsure of their own people's desire for war: 'In that event we should need to be most provident stewards of the national interest, and to take every step to ensure that we were not deceived.' One can hear Churchill's resonant tones in these words, which were an unmistakable shot across the bows of the Prime Minister and Foreign Secretary. By ignoring them and pointedly saying straight-away that he agreed with Halifax, Chamberlain showed that he accepted the challenge and by implication recognised that he might now be under closer scrutiny from his own colleagues.

Having no choice but to wait for Hitler's staged speech, with its likely proposals, the government thus rationalised their position as one of allowing Germany to make the running and thereby show its own weakness.[56] The concern was focused more on discreet diplomacy to prevent all the many non-belligerents who wished to see the war end from being swung towards the German camp by Hitler's initiative. At various points it was feared that Italy, the Vatican, the United States and the smaller neutrals would all be susceptible to what Hitler might say. Even India and the Dominions, already at war, might weaken in their resolve. At home, Lloyd George's speech on 3 October seemed to compound the atmosphere of apprehension, even 'defeatism'.[57]

The government as a whole were fully aware that the next stage in the war of nerves was to be Hitler's 'peace initiative', even if only a few in the Cabinet were fully up-to-date with the Dahlerus story. They were thus on guard for any possible attempt to confuse or humiliate Britain so soon after the hesitant entry into the war. Given the new presence in the War Cabinet of Churchill, and his self-appointed but also public role as guardian of steadfastness, there was little room here for innovation or flexible diplomacy on the part of Chamberlain or Halifax. Nonetheless, a good deal of finesse was still required on a day-to-day basis, and there was scope for both error and subtlety in the execution of the broadly agreed policy. Since the policy itself was inherently ambivalent, moreover, in its dismissal of the prospects of peace but willingness to listen to offers, the issue of collective responsibility and the Cabinet's control over diplomacy became central once more. Churchill (and Eden, a regular attender at, if not a full member of, the War Cabinet) would have been alerted to the need to follow events closely, when they heard the Prime Minister say on the eve of Hitler's speech, 'The present might be one of the most important psychological moments of the war, since there was evidence that Germany and perhaps other countries were now wavering in their attitude.' For his part Halifax was both enigmatic and optimistic: 'the main point was to secure the position in the present war, which it was reasonable to hope would be followed by a long period of peace'.[58] Clearly Hitler's speech was likely to determine the climate in which the British government would have to work out their still rather cloudy views on war aims and the nature of the British commitment. The scene was set for an important series of discussions, if not decisions.

When it came, Hitler's speech was skilfully pitched to appeal to international opinion without sacrificing the nationalistic *élan* which whipped up domestic support. Although it is universally referred to as a 'peace offer', in fact Hitler only sketched out a general preference for peace and said nothing about specific heads of agreement, which by contrast had been forthcoming through the von Papen feeler. He talked of the waste of war, the need for conditions in which prosperity could be achieved and the possibility of a conference in which to resolve outstanding questions. This could only take place after hostilities had come to an end. The Führer went through a long list of countries, stressing how he had no claims on any of them (pointedly omitting Finland and the remaining two British-guaranteed states, Greece and Roumania) but also making it clear that 'the Poland of the Versailles Treaty will never rise again' and that the German-Soviet agreement meant two new, exclusive, spheres of influence in central Europe. He also showed himself aware that Britain was now seeking to bring about a change of regime in Germany and finished with the threat that 'those who repulse my hand' would find that 'neither force of arms nor time will overcome Germany'.[59]

The question of how the British government reacted to this speech provides us with a classic example of collective foreign policy-making in a limited time-period, when basic values were at stake. If it had also been the case that a major turning-point was unavoidable at this juncture (it was not), then this would certainly have been a case of full-blown crisis decision-making.[60] The Cabinet was focused as a group on a major issue, it had sufficient time in which to consider carefully, although not so much that other issues supervened, and the final product (a statement) did not involve such a careful monitoring of long-drawn-out implementation as had, for instance, the Anglo-Soviet negotiations of the previous summer. And yet many complicated nuances of diplomacy were involved, which non-specialists in foreign affairs might be unaware of, or hesitate to intervene in. The British response to the speech of 6 October represents, therefore, a problem which could have facilitated *either* executive dominance of the Cabinet *or* a fully participatory process. Which model was to be borne out by events?

THE GOVERNMENT'S RESPONSE

The six-day period between Hitler's speech on the afternoon of Friday 6 October and Chamberlain's reply in the House of Commons on the afternoon of Thursday 12 October saw the War Cabinet meet daily, as usual, and hold four major discussions on how Britain should respond. Three members of the War Cabinet were fully involved in the drafting throughout, and another joined them in a formally constituted sub-committee after three days. The remaining five members, together with two of the three 'constant attenders' at the War Cabinet from the larger Cabinet body, had a number of opportunities to influence the drafting in the daily meetings, and played a fairly full part by that means.

On the substance of the issue, it was clear from the outset that there was to be no question of any positive response to Hitler's speech. The 'decision-making' did not consist in arguments about whether or not to make peace, and there is no evidence to suggest that anyone in the Cabinet (even Chamberlain, who was perhaps the most susceptible to temptation[61]) came anywhere near the position which Lloyd George had laid out so controversially a few days before. The reason the process was so long drawn out, and was seen as so significant by its participants, was rather because they were aware that the psychological and political balance of the war might be at stake. Partly in terms of the contest between the two governments, partly in terms of the struggle for the support of the 'neutrals' and partly in terms of the effects of both German and British public opinion, the Cabinet realised that a badly handled reply might hand important cards to their adversary.

Moreover, as had been evident on 5 October, the issue of the extent to which Chamberlain and Halifax could be trusted with the execution of foreign policy was not entirely absent from the atmosphere. Perhaps it was with this in mind, and also the events of 2 September, that the Foreign Secretary addressed his colleagues apologetically on the morning of 7 October. Halifax referred to the statement which had been broadcast on the previous evening and included in the morning newspapers as 'issued on the authority of His Majesty's Government': 'This statement had gone rather further than the general guidance authorised by the War Cabinet, but the Minister of Information had persuaded him that something on these lines was necessary.'[62] The War Cabinet had in fact agreed on the 6th that until 'careful consideration' had been made of Hitler's speech, 'nothing should appear by way of commentary which purported to give His Majesty's Government's views. Silence might well prove to be the most effective reply.' Yet 'while nothing could be said on questions of policy, the Ministry of Information should not be left without guidance . . . '. It should refer to the Prime Minister's statement of 3 October, when he had said in the Commons that peace proposals would be examined, but that the German government would have to meet the objection that they had proved their word to be unreliable.[63] The statement released immediately after Hitler's speech, however, was anything but brief or bland. It attacked in some detail Hitler's 'perversions of the truth', referred to 'Herr Hitler's open aspirations for world domination in *Mein Kampf*' and said that although the German leader's remarks would be given 'careful examination', no peace proposals could be acceptable which did not provide guarantees against future aggression, and guarantees based on 'something more than words'.[64] All this was undoubtedly a statement of policy, and one which was bound to affect the climate in which the War Cabinet settled down to its in-depth reply. It was an independent political act, if not such a dramatic one as Chamberlain's reversal at Munich of the Cabinet's decision to support Czechoslovakia.

The War Cabinet did not protest, however, at Halifax's action. This was rarely the way. They understood the pressures of events, so any resentments took time to build up and calculation to express. Rather, they accepted his lead for the immediate future. The Foreign Secretary said that time would be required for a reply, but he would favour pointing out the 'difficulties' in the speech, and would mention Poland, Czechoslovakia and disarmament in particular. The real problem was the impossibility of relying on the German government's word, and he was coming increasingly to the view that 'his chief war aim was the elimination of Herr Hitler'. Any eventual peace should not be 'vindictive'.[65]

In the discussion which followed, individuals are not recorded as having made their distinctive marks, but the point was made that 'the statement must be worthy of the occasion . . . rather full, and should contain the necessary historical background'. Clearly the issue was of central importance to the government. Despite the evidence of the Prime Minister's post-bag that 'a small section of opinion in this country held pacifist views', Hitler's speech was perceived as having fallen flat both in the UK and abroad. It was argued that the British statement should leave the onus on Hitler to answer certain questions or start the war 'in earnest in the West'.

The procedure for the next few days seems to have been easily agreed. The Prime Minister was to make a statement in reply to Hitler in the House of Commons, probably on 11 October. Halifax was to prepare a draft for the War Cabinet to consider on the 9th. Only after that point would the Dominions and France be consulted, although efforts were to be made to ensure that France did not act herself without consultation. In the interim, even the Ministry of Information was to say nothing.[66]

The next twenty-four hours or so were taken up with drafting and consultation. Cadogan produced a first draft reply for Chamberlain and Halifax after the Cabinet meeting on the 7th. On the 8th, the War Cabinet met in its usual Sunday truncated form, with only Simon, Churchill and Kingsley Wood present. The 'peace offensive' was not on the agenda. Outside the Cabinet room, however, Cadogan was fending off the suspicious French Ambassador, Corbin, and perusing Halifax's redraft of his own first attempt of the day before.[67] It was 'much longer – as Sam Hoare wanted – but I don't know that it's the better for that. Winston came over after the Cabinet – about 6. He thinks it's too long.'[68]

According to Churchill, Halifax asked him to come over that Sunday night and invited him to submit a draft of his own, after Churchill had said that Halifax's version was 'too long and too defensive'. Churchill then did so, and sent it to Halifax that night and to the Prime Minister the next day, saying that it 'does not close the door on any genuine offer, and does not commit us to any territorial arrangement'.[69] There is one reason why it is worth reflecting on whether this account is the whole story. After Churchill had left Halifax, he sent his draft with a covering note: 'I thought it was very kind of you to invite me to draft something.'[70] This slightly otiose gesture may be accounted for by Churchill's desire to have it on the record that he was not interfering gratuitously in the business of his senior colleagues. After all, he had already made this reputation, and on the same day Chamberlain wrote to his sister how he had been forced to dress down the First Lord for overstepping the mark in this respect. The latest missive (probably *not* the draft reply to Hitler, which the Prime Minister would not by then have received) 'went so far and looked so like a document for the book that I resolved to put an end to it'.[71]

Thus Churchill, perhaps with Halifax's connivance, may have been covering the tracks of his own initiative in breaking into the inner circle of Cabinet drafters. The point cannot be proved, and it may simply be the case that Halifax wanted to bring within the walls the one formidable character in the War Cabinet who might wreck a proposal drafted by the foreign policy executive.[72]

The three drafts up to this point – Cadogan's, Halifax's and Churchill's – differed on important details, if not in their rejection of the possibility of negotiation. Following the lines of Ivone Kirkpatrick's first briefing paper on Hitler's speech (Kirkpatrick was a Foreign Office expert on Germany), Cadogan established the structure of what was to be the final statement, in dividing his remarks into a commentary first on Hitler's various historical claims, and then on his proposals and demands for the future. Much of the content of this document found its way, in amended forms, into the statement made by Chamberlain to Parliament, and indeed the Prime Minister's amendments to his copy of the draft were largely stylistic. On the other hand he did not quarrel with a relatively conciliatory passage which was eventually excised:

His Majesty's Government have already announced that, if proposals for peace were made, they would examine them with care and measure them against the principles for which they had taken up arms, and they feel that it is due from them to make a statement of their views on Herr Hitler's utterance.[73]

The fact that the nature of the statement was a delicate matter cutting across obvious policy positions was illustrated by Vansittart's comments on Cadogan's draft. Although Vansittart was only interested in how to squeeze the maximum advantage out of the situation in terms of ultimate victory, he recognised that the need to play for time and discourage any German attack before the winter meant that Britain should avoid being 'snappy' with Hitler. He wanted to keep the Nazis talking and to lead them 'up the garden path'.[74]

On this, Halifax wrote to Chamberlain to say that he agreed with Vansittart's objectives, but that the tactic of delay and obfuscation would engender 'doubt and uncertainty ... in many quarters'. This was probably the domestic dimension, which Vansittart tended to overlook. The French view would also have to be taken into account (which was that Hitler was the symptom of a general problem with

Germany). Sir Horace Wilson drew this to Chamberlain's attention, and wrote 'it would not satisfy opinion over here' – the 'it' referring to the French line.[75] Halifax's own draft follows Cadogan, but adds one section on the horrors of the Polish campaign (Halifax's High Anglicanism probably made him particularly sensitive to the sufferings of a Catholic people) and another much longer one on Britain's reasons for rejecting Hitler's olive branch, as well as the principles which were governing British conduct.

The Foreign Secretary's version was more fulsome and repetitive, and where Cadogan emphasised that essentially Britain wanted a return to the status quo ante, with guarantees against its disruption, Halifax was prepared to envisage proposals for disarmament or other long-term reforms of the international system. This tension, between righting Hitler's wrongs and structural changes to avoid any repetition, was at the heart of the uncertainty as to whether the government should formulate detailed war aims, and it was increasingly to bedevil British policy as the war unfolded.

Halifax faced up to the conflict between basic values which was at issue. Britain recognised that war meant cruel losses, but that would be preferable to the annihilation of human progress. In particular he drew attention to the changes in Hitler's approach during the previous year. He was now forcing non-Germans to be included in the Reich, and he had gone back on his often-stated anti-Bolshevism. Both of these points, evidently of central importance to the government, were included in the final statement on 12 October. Halifax made a conciliatory gesture in Hitler's direction by agreeing with him that the world's political and economic ills required international solutions, but this had already been effectively negated by the firm statement that 'it is no longer possible to have faith in the word of the present German government'.[76]

Given the length, and typically agonised flavour, of this effort by Lord Halifax, it is not surprising that Churchill was eager to inject both his mastery of the language and his policy convictions into the reply. His four typed letter-pages were more positive in their denunciation of Hitler and the 'grievous crime in European history' which was the invasion of Poland. They stressed the centrality of the restitution for the victims of aggression (including Czechoslovakia) and 'solid and enduring guarantees against the renewal of German aggression'. A powerful statement, which was to find its way into the final version, followed:

Acts, not words alone, must be forthcoming before the Allies would be justified in ceasing to wage war to the utmost of their strength.[77]

Even Churchill, however, felt the need to avoid giving an impression of unbending belligerence. His draft argued that His Majesty's Government would 'at all times respond to any real and sincere effort by Germany to undo, so far as it be possible, the wrong that has been done and the misery that has been caused'. Moreover, Britain's sole aim would be 'to build a free, a peaceful and a prosperous Europe in which Germany, as one of its greatest nations, should play a leading and an honoured part'. It seems likely that Churchill included such passages both to distinguish between the German people and the Nazis and to anticipate the tone which he knew Chamberlain was likely to require. Although a formidable figure, Churchill was still only a Service minister, and he had been out of power since 1929. He was anxious not to alienate further the senior members of the government, and had succeeded to the point where that very night Chamberlain could write to his sister Ida that the Cabinet were 'working together very harmoniously and successfully': 'I constructed my Cabinet on no theory or rule governing its size or the nature of its composition whether departmental or otherwise. My sole purpose was to find a Cabinet that would work, which means that *personalities* must be taken into account, and in that I seem to have been successful.'[78] The War Cabinet met at 11.30 a.m. on 9 October to consider Halifax's draft reply. As usual, the matter was last on the agenda, but took up (if the length of the minuted discussions is a guide) nearly forty percent of the morning's discussion. All members were present, including Eden and Anderson, the 'constant attenders'.[79]

The Prime Minister set the tone by suggesting that the critical international reaction to Hitler's speech justified a rather 'stiffer tone' than might otherwise have been the case.[80] Moreover Hitler's assertion that Poland was now a *fait accompli* was unacceptable, although Britain would not commit itself to any 'specific solution of the Polish problem'. He would not rule out a sympathetic reference in his coming statement to Czechoslovakia, but Poland was the main concern. The proposals in Hitler's speech were hardly discussable because nothing the Führer said could be believed. Acceptable actions were necessary before that view could be modified. He was against any precise statement of war aims.

The 'peace offensive', October 1939   121

Churchill took the initiative in the discussion, relegating Halifax, who had actually written the draft asked for by the Cabinet, to the position of also-ran. He agreed with Chamberlain, and emphasised that opinion at home, in the Dominions and in neutral countries was against discussions with Hitler until his deeds changed. Despite this clear lead, there was in fact some uncertainty in the general discussion which followed. Halifax and Chatfield wanted to reassure the German people that the allies were not aiming for another 'dictated peace', but there was general agreement that war aims should not be stated in detail, with Eden (Secretary of State for the Dominions) pointing out that this would probably satisfy the Canadian Prime Minister, who had also wanted some reference to war aims in the reply.

It was also agreed that 'while the tone of the reply should be very firm, it should not definitely shut the door, but should make it clear that it was for Herr Hitler to give a reply to our answer'.[81] A further draft to take all this into account was to be prepared for the following day by a sub-committee composed of Chamberlain, Halifax, Churchill and now Simon as well. It should be noted that, again contrary to traditional notions about Chamberlain's 'inner Cabinet', Sir Samuel Hoare was not a member of this group. Even after this decision, however, there was some havering. Some unnamed ministers were concerned about the reaction of the 'average German' to a British statement which seemed to promise only 'a long and bloody war'. The German people should be encouraged to seek peace by getting rid of Hitler.[82] Then Halifax returned to the question of associating the non-belligerent powers with any peace conference. This would have to include Russia and the USA, and would be another way of attracting moderate opinion in Germany. Although this was jumping the gun somewhat, the only point made against the Foreign Secretary seems to have been that France would be suspicious of an American role, remembering the failure to ratify Versailles.

The details of the subsequent work by the sub-committee are not entirely clear. Cadogan's record for 9 October reads:

P.M. has produced new draft reply to Hitler. Spent 3–4 p.m. trying ... to graft on to it essential passages of H's draft. Meeting at 4 P.M., H., Winston, H.J.W. and self on draft. Quite useful – got it into shape, more or less. Adjourned 6–7 for Horace to have it retyped. Then met and approved it. Quite good, I think.[83]

Thus Simon was not present for the preliminary meeting of the sub-committee. He was chairing the Economic Policy Committee of the Cabinet at the same time. But he took a full part thereafter.[84] The following week Chamberlain recalled that the draft had been 'amended and polished and improved again and again by a committee of Halifax, Winston, Simon and myself'. Churchill had been particularly helpful, even listening to other people's suggestions.[85] Moreover the Transport Minister, Euan Wallace, outside the War Cabinet but watching its business closely, recorded when he received an advance copy of the statement on 11 October that 'it would be impossible to improve upon it. It bears every evidence of the collective mind of the best brains in the Cabinet.'[86] Clearly the formulation process was perceived as having been collective, and Sir John Simon, who as Chancellor of the Exchequer, ex-Foreign Secretary and future Lord Chancellor was undoubtedly one of the government's 'best brains', was fully involved.[87]

The sub-committee did not alter the existing draft radically, but they did act as a bridge between the lengthy Halifax and the pithy Churchill versions, as between the slight uncertainties of the early days of the process and the final statement, with which ministers were generally pleased. The sub-committee continued with the basic strategy of following the organisation of Hitler's speech and rebutting his main points in turn. They did, however, wrestle with the tone of their reply, eventually deciding to omit a reference even to the possibility that Britain might wish to 'crush Germany' and cutting out a paragraph talking about Germany's breach of 'pacts and conventions' on the use of arms. In general the drafting process slightly moderated the language of the British reply. For example, in the phrase 'it is no longer possible to have faith in the word of the present German Government', the term 'unsupported' was placed before 'word', suggesting that if only Germany would provide some earnest of its future good intentions (by, say, marching out of Poland), the door might not be fully closed to dialogue. Equally, a statement which could have committed Britain to a crusade for democracy ('the British people are resolved to make every effort in their power to win for themselves, as for others, liberty through respect for the law') was cut out during the committee stage.[88]

Much of all this was in the interests of presentation and tight drafting. Moreover the concern not to alienate all Germans, thereby driving a wedge between Hitler and his people, was an increasingly important part of British strategy for winning the war. But it is not too fanciful also to see in such inclusions the Prime Minister's own hand, as he tried rather forlornly to square the circle or reconciling his own deep needs to find non-military solutions with the new realities of prosecuting the war. Churchill and (to some degree) Halifax were ready to watch out for any back-sliding into excessive optimism about peace, but neither was sufficiently confident about the future of the war or the strength of his own political position to ride roughshod over Chamberlain's concerns – as even the crisis of May 1940 was to show.[89] Chamberlain certainly drafted a passage saying that Britain sought 'no material advantage', and that 'we desire nothing from the German people which should offend their self-respect', in place of the statement (a hostage to fortune) that 'we propose to make no territorial claims'. He was also responsible for the inclusion of a reference to France as 'our gallant and trusted Ally', put in to show Paris that French concerns were not being overlooked, despite the fact that Britain insisted on taking the Reichstag speech seriously. In general, Chamberlain's personal amendments suggest bitter resignation and shock about the turn of events, rather than any attempt to renew appeasement. Unlike Halifax, who wished strongly to include sections on long-term goals and the involvement of neutrals in any peace settlement, Chamberlain eschewed planning for the future, and fell back now on a mixture of hope and steadfastness.[90]

The sub-committee's efforts were examined by the War Cabinet on the morning of Tuesday, 10 October. This was no pro forma repetition of the informal meetings, as the draft was now subject to the renewed scrutiny of Hore-Belisha, Kingsley Wood, Chatfield, Hankey and Hoare – a numerical majority of the War Cabinet. This time the subject took up less than 20 per cent of the total discussion.[91] First Halifax conveyed some confidential information about a new promise from Dahlerus that concrete proposals were on their way from Berlin. Halifax had said all such information would be considered, but Dahlerus would not be permitted to come to London.[92]

The rest of the discussion was less rambling than at the previous War Cabinet, and a number of important issues came up. Chief amongst them was the matter of the Dominions' views. Eden reported that they wanted more time to consider and that the draft (that is, Halifax's first draft) 'went too far in the direction of slamming the door on further discussion, instead of putting questions that Herr Hitler would have to answer'.[93] After some debate, in which the point was made (it has the feel of Churchill) that 'the French government and a large section of opinion in this country' expected, *per contra*, an immediate summary refusal of any dialogue with Hitler,[94] it was agreed that the importance of maintaining unity with the Dominions 'outbalanced other considerations'. It was decided to delay the statement for a further day, until Thursday 12 October.

On the Dominions' substantive point about keeping open the possibility of discussion, several ministers pointed out that Paragraph 14 (that is, the 'Conclusions') of the draft was indeed 'a little too definite', and it was generally agreed that it 'might be put in a more questioning form'. A Canadian redraft of this section was handed round, and it was agreed that the sub-committee would attempt to rework the passage, incorporating some of the Canadian points. At this point, Halifax put his finger on the dilemma in which the government found themselves: any statement which did not fully 'slam the door' was likely to imply that there was in fact a basis for negotiation. In fact, as Daladier seems to have realised, the failure to dismiss the Reichstag speech out of hand at the outset had itself been a tacit admission of the continuing possibility of communication between the two sides. What the government was saying was slightly at odds with its procedure for saying it.

It is worth pausing for a moment here to note the overall role of the Dominion governments in the decision-making process with respect to the October peace offer. Our concern is with the functioning of the British Cabinet, and not the general interplay of historical forces, but there is a link in this case between the attitudes and inputs of the Dominions and the balance of discussion in the War Cabinet. This is partly because of the peculiarly intimate connection in foreign policy between the Dominions and Britain, and partly because of the exigencies of wartime, when the need for allied unity seemed overriding. The first of these two factors might be thought the more significant, given the distance, even coolness, between London and Paris on the issue. The French view was expressed forcefully, and French susceptibilities were soothed by Chamberlain, but France did not have the persistent access at the Cabinet level which personal contacts and institutionalisation (in the form of a Secretary of State) provided for the Dominions.[95]

The Dominions are also important in this case because they represented that tendency which hankered after regaining peace before it was too late, and therefore a counter-balance to the circumstantial pressures that Chamberlain was coming under to abandon his long-held belief in the possibility of negotiated solutions to international conflicts. There were, of course, nuances (even real differences) between the positions of the individual Dominion governments. Moreover the relatively short period of six days in which drafting took place meant that it was difficult for the Dominions to be very effective either in co-ordinating amongst themselves or in keeping up to date with the revisions being produced in London. This was a different order of exercise from the strong general input in favour of peace they had made during September 1938, and which had been influential in tipping the balance as Chamberlain and his ministers oscillated over whether or not to fight for Czechoslovakia.

Despite their inherent disadvantages in the drafting process, the Dominions still put together a coherent collective position and made their mark on British policy, first by delaying the statement by twenty-four hours, but more importantly by shaping some of its content. Briefly, they all favoured (unlike France) a proper reply being made to Hitler, and most (Australia was less concerned) stressed that no opportunity of an honourable peace should be spurned, however unlikely. Their main point was their strongly held opinion that the allies should state their war aims clearly, in order to appeal to neutral and moderate German opinion. By 12 October, they had all come round to the Canadian view that a conference of neutral powers should be proposed as a way of deciding on the boundaries of what they hoped would be the reconstituted states of Poland and Czechoslovakia.[96]

In making these points persistently and forcefully, the Dominions not only reminded the Cabinet of Britain's dependence on the Commonwealth; they also touched on differences of emphasis within the War Cabinet itself. For example, during the meeting of 10 October which decided to take another day over drafting to 'carry' the Dominions along with the policy and in which 'several ministers' agreed that Paragraph 14 was 'a little too definite', it is also recorded that Hoare, Halifax and Chatfield joined together to argue that part of the first draft should be reincorporated 'in order to appeal to the more idealistic elements both in this country and abroad'. This was a reference to a passage dealing in general terms with the kind of post-war settlement envisaged, and was both a sop to Dominion concerns over war aims and a case of Halifax returning to the charge over his own (and Hoare's) personal preoccupations. The War Cabinet would not, however, accept the associated idea of a conference of neutral powers.[97]

The content of the final statement thus reflected some of the Dominions' concerns. Horace Wilson minuted on 11 October that a sentence about the war being for the security not only of the smaller nations, but also of all freedom-loving countries was included after a telegram from Menzies.[98] Indeed the Australian Prime Minister had exerted the biggest single external influence. His phrases about aiming beyond victory towards a better international system also found their way into the statement ultimately made.[99]

But the War Cabinet's patience with consultations ran out as the process of formulation threatened to extend itself indefinitely. It was clear there could be no further postponements of the statement without the kind of furore in Parliament which had occurred on 2 September. At the Cabinet meeting on 11 October to consider a further redraft, therefore, with a final polished version still to come, Eden reported further Dominion anxieties about insufficient treatment of Allied war aims, only to be told by his colleagues that the existing version was not inconsistent with the Dominions' concerns, and that it could not be altered yet again. The Dominions should be told that their points could be covered in any future statements.[100] On this occasion Hitler's speech merited less than 10 per cent of the Cabinet session as a whole; the momentum was ebbing from the process.

On the morning of 12 October, the day in which Chamberlain was to make the statement in the House, the War Cabinet met to hear final details. Eden reported on his meeting with the Dominion High Commissioners (at which they had asked for a conference of neutrals) and the Prime Minister clearly had general support for turning this idea down flat, as both unprepared and impracticable. He pointed out that the statement 'left the door open' for Hitler, and that if he were to respond positively the Dominions would then have plenty more opportunities for consultation. No additions should be made to the draft, for example, by stating that Britain might negotiate over any satisfactory German proposals, as the aim of the statement was to put Hitler in the position of having to make a choice and take responsibility for war or peace.[101] The War Cabinet authorised the statement without further argument. It was delivered by

Chamberlain in the Commons that afternoon, and by Stanhope, on behalf of Halifax, in the Lords.[102]

IMPLEMENTATION

The Prime Minister's reply to Hitler went down well in British political circles. Clement Attlee for the Labour Party welcomed it warmly in the Commons, and said that no British government, whether on grounds of prudence or principle, could have made a different kind of statement. There was no serious dissent from the general line taken within it.[103] The Dominions also seemed happy in the event.[104] The fact that Hitler reacted angrily to the statement as tantamount to a declaration of war[105] for once confirmed Chamberlain in a sense of the rightness of having taken a firm stand, and the image of Cabinet unity was quickly projected onto the whole country. Whereas on 7 October worries had been expressed about 'a small section of opinion' which held pacifist views, by 16 October the War Cabinet felt that 'public opinion in the country was practically unanimous in support of the Government's war policy'.[106] The Prime Minister was privately less certain about public opinion, but his success did increasingly lead him to think that Hitler was now at a disadvantage. By 5 November he saw Hitler's 'silence' as the product of 'abject depression' at his own impotence, and felt that German support for the Führer would crumble: 'I have a hunch that the war will be over before the Spring.'[107]

Thus the implementation phase of the response to Hitler's Reichstag speech was fairly short and unproblematical, unlike those of many major foreign policy decisions,[108] even if there were still to come a number of alarums and excursions on the issues of war aims and peace feelers (particularly behind the scenes) before the end of the Phoney War.[109] But how are we to interpret the pattern of Cabinet decision-making revealed by this week of hectic activity? We have observed the forging of a strong consensus among ministers, but also some important hesitations and differences of outlook. What were the determining elements in producing the outcome which prevailed?

ANALYSIS

Overtly, War Cabinet decision-making in response to the October peace offer was highly participatory, with the habit of daily meetings facilitating involvement by all nine members of what was designed to be a small and cohesive group in comparison with normal peacetime Cabinets. The proprieties were observed, with the constitution of a drafting sub-committee and its reporting back leading to further instructions and redrafts. The result was a statement which was as near to being genuinely agreed as any collective piece of writing can be. There is, therefore, a good *prima facie* case for seeing this episode as supporting the classical view of the Cabinet as an internally democratic institution in which power as well as responsibility is shared.

Before this conclusion can be established, however, it is important to look at certain particular aspects of the problem in more detail, namely the relationship between the War Cabinet and the Cabinet proper, the role of the 'foreign policy executive' and the impact of certain key individuals on the development of attitudes in the group.

Cabinet and War Cabinet

So far as the main Cabinet were concerned, that is, the fifteen in the 'outer circle' but 'above the line',[110] there were relatively few opportunities to become involved in the formulation of a response to Hitler. The special weekly briefings by a senior minister, or what eventually became known as 'the children's hour',[111] did not begin until two months later, and most ministers followed a routine of concentrating on their particular task, relating mostly to officials, Parliament and the press. The papers which survive from this group of ministers suggest a general rather than an intimate familiarity with War Cabinet business, and a straightforward acceptance of the latter's ultimate supreme authority. For junior ministers, of course, even those like Harry Crookshank at the Treasury, the War Cabinet was like some distant star, dictating their orbit but only dimly visible.[112] The Inskip Diary – Sir Thomas Inskip had become Viscount Caldecote on the outbreak of war and had been appointed Lord Chancellor, outside the War Cabinet – shows its author increasingly reliant for his knowledge of policy on his reading of regularly circulated Cabinet papers, rather than access to the inner sanctum. Indeed, Caldecote only attended the War Cabinet on one occasion, and that for one agenda item (on contingencies for a new meeting-place for Parliament) in the whole of the time up to the fall of the Chamberlain government. That detachment probably accounts for his comment on 20 September that 'The War Cabinet has woken up to the fact that a little more news should be given to the ordinary Cabinet members, and the COS reports are to be circulated.'[113] Caldecote's sole comment on the reply to Hitler shows an accurate but rather general appreciation of what was going on:

> The Dom. Govts. all wished the PM to make a more definite statement of war aims. The PM reacted rather irritably to this, partly because it meant more delay, partly because it would alter the tone of the document which was meant to put H. in a dilemma. The PM thought the Dom. Govts. showed a lack of the sense of realism.[114]

Nonetheless, the very separation of the two groups of ministers, the one subordinate to but larger than the other, had the potential for slippage possessed by any two centres of decision. On the day of Hitler's speech, for example, the Home Policy Committee, which some thought 'as near as may be the old Cabinet',[115] met to discuss morale and propaganda:

> we all agreed on the desirability of a series of pronouncements by the Prime Minister or Foreign Secretary on major issues which could be used subsequently as texts for the smaller fry. The great difficulty at the moment seems to be the precise definition of our war aims, and there is no doubt that there is in the country a very great sense of bewilderment. Every Minister present had been impressed with the doubts, and in many cases apathy, expressed in conversation during the past few weeks and by no means least in the House of Commons itself.

There was further comment on the lack of liaison evident in the fact that the Ministry of Information had been given no instructions on how to handle Hitler's speech that very day, and unrest at the lack of co-ordination and initiative in the handling of the matter. Hoare was deputed to inform the War Cabinet of these views when they met later that morning, which he did.[116]

The War Cabinet took their colleagues' views seriously but, as we have seen,[117] decided that time was necessary to respond to Hitler, and that silence might be effective in the meanwhile. They may have had something of the same view as Crookshank, who had also been present at the Home Policy Committee but who, by contrast, regarded its discussion as 'all blah'.[118] Still, such assertions of authority could incur a cost, and the determination of the Ministry of Information to put out something substantive led to Halifax's authorisation of the breach of the War Cabinet's decision that he reported on 7 October.[119]

This may have been an isolated instance of influence from below, as the Home Policy Committee's chairman, Hoare, later complained to the Prime Minister's office that important matters were virtually settled before coming to the Committee.[120] Its importance lies rather in its demonstration of the fact that cohesiveness in the War Cabinet did not guarantee the smooth running of the overall direction of high policy.

The experience of the 'constant attenders', who were clearly intended to act as a form of bridge between the two parts of the Cabinet, pointed in the same direction. Table 4, below, provides a sample of one month in the attendance record of Chamberlain's War Cabinet. The impression it gives of other ministers having considerable, if irregular, access to the War Cabinet is slightly misleading in that most of the isolated instances refer to occasions when a minister attended for a particular agenda item, and did not stay for matters outside his remit. This applied even to the slightly more familiar figures. In October there were thirty-four meetings of the War Cabinet, but five of those were on Sundays when only three full members were present and no outsiders.[121] Thus there were twenty-nine possible meetings to which ordinary Cabinet ministers might hope to be invited. Most came to one or two meetings for one item. Burgin, Brown, Gilmour, Morrison and Zetland attended between five and eight on the same basis.

Oliver Stanley, President of the Board of Trade, also usually came along only for particular items, although he did attend parts of no fewer than eighteen out of the twenty-nine meetings. It may be, however, that his presence was becoming seen as increasingly valuable outside his area of expertise, as in the following January he was brought fully into the War Cabinet to replace Hore-Belisha. Two other ministers remain. Anderson and Eden were the real 'constant attenders' of Cabinet Office lore, both being present at twenty-eight meetings in October, without being restricted to particular subjects.[122]

Such a special privilege was not granted by Chamberlain unequivocally. So far as Eden was concerned, the Prime Minister had said at the onset of war that the Secretary of State for Dominion Affairs would need to attend 'whenever matters were discussed of which it was necessary that he should be aware in order to be sure that the Dominions were properly supplied with information'.[123] In practice this meant all the time. Eden himself, however, later described his position as 'humiliating'. He remembered Chamberlain as having been embarrassed at not being able to offer his ex-Foreign Secretary a place in the War Cabinet, and having said that he should be a constant attender. Strictly speaking this meant that Eden would only be able to speak about the Dominions, but the Prime Minister 'did not expect that this restriction would be strictly enforced'. Not surprisingly, Eden did not feel at ease with this arrangement, and recalled that he had been a 'spectator' of most proceedings, not a participant.[124]

Anderson, as an ex-civil servant, was in a totally different position to Eden, who had been propelled into the Cabinet largely by his public following and having been seemingly vindicated by events. Anderson was becoming increasingly important as an administrative linchpin on the home front, and was eventually to become Chancellor of the Exchequer under Churchill in 1943. Perhaps also because he had had to swap posts with Hoare on 3 September to allow the latter a seat in the War Cabinet, he too was given the status of constant attender as a form of compensation.

Churchill, looking back, saw Anderson and Eden as *de facto* members of the War Cabinet – 'thus our total was eleven'.[125] In general the Conclusions of the War Cabinet are more terse than those of the prewar period, so that it is difficult to say whether in fact the constant attenders were able to participate in wide-ranging discussion. Eden's testimony suggests not, that he felt ham-strung and that 'I was only there on condition that I took no effective part in anything outside the work of my department.'[126]

Yet Eden was jaundiced about Chamberlain after the events of 1937–8 and in retrospect would not have been eager to associate himself with the work of the latter's War Cabinet. Moreover in the nature of things the Cabinet Conclusions would not refer to contributions by non-members, nor to the informal interchanges which are crucial in shaping moods and attitudes.[127] On balance it seems likely that the two constant attenders were seen as significantly elevated above other non-members. The Cabinet Office certainly did not want to encourage others to seek to emulate them. They wanted to restrict the circulation of Cabinet agendas among ordinary ministers, because 'nothing ought to be done to whet their appetite for attending', and the Prime Minister was already under fire for having too big a War Cabinet: 'if one or two get a regular right of entry, there will be trouble with, e.g. *The Times*'.[128] In this new environment, decisive leadership was expected.

Table 4. Attendance at the War Cabinet by ministers of Cabinet rank but not full members of the War Cabinet, 1–31 October 1939

	JA	LB	VC	DS	AE	EB	JG	MM	LM	WE	EW	DLW	WSM	LZ	OS
October 1															o
2		o			o										o
3	o/o				o										o/o
4	o	o		-/o	o/o										o
5	o									o/-		o/-			
6	o				o										
7	o				o										
8															
9	o	o			o										o
10	o				o										
11	o				o				o						
12	o				o										
13	o				o			o							o
14		o					o								
15	o				o		o				o				
16			o												
17	o				o	o/o	o/o								o
18	o/o	o			o/o	o/o	o/o						o/-	-/o	o/-
19	o	o			o		-/o								o
20	o				o										
21															
22		o													
23	o				o		o				o				o

24		o		o
25		o/o		o/o
26		o/–		
27		o	–/o	o
28		o		
29				
30		o		o
31		o		

Notes:

1. JA = Sir John Anderson; LB = Leslie Burgin; VC = Viscount Caldecote; DS = Sir Reginald Dorman-Smith; AE = Anthony Eden; EB = Ernest Brown; JG = Sir John Gilmour; MM = Malcolm MacDonald; LM = Lord Macmillan; WE = Walter Elliott; EW = Euan Wallace; DLW = Earl De La Warr; WSM = W. S. Morrison; LZ = Lord Zetland; OS = Oliver Stanley.

2. 'o' means present at a particular meeting of the War Cabinet, although it should be noted that many ministers attended only for particular items. 'o/–', 'o/o', and '–/o' refer to the days on which there was more than one meeting of the War Cabinet, and are designed to show whether a minister was present at one or both on that date.

The foreign policy executive

There were, however, limits on the directions in which leadership could be exerted. The structural position of advantage for the foreign policy executive that we have observed in certain previous instances was attenuated once war had broken out by the reduction in size of the War Cabinet and the almost exclusive public focus on matters external. Moreover any tendency by the Prime Minister and Foreign Secretary to improvise policy was likely to awaken memories of the now-discredited past. The climate of wartime might seem to be favourable to the personalisation of government, but the challenge it represents can also undermine a Prime Minister who is unable to adjust to the new circumstances, as it was to do with Eden in 1956.

Chamberlain's confidence was dented,[129] and it is possible, as Cameron Watt argues,[130] that he was beginning to give ground somewhat to Halifax, who had shown some subtle signs of wishing to distance himself from appeasement during the previous twelve months. Nonetheless the two men were still very close, and indelibly associated with the old policy, as Halifax's exile to Washington soon after Chamberlain's death in November 1940 bears out. Although the War Cabinet here was rather like the Foreign Policy Committee during the consideration of the Soviet offer of an alliance during the previous spring, in that it was focused on a particular issue of high salience, documentary character and divisive potential, there seems to have been nothing similar to the crucial isolation of the Prime Minister which took place through Halifax's conversion to the idea of an alliance on 19 May. Chamberlain and Halifax seem to have been broadly of one mind on how to respond to Hitler.

It is possible to read some nuances into the record of discussions to the effect that Halifax was taking a slightly more firm line against the peace offer than he feared Chamberlain might be about to do, such as the fact that he allowed the Minister of Information to issue a strong condemnation of Hitler's speech when the Cabinet had decided on silence.[131] It may also be significant that Cadogan recorded, on 7 October, that 'the line, according to me, is to say frankly (and PM hesitates to say this) that *we won't make peace with Hitler.*'[132] On the other hand, this statement could easily centre on the notion of 'saying frankly' that this was an aim, that is, on a tactical rather than a strategic issue. Chamberlain's letters of the period and his contributions to Cabinet as recorded by Bridges all show a weary but definite commitment to the war until Germany should meet certain basic agreed conditions, such as pulling out of Poland.

Moreover, insofar as differences between the Prime Minister and the Foreign Secretary can be discerned over this issue they derive as much from Halifax veering off the purely military track as from Chamberlain doing so.[133] Halifax was one of those in the War Cabinet who believed that a reply to Hitler should go some way down the road of defining British war aims, so as to appeal to neutral opinion and moderates inside Germany. At this time Chamberlain was slightly hysterical about the prospects of an early victory (he told his sister that he expected an end to the war on the basis of a crumbling of Nazism by spring 1940![134]) but he did not show great urgency about the question of what to do when peace came.[135] Halifax, by contrast, was foremost among that group in the War Cabinet which pushed for 'making clear the general nature of our aims at any Peace Conference'.[136]

The foreign policy executive of the government was not therefore seriously divided against itself on how to respond to the Reichstag speech. A difference over spelling out basic assumptions was as far as it went. Indeed, good personal relations put a limit to the extent of disagreement. According to Chamberlain (easily flattered, it is true), Halifax had said about the Cabinet 'mutiny' of 2 September that other ministers' behaviour had been 'unbearable', while in the build-up to war Chamberlain had told Hankey that 'Halifax meant so much to him that he must be a member' (of the coming War Cabinet).[137]

Yet, equally, the executive were not able to dominate the making of foreign policy as they had done in the crisis of the previous March. As we have seen, the idea of reneging on agreed policy was ruled out both because neither man had any serious desire to do so and because the events of 1–3 September meant that their ministerial colleagues were more alert to their collective responsibilities. Nor, in the nature of the problem at hand, were there real opportunities for creative initiatives. It was Hitler who was setting the pace, and the British government who were cautiously responding. There was some room for tactical creativity, such as the attempt to make Hitler answer yet more questions, but the technical expertise of the Foreign Office behind Chamberlain and Halifax – normally a significant advantage – was not indispensable here. Churchill, for example, would have been quite capable of handling the whole episode on his own, had he been allowed to do so. Moreover, the fact that there was a limit to the time which could be taken for a reply paradoxically meant that the process of consideration and drafting was structured and susceptible to monitoring by the group as a whole, unlike the rushed extemporising of 15–30 March, when the pace of diplomatic activity by the executive had wrong-footed most other ministers.

Inside the War Cabinet

The experience of October 1939 confirms again that the existence of a settled 'inner Cabinet' during the Chamberlain years is largely a myth, at least with respect to foreign policy. All the members of the War Cabinet seem to have been important in various ways in this decision, and they do not divide easily into insiders and outsiders. In particular, the 'big four' grouping of Chamberlain, Halifax, Simon and Hoare so often assumed to have been the driving force of government in these years, is not to be found here, any more than it was in our earlier cases. As was so characteristic, Simon's oral contributions were very limited, and in any case he had been the leader of the 'rebels' on 2 September. [138] Moreover he and Hore-Belisha had drafted a joint note suggesting that the Allies declare that they would 'pursue unflinchingly the fight for the overthrow of Nazi dictation in Europe'.[139] This meant that when Simon was appointed a member of the four-man drafting group set up on 9 October (after the two drafts by Halifax and Churchill had established the parameters of discussion) it was hardly the act of an appeasing cabal.

Hoare proved once more an unpredictable case – and thereby probably a far more interesting figure than he has generally been given credit for.[140] It is noteworthy that he was not a member of the drafting committee. This may have been because he did not get on well with Churchill,[141] but it seems more likely that it was because the range of views in the War Cabinet (except those of the Dominions, as Eden was not a member) were already represented on the committee, and his presence would have been superfluous. In his diary 'notes' for 2 October, Hoare recorded that 'Winston', Hankey and Chatfield had come to dinner: 'agreement over peace offensive. Our position clear. What do the Germans mean by their proposals? No need for hurry in reply. Time on our side.'[142] Hoare's position was made clearer in entries for the period 6–8 October. On the Saturday he put down, somewhat obscurely, his personal views on Hitler's speech, saying again 'our position clear', but 'German position not clear . . . ask time. Germans to clarify it . . . even if they do, what are the sanctions?' On Sunday 8 October, Hoare lunched with Chamberlain at Chequers, with the only other guests the 'nuisances, i.e. Runciman and Londonderry'. Referring to 'Neville', Hoare noted 'his view of war probabilities the same as mine'.[143] Hoare was not therefore so much at odds with the Prime Minister as he had been in the previous April, even if, as we have seen,[144] he tended to share Halifax's hankering after a war aims statement.

Relationships in the War Cabinet at this stage, and perhaps throughout the time until Chamberlain's removal, were fairly fluid, and did not coalesce into antagonistic sub-groups. Perhaps the most important implicit grouping was that of the senior figures who actually had experience of the machinery of government in wartime, namely Chamberlain, Churchill, Simon and Hankey. Apart from Chatfield, these were also the older members of the War Cabinet, at sixty and above. If we include Halifax through the weight of his office (his first ministerial appointment was in 1921, compared with Chatfield's debut in 1939) and Hoare (who served in intelligence in Russia during the Great War) we find that the remaining three ministers were responsible for military matters (the Secretaries for War and Air, plus Chatfield), and were all relatively inexperienced. They were all also to be either sacked or moved *before* the crisis of May 1940.[145] If we are to distinguish at all, then, among members of the War Cabinet, it might be as well to do so on the basis of the politically weighty six, who were themselves divided by their degrees of personal distrust of Churchill, the Odysseus returned.

In the four key War Cabinet meetings between 6 and 11 October, attendance was 100 per cent among full members (it was normally over 90 per cent in any case), while Eden and Anderson were also ever-present. The importance of the issue concentrated all minds, and there were opportunities for genuine influence to be exerted through discussion. In fact there were two significant attempts made to shape the eventual statement, the one a pre-emptive move to set the tone of debate and the other an attempt to salvage points which were in danger of being abandoned.

The first of these we have already come across – Churchill's seizing of the initiative early in the proceedings by submitting his own draft. At least as important as the possibility of collusion between Halifax and Churchill on this initiative[146] is the impact of Churchill's draft on the balance of discussion in the War Cabinet. Martin Gilbert has told the story of how, on 11 October, the *Daily Mirror* published an article stating that 'it was only Churchill's "brilliant memorandum" that had persuaded the Cabinet to stiffen Chamberlain's proposed reply to Hitler'. Churchill immediately wrote to the Prime Minister saying that 'I spoke to no one about my draft article outside the secret circle. I gave copies of it to five Cabinet colleagues including yrself & Edward.'[147] Leaving aside the possibly Freudian slip of referring to the draft as an 'article', there remain the issues of who received the 'note' (as it was actually titled[148]), who leaked it and whether the *Mirror*'s analysis of its effect was right.

The five 'Cabinet colleagues' included, we know, Halifax and Chamberlain. There is no evidence as to the recipients of the other three copies, but it seems likely in the light of Hoare having discussed the peace offensive with Churchill on 2 October that he was one. Hankey was probably another, as he had circulated his own 'War Appreciation' only a week or so before. Since Churchill is known not to have had great respect for either Hore-Belisha or Chatfield, it is probable that the last recipient was either Simon or Kingsley Wood.[149]

If it is difficult to find out who is responsible for a contemporary leak, it is virtually impossible to discover the truth in an historical instance. Any member of the Cabinet inclined to reply in strong terms to Hitler could have been responsible. Foreign Office officials with access to the drafting process are also potential culprits. But despite Churchill's denial, the person with the strongest interest in the leak, and with the closest contact with the *Daily Mirror*, was the First Lord himself. His entourage of Brendan Bracken, Lord Beaverbrook and Duncan Sandys, was certainly capable of providing built-in deniability by taking the responsibility on themselves. Moreover Churchill was well known for being unable to resist using the press to release news of his triumphs, as at the start of the war: 'He has let it get into the Press that he will be in the War Cabinet – to the great annoyance of many.'[150] He seems also to have been suspected by Chatfield only two months later of leaking material critical of the latter to the *Sunday Express*.[151] In broad political terms, Churchill only benefited from his image as the backbone in the body politic, especially as Chamberlain accepted his assurances of innocence over the *Mirror*'s story in October. More immediately, he was satisfied with the final version of the reply to Hitler, and probably felt that his contribution had had some real impact.

It cannot be argued plausibly that without Churchill the Chamberlain Cabinet would have run for cover and taken a positive line in reply to Hitler. Both their own documented views and the broader political climate would have made it difficult to do that. The truth is more subtle, namely that a leadership committed to the war but heavy with the sense of its own failure was still uncertain as to how to proceed, on both military and political fronts. Its members were also still susceptible to the disease of wishful thinking, in that hope had not been extinguished that the war might end soon with some upheaval in Germany, or even that Hitler might come to his senses and relinquish his conquests. Only thus can we explain on the one hand the weight placed on the secret contacts with German 'Generals' which led to the Venlo disaster,[152] and on the other the continuing on–off–on Dahlerus saga (see Table 5).[153]

In this context Churchill certainly signalled to his colleagues that he would be vigilant against any loss of nerve. His influence can be traced from the anticipatory discussion of the 'peace offensive' on 5 October, when he had warned of the need to be 'provident stewards of the national interest'.[154] The Conclusions for the first meeting after Hitler's speech do not record any particular contribution from Churchill, although 'various points were made in the discussion'. But the decision to delay a statement until the 11th and to consult the Dominions (after the 9th), together with the expression of the view that the British reply should end 'on a note of enquiry rather than a direct rejection',[155] would certainly have left alarm bells ringing in his mind.

Thus, whether or not with Halifax's encouragement it was not surprising that this statesman *manqué*, already in the habit of deluging his colleagues with memoranda over the whole range of government business, should have gone away to compose his own strong statement of policy for ministers to consider. This had the effect at its next meeting of getting him appointed to the drafting committee, and may have been responsible for Chamberlain's view that 'we should [now] be justified in taking a somewhat stiffer tone in our reply than if the speech had revealed any serious cleavage of opinion', although the Prime Minister was ostensibly referring here to world reactions, and may well have stood firm even without Churchill's presence.

As it happened, the views of Chamberlain and Churchill did not

Table 5. *Contacts between the British government and Mr Birger Dahlerus, 3 September–31 December 1939*

September	5	Dahlerus (D.) sees British Ambassador and Sir George Ogilvie-Forbes (ex-Counsellor in the Berlin Embassy) in Stockholm
	12	Ogilvie-Forbes sees D. again
	18	D. reports that Göring still positive about the possibilities of peace
	22	D. visits Ogilvie-Forbes in Oslo, prior to travelling on to Berlin and London via The Hague
	28–30	D. visits London, to see Cadogan, Halifax and Chamberlain, after two days in Berlin seeing Göring and Hitler
October	3–4	D. telephones from the British mission at The Hague about a possible visit to London. Told that arrangements could be made if necessary
	5	Halifax informs a displeased French Ambassador of the contacts with D.
	11	D. telephones for news of Britain's reply to Hitler, from The Hague
	12	D. telephones for 'guidance' on British reply, but Cadogan refuses contact. D. nonetheless transmits detailed peace proposals, apparently at German behest
	13	Telegrams from D. with news of Göring's response to Chamberlain's speech of 12 October
	14	Telegram from D. talking of a 'more hopeful atmosphere' in Berlin. Kirkpatrick notes that D. is becoming 'tiresome'
	17	More messages from D., annoyed at not being encouraged by Cadogan to visit Britain again
	19	D. 'still bothering, but I drafted a quietus' (Cadogan, signed by Chamberlain and Halifax)
'late October'		D. shows British embassy in Stockholm a letter from Göring thanking him for his efforts, and again makes detailed proposals for a settlement
November	23	More news from D., who has just visited Berlin, and is again (via British embassy in Stockholm) suggesting a secret meeting on neutral ground
December	6	Cadogan talks to Halifax about D. and Villard (an American journalist, just back from Germany). Halifax apparently hankering after 'peace' again; Cadogan counters
	8	Cadogan surprised to hear that D. arriving in London that day
	28	D. in London, and sees Cadogan, who reinforces D.'s tendency now to focus more on the Scandinavian dimension of the war. Nonetheless, D. still talking of Göring wanting to know what guarantees Britain would require for ending the war.

diverge significantly during the drafting process, and the actual contents of Churchill's short draft barely survived into the final text.[156] This was partly because of the element of mutual deference and partly because Churchill was satisfied with the Prime Minister's new firmness. It was also, however, due to agreement on the basic point that attention had to be concentrated on immediate events, leaving the future to take care of itself – even if the two men differed greatly in their expectations of how the war was likely to proceed. In this they found themselves at odds with the second major effort made to influence the statement from within the War Cabinet, back towards a more philosophical approach.

Halifax was the main mover in this. He and Chatfield were concerned that the question of 'aims at any Peace Conference' should not be lost sight of, while Eden confirmed that the Dominions wanted a general statement on values and war aims. Halifax returned to the importance of associating non-belligerent powers with a peace conference, even after the Cabinet had agreed to ask for a further draft, and had accepted that 'while the tone of the reply should be very firm, it should not definitely shut the door'.[157] Thus there was a contest going on in the War Cabinet, in however understated a fashion, over whether the reply to Hitler should be dismissive, in the interests of getting on with fighting the war, or open-ended and discursive about longer-term political goals. Halifax did not give up his draft, with its wordiness but also its willingness to introduce ideas into the discussion, without a struggle in which he was partly successful.

Note to Table 5
Sources:
1. FO memorandum of 24 February 1941, C4216/610/G (in PREM 4/100/8), 'Summary of principal peace feelers September 1939–March 1941', pp. 2–3
2. *Cadogan Diary* (Dilks edition and MS)
3. Foreign Office files: FO 371/23098, 23099, and FO 800/317. Some of this material has been printed in Nicholas Bethell, *The War Hitler Won* (London: Futura, 1976), chapter 9
4. CAB 65/3, Confidential Annexes of Cabinet Conclusions
5. Bernd Martin, *Friedensinitiativen und Machtpolitik in Zweiten Weltkrieg* (Dusseldorf: Droste, 1974).
Note: Dahlerus was still prominent in May 1940, when his offer to find a way out of the crisis in Norway was considered by the War Cabinet (CAB 65/13, WM 135 (40), item 9, 23 May 1940).

For this difference of emphasis was part of the wider general debate on whether war aims should be outlined so early in the war, an issue on which Chamberlain and Churchill found themselves in unusual (and negative) agreement. Thus the reply to Hitler was affected by the views already half-articulated by certain ministers. Hankey, for instance, had produced a lengthy 'war appreciation' on 12 September, which he revised on 29 September. Both versions were circulated widely among senior figures, and each showed a deep ambivalence about the war and any peace offer which might be forthcoming.[158] The 12 September version thought there was no 'over-riding consideration which would justify the War Cabinet in re-canting the attitude of the Government that preceded it to the extent of accepting a humiliating peace offer', and anticipated the declaration of 12 October by saying that Britain should say – but 'in terms of sorrow rather than anger' – that it could not deal with the Hitler regime. This circumspect, even loaded, language was matched by some pointed references to the questions which historians would ask about whether the War Cabinet realised fully the serious ramifications of the decision they had made for war.

The revised appreciation of 29 September was somewhat more confident, in terms of thinking that Britain's military hand was the stronger and that the War Cabinet should not therefore be deterred from 'giving as stiff a reply as we think fit to the coming peace offensive'. It built on the joint conclusions of the secret ministerial meeting of 26 September: 'Hard as the conditions are we have no alternative but to fight on to victory unless we can *per impossibile*, obtain acceptable terms and conditions.' A reply to a peace offer would not be difficult: it should concentrate on appealing to world and moderate German opinion. But if the German government were to offer such – admittedly unlikely – guarantees as putting part of its air force temporarily under neutral custody or withdrawing its armies from occupied territory, then the Allies should show themselves willing to grant reciprocity – for example, by a temporary French withdrawal from the Saar, or handing over some of their air forces to neutrals. Hankey could not see any obvious way by which victory would be obtained; he ended on the proposition that in the long run Britain and France might end up fighting with Germany 'to keep Russia out of Europe' (thus anticipating the Cold War).

Thus one of the most experienced hands in the government was preaching the message of dismissal towards a peace offer, but in language which both conveyed great doubts about the wisdom of an unqualified rejection and speculated wildly about the future. This was far removed from what, by comparison, was Churchill's 'superb, stark, confidence'.[159] Hoare, too, though basically expecting 'a long and grim struggle', believed that Hitler's position was not yet clear, and 'before we even contemplate the possibility of a peace conference, we must have it much more clearly explained than has been done in his speech. This would seem to be a wiser course for us to take rather than to meet his speech with a curt and immediate refusal.'[160]

The desire not to 'shut the door', as it was habitually referred to in these discussions, was echoed in a letter from Anderson on 11 October, which the Prime Minister saw. He enclosed an articulate letter from a constituent, displaying a strong desire for peace, and argued 'The number of people – decent and thoroughly loyal – who are thinking like the writer of the enclosed is I believe very large. These people will not mind how firm the reply to Hitler is, provided it is also constructive.'[161] Even Churchill's own draft was a product of its time, with its gestures towards Germany and its hint of hesitancy before committing the country to all-out war.[162] Victor Cazalet recorded at the time, after seeing a good deal of Churchill, 'There is absolutely no prophesying how the war will develop. Winston is at just as great a loss as anybody else.'[163]

Thus ministers anxious not to foreclose on the last faint hopes of avoiding world war were not so far removed from their temperamentally more robust colleague. It was into this situation of rather nervous debate that the Dominions factor discussed above entered. The War Cabinet meeting of 10 October which led to a further day's delay to enable the Dominions to be 'carried' saw 'several ministers' wanting Paragraph 14 to be made less definite and more questioning, along the lines of a Canadian suggestion. At the same time, Hoare, Halifax and Chatfield suggested reincorporating parts of the earlier draft which dealt in general terms with the kind of post-war settlement Britain might like to see.

In effect, therefore, the Dominions not only found a sympathetic ear in London for their own difficulties; they also acted upon some existing differences of outlook within a generally consensual War Cabinet. The very prolongation of the decision-making process which this involved came near to producing a minor crisis, as it gave the impression of procrastination, even argument, inside the British government. By contrast, the actual evidence of this crucial week of discussion shows not that there were ministers who wanted to accept the *fait accompli* of the loss of Poland, but rather, as Bethell says, that the Government 'made heavy weather over the rejection of Hitler's offer'.[164] Collective uncertainty was the order of the day.

CONCLUSIONS

The period of six days in which the War Cabinet agonised over its reply was probably inevitable, because policy on the nature of the war, and the kind of peace which might be possible, was being made up as the Government went along. In these circumstances the final text of Chamberlain's statement was necessarily a compromise between the different values and tendencies evident within the alliance of anti-Hitler states, the War Cabinet and even the heads of individual ministers. It turned out to be a successful compromise, in that it had a good reception in the Allied camp, and did not provide openings which Hitler could exploit. Moreover, even if it was not quite 'the maturely considered statement' that Churchill later claimed,[165] it was certainly the product of a more effective collective process than many foreign policy decisions in Cabinet. As Simon noted, 'the War Cabinet had put in a great deal of work on the text of the statement'.[166] The working conditions of semi-crisis, combined with the smaller size of a War Cabinet, had enabled all members of the group to participate effectively in discussion and even to influence the detailed drafting of a carefully weighed document. At the same time, in its basic format the statement was not far removed from the earliest drafts of the Foreign Office and even Hankey's 'war appreciation' of 29 September. The process of drafting had not been captured by any single strong view or sub-group within the War Cabinet. The finished version therefore reflected both a determination to resist Hitler and the desire not to 'slam the door', a concern for tactics while also looking forward to a post-war world.

If, like all committee prose, the joins were all too evident in places, at least the statement of 12 October (see Appendix 3, below) did not bear the scars of the kind of prolonged battle which had been necessary before an alliance with the USSR had been contemplated. Nor was it an ill-thought-through initiative foisted by a hasty foreign policy executive on the Cabinet, like the Polish Guarantee. The reply to Hitler's peace offer does not live up to the classical model of collective responsibility, but it does represent the realities of joint decision-making at the highest level, which involves playing politics inside and outside the Cabinet room, and at best an uneven pattern of ministerial influence. As such, it was able not only to establish the lodestar to which all future considerations of the peace issue were referred, but also to sustain a political consensus inside the government and the country as a whole – which was looking doubtful to some insiders at the time[167] – at least until military disasters wreaked their havoc in the following spring.

6. TO CONTINUE ALONE? MAY–JULY 1940

The period of May–June 1940, the months of the fall of France, was a time of the highest stress and instability for all those who lived through it in Europe. By the same token it raised once more the most basic and prominent questions with which decision-makers are ever likely to be confronted – those of war or armistice. It would seem that, as in the previous September, the problem facing British ministers could not have been more conducive to uninhibited debate. The crude facts of physical danger and potential resistance were apparent to all: there existed only a narrow and defined range of available strategies; there could be no question of taking any imaginative initiative such as that of the guarantees of 1939 to transform the political environment. With Hitler in a position of military invulnerability, and with no immediate prospect of attracting new allies by diplomacy, all proposals raised inside the British government would inevitably be subsumed under the crude but clear alternative of fighting on until the situation changed or of coming to terms of some kind with Hitler. Since the War Cabinet met at least once daily,[1] it might be thought that in mid-1940 suitable conditions existed for full Cabinet participation in the making of these major political decisions.

Despite these factors, the data present a different picture. It will be argued here that the period in which France left the war demonstrates how an energetic Prime Minister (in wartime necessarily absorbed by military and foreign policy) could lead the opinion of his colleagues into channels of which only he and perhaps a small circle had a very clear advance idea. In practice this happened in two ways: first by systematically excluding the genuine consideration of some options, and secondly by successfully transforming an existing policy to meet dramatic new circumstances and pressures. The ability of the Prime Minister to play such a role was made possible by the profound impact of external events on existing attitudes, in such a way as to precipitate a highly fluid situation in which uncertainty and shock were the predominant mood. Churchill – who had replaced Chamberlain as Prime Minister on 10 May after a crisis of confidence within the Conservative party over the handling of the war – was thus presented with opportunities which enabled him to direct the nature of the debate into the areas which he judged important. That he formed very definite personal ideas on how to deal with the new problems was partly the result of necessity, partly of predisposition and partly of character;[2] it also meant that the Prime Minister took advantage of the opportunity inherent in the crisis to exert executive leadership. (See Table 6 for the composition of the new Cabinet led by Churchill.)

One clear example of the routine freedoms of the foreign policy executive in implementing policy was Churchill's direct approaches to Roosevelt, outside the scope of Cabinet business and building on the contacts established since Churchill had become First Lord of the Admiralty at the outset of war. These were the famous 'Former Naval Person' letters and telegrams which continued throughout the war at an average of nearly four a week, on many and varied subjects.[3] Between 15 and 20 May the content of these declarations gave clear indications that the Prime Minister intended to make it very difficult for his colleagues within the government to renege on their commitment to the war. Indeed he distributed the telegrams for information to members of the War Cabinet, which was not always routine procedure.[4]

Churchill's messages made important presumptions about the content and consistency of his government's policy at this time. On 15 May he asserted that 'If necessary, we shall continue the war alone', and went further on 18 May in stating that 'We are determined to persevere to the very end, whatever the result of the great battle raging in France may be.' Churchill reiterated this determination two days later with the argument that any British 'parley' with the Germans could only take place after the fall of the present administration, since 'in no conceivable circumstances will we consent to surrender'.[5]

Clearly these gestures of defiance were in part calculated to encourage Roosevelt into giving Britain diplomatic support – and in particular to entice steel, destroyers and ammunition from the USA. Churchill could not technically commit his government to acting in

Table 6. *Membership of the War Cabinet in the Coalition Government, 11 May 1940–22 June 1941*

Prime Minister	Winston Churchill (C)
Minister of Defence	Winston Churchill (C)
Lord President of the Council	Neville Chamberlain (C); from 3 October 1940, Sir John Anderson, (Independent National MP for Scottish Universities)
Chancellor of the Exchequer	Sir Kingsley Wood (from 3 October 1940) (C)
Lord Privy Seal	Clement Attlee (Lab.)
Foreign Secretary	Viscount Halifax (C); from 22 December 1940, Anthony Eden (C)
Minister of Aircraft Production	Lord Beaverbrook (C) (in War Cabinet from 2 August 1940; out of War Cabinet again when J. Moore-Brabazon took over on 1 May 1941)
Minister of State (from 1 May 1941)	Lord Beaverbrook (C)
Minister of Labour and National Service	Ernest Bevin (Lab.)
Minister without Portfolio	Arthur Greenwood (Lab.)

Note:
As we have seen with Chamberlain's War Cabinet, many other ministers attended the War Cabinet from time to time, and some can be categorised as 'constant attenders', particularly Eden as Minister of War before 22 December 1940, and Duff Cooper as Minister of Information.
Source:
David Butler and Anne Sloman, *British Political Facts 1900–1979*, 5th edn (London: Macmillan, 1980), pp. 26–31.

the way that he had baldly outlined. He could impose no physical constraints on future choices, such as those which might be imposed by irrevocable steps like a declaration of war, or a running down of the armaments industry. But this is not to say that the declarations were devoid of commitment, in terms either of Anglo-American relations or of the thinking of his own colleagues about the future of the war. Just as the Anglo-French military conversations of 1905 and beyond had created an increasing expectation in France of alliance with Britain, and had helped to impregnate the minds of Asquith, Grey and Haldane with the same belief,[6] so Churchill's solitary diplomacy fostered an increasing closeness of Anglo-American relations that in its turn may have encouraged his fellow ministers to hope first for survival, through the prospect of endless material supplies, and then for victory, through a reliance on an American entry into the war.

Furthermore, Churchill's automatic assumption that future policy would be to continue the war, and of his right to anticipate it, was a difficult initiative to resist, for both tactical and psychological reasons. By asserting first that Britain would continue to fight despite the likely defeat of France and then that the present government would not consider compromise in any form, despite her apparently desperate military situation, Churchill was placing the onus on his colleagues to challenge his prejudgement of the issue, while at the same time directing their attention away from any balanced consideration of the pros and cons. Through presenting his opinions as facts and moral imperatives, the Prime Minister created a momentum for his interpretation of British interests that would have required a major confrontation within the Cabinet to stop. With the implication that argument was unthinkable, Churchill had begun to pre-empt his government's decision on the issue of fighting alone.

MILITARY DISINTEGRATION

Even at this early stage, Churchill was becoming aware that the bases of British war policy were on the verge of dissolution, and that the government might imminently be faced with a totally changed set of circumstances, demanding the rapid reformulation of expectations long-established but now rendered obsolete by the destruction of the Western Front. For although Allied military opinion had long anticipated a German attack in the west, even possibly as the first stroke of war,[7] it quickly became clear after the invasion of 10 May that a new scenario had to be considered: that of a rapid French defeat. On 13 May Guderian's armoured forces crossed the Meuse and broke through the French defences where they had been least expected to do so. By the evening of the next day Churchill was reading a message from Paul Reynaud to the War Cabinet which warned that the breach in the defences had allowed the Germans to drive for Paris and which thought that the only hope of preventing them was by massive attacks on the supporting German bomber force. The outlook had evidently deteriorated very quickly.[8]

Even so, neither Churchill nor the Cabinet yet regarded the situation as sufficiently grave to require the dispatch of home-based fighter squadrons. After Paul Reynaud's statement to Churchill on 15 May that France had effectively been defeated, the Prime Minister gave the distinct impression to his colleagues that the outlook was not disastrous. In those days of hectic military activity, the Cabinet relied on Churchill for its sources of information; now he told them that Reynaud's message had been 'alarmist', and that in personal telephone conversations with Generals Georges and Gamelin it had been clear to him that they remained calm, and believed that the German advance in the south had been halted. Supported by Air Marshals Newall and Dowding, Churchill directly opposed the dispatch of further fighters to help the French, and the Cabinet took a decision to this effect.[9]

But it took less than twenty-four hours to reverse their decision. Information from the front about renewed German penetration indicated that, in General Ironside's words, 'the situation was critical ... All now depended on whether the French will fight with vigour in the counter-attack which General Gamelin proposed to launch.' Halifax said that Reynaud feared the German attainment of Paris that night.[10] In the evening Churchill arrived in Paris, and heard for himself about the vulnerability of the French military situation; losses of artillery and fighter aircraft had been severe, and the German tank corps was in a position either to move on to Paris or to advance to the coast so as to split the Allied forces. He passed on this information to the War Cabinet, which met without him at 11 p.m. so as to authorise the second reinforcement that day of fighters to France, a volte-face in policy.[11] The Cabinet, however, only sent half the number of squadrons to French bases that Churchill had asked for (admittedly in an unusually decisive tone),[12] since otherwise Britain would have been left without any fighter defences itself. The discretionary powers that military operations often confer did not always work in favour of the Prime Minister.

Thus by 17 May it was clear that France was in an extremely serious military situation. If her defeat and exit from the war were not yet seen as certain in London, ministers could not fail to realise that this was now a distinct possibility. Within a week of the German move against the Allies, the balance of strength had been transformed, and British policy-makers were increasingly and rapidly faced with a new series of conditions to be accepted, understood and processed into attitudes or policies. However, the full impact of the changed situation did not take effect immediately, despite French defeat having been made militarily probable by the German advance on Amiens and Arras.

This was partly because, without the benefit of hindsight, few of the participants could clearly see the pattern of the battle, and its inexorable conclusion. It was also because Churchill's interpretation of developments continued in an optimistic vein, in the belief that the trend of the conflict could still be reversed, given will, effort and the correct strategy. On 18 May, he praised to the Cabinet the efforts of the RAF and of recent French resistance, saying that 'On the whole the military situation in France is better.'[13] During the next few days, further Allied reverses, culminating in the German arrival at the Channel coast on the 20th, made the likelihood of defeat more clear. Yet those responsible for British policy were still cushioned from the direct implications of the changes. Not until late on 25 May did the Service ministers and Chiefs of Staff take the decision that Lord Gort should make haste to evacuate as much of the British Expeditionary Force as he could salvage from France.[14] Right through the previous four days Churchill had hoped that the trapped forces would be able to fight their way southwards to meet a new French army advancing to the north. On the 21st the Prime Minister told the War Cabinet that 'The situation is more favourable than certain of the more obvious symptoms would indicate . . . We must now be ready to fight hard under open warfare conditions.'[15] The next day he described the plan in more detail for the Cabinet after seeing Weygand, and forecast a crucial battle for 23 May, despite doubts from Ironside and a gloomy report from Gort's staff.[16] On the 23rd itself, frustrated by the lack of any sign of a reversal of the campaign, Churchill cabled Reynaud demanding the immediate implementation of Weygand's pincer plan, which could 'turn defeat into victory'.[17] It was thus partly due to Churchill's refusal to accept that the battle was lost and the BEF should cut its losses that the excision of France from the contest did not become more plain at an earlier stage.

Another major factor, however, was the failure of the information and co-ordination process between London and the battlefront. Ministers did not realise the extent of the German advance or the weaknesses of the Allied forces and positions. Liaison with the French army was bad. There was always an important time-lag between events on the continent and decisions in Whitehall. Towards the end, on 24 May, Churchill and Ironside had believed that Gort was still trying to strike to the south, when in fact he had begun to retreat to the ports. The information was finally conveyed to them by the French.[18] Political and military decision-making were right out of phase; Gort did not even know that Belgium was about to surrender. But the lack of synchronisation was compounded so far as the Cabinet were concerned by their reliance on Churchill for what up-to-date knowledge there was, and for an overview of the general trend of the conflict. As far as we can see from the continuing decisions to approve the counter-attack to the south, the Cabinet were no more convinced than Churchill of the irrevocability of French defeat until 26 May, when the BEF was already preparing for embarkation. In any case being even more out of touch they had little choice but to accept the Prime Minister's version of events. This was particularly true for ministers outside the War Cabinet, who attended the latter's meetings only on an occasional basis, and by grace of the Prime Minister. Moreover those in the War Cabinet by right (Halifax, Chamberlain, Attlee and Greenwood) were still recovering from the change in government, although not all for the same reason.

A POLICY VACUUM: THE IMPACT OF CRISIS

This outline of the military events of May 1940 is designed both to make clear how the world of British policy-makers at the time was suddenly overturned, and to show how that catastrophe generated the greater impact by being partially disguised until its final dénouement. It may also serve as a secondary example (because to do with military rather than foreign policy) of the way in which the Prime Minister could, by strength of leadership, influence strongly the conclusions of his Cabinet. But primarily it is important to realise the fluidity of the events into which the Cabinet found themselves plunged, with little mental preparation. Ministers were faced with the immediate need to reassess the factors on which they had pinned their hopes for survival and ultimate victory. Previous images of the way the war would develop, with Britain and France jointly draining off the German military effort and isolating the German homeland by blockade,[19] were inevitably dissolving under the pressure and speed of events. They had to absorb the fact that to all intents and purposes Britain would now have to fulfil her war aims entirely alone, being deprived not only of French manpower and *matériel*, but also of the strategical advantages of a Western Front and a long stretch of European coastline from which to administer the vital blockade.[20] As a result of this increasingly obvious circumstance, there arose the problems of deciding whether in practice Britain should (or would be able to) continue the war in the new environment and, in the event of an affirmative answer to this first question, of determining the ways in which it could be done. It was a time which required a fundamental yet expeditious change in focus.

This task presented little difficulty for Churchill, despite his belated recognition of the collapse of France. His attitude to the war was clearly defined, strongly held and consistent. Simply, it added up to a determination to prolong the fight in all foreseeable circumstances, and to a preference for complete defeat over the stigma of a compromise peace, which would mean accepting that victory was impossible without avoiding what he believed would be subjugation. Thus for the Prime Minister defeat in France constituted only a severe setback, and by no means an irresistible pressure to rethink Britain's position. He believed that Britain should fight to the death, however imminent annihilation might seem.[21]

For some of his colleagues, however, the issue was less clear. They had held no brief for a compromise solution to the war while the Allies remained in a position from which the achievement of their objectives remained possible, given sufficient patience, even if the exact methods of this success could not yet be predicted. Since defeat seemed remote, there was good reason to hope that the means of victory would eventually be engineered. Because they were willing to allow Britain to undergo the toils and suffering of war as such, there was no reason for ministers to consider the possibility of a settlement which satisfied their aims less than completely, so long as the danger of defeat did not figure in their thinking. But in May 1940 that danger appeared with a vengeance.

In this inchoate environment the Prime Minister set a clear lead on the attitude he expected the government to adopt. Although Churchill was determined not to believe the worst of any situation until it was inevitable, he did not blind himself to the possibility that the worst could in fact occur. As early as 17 May he had initiated a special ministerial sub-committee under Chamberlain to consider the consequences for Britain of the fall of France.[22] But, as Chamberlain, the new Lord President of the Council, told the Cabinet, its brief did not involve a discussion of whether Britain would be able to continue the war, or of whether she should revise her whole expectations of the conflict: 'He had been concerned in the main with a situation in which we might find ourselves *obliged to continue our resistance single-handed in this country* until the United States of America could be induced to come to our help.'[23] Thus Chamberlain went on, because of the above premise, merely to describe the extensions of government powers over internal activities which the sub-committee had recommended as a necessary means of continuing the resistance – and this although a day later Chamberlain was to write in his diary that although a German ultimatum to Britain would be rejected, 'we should be fighting only for better terms, not for victory', considering the Americans to be Britain's 'only hope' and that even they 'can do little to help us now'.[24] By 22 May the Lord President had come to regard the crisis as 'the gravest moment in our history', and anticipated 'an attack on this country very shortly'.[25] Yet, emasculated by his recent fall from leadership and possibly by a fear of reviving the accusation of appeasement, Chamberlain took no initiative towards raising the issue of what Britain should do in her new position, in any wider context than that of providing efficient domestic powers to meet the emergency of a German attack. Nor, as we shall see, was this because he was as resolutely determined as Churchill to continue the war even when defeat might appear certain.

The Prime Minister took a further initiative on 26 May, when he asked the Chiefs of Staff directly to describe what situation would arise if France were forced into an armistice after Belgium had capitulated but also after the BEF had reached the coast (and were in the process of escaping). The Chiefs of Staff were given formal terms of reference, of which it is worth quoting the rest in full:

[what situation would arise] in the event of terms being offered to Britain which would place her entirely at the mercy of Germany through disarmament, cession of naval bases in the Orkneys etc.; *what are the prospects of our continuing the war alone against Germany and probably Italy. Can the Navy and the Air Force hold out reasonable hopes of preventing serious invasion, and could the forces gathered in this Island cope with raids from the air involving detachments not greater than 10,000 men*; it being observed that a prolongation of British resistance might be very dangerous for Germany engaged in holding down the greater part of Europe.[26]

As will be observed, the purely military question on which the Chiefs of Staff were uniquely qualified to pronounce occupies only part of these terms of reference, that is the two italicised sentences. The rest of the document consists of value-judgements which intrude on the neutrality of the question, and seek to pre-judge the issue. It is clear what answer Churchill wants to his question, about the prospects of holding out. His mention of the terms which Britain might be offered is couched in the language of a Carthaginian peace; Germany is seen as incapable of offering terms other than those which would put Britain 'entirely' at her mercy. The examples chosen strike at the most sensitive points of British conceptions of her national interests – the capacity for self-defence and the sea-power on which her commercial and Imperial safety was based. This political pre-judgement is followed at the end of the terms of reference by an equally direct attempt to load the question, this time on the military side. The Prime Minister was so eager to anticipate a conclusion from the Chiefs of Staff to the effect that Britain would be able to carry on that he tried to begin their task for them by stating one of the main arguments in favour of the capacity to continue the fight; he did not balance this out by an example from the other side of the question.

It would be impossible to show whether the form in which Churchill cast the question in some way predetermined the Chiefs of Staff's eventual conclusion (proved correct by a hair's breadth as the year wore on), which was that the outcome would depend on the ability of the British aircraft industry to withstand bombing and provide the RAF with constant superiority in the air, and that the Chiefs believed in this ability.[27] Conversely, it is impossible to show that it did not help to condition their findings. In any event, that is not the only relevant issue. Just as important is the effect of Churchill's lead on the direction and tone of the discussion within Cabinet in general. (The Chiefs of Staff's answer was not delivered until the next day, two Cabinets later.)[28]

As we have seen so far, Churchill was the source of the only two initiatives in the government for discussing the effect of the possible fall of France on Britain's position. Moreover he formulated the questions which sprang from these moves in such a way as, in the first case, to delimit the scope of the issue under consideration and, in the second, to indicate strongly the form of answer that he expected and desired. The rest of the Cabinets for May 1940 show Churchill continuing to give a clear lead on the attitude he wanted from the Cabinet, and finally achieving the agreement of his colleagues after a period of some considerable doubt and uncertainty.

Soon after Churchill had posed his question to the Chiefs of Staff on 26 May, and in the same meeting, Halifax indicated that for him at least recent events had deeply disturbed the notions about war aims which had been evident in the discussions of the previous October. He stated that 'we had to face the fact that it was not so much now a question of imposing a complete defeat upon Germany but of safeguarding the independence of our own Empire and if possible that of France'.[29] The implication was that this implied that the Foreign Secretary was coming to think that a compromise settlement might be preferable to a German invasion of the United Kingdom and possible territorial gains in the Mediterranean, particularly since he went on to recount his conversation of the previous evening with the Italian Ambassador, in which he had told Bastianini, after the latter 'had clearly made soundings as to the prospect of our agreeing to a conference', that 'peace and security in Europe were equally our main object, and we should naturally be prepared to consider any proposals which might lead to this, provided our liberty and independence were assured'. Bastianini was coming for a further interview that morning, 'and he might have fresh proposals to put forward'.[30] The trend of Halifax's thought – towards an acceptance of a dramatically changed balance of power – was confirmed nearer the end of the meeting. He observed that if France collapsed the Germans would be able to switch their productive effort *en masse* towards the construction of aeroplanes. Since Halifax and the Chief of the Air Staff had just agreed that Britain's ability to survive, as argued in the first Chiefs of Staff draft on the question, would depend on preventing the Luftwaffe from achieving sufficient air superiority to mount an invasion, the pessimistic inference of this remark was that the outlook for survival might be poor.[31]

None of Halifax's fellow-ministers attacked either his pessimism or the particular implications of his remarks. On the other hand, they did not express positive support. They were in a state of genuine indecision, open to formative influences in either direction, from both the course of events and the nature of the leadership exerted in Cabinet. Clement Attlee, the Lord Privy Seal, merely made two piecemeal observations to the effect that Italy might be nervous about the prospect of a German hegemony in Europe and that the best way of keeping France in the war would be to convince her of the fact that 'destruction' would ultimately follow capitulation. He thought the Cabinet should await the Chiefs of Staff's report. Chamberlain, similarly, had no positive views. He confined himself to some low-key remarks on the best way to keep Italy from attacking France, suggesting that France might be able to buy Mussolini off with concessions. Finally he added that undertakings by the French not to make available their productive capacity to Germany would be useless, since the Germans would impose terms designed to prevent such an arrangement. Arthur Greenwood, the remaining member of the War Cabinet, seems to have made no comment.[32]

Churchill agreed that there could be no reliance on France to obstruct Hitler once it was out of the war. However, he showed no sign of backing down from the view he had expressed in the messages to Roosevelt of a week earlier. On the contrary, he stressed that Halifax's criteria of 'peace and security' were insufficient. Both aims 'might be achieved under a German domination of Europe'. For the Prime Minister it was a question of a different interpretation of national interest: 'We must ensure our complete liberty and independence.' Whereas Halifax had been willing to define these terms on the one hand widely enough to admit the possibility of recognising an immovable German domination of Europe, and on the other within sufficient limits as to avoid any danger of a complete loss of security, Churchill would accept nothing less than 'complete' independence, or positive liberty. He would envisage no solution which demoted Britain from her apparent pre-war status of a great power, subject to the will of no other single power: 'He was opposed to any negotiations which might lead to a derogation of our rights and power.' This was a conception which at the time none of his colleagues in the War Cabinet shared with such implacable enthusiasm.[33]

The Prime Minister did not contribute a great deal to this meeting in quantitative terms; what he did say, however, was couched in positive language: 'we could *never* accept . . . *our complete liberty and independence*'. Whereas Halifax now felt the pressure of conflicting criteria (survival versus 'liberty'), and other ministers felt sufficiently unsure of their views as to want to await the outcome of further developments and information, Churchill had an uncomplicated and internally consistent picture of the future. Having entered the war for the right reasons, his ideas ran, Britain should continue the fight until her aims had been fully realised. Military setbacks were inevitable in some form or other. So long as Britain remained actually undefeated, she possessed the potential capacity to achieve victory, since time would inevitably work against Germany.[34] These opinions could not but stand out in a small War Cabinet in which others neither adhered as fiercely to ideas they had formulated in a previous and now remote situation or could conceive of any compelling alternatives. Churchill was the only member, and one in an institutionally powerful position at that, with an exceptionally sharp definition of how Britain should act.

It would be possible to trace the whole development of this formulation of policy by describing the events of each individual Cabinet, in sequence. This would not only be repetitive and space-consuming, but it would not bring out clearly the basic structure of the debate, or how its outcome was affected by the way in which the argument was conducted and the limits within which its propositions were cast. Such phenomena can be better demonstrated by a direct analysis of the principal issues discussed throughout what is already a short time-span – from 26 May to 19 July (the date of Hitler's second 'Reichstag' peace offer, whose rejection marked the end of a phase of uncertainty in Cabinet policy-making).[35]

As will be clear already from the events of the 9 a.m. Cabinet meeting on 26 May, the main question involved the way in which the government might or might not adapt its attitude to the war as a result of the projected loss of her ally. To a large extent, however, this issue was entangled with the particular point from which it sprang, that of a possible bribe to Mussolini to keep Italy out of the war. Strictly speaking, the attempt to influence Italian policy was principally the concern of France – for two reasons. The security of the French homeland would be immediately threatened by an Italian declaration of war and the doubt as to Mussolini's intentions only lasted as long as there was a prospect of France herself escaping defeat. Nevertheless Britain was also very concerned with Italy, as she had been throughout the 1930s, and the British government was continually consulted during the French deliberations over whether to make an approach.[36] But in the discussion within the British Cabinet, the issue was quickly blurred into that of a more general settlement. After the initial French suggestion of a *démarche* and the first, fairly open-minded, reactions from the Cabinet as to its utility,[37] both Churchill and Halifax showed signs of a willingness to discuss the question of negotiations in terms which went beyond Mussolini to Hitler – although for diametrically opposite reasons.

The Prime Minister himself felt under no illusion about the buying off of Italy being separate from the Anglo-German dispute. He wanted to alleviate France's difficulties, but 'At the same time we must take care not to be forced into a weak position in which we went to Signor Mussolini and invited him to go to Herr Hitler and ask him to treat us nicely.'[38] He was afraid that France would 'drag us into a settlement which involved intolerable terms'. This was because, as he remarked slightly later, of the suggested approach to Mussolini, 'it implied that if we were prepared to give Germany back her colonies and to make certain concessions in the Mediterranean, it was possible to get out of our present difficulties'. Churchill saw this as unacceptable: 'He thought that no such option was open to us. For example, the terms offered would certainly prevent us from completing our rearmament.'

Halifax was equally prompt in raising broader considerations than those of Franco-Italian relations. *Vis-à-vis* any offer to Mussolini, he said 'that he attached perhaps rather more importance than the Prime Minister to the desirability allowing France to try out the possibilities of European equilibrium'. As we have seen, the Foreign Secretary had already told Bastianini the previous day that he was free to tell Rome 'that His Majesty's Government did not exclude the possibility of some discussion of the wider problem of Europe in the event of the opportunity arising'.[39] This elision of the Italian problem into that of the wider war is not an academic mirage. Halifax himself noted it in his papers, with regard to the continued discussion on 27 May: 'At the 4.30 Cabinet we had a long and rather confused discussion about, nominally, the approach to Italy, but also largely about general policy in the event of things going really badly in France.'[40] The Foreign Secretary was not optimistic about an approach to Mussolini, but did 'not wish to give the French an excuse for complaining'.[41] At least this is how he justified it to himself. Halifax was grasping at the broadening of the debate because of his growing feeling that hostilities were no longer the unquestionably right course. Chamberlain thought that his friend's view was that 'there could be no harm in trying Musso & seeing what the result was. If the terms were impossible we could still reject them. I supported this view.'[42] The probing of Italy was an opportunity to test the ground, just as Ciano's intervention on 2 September 1939 had been a (spurned) opportunity to delay a declaration of war. Indeed, he was positively anxious to avoid particular issues, and to concentrate on a general focus, in which difficulties might more easily be accommodated. He thought that any approach should avoid 'geographical precision' when touching on the problem of terms.[43]

But this very difficulty about the requirement of detail which Halifax felt when developing his argument is an indication of his basic disadvantage in this situation relative to the Prime Minister – that is, the disadvantage of a minister feeling his way to a new argument and general position, in a Cabinet where the majority of his colleagues were undecided, but where he was opposed by the one individual on whom custom and the nature of the institution conferred the role of leadership, and who in this case had an especially positive personality and idea of policy.

It is true that as Foreign Secretary Halifax was still in a position of privileged 'executive' responsibility over external relations, as I have argued before in this chapter. Moreover, he represented continuity and experience at a time when a new Prime Minister might have been expected to defer somewhat to his most senior colleagues in the interests of preserving harmony within the government. While Halifax had nothing of Churchill's charisma, he was not over-awed by his tempestuousness and theatricality – indeed he seems to have harboured a quiet contempt for it.[44] But circumstances had changed radically with the fall of the old administration. The War Cabinet, itself less than half the size of the peacetime body, had shrunk further (to five members) to the point where a 'foreign policy executive' of Prime Minister and Foreign Secretary was less practicable – unless the two individuals were already close, as Churchill and Halifax were not. An insulated executive was particularly unlikely since two of the other three members were now drawn from the Labour Party and could not be left on the sidelines.[45] Furthermore, Churchill's personality was well suited to the taking on of major responsibilities from the moment of kissing hands. Encouraged over the previous twelve months by admiring friends, Churchill undoubtedly felt that history and the British people required great leadership from him. He was constitutionally ill-fitted to working in harness with anyone, let alone Halifax, newly discredited by his past association with Chamberlain and a man prone to vacillation and crises of conscience even in less catastrophic times.

Halifax's problem was heightened by the fact that because the external environment of British foreign policy in mid-1940 presented unparalleled dangers and uncertainties, Cabinet discussion placed a premium on recommendations which were well-known, clear and strongly argued. The views of Lord Halifax at this stage were new, vague and ambivalent. His belief that France should be able 'to try out . . . European equilibrium' was hardly likely to convince the Cabinet that there existed a definite alternative to the line argued by Churchill which was worthy of serious consideration. Equally his eagerness to discuss the need to keep Italy out of the war in conjunction with the issue of whether to cut Britain's losses in the conflict with Germany (encouraged by both Churchill and French policy) could only increase the unsureness of his colleagues as to the right course on both questions.

Yet this ineffectiveness was more a function of the basic dilemma facing the Government than of personal failings in Halifax. It was soon clear that since the Italian question intrinsically involved that of 'general policy', confusion between the two was difficult to avoid. The comments of other ministers made the point. The Minister without Portfolio, Arthur Greenwood, believed that concessions to Mussolini would mean 'we should soon get to the point at which demands were being made which affected the security of the British Empire'.[46] This would obviously impinge on British abilities to fight Hitler, particularly as 'He doubted . . . whether it was within Signor Mussolini's power to take a line independent of Herr Hitler'. At a later stage, Greenwood spelt out the nature of the 'demands' Italy might make: 'Signor Mussolini would be out to get Malta, Gibraltar and Suez. He felt sure that the negotiations would break down; but Herr Hitler would get to know of them, and it might have a bad effect on our prestige.'

In Cabinet on the day following, Sir Archibald Sinclair, the Secretary for Air (and leader of the Liberal Party) took this point up in agreement: 'the suggestion that we were willing to barter away pieces of British territory would have a deplorable effect and would make it difficult for us to continue the desperate struggle which faced us'.[47] Attlee supported this argument; he thought the approach would be 'very damaging to us. In effect, the approach suggested would inevitably lead to our asking Signor Mussolini to intercede to obtain peace-terms for us'.[48] It is therefore clear that the objections to pursuing an approach to Italy rebounded by their very nature onto the issue of peace with Germany, and helped to associate the latter in the minds of ministers with damage to British prestige and security, as well as to confuse the issue in general. It was felt that an approach in Rome would pre-judge the problem of what attitude to take to Germany, first by 'inevitably' leading Mussolini into interceding with Hitler (although it is not clear why this should have mattered in itself, given that the Cabinet certainly would have felt that it was free to take up or reject any terms offered by Hitler),[49] and secondly by irretrievably damaging Britain's bargaining position in the war, *before* the government had even formulated its final attitude to the effects of the defeat of France. It would have apparently constituted in itself a setback of near-military proportions. Undeniably, therefore, since the two problems were very easily and thoroughly blurred in the Cabinet's discussions, Halifax's arguments for a serious consideration of a compromise peace were weakened at the same rate as the proposal about Italy fell into disrepute, by a process of close association and confusion.

The Prime Minister's position and viewpoint was also strengthened by the pressures against challenging the leadership and splitting the government, in a wartime crisis of such severity and fluidity. After the long and divided Cabinet meeting of the afternoon of 27 May, Halifax was near to resignation. The Foreign Secretary's record reads:

I thought Winston talked the most frightful rot, also Greenwood, and after bearing it for some time I said exactly what I thought of them, adding that if that was really their view, and if it came to the point, our ways must separate. Winston, surprised and mellowed, and, when I repeated the same thing in the garden, was full of apologies and affection. But it does drive me to despair when he works himself up into a passion of motion when he ought to make his brain think and reason. But none of these things, of course, really matter in comparison to the military events.[50]

Cadogan's account confirms that Halifax felt, 'I can't work with Winston any longer', and that Churchill had been 'v. affectionate' afterwards. Cadogan adds that he advised Halifax not to give way to the annoyance 'to which we were all subject' over Churchill's 'rhodomontades', and to consult Chamberlain before acting: 'He said that of course he would and that, as I knew, he wasn't one to take hasty decisions.'[51]

As is evident, 'it' never did come 'to the point', even though Churchill's 'sentimental' views were to represent the actual course of British policy far more closely than Halifax's 'reasoned' opinion. It seems likely that Halifax reluctantly gave voice to feelings which he was partly repressing, and that Churchill gave him an easy exit from his threats of resignation, by a personal conciliation which did not concede the substance of the dispute (as we shall see). Despite the strength of his views, the Foreign Secretary found it an impossible strain to precipitate a major confrontation with his Prime Minister at such a hazardous time, let alone to take the issue to a more public arena, despite resentments which had their roots in the fierce arguments of the 1930s over first India and then appeasement.[52] Purged by his outburst, Halifax allowed himself to be talked out of any 'hasty decision'.[53]

THE ASSERTION OF LEADERSHIP

The surprise, danger and urgency of the new problems meant that decision-making was taking place in true conditions of crisis. The consequent hesitancy felt by most ministers, especially those serving in office for the first time, invited dominating, executive leadership. And Churchill was not a Prime Minister to pass up circumstances which particularly seemed to require creative action on his part. He was personally willing to broaden the question of the approach to Mussolini because of a genuine fear that Britain might be insidiously trapped into the compromise peace to which he was so strongly opposed. By 28 May he was certain that 'the French purpose was to see Signor Mussolini acting as an intermediary between ourselves and Herr Hitler. He was determined not to get into this position.'[54] Churchill went on to describe the grounds on which he opposed Reynaud's apparent attempt to get Britain to the conference table and end the war: 'If we once got to the table we should then find that the terms offered us touched our independence and integrity. When, at this point, we got up to leave the conference-table, we should find that all the forces of resolution which were now at our disposal would have vanished.'[55] The Prime Minister summed up his views of negotiations with the Axis by the political cliché of 'the slippery slope' onto which Britain would be enticed. The metaphor illustrates well the technique by which Churchill continually presented the problem in extreme terms: one move towards communication with Hitler, the phrase implied, would begin an inexorable draining away of the remaining strength of Britain's position. There could be no middle way. Because of his own strong views, Churchill's natural tendency was to use his position as Chairman to polarise the argument between his own advocacy of a fight-on-with-no-compromise attitude, and what he cast as the only alternative, that of negotiations involving the surrender of British interests and security. Favouring one extreme, he preferred to argue against the other, rather than against an attitude of moderate compromise, since he could then more easily cast Halifax's arguments as an attempt at complete surrender and more firmly identify his own attitude with that of the status quo position, which was at least known and associated with patriotic sentiments of heroic defence. The opposite case, in its straw-man form, amounted not only to virtual defeat, but to the notably worse fate of dishonourable defeat.

For when it had finally been acknowledged that France was likely to suffer military defeat, Churchill had told Reynaud that 'We would rather go down fighting than be enslaved to Germany.'[56] This was not just to encourage French morale; twenty-four hours later Churchill informed his Cabinet that 'Even if we were beaten, we should be no worse off than we should be if we were now to abandon the struggle ... If the worst came to the worst, it would not be a bad thing for this country to go down fighting for the other countries which had been overcome by the Nazi tyranny.'[57] As a mere Service minister under Chamberlain, Churchill had not been able to set a strict moral example in this way. Then, his views only constituted one input among several, as to the criteria which ought to be adopted for the making of any given policy.[58] But now, as Prime Minister, he was able to use his stature and right to lead the discussion to get a special hearing and to put the onus for disagreement on his colleagues. In this same monologue, he asserted that the only way to reflate Britain's punctured prestige in the world was by remaining unbeaten, thus assuming that the need to boost prestige was a first priority. It was this natural appropriation, on Churchill's part, of a high moral authority which so much put his fellow Cabinet members at a disadvantage when they were in the process of reconsidering their attitudes, and possibly of feeling their way towards a new position, with all the attendant justification which that would require.

A prime example of this is Churchill's reaction on 28 May to the suggestion that the British Empire should directly appeal to the USA for the latter's entry into the war. The Prime Minister thought that this would be 'altogether premature': 'If we made a *bold stand* against Germany, that would command their *admiration and respect*; but a *grovelling appeal*, if made now, would have the *worst possible* effect.'[59] Here Churchill both polarised the debate by casting the options in extreme form, and again adopted for his views the terminology of moral approval; for the opposing alternative, his tone was little short of demagogic. The importance of this does not lie in any argument that the use of such language is itself enough to give a minister a determining role in policy formulation; clearly most others expressed strong feelings of approbation or denunciation at various times. Nor is it argued that a Prime Minister has only to handle a discussion in this way in order to dominate his Cabinet. That would imply that low-key Premiers like Stanley Baldwin or Clement Attlee were never able to exert strong leadership over their peers. The point is rather that where the pace of events was so fast, where the data-base of previous policy-assumptions was in the midst of disintegration, there occurred, before the re-emergence of a definite set of attitudes in Cabinet, a crucial hiatus in which the Prime Minister was especially well placed to take an influential initiative should he wish to do so. And where a system is structured so as to give certain special opportunities to particular actors, it is not usual for those openings to be ignored. The strong moral line and polarisation of argument which characterised Churchill's behaviour on this occasion were the ways in which this Prime Minister took the opportunity. In so doing, he fulfilled a necessary function from the point of view of the Cabinet as collective organisation. Without an agreed and clear perspective during the disintegration of the Western Front, it vitally required an initiative from somewhere to clarify the issues. Because the environment was one of crisis, there was also an intrinsic need for rapid resolution of the issues into a single, settled policy, whatever its form. Churchill's immediate provision of a clear-cut opinion and his consistently strong inputs on its behalf were the relevant response to this need. The actual arguments employed were, in this one sense, of lesser importance for the final decision.

However, the Prime Minister's lead did not only take the form of righteous exhortation. He also annexed the arguments of practicality to his views. Halifax had made no pretence that a readjustment of war policy would carry any moral weight; his advocacy rested on tangible reasons of necessity. But here too he was outflanked by Churchill. Halifax based his argument by definition on the *prediction* that Britain could secure acceptable peace terms from Hitler.[60] Churchill argued from statements which were also essentially speculative, but which he presented as indisputable objective facts, by basing them on the current scenario, in which Britain was still undefeated and had suffered no irreversible military losses. In this he was aided by the fact that the Foreign Secretary's prediction conflicted with the undividedly hostile image of Hitler and the Nazis which was common to all British policy-makers by this time. To gain acceptance, it would have to have achieved the reformation of an established image – albeit one hardened by the sense of having come belatedly upon the truth. Such an achievement was obviously not impossible, since general perspectives must and do change over time if policy is not to fall disastrously out of phase with the continually evolving external environment. But in this context most factors worked against any minister other than the Premier being able to shift the general focus of policy. Moreover, in this specific instance, the Prime Minister was not competing to gain acceptance for a new set of attitudes, but was rather seeking only to reinforce and perpetuate the existing criteria for war policy.[61]

The 'facts' and practical arguments which Churchill presented in support of this line added up to an optimistic picture of apparently disastrous events, by a selective interpretation of the value of allies. As we saw earlier, the Prime Minister was eager to represent any small sign of resistance to the German invasion as evidence of the continued ability of France to stay in the war. Yet when it ultimately became clear that this was not in fact the case, he quickly turned the implications of French defeat also to Britain's advantage. On 26 May, when it was realised that counter-attack was impossible, Churchill remarked that 'From one point of view, he would rather France was out of the war before she was broken up, and retained the position of a strong neutral whose factories could not be used against us.'[62] Cadogan noted this switch of view in his diary that night, with some scepticism. Five days later, however, he had come round to the same opinion.[63] It was a natural rationalisation to make. But Churchill had come to it first among those present at Cabinet, and because of the natural attention accorded to his reactions, he probably played a decisive part in setting the tone of the collective governmental feeling about Britain's new isolation, by affecting the delicate and momentary balance between pessimistic and optimistic perceptions.[64]

In similar vein, Churchill moved towards a position of regarding recent developments as positively beneficial in terms of their effects on American policy towards the war. British policy-makers had been sanguine from the beginning about the back-up resources which the USA could provide for the Allied war effort,[65] but now there emerged a significant propensity to regard an American entry into the war at some stage as likely and even inevitable. Right back on 15 May the Prime Minister had said that 'American sympathy had recently been veering very much in our favour.'[66] The Cabinet naturally looked to Churchill, with his transatlantic connections, for its interpretation of Foreign Office data on American intentions – especially now that Hoare and Chatfield, who had both corresponded on a regular, private basis with the British Ambassador to the United States Lord Lothian about the war, had left the Cabinet.[67] Even the Foreign Secretary recognised the special advantages which Churchill possessed through his correspondence with Roosevelt. Halifax said, with regard to Britain's need for American planes 'that in his opinion the only chance of obtaining the equipment we required was through a direct approach from the Prime Minister to President Roosevelt'.[68] Halifax had become sidelined even in the process of bilateral diplomacy with a friendly power.

We have already noted how Churchill stressed the need to win America's 'administration and respect'; on that occasion the War Cabinet had agreed with him that there should be no appeal to the USA for fear of confirming any fears as to British weakness.[69] As time went on Churchill could argue that positive American intervention was near at hand. On 9 June he brought up in Cabinet a complaint from General Smuts that the Dominions Office had urged the propagation of the idea that it was neither Britain's wish nor interest to involve the USA in 'totalitarian warfare'; Smuts believed that 'as events were now moving any day anything might happen to precipitate the United States into the war. Why should we arrest this process of conversion by the logic of events?' The Prime Minister said that he entirely agreed with the view expressed by General Smuts. He had therefore already ordered the sending of a telegram to the Dominions to correct the impression given in the previous dispatch.[70] Thus Churchill got his way on two diametrically opposed decisions twelve days apart. After a further three days, the question of the war itself was almost subordinated to the acquisition of American aid. Churchill stated: 'A declaration that we were firmly resolved to continue the war in all circumstances would prove the best invitation to the United States of America to lend us their support.'[71] The circular argument here, that Britain should commit herself to the war so as to encourage America to help it continue the war, seemed to pass unnoticed.[72]

Thus, when Roosevelt sent a message of encouragement to Reynaud on 13 June, the Prime Minister was ready to interpret it as a virtual declaration of war – that is, as far as the President could go without Congress. He thought that Roosevelt would hardly urge France to fight on if he did not intend to join her. He expected America's entry 'in the near future'.[73] Churchill's friend Lord Beaverbrook agreed: 'It was now inevitable that the United States of America would declare war.'[74]

There seem to have been some in the Cabinet who were less convinced than Churchill of this likelihood,[75] but if so their doubts were inconsequential in the absence of hard information to place against Churchill's convictions. (In 1940 the British political class, especially on the Labour side, had a far less intimate knowledge of the American political system than was to become the case after 1945.[76]) Although it was pointed out in discussion both that Roosevelt 'had not stated in terms that the United States would declare war' and that the implications of the message might not be as clear to the French as to the 'Anglo-Saxon mind', Churchill relentlessly stressed the significance of the declaration. Hitler might 'turn on' Britain 'very quickly, perhaps within a fortnight; but before that the United States of America would be in the war on our side'. Ultimately the War Cabinet tended to agree, although they still 'generally felt' that it needed pointing out to France that the President's message 'contained two points which were tantamount to a declaration of war – first, a promise of all material aid, which implied active assistance, and second, a call to go on fighting even if the Government was driven right out of France'.[77]

It will be noted, with hindsight, that these hopes and inferences were wildly unrealistic, and indeed that they were soon replaced by a more sober assessment. In May–June 1940, however, they were both a typical product of the sense of crisis and one of the means by which the strain was alleviated. Churchill inspired and inflated the feeling that Britain might soon have a new ally, by his positive introductions of the possibility during discussions on war policy and by the way he presented Roosevelt's evident sympathy for the Allied cause as proof of an almost immediate American declaration of war – despite his simultaneous acknowledgement of the restraints imposed by

Congress on US foreign policy, and the general feeling that this interpretation would not be obvious to the French.[78]

THE EXECUTIVE DIVIDES

Halifax was thus confronted by a Prime Minister who fully utilised the opportunities inherently open to him in this particular development of the war, first to determine the direction of Cabinet thinking and then to consolidate tentative preferences into general policies. It was not surprising that Halifax failed to gain Cabinet support for his differing views. The actual course of the major confrontation between the two men (from 26 to 28 May) illustrates the way in which Churchill was able to identify his views with the maintenance of the status quo, and to place the onus of proof upon Halifax: that is, he took refuge in non-decisions, as those holding the reins of power are often able to do when faced with those who would revise policy. The power to ignore can be the most difficult of all ploys to counter.[79]

The disagreement centred on the likely nature of any German terms. Halifax raised the subject during discussion of the approach to Mussolini: 'He was not quite convinced that the Prime Minister's diagnosis was correct and that it was in Herr Hitler's interest to insist on outrageous terms. After all, he knew his own internal weaknesses.'[80] The Prime Minister did not respond immediately to this challenging of one of his fundamental assumptions. However, later in the proceedings, as I have already noted, he stressed that any terms offered would certainly involve unacceptable conditions, such as a limitation on British rearmament. Halifax agreed that this condition would be unacceptable – but Hitler might not seek to impose it.

The next day Halifax pressed the point again, but by then he had been put on to the defensive. Inevitably in such a dispute, the Foreign Secretary was forced to answer objections from the Prime Minister, and not vice versa. For Churchill refused to take seriously the possibility of Hitler offering reasonable terms or of Britain negotiating them. Halifax had to deny that he proposed suing for terms which would lead to disaster and constantly to reiterate that realistic terms were not an impossible contingency, solely to keep the idea in the forefront of the debate.[81] Halifax's central points through the arguments of the five relevant meetings were, in summary: (1) that the terms which Germany might offer need not be unacceptable, as such, to Britain, and (2) that in the event of terms being offered which did not promise to destroy British independence, the risk of fighting on might become too great given the strength of Germany's new position.

In fact at this time even Churchill was able to conceive of British war aims less ambitious than those of October 1939 – because of the desperate military situation – but he did so in a purely hypothetical context. He would not allow the issue an important place in policy-formulation:

THE PRIME MINISTER said that he thought the issue which the War Cabinet was called upon to settle was difficult enough without getting involved in the discussion of an issue which was quite unreal and was most unlikely to arise. If Herr Hitler was prepared to make peace on the terms of the restoration of German colonies and the over-lordship of Central Europe, that was one thing. But it was quite unlikely that he would make any such offer.[82]

After another twenty-four hours and three Cabinet meetings, Halifax was still arguing that the present might be the best opportunity of getting good terms, and that he had again been misrepresented as pursuing 'ultimate capitulation' (so successful had Churchill been in polarising the issue). But by this time he was reduced to a mere restatement of the desirability of 'trying out the possibilities of mediation'; the fact that he was requesting a major change in policy was inhibiting even the development of his case.[83] Churchill could contrast the physical fact of Britain's survival, however temporary it might be, with the speculation of the Foreign Secretary's point. The Prime Minister thought 'that the chances of decent terms being offered to us at the present time were a thousand to one', and that 'it was impossible to imagine that Hitler would be so foolish as to let us continue our rearmament'.[84] By continuing to assert flatly that any German terms would enslave Britain, and that negotiation *in itself* would be harmful, Churchill was drawing attention to the inherent difficulties of Halifax's standpoint, that it contravened the generally held image among ministers of a dynamically aggressive Nazi regime and at the same time raised the spectre of previous and apparently mistaken negotiations with Hitler. In short, his was – in context – a very strong case. Moreover since he had been accepted on all sides as the new Prime Minister only two weeks before, Churchill was in a powerful position to demand the rejection of Halifax's viewpoint – especially as he along among major political figures had escaped the retrospective 'shame' of both Munich and the failure to support rearmament.[85]

No less on the argument that Britain should not ignore a chance to avoid the costs of a German attack was Halifax fighting a losing battle. Even when it seemed that the BEF might be lost, Churchill compared Britain's intact strength with the disintegrating powers of France (rather than with France's position before the German attack, which would have been a truer comparison). He believed that Britain's situation could only improve, and because of rather than despite an attempt at invasion. In opposing what he saw as French attempts to entangle Britain in negotiations, Churchill argued that 'the position would be entirely different when Germany had made an unsuccessful attempt to invade this country'. Thus the only incentives were to continue in the war: 'We should get no worse terms if we went on fighting, *even if we were beaten*, than were open to us now. If, however, we continued the war and Germany attacked us, no doubt we should suffer *some damage*, but they also would suffer severe losses. Their oil supplies might be reduced.'[86]

It is clear that Churchill's argument was based at least as much on assertion as that of Halifax – an invasion attempt will be unsuccessful, Hitler's terms will be crippling (yet no more so after a total defeat of Britain), Germany will suffer 'severe losses' but Britain only 'some damage'. These were desperate rationalisations. Nevertheless, it was here that the innate advantages of the Prime Minister counted in his favour. Because of the premium on a positive and formulated policy at this time, and because of the opportunity Churchill had to determine the terms of reference of the discussion, his assertions were likely to be more influential in Cabinet than the assertions of any colleague, particularly as the Prime Minister was hardly reluctant to capitalise on the privileges which his institutional status conferred on him. For example, stimulated by reports that the Australian High Commissioner was spreading counsels of 'defeatism', Churchill both admonished his ministers and wielded the idea of public support as a further means of exhortation:

THE PRIME MINISTER thought that it would be as well that he should issue a general injunction to Ministers to use confident language. He was convinced that the bulk of the people of the country would refuse to accept the possibility of defeat.[87]

The War Cabinet 'completely agreed' with Churchill. But once again they were following in the Prime Minister's wake, not sharing in the initiative.

Moreover Churchill was able to mobilise ministers outside the War Cabinet as another way of weighting the balance of argument within it. In between the two halves of the meeting which began at 4 p.m. on 28 May and was adjourned for three-quarters of an hour in its midst, he saw the group of other ministers and gave them the most recent information:

They had not expressed alarm at the position in France, but had expressed the greatest satisfaction when he had told them that there was no chance of our giving up the struggle. He did not remember having ever before heard a gathering of persons occupying high places in political life express themselves so emphatically.[88]

Thus the Prime Minister not only pre-judged the outcome of the Cabinet's deliberations, but also communicated to the Cabinet the views of other ministers in the form of a uniquely homogeneous and emphatic endorsement of his own position. The previous practice with such meetings had been simply to disseminate information, not to involve a wider circle in disputes internal to the War Cabinet. While the views of the below-the-line ministers were generally in favour of fighting on, it is reasonable to wonder how far Churchill over-estimated their enthusiasm, and also whether he would have reported their views so readily had they taken another form. Dalton's private account confirms the meeting's agreement with the Prime Minister, but also gives the impression that its response was much more passive. Churchill had said that if Britain were to face defeat, let her face it not through surrender, but 'only when each one of us lies choking in his own blood upon the ground'. In response:

There was a murmur of approval round the table, in which I think, Amery, Lord Lloyd and I were loudest. Not much more was said. No-one expressed even the faintest flicker of dissent. Herbert Morrison asked about evacuation of the Government, and hoped that it would not be hurried.[89]

Churchill had thus verged on hysteria when addressing the junior ministers and exaggerated their enthusiasm when reporting back to the War Cabinet. Such was the force with which the Prime Minister was arguing for a continuation of the war. His colleagues, whether they disagreed or were simply less certain in their judgements, were under extreme pressure to follow Churchill's lead, since he would not admit even the possibility of doubt. Anything less than unqualified belligerence was in danger of being cast as treason. At that delicate point in the formation of a consensus within the War Cabinet, the Prime Minister's armoury of weapons in discussion may have been of some significance.[90] On 29 May, indeed, Churchill overtly waved the big stick, by circulating the general minute which he had had in mind to all Cabinet colleagues and high officials. This enjoined them to maintain 'a high morale' in their circles and show an 'inflexible resolve to continue the war until we have broken the will of the enemy to bring all Europe under his domination'.[91] In a military crisis he used the language of command naturally, and his civilian colleagues could not help but be affected by it.[92]

WAR CABINET COLLEAGUES

At this point we should turn to the opinions of the other three members of the War Cabinet, and of those who were occasionally present. The two main protagonists monopolised the dispute, but not the discussion. However, the meetings of the Cabinet at this time reveal Attlee, Chamberlain, Greenwood and the few other major contributors as moderate, hesitant and influenced by the arguments of Churchill and Halifax. Although they all held individual views on the situation, these were nothing like so consistent or strongly affirmed as those of the Prime Minister and the Foreign Secretary.

At the height of the crisis, for example, on the morning of 27 May, Chamberlain told the Cabinet that he had replied to Stanley Bruce (the Australian High Commissioner) and his pessimism about British prospects by pointing out 'that it was too soon to give any definite opinion in the matter'. The lack of conviction in his language, albeit due to his crushed psychological condition, can hardly have reassured Bruce: 'Our dangers were clear, but Germany would have her difficulties also, and *even fighting single-handed we might well outlast her.*'[93] Chamberlain implicitly recognised that *not* 'outlasting' Germany was at least a serious possibility, to be weighed in advance when determining policy – an admission Churchill would never have conceded. On the 27th Chamberlain went on to develop this attitude further. In terms of sheer survival, he was determined and sanguine about fighting on; but he was not so certain about the ultimate wisdom of continuing to exclude a compromise peace from the range of possible futures. Chamberlain suggested, and the Cabinet agreed, that he should see the Dominion High Commissioners again, to inform them that 'even if France went out of the war, there was no prospect of our giving in. We had good reason to believe that we could withstand attack by Germany, and were resolved to fight on.' (This statement would apply of course to the immediate situation arising out of the hypothetical collapse of France. It would not mean that if at any time terms were offered they would not be considered on their merits.)[94] Such a position represents an important *via media* between the two extremes of (1) fighting until the war ended in total victory or total defeat, and (2) being willing to contemplate immediate negotiations for peace so as to avoid the risks of bombing and attempted invasion. Chamberlain was still looking at external policy through the lens of compromise, even if the parameters of choice were now deeply changed. The other ministers seem to have endorsed his approach. While the First Lord and the Dominions Secretary spoke against Bruce's 'defeatism' about Britain's chances of survival in isolation, the Cabinet approved Chamberlain's remarks in their entirety, including the new qualification on Britain's ability to achieve victory and keep out of negotiations with Hitler. Ministers were against 'capitulation' before the first stone had even been cast, but equally they were no longer wholly confident about an irrevocable, open-ended, prosecution of the war.[95]

The lengthy discussion on 28 May makes this clearer. Again the Cabinet Minutes give the impression that it was Chamberlain of the uncommitted ministers who contributed the most. First he stressed that 'mediation at this stage, in the presence of a great disaster, and at a time when many people might think that we had no more resources left, could only have the most unfortunate results. We in this country felt that we had resources left to us of which we could make good use.' Yet there was no doubt that Chamberlain was here arguing for the continuation of the war on the criterion of achieving a better ultimate compromise peace, rather than on that of pursuing total victory. He agreed with Churchill that resistance to invasion would improve Britain's position, but where the latter believed that any terms offered thereafter could not be worse than at the present, and essentially hoped that time would bring Britain allies who would restore her capacity to defeat Hitler, the Lord President thought that Britain's ability to resist would secure for her an acceptable settlement which should be considered seriously the moment it appeared on the horizon. The following records of Chamberlain's statements express this view fully:

There could be no question of our making concessions to Italy while the war continued. The concessions which it was contemplated we might have to make, e.g., in regard to Malta and Gibraltar, would have to be part of a general settlement with Germany... It was clear to the world that we were in a tight corner, and he did not see what we should lose if we said openly that, while we would fight to the end to preserve our independence, we were ready to *consider decent terms if such were offered to us* ... THE LORD PRESIDENT OF THE COUNCIL said that it was our duty to look at the situation realistically. He felt bound to say that he was in agreement with the Foreign Secretary in taking the view that *if we thought it was possible that we could now get terms which, although grievous, would not threaten our independence, we should be right to consider such terms* . . . If, as we believed, we could hold out, we should be able to obtain terms which would not affect our independence.[96]

These arguments have the appearance of consistency. But even aside from the fact that they were a loose amalgam of the two different standpoints of survival at all costs and victory at all costs, it will have been observed that their attitude to the prospect of immediate negotiations was distinctly ambiguous. At various points Chamberlain emphasised that mediation would harm Britain's bargaining position and morale, and that better terms would be available once the contest had been joined. At others he suggested (as in the italicised passages above), that the possibility of an imminent settlement should not be ruled out. Given the events of 2 September 1939, and the tide running against the 'guilty men', he was hardly in a position to press strongly for negotiations – assuming that he was inclined so to do.[97]

Dalton colourfully expressed his impression after the meeting of below-the-line ministers that the War Cabinet might not be completely or actively behind Churchill: 'It is quite clear that whereas the Old Umbrella – neither he nor other members of the War Cabinet were at this meeting – wanted to run very early, Winston's bias is all the other way.'[98] And indeed Attlee, Greenwood and Sir Archibald Sinclair seem to have shared Chamberlain's rather diffuse and tentative attitude, even if 'running very early' caricatures Chamberlain's position crudely. None of the three figures prominently in the Cabinet Minutes, and unless for some inscrutable reason the Secretary to the Cabinet, Sir Edward Bridges, decided to pare down their contribution to the debate, it is reasonable to infer that they did not feel sufficiently certain or positive in their views to speak forcefully and at length. (All three were relative newcomers to government, and representatives of the former Opposition[99]). Generally speaking, we may say that they were definitely opposed to peace negotiations merely on the grounds that France was certain to be defeated – and in any case sceptical about their likelihood. Attlee tended to take his lead from others. He felt that Hitler would be in a worse position if he had been frustrated in his plan for victory by the end of the year, and that approaches to Mussolini should be avoided because they would lead to an immediate attempt by him to intercede between Britain and Germany. His views were expressed in the most clipped way, but it is clear that he was opposed to such a move in part because of the great damage it might do to the morale of the British people and their consequent ability to survive a German onslaught.[100] As Chamberlain had noted on the 26th: 'Attlee said hardly anything but seemed to be with Winston.'[101]

Greenwood also subscribed to these two points. He believed that any course of action open to the Cabinet would be highly dangerous, but still came down just about in favour of continuing the war, for the present: 'The line of resistance was certainly a gamble, but he did not feel that this was a time for ultimate capitulation.' In the 2 p.m. meeting of 26 May Greenwood had been willing to see Halifax's 'line of approach' (about Mussolini and general 'European equilibrium') tried. Two and a half hours later, however, when he joined Churchill, Attlee, Halifax and Chamberlain in the Admiralty after their discussions with Reynaud, he gave Chamberlain the impression of not having thought things through, although he saw 'a good chance of outlasting Hitler'.[102] On the 28th he remained aware of the fragility of Britain's position but wanted no 'weakening' in the immediate crisis.[103]

The only other participant in high-level policy formulation within the Cabinet at this time (as opposed to the intermittent attenders) was Sinclair, in his function of representing the minority party in the National Government. The Liberal leader was equally opposed to any concessions while the outcome of a German attack on Britain still remained to be determined; in any case, he thought that 'there was no possible chance of acceptable terms being open to us at the present moment'. Sinclair's clear pronouncement nonetheless carried the implication that at some future stage, 'acceptable terms' might conceivably be available to Britain. The two Labour ministers also accepted the implication, endorsing Chamberlain's remarks to that effect. The Minutes explicitly and repeatedly record that 'There was complete agreement with the views which had been expressed by

... The Lord President of the Council' that (after Chamberlain's statement that making peace soon would involve a 'considerable gamble', but equally that Britain should be ready to consider 'decent terms') 'The War Cabinet agreed that this was a true statement of the case', and that 'In further discussion, general agreement was expressed with the views put forward by the Lord President.'[104] Chamberlain, as in so many different contexts, saw himself as the broker or peacemaker, and after the 'rather stormy discussion' in Cabinet on 28 May it was he who drafted the reply to Reynaud on which all finally agreed.[105]

Ultimately Attlee and Greenwood went along with the low-profile stance articulated by Chamberlain. They were willing to state positively their opposition to joining France in an imminent armistice, but they also bestowed approval on Chamberlain's further comments about the need to consider any reasonable terms – as did Sinclair. Essentially they were reluctant to voice such sentiments positively, their expressions of opinion being generally tentative and piecemeal.[106] Their muted agreement with Chamberlain's compromise position was based both on a recognition that peace might be an *eventual* hard necessity, and on the history of their own previous commitment to make no more 'dishonourable' agreements, and to vanquish Nazism completely.[107]

THE WIDER CONTEXT

Thus after intensive debate in the last week of May, a pattern of attitudes had emerged in the War Cabinet: Halifax and Churchill in basic conflict, with the other senior ministers pulled both ways and tending towards compromise as much through a desire for consensus as through any conviction about the precise policies to be followed in future.[108]

Of course, the progress of the war, France's collapse and many other factors outside Britain's control were the major determinants of the history of this period. Put in a wider perspective, arguments within the War Cabinet of the kind we have plotted may seem of only passing significance. The assumption behind any analysis of decision-making, however, is that external forces continually interact with domestic variables to produce choices whose character and outcomes are far from being predetermined. There will always be a variety of ways in which a country may react to a given international development, according to the state of her own politics and government at the time. In the case under review here, hindsight has tended to distort our understanding by making the path that Britain did follow in 1940 seem obvious and inevitable. The Cabinet records make it clear that policy-makers did not, of course, see it in that way. Fear, uncertainty and speculation abounded in a 'world turned upside down'. The meaning for Britain of the terrifying events in France was obscure, except in their demonstration that nothing could be taken for granted about the war. Recommendations about policy were bound to be even more subjective than usual. In these circumstances, then, choices were especially crucial and problematical, and the decisions which did emerge are worthy of the closest attention. As it was, the very unpredictability of events contributed to the strengthening of Churchill's arguments, precisely because the latter resembled articles of faith more than a detached measuring of pros and cons. Behavioural research suggests that when decision-makers perceive external threats to be severe, they tend to fall back on conviction far more than logic, thereby resolving some of the anxiety that might otherwise paralyse decision.[109] In May 1940 Churchill enjoyed not only the powers of prime ministerial office, but also a capacity for conviction unrivalled among his colleagues.

Moreover, the absence of certain pressures worked in the Prime Minister's favour. It was important, for example, that there had been no *German* peace offers made during the crucial last weeks of French independence, and especially in the week before Dunkirk, when the course of the campaign had become clear, including the prospect for Britain of the loss of her entire army, and the Cabinet had been in the midst of its anxious discussions about a possible end to hostilities.[110] There was a strong inhibition in the British government against beginning contacts with Germany about peace. Such a positive step would have been an overwhelming responsibility at such a time of tension between basic aims and values on the one hand and apparent lack of capabilities on the other. It would have meant a risky pre-judgement of Hitler's interest in a moderate peace. It would also have involved massive humiliation at home and abroad.

Finally, the way in which such a step might be taken had particular complications. The raising by the French of the question of a possible bribe to Italy inevitably introduced for Britain the added unpleasantness of likely concessions in the Mediterranean to a country not yet at war, as part of the price for achieving a general settlement with Germany. The Mediterranean, furthermore, was an area of long-term strategic importance to the British Empire.[111]

Given that these factors militated against a positive move by the Cabinet for an armistice, a *démarche* by the Germans themselves, on the relatively moderate lines of the July feeler in Berne,[112] would at least have brought an important new element into play during the formulation of British policy. It would have relieved the government of the responsibility for initiating distasteful contacts with Nazism, and it would have removed the difficulties of having Mussolini as middle-man. At the same time a serious proposal would have forced on the War Cabinet detailed consideration of a scenario based on peace, at the very point when they were most in a state of flux over attitudes to that question and when a specific decision in either direction was being avoided. As the American Ambassador in London actually reported on 27 May, a German offer of peace to both Britain and France would have produced 'a row among certain elements in the Cabinet here; Churchill, Attlee and others will want to fight to the death, but there will be other numbers who realize that physical destruction of men and property in England will not be a proper offset to a loss of pride'.[113] Kennedy's own pessimism about Britain's chances of survival probably led him to play up the existence of a defeatist camp, although his failure to mention names indicates the difficulties they would have been in, but he was correct in seeing the reaction to the defeat in France as a critical point of political as well as military decision.[114]

In the light of this, Hitler's non-decision on a serious peace offer at the end of May, and the timing of his eventual peace offensive in July, were tactical errors comparable with the military failures to press home both the attack on the BEF before Dunkirk and the blitz of British fighter bases during the Battle of Britain. On the other hand even a generous offer around 27 May would probably have done no more than strengthen Halifax's hand without changing the policy, while it is likely that Hitler saw the developing options no more clearly than did his victims.[115]

Too much should not be made of this point. There is no strong case for believing that a German peace proposal at, say, the start of June would have led to a compromise settlement of the war. The relevance of the absence of such a proposal is more limited to illustrating the truism that policy formulation within the Cabinet does not exist in a vacuum: that where internal considerations of power or personality may favour one point of view but still be finely balanced, outside changes or the lack of them will have the capacity at least to tip the balance of decision-making.[116]

The opinions of the Chiefs of Staff were more predictable than the actions of Hitler, but they too constituted a form of external pressure on the sorts of conclusions which the Cabinet might come to. Had the Chiefs, when they presented their revised views in reply to Churchill's slanted brief of 26 May, argued that Britain's thinly stretched resources were regrettably insufficient to survive an attempt at invasion, more ministers than Halifax might have been nervous of putting the matter to the test. While it is true that Churchill only asked for the opinion because he was fairly sure of the answer,[117] even he could not have kept the Chiefs of Staff's views from the Cabinet had they been adverse. (Eleanor M. Gates suggests plausibly that Churchill revised his brief to the Chiefs after preventing ministers from seeing the first, rather pessimistic paper – 'a possibly significant bit of shuffling which no doubt helped Churchill to control his Cabinet'.[118]) As it was the Chiefs of Staff came down on the side of Britain's ability to survive, but made clear the element of subjectivity in this knife-edge judgement. After outlining the difficulties facing Britain, with only her bombing fleet as a countervailing force (the substance of the report already prepared), they ended on a note of faith and hope more than conviction:

> To sum up, our conclusion is that *prima facie* Germany has most of the cards; but the real test is whether the morale of our fighting personnel and civilian population will counter-balance the numerical and material advantages which Germany enjoys. We believe it will.[119]

Bearing in mind the even more negative tone of their first paper, the conclusion is irresistible that the military were distancing themselves as far from a prediction of success as was possible without being actually defeatist. Of the ten substantive paragraphs in the report which preceded their rather depressed summation, five were pessimistic, two optimistic and three neutral. Nevertheless Churchill had the definite opinion that he wanted, 'to be able to assure Parliament that our resolve was backed by professional opinion'[120] and it closed off an important line of argument for those, like Halifax, who might have been considering the possibility of compromise as a response to harsh necessity.

Dunkirk provided a more positive boost to Churchill's outlook of uncompromising resistance. The rescue of the greater part of the BEF from enemy hands was a great objective contribution to Britain's home-defence capacity and even, in the far-distant future, to the reconstruction of a force for continental invasion.[121] Yet there were also psychological benefits. It was not difficult for the Prime Minister to use the success of the evacuation as a means of reinforcing his strenuous arguments of the previous week, and of proving Britain's basic resilience (in the particular form of her air-power) in the face of the forthcoming adversity. Chamberlain's diary shows how much better things had turned out than had been assumed at first.[122] Paradoxically defeat meant that the talk of 'resolve' now had greater plausibility. On 11 June Churchill reported that he would impress on Reynaud that if France could delay a German success 'we should hold out, even if the whole resources of the enemy were turned on the United Kingdom'.[123] A day later the War Cabinet decided that a study should be made, on the assumption of French collapse, of the economic harm that Britain could do to Germany and of the aid that Britain would require from the USA both to survive and to defeat Germany.[124] Horizons were widening once more; the question of an imminent peace was no longer an issue.

Perhaps the most important way in which Dunkirk reinforced Churchill's arguments, however, was in the negative respect of the prevention of a disaster. Had the BEF in fact been lost, Britain's military position would have seemed irredeemable. That it came so near to disaster was a measure of her intense vulnerability. The Chiefs of Staff had reported that the primary conditions for repelling an invasion were air superiority and the morale of the work-people who manufactured aircraft. If the army had been captured, it would both have demonstrated that the RAF could not dominate the air over the Channel and have been a major blow to civilian morale, with the loss of a key symbol of defence and one that was largely made up of the friends and relatives of industrial workers.[125] As it was, the assumptions of the new policy were fortunately reinforced.

Yet, even without the turn of events, Churchill had effectively managed to impose his strategy upon the Cabinet. For the very nature of the compromise which we have described was weighted against the conclusion of a negotiated peace. The War Cabinet had come to an informal decision to continue the war, wait on events and delay the consideration of peace terms to a later stage, when the blunting of an invasion would have restored the semblance of a bargaining position. In practice this solution meant that British policy was likely to follow one or other of the two scenarios set out by Churchill – glorious defeat or the open-ended continuation of the war. For if an invasion were to be repelled, then the Prime Minister would be able to capitalise on the relative improvement in British futures to encourage the belief that if survival was possible, then victory could be also. The prospect of imminent defeat would no longer exist to provide an incentive for accepting negotiations. Alternatively, if an attack on Britain began to prove successful, it is implausible that a satisfactory compromise peace could have been achieved at such a late stage, with even less leverage than in June. Once an air bombardment and an invasion had been launched and was bearing fruit, Hitler was unlikely to accept an armistice on anything less than the most favourable terms. At worst, the momentum of the military campaign would carry him on to achieve complete victory by conquest.

DENOUEMENT

In the event, the way the war unfolded during the next three months conformed with the first of Churchill's preferences. The War Cabinet moved naturally away from their original opinion that successful resistance would lead to a better position from which to obtain independence-without-victory, even though the latter had seemed the best possible outcome after the loss of France. The Battle of Britain and the abandonment of Operation Sealion enabled Churchill to recruit ministers to his belief (and their own, prior to May 1940) that Britain must and could continue to strive for complete victory.[126]

Thus neither Halifax nor the cautious centre of the War Cabinet ultimately had a decisive influence on the attitude of the British government to the war after the attack of France. The Foreign Secretary failed to convince his colleagues of the need to work for peace before an invasion; Chamberlain, with Greenwood and Attlee in train, appeared to have kept open the option of an 'honourable issue' at some point in the future, but by siding with Churchill against Halifax on the immediate issue, they had in fact rejected the idea of peace negotiations at the very point when they might have been most seductive.[127]

During June Churchill actively consolidated his implicit success in preventing the consideration of a compromise peace. As it became finally clear that France was lost, the Prime Minister began to cast any discussion of the future more in the optimistic terms of prospective victory. The recent past had been catastrophically unsuccessful; accordingly Churchill stressed that a 'new phase' was commencing, and one that he viewed with confidence: 'we should maintain the blockade, and win through, though at the cost of ruin and starvation throughout Europe'. He added that such resolution would attract the support of the USA.[128] In other words Churchill was no longer paying even lip-service to the idea that a hard-fought compromise might be the best realistic goal. He resurrected the idea of military victory on the basis that Britain's retreat behind the safety of her coasts would of itself assure eventual victory through the working of time and a blockade against Germany. He reported to the Cabinet his words to Reynaud of 13 June, without a trace of disingenuousness: '[Britain] believed that Hitler could not win the war without overcoming us. Our war aim still remained the total defeat of Hitler, and we felt that we could still bring this about.'[129] This was despite the clear scepticism among his own colleagues about total victory, expressed in the War Cabinet only two weeks before, and despite the circumspect Chiefs of Staff paper of 25 May, which had said that success was only likely on the twin assumptions of (1) 'full economic and financial support' from the USA, and (2) the accuracy of the Ministry of Economic Warfare forecasts as to German economic weaknesses.[130]

In this highly unstable environment, where most other predictions and options were highly tentative, Churchill fully exploited his institutional privilege of collecting the voices within the War Cabinet, his penchant for certainties becoming even more pronounced. Statements to colleagues came to resemble orders more than suggestions. On 6 June, in the midst of a quite specific discussion about the French armistice, Churchill announced that 'in no circumstances whatsoever would the British Government participate in any negotiations for armistice or peace' and 'At the present juncture all thoughts of coming to terms with the enemy must be dismissed as far as Britain was concerned. We were fighting for our lives and it was vital that we should allow no chink to appear in our armour.'[131]

During this kind of pressure the Prime Minister's colleagues, who had only ever been concerned to qualify his arguments by postulating a later consideration of the peace issue, were unlikely to voice any disagreement. Yet by supporting Churchill's dismissal of an armistice before the invasion attempt they were also drawn into a tacit approval of the whole burden of the Prime Minister's remarks, including the implication that a compromise peace would be possible 'in no circumstances whatever'. Once Churchill had elided the two issues, of unmitigated resistance to attack and of unyielding commitment to final victory, it was impossible for other ministers to disentangle them without appearing both premature and fainthearted. Certainly Halifax had come round to follow Churchill's lead. Two weeks after his advocacy of peace to the War Cabinet, he remarked that France ought to realise that 'if they made an armistice, they would embark on a slippery slope which would lead to the loss of their fleet and eventually of their liberty'.[132] Three days later he expressed the belief that if Hitler forced onerous terms on France, then the United States would enter the war.[133] Without Churchill's leadership and exhortation it is unlikely that the Foreign Secretary would so easily have abandoned his belief in the feasibility of peace. Nothing in the meantime had happened in the war to undermine his previous argument that reasonable terms might be available. Indeed, if anything, Dunkirk should have led to some speculation about whether Hitler had deliberately allowed the BEF to escape in order to improve the chances of peace with Britain. It did not, largely because it was no longer easy to think of Hitler as a rational actor, but also because Churchill was inspiring a psychology of defiance in which a successful evacuation became the apprehension of victory, the loss of France a palpable advantage and optimism a test of loyalty.[134]

For himself Churchill was increasingly concerned to shift his government's attention away from the difficult present: 'It might well be to our advantage that the Germans should have to hold down all these intelligent and freedom-loving people; the task of this holding down all Europe should prove beyond even the strength of a Gestapo, provided England could retain her liberty.'[135] While it was probable that his colleagues held hopes along these lines, the Prime Minister relentlessly expressed such views with complete confidence. Each turn of events was presented through the same filter of inflexible optimism and determination, despite the fact that a prediction six months previously of the current difficulties would have made even Churchill pause for thought. The peace terms offered to

France, for example, were cast as 'murderous' and depriving that country of 'all liberty'.[136] Apparently unaffected by his frenetic involvement in detail of all kinds, Churchill also took care to monopolise interpretations of the general outlook. The Cabinet was rarely allowed to forget the spirit in which it and the populace at large ought to be approaching the future. The Prime Minister was strongly opposed to the evacuation of children to North America: 'A large movement of this kind encouraged a defeatist spirit, which was entirely contrary to the true facts of the position, and should be sternly discouraged.' As a consequence of these remarks the Cabinet gave its approval to a stern prime-ministerial warning to higher officials 'to maintain a spirit of alert and confident energy' since 'there are no grounds for supposing that more German troops can be landed in this country . . . than can be destroyed or captured by the strong forces at present under arms'. The RAF was said to be at the zenith of its strength, and the German Navy at its nadir. Subordinates who were deliberately exerting a 'disturbing or depressing influence' should be removed or reported.[137] In such ways did Churchill display the powerful prime-ministerial leadership for which he has so often been praised.

In the light of the way opinions on the future of the war had been dominated by Churchill, and their subtleties submerged by the cumulative effects of his 'never surrender' reprovals, such German initiatives as there were for a settlement came far too late to have any impact within the Cabinet. Whereas an offer in late May or early June might have further disturbed the uncertain feelings of Churchill's colleagues, by the end of June peace feelers encountered a government once again operating on a basic consensus. As a result the Prime Minister was able to set in motion a negative response with little collective deliberation.

The Papal suggestions for an agreement of 28–30 June did not even get as far as the War Cabinet, despite the fact that 'Silly old Halifax [was] evidently hankering after them.'[138] According to Cadogan, Churchill did not allow the Foreign Secretary to begin talking seriously again about peace. He minuted: 'I hope it will be made clear to the Nuncio that we do not desire to make any inquiries as to terms of peace with Hitler, and that all our agents are strictly forbidden to entertain any such suggestions.'[139] The Prime Minister here interpreted the Cabinet's general feelings about a settlement, never expressed in a formal decision, with a certain licence. As with the Prytz affair around the same time, this was a good example of the Prime Minister's capacity to remove all doubt as to the implications of a general attitude formed in Cabinet, by acting decisively on his image of that attitude when a specific occasion arose.[140] By acting in this way a Prime Minister could create a *fait accompli* in a particular instance, and possibly lead his colleagues into a view of their own policy which might not have been fully formed until that point.

On 10 July, the War Cabinet did get the chance to consider a possible German peace move, when the Foreign Secretary reported a conversation in Berne between the British Minister and the Acting President of the Red Cross, Dr Burckhardt, who had communicated that Hitler was once again urging 'a working arrangement' with the British Empire, and a 'white peace like Sadowa'.[141] By this stage Churchill had given sufficiently clear expositions of British policy to leave even Halifax in no doubt of the response which should be made. He suggested, and the Cabinet agreed, that no reply should be made to the feeler. (Although it should be noted that there was at least enough interest to rule out 'a flat negative', in the thought that silence might lead Germany into confirming the sounding.[142]) There was no deliberation of any length on the issue, and the predominant impression is that of a pre-formed attitude applied automatically as the occasion arose.

The War Cabinet's reaction to the major peace initiative of this period, Hitler's speech of Friday 19 July,[143] confirms this picture. Ministers did not consider the speech until 22 July, by which time Churchill had acted quickly to ensure that the parallel attempt to contact the British Ambassador in Washington about peace was given no encouragement. He had sent the following telegram on Saturday the 20th: 'I do not know whether Lord Halifax is in town today, but Lord Lothian should be told on no account to make any reply to the German Chargé d'Affaire's message.'[144] When ministers did meet, there was no serious consideration of Hitler's 'appeal to reason', but rather a discussion of whether it would be best formally rejected in Parliament or simply ignored. In the event, Halifax made a radio broadcast on the same night which dismissed the peace offer by announcing that 'we shall not stop fighting until freedom is secure'.[145]

By the end of July the Prime Minister's consistently forceful advocacy had united the Cabinet behind him after a short but important period of uncertainty and division. Churchill had succeeded in maintaining the bases of British war aims, despite a massive upheaval in both the operational and psychological environments. The confusion into which British policy was plunged in May 1940 had allowed full scope to the clear definitions of goals that in this instance the Prime Minister alone possessed. Churchill was no Machiavelli; although far from being innocent of the political skills needed to acquire and hold onto power, he preferred the risk of rejection implicit in offering emotional leadership to the stratagems of palace politics. For once in his career this proved a positive advantage.[146] In the critical early months of Britain's isolation, circumstances and personality conspired to produce a concentrated period of prime-ministerial government.[147]

7. THE LONGER TERM: WAR AIMS AND OTHER COMMITTEES, OCTOBER 1940–JUNE 1941

Survival and the dramatic transformation in the character of the war were the issues with which the Cabinet struggled throughout the twelve months from the fall of France to Hitler's ultimately fateful attack on the Soviet Union. In policy-making terms, this produced a tension between the inevitable involvement of all ministers in a period of prolonged, unprecedented national crisis and the circumstantial needs for decisive personal leadership and diminished accountability from those responsible for grand strategy. In the first phase of the crisis, as we have seen, this led to emotion and uncertainty in Cabinet, resolved by the strength of Churchill's will and vision in a situation which was conducive to the assertion of prime ministerial initiatives. After the first febrile weeks, however, while the crisis remained, its temperature was sufficiently lowered to enable ministers to take a longer perspective on the war and its prospects. In particular, this meant that the discussion of war aims rose once again to the surface, and the coalition Cabinet wrestled for the first time with the strains of conducting day-to-day military campaigns at the same time as debating a putative post-war order. They attempted this task largely through the device of delegation to Cabinet committees, and it is the performance of these committees which forms the subject of this last case-study chapter. To what extent did they provide the means for a genuinely collective consideration of war aims, or for the mobilisation of special views and interests? How far, by contrast, could they be manipulated or ignored by a Prime Minister who was taking increasing strength from his evident indispensability?

'As the time passed at the gallop of war, the ideas of one year were over-ridden by the facts of the next.'[1] So Churchill caught vividly in 1947 the rapid changes in 'mentalité' brutally imposed by military defeat. 'War aims', almost by definition, were more likely to be affected by this process than any other area of policy. There were debates about what they should be, how far they could be distinguished from 'peace aims',[2] what their relationship was to the prosecution of the war and whether, indeed, they were a luxury and a distraction. The one certain fact about war aims, however, is that they could not be kept down for long. In whatever different forms, and despite various forms of hostility to them, war aims continued to find their way back onto the Cabinet's agenda.

There is a distinction, of course, between the *de facto* formulation of war aims, by way of reaction to some outside stimulus, and more formal attempts to reflect on the general purpose of Britain's commitment to the war and the terms on which it might end. In the former category fall the subjects of two previous chapters, that is, Britain's reactions to Hitler's two major peace offers, of 6 October 1939 and 19 July 1940. Into the latter fall the campaigns by parts of the press in conjunction with certain interest groups during the last three months of 1939 to force the government to go beyond the cautious generalities of Chamberlain's statement of 12 October towards a more explicit idealism about the future of international relations.[3] This led the junior minister Captain Harry Crookshank to observe about war aims in February 1940, 'There is no subject about which more has been said during the last six months.'[4] This first phase of the discussion of war aims, then, both public and intra-governmental, was broadly co-terminous with the Phoney War period, although so far as the Cabinet were concerned it was mostly a question of coping with Hitler's offer of peace and attempt to put the burden of blame for the war onto the Allies.

The campaigns in Norway, France and the Low Countries for a time froze all longer-term thinking about the war, except insofar as the agonising over whether or not to fight on depended on certain half-explicit notions of what British purposes and interests were. But the revival of debate was, surprisingly, not long postponed. This time Hitler's speech of 19 July offering peace was not the main focus. It was dismissed without serious attention by the government, whose crisis over the war had already taken place and been resolved.[5] The new phase of discussion, which was longer drawn out and therefore less dramatic than that of 6–12 October 1939, was both more concrete and more proactive.

It was more concrete in its primarily instrumental, rather than philosophical, approach. A statement of war aims was increasingly seen as desirable because it could help to win the war. On the home front, it would imbue a bewildered population with the sense of a struggle for civilisation, and for a Britain worth securing. This time the values and objectives would have to be spelt out rather less cheaply than the 'homes fit for heroes' slogan of 1918. Morale was vital to the survival of an embattled, isolated Britain in late 1940, and it might be necessary to reinforce it by various official clarion calls, even bribes about post-war reforms.

So far as the external environment was concerned, it was beginning to be thought that a more effective British propaganda was required, so as to win over neutrals such as the United States. Only if outsiders were clear about British goals, the argument ran, and in particular if they understood how the British were fighting for something more profound than a selfish set of national and imperialist interests, would they listen sympathetically to Britain's requests for the many and varied kinds of assistance needed.

As well as these quasi-military reasons for considering a new war aims statement, however, there was a reflective dimension. This produced for the first time the more positive attitude in governmental circles that commentators had been pressing on them from the start of the war, namely that Britain had to be prepared for the post-war world, which would inevitably come, and that its process of thinking through strategies for the future would itself inform and refine political decisions in the short term. The 'lessons of history' demonstrated the importance of thinking through in advance the link between rapid military developments and new political opportunities (as in 1918–19), so as not to risk such apparently disastrous mistakes as Versailles and reparations (it was significant that J. M. Keynes was brought into the official process of war aims formulation at this stage).[6] The rare historical opening for change which the end of a major war represented should not be missed this time round, whether at home or abroad. As the influential outsider Lionel Curtis put it in correspondence with Halifax in the midst of the May crisis in 1940, 'We shall either lose or win this war this summer. If we lose, nothing matters. If we win, then some cool thinking *now* as to what is to be done when the fighting is finished will make all the difference.'[7]

This kind of approach did not find many echoes in government before July 1940. The government was by no means silent on war aims after October 1939, but in frequent speeches and parliamentary statements they had the intention more of 'informing the country of the purpose of the war' than of taking part in an exchange of views.[8] This meant taking the 12 October statement – which had been so carefully constructed – as the baseline, and barely departing from its generalities. It is true that there was some slight shift so as to conciliate the French, away from the early emphasis on the Nazis as the main source of aggression and towards the view that the German people, too, had to face responsibility for their support of Hitler.[9] But in general the government were anxious not to be drawn into detailed commitments. They could not avoid the subject altogether, as Ivone Kirkpatrick observed: 'While we originally considered it desirable to damp down all public discussion of war aims, it proved quite impossible to do so in this country, and equally impossible to prevent the views over here being reported in France.'[10] Moreover there was some natural uncertainty even in the minds of senior Foreign Office professionals. Cadogan, for example, fearing another German 'peace offensive' in January 1940, wished:

when we turn that down – that we might have some terms that we could attach to our refusal. We have said repeatedly, that we must have 'guarantees' for the future. If I say that I must be 'assured' of something, it is not quite reasonable of me to refuse to disclose what will give me the required degree of assurance . . . At present the German government can represent to their people that we refuse to disclose our position – because our real aim is the annihilation of Germany . . . The real difficulty begins when we try to see whether we *can* define our minimum conditions in any way.[11]

Not long before, the British Ambassador in Washington, Lord Lothian, had made a speech in which he touched on the linkage between the struggle against the use of force in international relations and the need for a better set of economic dispositions at home, so as to strengthen democracy and the example it set in the world.[12] This was perhaps the first time a British spokesman had made such a connection in public.

In April, on the verge of the war proper, the government proposed a summit meeting to the Prime Ministers of the Dominions to discuss the joint war effort, 'and an opportunity might be afforded for, at any rate, the preliminary consideration of the problems of post-war reconstruction'.[13] This early reference to 'reconstruction' was an indication that, willy-nilly, the war aims debate, fuelled by outside pressure-groups and academics, was beginning to creep up on the government. At about the same time, Halifax had two meetings with Lord Lytton of the League of Nations Union, to discuss general matters relating to war and peace.[14]

It is not wholly surprising, therefore, that after the impossibility of such reflections during May and June, the perceived need for political planning ahead should creep up once more. That it should begin to happen even during the invasion crisis of July–October 1940 shows how a priori arguments were beginning to take on extra strength through being fused with practical arguments about morale and propaganda.

It was these arguments which ensured that the question of war aims rose once again to the level of the War Cabinet. The initial stimulus came from the Foreign Office Political Intelligence Department, which was one of the means by which the expertise of certain academics could be drawn into the policy process. In late June 1940 the historian Llewellyn Woodward drew attention to rumours that Hitler was on the verge of convening a European Economic Conference, which would demonstrate the supposed benefits of sheltering inside a German- and Italian-led system while Britain attempted to blockade the continent. Hitler was likely to announce his plans for the economic recovery of Europe. Woodward thought therefore that Britain was making 'a most grave and dangerous mistake in refusing to make any statement about our plans for the future economic and political organisation of Europe'.[15] Woodward quickly obtained the support of Rex Leeper, the Head of the News Department,[16] while the Deputy Under-Secretary Orme Sargent reacted quickly. He argued that Britain should put forward an economic plan of its own, to prevent Hitler wooing 'large sections of the American public', and suggested that a high-level committee be formed to report to the War Cabinet on the matter as soon as possible.[17] Cadogan and Halifax were drawn in immediately. They agreed that Roosevelt should be warned of the likely turn of events, while the Foreign Secretary thought 'we should prepare opinion so far as we can by letting the idea "leak"'. At this stage, however, he was sceptical about the need for a committee.[18]

Discussions continued within the Foreign Office during the first few weeks of July (with a certain irritation at Lothian's failure to carry out his instructions by sufficiently alerting the highest levels of the US government) and on 11 July the Ministry of Information was brought into the process of policy-formulation. The essence of British action would have to be counter-propaganda: 'We have to convince the countries of Europe that, when we do win, with the resources of the New World behind us, we are not going to retire into our own shells and leave them in their chaos and misery.' Otherwise Britain would not be able to encourage effective resistance to Hitler on the continent of Europe.[19]

Thus an initiative at Cabinet level was being pulled together, for which the final and necessary precipitant was Duff Cooper's paper of 20 July, which came before the War Cabinet six days later. It was significant that it was the Ministry of Information, rather than the Foreign Office, which led on this renewal of interest in the war aims question, as the most significant motive was now that of effective propaganda, rather than the a priori benefits of long-term planning. In his paper, Duff Cooper pointed out that if British morale were to worsen, it would be vital to have 'a clear and definite picture of the cause which was at stake' if the peace movement were not to gain renewed strength under a German peace offensive – which 'would be more dangerous than any invasion'. Thus 'the government should now formulate in their own minds, with a view to conveying it to the people, a clear and definite picture of the cause that is at stake'; the public's hearts might fail them if they thought 'we are fighting merely to restore the Europe of Versailles and the England of the last two decades'. Equally, the neutrals would be more likely to be inoculated against Nazi seduction by a British willingness to envisage a new united, even Federal Europe, based on co-operation and goodwill.[20]

This expression of ruling-class guilt and anxiety about Hitler's effect on opinion at home and abroad was clearly introducing a powerful political element into the discussion. It was not surprising, therefore, that officials were only too glad to see the politicians take the responsibility. N. B. Ronald and T. N. Whitehead in the Foreign Office, for example, argued that the War Cabinet would have to issue general instructions on how to counter German propaganda, especially as American demands for a clearer British definition of war aims were likely to grow.[21]

This was, of course, no less a difficult and delicate matter for the War Cabinet itself. Halifax, prompted by Cadogan the day before, reminded his colleagues that Britain had, from the start, tried to play this down to appease the French. In the interests of more effective propaganda, he now thought it important to revert to the earlier position. The War Cabinet agreed and then backed Duff Cooper's paper but asked for a further development of its ideas, 'by various groups of ministers'. Churchill – at this stage at least – does not seem to have been unsympathetic, as he 'sketched out certain ideas which might well take their place in my scheme for the reconstitution of Europe'.[22]

Ministers were, however, under no illusions that the collective development of their ideas was going to be any easier than when they had shied away from the task at the end of 1939. Duff Cooper himself wrote to Halifax that 'It is an awfully difficult matter, this formulating of war aims', and argued that the government would have to avoid the two extremes of 'a lot of professors, out of touch with reality' and 'purely opportunist propagandists'. He then laid down the typology which was to resonate throughout the discussions of the following months and years. He wanted 'People who do know what is going on and can keep closely in touch with the course of events, but who are also capable of taking long views, and planning for the future. We want this done in two spheres, foreign and domestic.'[23]

Duff Cooper's analysis looked at war aims in two inter-related dimensions: their relation to home or abroad and their focus on practical relevance or long-term planning. Any discussion of war aims would have to involve some pairing of these dimensions. Long-term planning would be necessary on both domestic and foreign subjects but, equally, the analysis of objectives in both areas would have to be rooted firmly in contemporary circumstances.

It is important to realise that at this stage the revival of the war aims question was taking place as a by-product of other factors. Cooper's paper, after all, was a Ministry of Information production (if skilfully fostered by the Foreign Office), and bore the title 'Propaganda for the Future'.

Yet the inherent political context of most of what was at issue was bound to come out, and to generate the disagreements which ultimately were to inhibit the flourishing of debate at Cabinet level. Nor was it simply a fact of the (important) question of propaganda raising problems about the values which were being fought for. The increasing complexity of the war itself threw up problems of 'war aims', even if it was convenient to avoid describing them as such. On 5 August, for example, the Cabinet wrestled with the question of a draft agreement with the Free French, caught in the dilemma of wanting to encourage General de Gaulle and at the same time to avoid any commitment to the exact restoration of the territorial status quo ante.[24]

The Foreign Secretary's increasing involvement bolstered a recognition that the matter went far beyond technical judgements on the efficacy of propaganda. In replying to Duff Cooper's letter (see n. 23, above, this chapter), Halifax explicitly referred to their coming conversation on war aims, and agreed that policy formulation would have to be at the highest level: 'Ministers must tackle this question themselves. This being so, I rather hope that in the paper you are preparing for the Cabinet you may suggest that a Ministerial Committee should be set up, which would study the question in all its aspects.' There ought to be a 'long-term programme for use after the war, and at the same time an *ad hoc* programme ready for use here and now to counteract Hitler's propaganda'.[25]

Duff Cooper perhaps slightly resented Halifax's behaviour as puppet-master, because in his next communication he took care to distinguish his own suggestion: 'my idea is that a Committee of Cabinet Ministers should be set up, on which, of course, all three political parties must be represented'. He was not blind to the obstacles ahead: 'Frankly, I foresee tremendous difficulties. Nevertheless, let us have a talk about it as soon as possible.'[26] A week later, Cooper's revised paper was ready for the War Cabinet. It referred to consultations with Halifax and the Lord Privy Seal, and formally suggested setting up a ministerial Committee to examine war aims.[27] This was rapidly followed by a paper from the Foreign Secretary, which re-drafted the terms of reference envisaged by Duff Cooper, so as, for example, to exclude a reference to the 'importance of Federation' in any post-war international system.[28]

The issues – and the two memoranda – came before the War Cabinet on 23 August, and this was the occasion at which the War Aims Committee, which was to be so short-lived but so influential in what it unleashed, was actually set up. Once again, the agenda item was entitled 'Propaganda – future policy', but it was now finally agreed 'That there was a growing demand for some statement of what we were fighting for. We must make our aims clear, not merely to our own people, but also to the peoples of Europe whom we were trying to free.'[29] The Prime Minister (who was soon to become hostile to further expatiation on these themes) was still personally interested enough to contribute some substantive points, referring to a possible future balance between 'the Four Great Powers of Europe' and 'Three groups of smaller states – in Northern Europe, Middle Europe, and in the Balkans'. Typically, he displayed considerable prescience even in these throw-away remarks, referring to the possibility of a Council of Europe and a Court – even if he also referred to an 'international airforce' and a scheme for the 'fair distribution of raw materials'. He stressed that 'there should be no attempt at a vindictive settlement after the war'. Perhaps sensing that he was running ahead of himself, Churchill added that as ministers were too busy to be able to devote much time to all this, delegation would be necessary.

Thus the question of war aims had finally been taken up seriously by the War Cabinet, initially as the spin-off of concerns about morals and propaganda, but in a more open-ended way than in the previous deliberations on how to respond to Hitler's speeches. The new committee gave ministers the rare opportunity for creative, long-term thinking, if paradoxically in the most straitened of circumstances, with an invasion threatening. The importance of this new development, and indeed more of the reasons for it, were reflected in both the terms of reference of the Committee and its composition.

The importance of war aims as an issue was demonstrated by the decision from the outset to have all three political parties represented on the Committee. If consensus could not be achieved at the apex of the British political system, then it would be difficult to appeal to public opinion for unity or to foreigners for support. The initial list of members, so far as Duff Cooper was concerned included the Lord President (Chamberlain) as Chairman, with the Lord Privy Seal (Attlee) and the Secretary of State for Air (Sinclair) representing the other two parties of the Coalition. The other members were to be Halifax and Duff Cooper (as progenitors of the Committee) and the Minister of Labour (Ernest Bevin) who had impressed Halifax with his forceful talk at a recent meeting of the 'below the line' ministers about the need to counter Hitler's economic offer to Europe.[30]

There were to be considerable changes in this proposed membership before the Committee met, and indeed during its brief life. From before its setting up by the War Cabinet, for example, Viscount Cranborne (Paymaster-General, but to become Secretary of State for the Dominions on 3 October)[31] was becoming involved, Halifax determining that he should see a memorandum sent in by Professor Huxley which caused quite a stir in the Foreign Office.[32] Towards the end of August, Orme Sargent (while admitting that 'it is entirely outside my sphere') minuted Halifax to the effect that Cranborne should be added to the Committee, and he was supported by

Cadogan. Halifax, clearly not offended by an official interfering in the political realm (it seems clear from previous minutes in this file that Sargent wanted Cranborne on the Committee partly because the latter shared his own anti-collectivist views on economic reform), said that Duff Cooper had such an addition in mind, and he should be reminded to raise the matter in the Committee itself.[33]

The War Cabinet set up the Committee as Duff Cooper requested, but it never met with its original chairman, as Chamberlain's terminal illness forced him to retreat from London in mid-September and to resign from office at the end of that month.[34] Attlee took over as Chairman. The Committee was to meet five times, all before the end of the year, and at its second meeting settled down with seven members, more than originally intended. Of the six initially cast, only Attlee, Bevin, Cooper and Halifax remained. Apart from Chamberlain, Sir Archibald Sinclair also never made an appearance. Presumably with his agreement, he was replaced by a more junior Liberal, Harcourt Johnstone, the Secretary of the Board of Overseas Trade. It may be significant that the latter was a personal friend of Churchill.[35] Sinclair was, in any case, to receive all the Committee's papers.[36]

As various elements in the Foreign Office had wished, 'Bobbety' Cranborne was added to the Committee in time for its second meeting on 31 October.[37] Cranborne had resigned with Eden in February 1938, and represented the successor generation of Conservatives, as Churchill weeded out the appeasers. As the new Dominions Secretary, he also represented a constituency with a vital interest in war aims. The other addition was less predictable, and more senior. The Chancellor of the Exchequer, Sir Kingsley Wood, also joined in time for the second meeting, and at Churchill's request.[38] The War Cabinet no doubt became aware of these changes to its decision of 23 August, but it would not have been asked for further approval.

As Table 7 shows, the War Aims Committee was set up as a significant body. Indeed half of the full War Cabinet were members of the Committee, which contained the Foreign Secretary and the Chancellor of the Exchequer, as well as the leader of the Labour Party and his most able colleague, a representative of the Liberals and two other Conservatives. Furthermore, three other ministers – Leo Amery (Secretary of State for India), Hugh Dalton (Minister for Economic Warfare) and Lord Reith (Minister of Works and Buildings) – also asked to join. To these requests Duff Cooper and Attlee

Table 7. *Membership of the War Cabinet, and of the War Aims Committee, October–December 1940*

War Cabinet	War Aims Committee
Winston Churchill	
Clement Attlee	Clement Attlee (Lab., Chairman)
Viscount Halifax (Anthony Eden (C) from 22 December)	Viscount Halifax (C)
Sir John Anderson (Independent National MP for Scottish Universities)	
Ernest Bevin	Ernest Bevin (Lab.)
Sir Kingsley Wood	Sir Kingsley Wood (C)
	Viscount Cranborne (C)
	Harcourt Johnstone (Liberal)
	Alfred Duff Cooper (C)
Arthur Greenwood (Lab.)	
Lord Beaverbrook (C)	

Note: Also often present as 'constant attenders' at the War Cabinet were A. V. Alexander, Cranborne, Eden, Morrison and Sinclair.

had 'no objection' but wanted to keep the Committee 'as small as possible'. They were therefore told, with the Prime Minister's approval, that certain subjects could be remitted to particular Committee members for consultation with other ministers, as appropriate.[39] The Committee's significance was also evident in its far-reaching terms of reference, which added a third dichotomy to the short-run/long-run and home/abroad axes for debate originally outlined by Duff Cooper, namely that of the interplay between political and economic factors. The brief was twofold:

(1) to make suggestions in regard to post-war European and world system with particular regard to the economic needs of the various nations and to the problem of adjusting the free life of small countries in a durable international order.
(2) to consider means of perpetuating the natural unity achieved in this country during the war through a social and economic structure designed to secure equality of opportunity and service among all classes of the community.[40]

Thus the pitch was now at objectives for reform inside Britain and in the wider international system; for the economic needs of small countries and of all classes in British society; for the security of the weak at whatever level of political life. It was asking a lot of even a high-powered Cabinet committee, especially at a time of grave crisis, to come up with plausible options for such changes, but this was not, of course, the primary purpose. The principal concern was to convince the British, American and European publics that a genuine change of heart had taken place at the highest levels of the administration in London, and that the war was not being fought for a narrow, self-regarding class who, once victory was attained, might continue to inflict unemployment at home while endangering British security in the wider world.

Events had played a major part in making Churchill's government take this position. The loss of France, the isolation, the prospect of a desperate struggle for survival, all put party-political differences into perspective and helped to create the grateful image of a loyal working class which had shown itself worthy of better than the subordination and unbending discipline which it had endured throughout the 1930s. The urgent need for the unity of a National Coalition government put the Labour Party, with its crucial influence over the trades unions, in a position to bargain for influence over future policy if the Prime Minister, as he clearly wished, was to concentrate on the prosecution of the war, and the experience of other Conservative ministers gave them a disproportionate impact on day-to-day affairs.

It was, therefore, the combination of the Labour Party's presence in government with a mixture of realism and guilt on the part of some Conservatives which led to the relatively progressive climate in which the War Aims Committee was born and worked. If Foreign Office and Ministry of Information concerns were reflected in the first of the Committee's terms of reference, then the second represented the fusing of the Ministry of Information's preoccupation with domestic morale and the Labour Party's determination (increasingly also expressed at the grass-roots of the army and civilian population[41]) to use the prospect of victory to legitimise the idea of radical reform in British society.

The Conservatives sympathetic to this new spirit of change and cross-party consensus were indispensable in bringing about the momentum of war aims discussions and the preoccupation with 'reconstruction' which followed it. Lord Halifax in particular, possibly motivated by religious conscience among other things, made a distinctive move to the left, which ultimately did not strengthen his position with Churchill.[42] After the meeting with 'below-the-line' ministers on 30 July Halifax recorded:

a good many of us felt that in the future days of peace – if we ever get there – as well as in the days of war, it was necessary to have greater regard to the human values and not allow them to be smothered by consideration of old-fashioned financial purity... I am quite certain that the human conscience in this country is not going to stand for a system that permits large numbers of unemployed...[43]

This shift in political philosophy meant by definition that Halifax and those who thought along similar lines became more sympathetic to the idea that war aims should be thought through in detail. As the Foreign Secretary commented when accepting the idea of a conversation with Duff Cooper on the subject, 'From the Foreign Office point of view, I am becoming increasingly conscious of the need for His Majesty's Government to have some definite programme.'[44]

At an early stage, therefore, the coming together of the procedural issue, which was whether or not war aims should be redefined, with the substantive point about the need for reform in the post-war order of things had already taken place. This conjunction was to characterise the war aims question for the rest of the conflict, and certainly during the period of our concern, up to Barbarossa. It was to be the source of much intellectual fertility, but also of disagreement in the Cabinet, particularly between the supporters of war aims discussion and the Prime Minister.

THE WAR AIMS COMMITTEE: ITS ACTIVE PHASE

In one respect, the creation of a national Coalition Government had simply altered the balance of power on the war aims argument. The Labour Party, which had called for a proper formulation of war aims in the previous October, was now inside the government and in a position to help bring about that formulation. Equally, the outsiders – whether pressure-groups or individual experts – who had made much of the running nearly a year before now had a focal point inside the government, and in some cases direct access. Arnold Toynbee, for example, the Director of Studies at the Royal Institute of International Affairs (Chatham House), the increasingly influential think-tank based in St James's Square, attended (at least) the second meeting of the Committee, having been asked to write a paper for it, and other academics were also closely involved.[45] Furthermore this new proximity to the centre of power acted to support the continuing desire of the Dominion governments for a more detailed consideration of war aims, although paradoxically it may also have supplanted the Dominions and their High Commissions at the centre of the policy-making process. There were now more actors, and other vocal advocates, involved inside the system.[46] This meant that there was a sufficient consensus, and a coalition within the War Cabinet in the late summer of 1940, to get war aims discussions off the ground once again. As we have seen, it was also sufficient, perhaps combined with his own reactions to the movement of events, to make Churchill relatively co-operative about the venture at first.[47]

The life of the War Aims Committee lasted effectively until January 1941 when it was transmogrified into the Reconstruction Problems Committee, with significant changes of scope and personnel. The four months of its existence was a period when the Prime Minister was at first cautious about trespassing against the proprieties of Cabinet government. In October and November, indeed, there were rare minuted discussions of the conventions in relation to the power of the Cabinet over the implementation of its decisions. The War Cabinet made it clear, in connection with a failure to implement 1938 instructions to increase chemical weapon stocks, that any department which would not or could not fully implement a decision of the War Cabinet was under an obligation to report the matter immediately.[48] This unusual reminder can be interpreted either as a problem of bureaucratic inertia and standard operating procedures, or as a shot across the bows from a Prime Minister determined to run a tight ship. Another incident suggests that Churchill was still not yet fully confident in his handling of the multi-party War Cabinet, even if his instinct for leadership often got the better of him. On 21 November the War Cabinet discussed the possibility of seizing ports in Southern Eire, given De Valera's refusal to allow the Royal Navy to use them. There was pressure in Parliament for a statement, which the Government was trying to avoid. The Prime Minister acknowledged that 'clearly [however] no reply or statement should be made without further discussion in the War Cabinet'.[49]

On the matter of the War Aims Committee itself, and its obligation to report back, the War Cabinet kept only a very intermittent eye on progress, awaiting the culmination of the Committee's work in the form of a draft public statement which the government might make in the New Year. On 20 November there was once again a lengthy discussion in the War Cabinet on propaganda and war aims. In particular this was because ministers had before them a joint Dalton/Duff Cooper paper (with a note of approval from the Chiefs of Staff), whose Paragraph 5f argued that 'from the point of view of our propaganda there is a real need for the formulation of post-war aims in broad terms'.[50]

The minute for the item gives no clue as to personalities, but the general arguments seem to have been rehearsed fairly at the meeting, that is, that any statement should take the middle course between platitudes and embarrassing commitments, while on the other hand 'our military position did not at present justify us in launching ambitious schemes for a post-war settlement.' Yet 'the general feeling was that there was much to be said for some general statement of the essential fundamentals of our thought which could be so expressed as to have a wide appeal in this country and elsewhere'.

This was on the grounds that, otherwise, Hitler's plans would establish the idea of German economic dominance in Europe, and Roosevelt might also seize the initiative in his inaugural speech in January 1941. The Cabinet generally approved the memorandum before them, subject to their own discussion.[51] The same day Hugh Dalton recorded that the Prime Minister felt that he was 'being pressed to make a statement on war aims'.[52]

The Committee was thus reinforced in its work (if rather back-handedly) only six days before the third of its meetings. It was in the midst of an active programme of work which was to produce sixteen memoranda in less than four months (but not, ironically, a prime-ministerial statement).

The life of the Cabinet Committee on War Aims, as shown in Table 8, is worth looking at in a little more detail.

The first meeting of the Committee, on 4 October, surveyed the issues widely, in both geographical and functional terms. Bevin talked of the need to woo Japan and China, while not forgetting India and the Dominions. Halifax, recapturing momentarily the spirit of Munich, argued that in respect to Europe 'it was anomalous and absurd that quite small countries should be in the position to be tiresome. There must be some organisation to over-ride these small obstructive minorities.'[53]

The Committee did, however, soon move beyond the pursuit of hobby-horses and on to its essential concerns. Bevin seems to have been the first to touch on the 'essential linkage' between domestic

Table 8. *Meetings of the War Aims Committee, October–December 1940*

4 October	10 a.m.	
31 October	3.30 p.m.	(attended by Arnold Toynbee. Sir Kingsley Wood and Lord Cranborne joined the Committee)
26 November	4.30 p.m.	
11 December	4.30 p.m.	
13 December	12 noon	(Ernest Bevin missed this meeting)

Notes:.
1. Sir Edward Bridges and A. M. R. Topham acted as the secretaries of the Committee throughout its life.
2. On 21 February 1941, the War Aims Committee was superseded by the Reconstruction Problems Committee, under the chairmanship of Arthur Greenwood (for its membership, see Table 9, below, p. 219). This Committee met first on 6 March, and then three more times in 1941, on 21 and 28 May and 6 November. It was then reconstituted with a smaller membership in early 1942, assessing the reports of the Committee on Post-War Internal Economic Problems. In 1943 it ran parallel with the Lord President's Committee on Reconstruction Priorities until 12 November 1943, when Woolton's Reconstruction Committee replaced them both. (See CAB 117, list of files, CAB 87/1, and S. S. Wilson, *The Cabinet Office to 1945* (London: HMSO, 1975), pp. 107 and 230–9.

and foreign war aims (fast to become the intellectual hub of the whole exercise), saying that economic change would be an important priority at the end of the war. Indeed the formal minute records that the Committee would proceed 'bearing in mind the essential linkage between our aims for a new world order and for improvement in our social and economic structure'.[54] It was generally agreed that there was no 'demand' for an early or detailed statement on war aims, but that there was 'a widespread demand for a statement of general principles and objectives, and that it would be desirable for such a statement to be issued as soon as possible, consistently with the great care and attention called for in the preparation of such an important statement'.[55] The repeated references to the 'demand' or lack of it for a statement betrayed the continuing concern for public opinion and morale, which had been one factor (but not such a serious one) twelve months before.

The procedure agreed to at this first meeting was that Attlee and Duff Cooper would draw up the heads for 'limited statement of objectives', while Professor Toynbee should be asked to provide an overview (no doubt on the basis of the preliminary paper he had already submitted to Duff Cooper). Other outsiders mentioned as possible helpers were Leonard Woolf, 'Macdougal' (probably Frank McDougall) and S. M. Bruce from Australia House and a Mr Phelan of the International Labour Organisation.[56]

Halifax thought that this first meeting 'didn't achieve much except [reveal] the difficulty of drawing a picture of the post-war world', but before the next, on 31 October, he was to send Attlee, as acting Chairman of the Committee, two papers on 'the spiritual basis of our war aims', one by Toynbee and one from his own pen. Toynbee's sweeping outline of 'the principles that inspire our way of life', with its reference to the Christian belief that 'God is love' and the principles held in common with 'the good pagans' of certain other religions, was perfectly consistent with his academic status and interest in the comparative study of civilisations. Halifax's similar draft (reproduced in Appendix 4, below), was, however, one of the most extraordinary documents ever to have been written by an incumbent Foreign Secretary, and it may well have further damaged his credibility in Churchill's eyes. Some of its ideas found their way into the Committee's final draft of a statement on war aims, and may have been a further factor in preventing it from ever reaching the public eye.

Halifax had been talking in the interim to William Temple, the Archbishop of York, and to Professor Julian Huxley, both radically minded, and had decided that 'much common ground is emerging in the minds of all those who are thinking about what after the war ought to be like when we get there'.[57] Halifax thought that 'millions of people all over the world' were wanting a statement of British principles of the kind which his draft was intended to preface. His document — which Harold Nicolson referred to incredulously as 'a pathetic little draft of peace terms . . . all about God'[58] — began by asserting that the allies were defining not 'material goods' but 'a way of life' which 'flows from the belief that all men are brothers, because they are all children of God, who loves them and wants them to love one another'. The Foreign Secretary then deduced three principles — the absolute value of each soul, the respect for conscience and the importance of individual liberty — from this belief, and claimed (with Toynbee) that other religions shared the political outlook which derived from Christianity. By contrast, Hitlerism represented slavery and had to be overcome, 'but we know that a military victory over it will not dispose of it completely. It will not have been eradicated until the idolatry from which it springs has lost its hold upon Men's minds and hearts.' It can easily be imagined how this ecclesiastical think-piece must have been received in late 1940 by the tough-minded realists of all parties who were wrestling with the military survival of Britain.

The Foreign Secretary's draft was not a formal Committee paper, and it was in addition to the five WA(40) memoranda put before the next meeting, consisting of various papers by Bruce, Duff Cooper, Attlee, Toynbee and Amery, on how the Committee's terms of reference should be interpreted, and what plan of work should be adopted. Toynbee's hand, indeed, can be seen in a good deal of the Committee's material, and he attended this second meeting.[59] A decision was reached at this meeting to produce a general statement on war aims within two months, to counter Hitler's propaganda. Attlee was already beginning to assemble the elements of such consensus as he could identify, and Halifax undertook to write a further note on the political mechanisms and principles necessary to ensure the survival of a democratic way of life. Bevin announced he intended to write something on the economic priorities (there is no evidence that he did so for this Committee), and seems to have tried to impose himself on this occasion, to judge from Halifax's disapproving diary entry.[60]

The process of thinking about grand political strategy was now well under way, with such big issues raised in the various papers before the Committee as world economic reform, human rights and what was later to be referred to as 'Anglo-America', or the prospect of a benevolent Anglo-American condominium.[61] On 1 November, for example, S. M. Bruce circulated another memorandum, calling for a commitment to a new highly progressive (indeed neo-idealist) order at home and abroad. If Churchill were to make a speech on this basis, Bruce thought, it would give hope to both the British working class and the oppressed people of Europe.[62]

Unlike many issues before a Cabinet, the subject of war aims was open-ended, and could, without particular impetus, either expand exponentially or fade away. In this first phase, at least, rapid growth was evident. In November the question arose of whether a special secretariat needed to be set up for the Committee, to undertake long-term research projects on the nature of the changes which might have to be engineered as soon as peace arrived, in the 'convalescent stage', as contemporary insider jargon had it.[63] This detailed work would 'enable the War Aims Committee to take the necessary decisions on policy'.[64] Attlee saw that this could easily become a Ministry of Reconstruction without a minister, and warned against it. A secretariat's functions 'should be in the main analytic and collative' while the Committee's own task 'should be that of deciding broad principles, the detailed application of which should be worked out by others'. The Lord Privy Seal went on to describe the role of a Cabinet Committee in the kind of terms often applied to the full Cabinet itself: 'The strength of a body of Ministers in committee does not consist in the expertise of individuals on particular problems, but on the capacity of all of them to take a balanced view of the subject on which they have received information from experts.'[65] Attlee was even prepared to envisage the use of outsiders, 'young dons' from Chatham House and elsewhere, which official advice had been only in favour of under controlled conditions.[66]

At the third meeting of the Committee, on 26 November, ministers agreed to follow Attlee's lead, as expanded on by Sir Kingsley Wood, who envisaged the secretariat collating the suggestions on war aims of various interested groups, thus enabling the Committee to draw up a list of priorities in terms of subjects on which they wanted a balanced report made. These reports would then return to the Committee for decision 'in the light of broad principles'. The Committee then looked at Bruce's paper, and another by Halifax, which they welcomed as a good basis for an eventual statement on war aims. Amendments to the draft were invited, to be submitted in writing to Halifax. The minutes record various ministers as having made verbal points which varied predictably according to party position, with Cranborne emphasising the importance of great power discipline over small states, Bevin the importance of a welfare net at home and Harcourt Johnstone (the sole Liberal) the need for European unification (*plus ça change...*). There was also a good deal of very general and abstract talk about 'rights', 'truth' and the like, but also an explicit decision to avoid the 'fundamental question' of tariffs and trade policy.[67]

Halifax's draft statement of 25 November is revealing of both the personality of the Foreign Secretary and the general handling of war aims within the Cabinet. His covering note was as diffident as it had been in October 1939, and talked about him being 'greatly daring' in attempting a draft, for 'Discussions in the War Cabinet and the

Committee would seem to have made it plain that we shall get into great difficulty if we attempt more than a general statement.' His basic preoccupation with the 'moral reinforcement of our national thought' remained, but some of the spiritual excesses of his previous 'preface' had been removed, and the statement was now as much directed towards the original purpose of countering German propaganda as to solipsistic metaphysics.

Halifax's memorandum provided the basis for the Committee's eventual draft statements.[68] There was, however, still a good deal of detailed revision to come, and this preoccupied the Committee in what turned out to be its last two meetings, during December 1940. On 11 December the Committee considered various documents, including a revision of Halifax's draft which took into account suggested amendments, and a version prepared by Toynbee seeking to incorporate the various memoranda submitted, including those by Bruce and one by Harcourt Johnstone which was barely completed.[69] The Committee discussed the possibilities in some detail and agreed that Halifax should prepare a final version in the light of discussion. The Foreign Secretary, however, was not as influential as he might have been. Duff Cooper had disclosed before the meeting that 'I do not send any amendments to Halifax, as . . . while I found very little to quarrel with in his paper which we had under consideration, I had a general feeling of dissatisfaction with the whole of it which I felt I could not express without being impolite.' Toynbee's document had been 'much more business-like and satisfactory', and gave 'a sensation of solid ground rather than airy visions'.[70]

The Committee decided that the Prime Minister would need to see all of the last few documents they had considered, and that he should be invited to broadcast a statement on war aims around Christmas or the New Year based on them. Their Chairman was privately convinced that it was 'of the greatest importance' that the Prime Minister should make such a speech before 4 January 1941.[71] Halifax thought that progress was being made, but as to whether Churchill would 'play', he reserved judgement.[72] Consultation with the Dominions would only be necessary if a statement were to be made to Parliament (so much for the promises to the Dominions in October 1939 that there would be plenty of time in the future for them to join in on war aims formulations.[73])

Two days later, the Committee met for the last time, to consider a revised draft, and after discussion authorised further changes following on from which the Lord Privy Seal would present the Committee's finished version (together with the other late drafts) to the Prime Minister around 20 December.

Thus the War Aims Committee of the Cabinet, though of short duration, burned brightly on the policy-making landscape, and by producing a draft statement on war aims fulfilled the War Cabinet's instructions. The final version was as near to being the product of genuine collective discussion and imagination as is possible in a politico-bureaucratic environment, although there were certainly some particularly persuasive voices, namely those of Halifax, Duff Cooper, Toynbee and Bruce. 'The system had worked', in Gelb's and Betts' careful phrase about American policy-making during the Vietnam War.[74]

In substance, the draft statement[75] eschewed precise definitions of objectives, as had always been the intention, and concentrated on principles. To Halifax's original three principles was added a fourth, 'the sanctity and solidarity of family life'. Together they were seen as the basis for individual 'rights' which, it was naively asserted, were common ground between the various religions of the world.[76] Nazi values were placed in antithesis to this democratic individualism, seen as crucially shared by 'America' and the British Commonwealth. The appeal to the western hemisphere was extended further by talk of Hitler's global ambitions, even across 'the Straits of Dakar' (*sic*). By contrast, Britain was aiming towards a post-war 'community of nations' freely negotiated between big and small, on the model of the British Commonwealth.

The draft statement contained a number of important new acknowledgements or emphases. We have already noted the 'essential linkage' between international and domestic reconstruction, which this predominantly Conservative Committee was now prepared to accept would involve widespread international economic co-operation,[77] especially in the period of 'convalescence', and an end to 'abject poverty and unemployment'. The younger generation was characterised as 'virile, imaginative and alert' just as German youth was seen as having been misled by its rulers for a century or more. Elites on both sides of the conflict were seen as having failed. There is a clear feel of *mea culpa* coming from this document, inspired by a conscience-ridden Halifax and worked out in the Committee by the successor generation of Labour leaders and Edenite Tories. Only thus could such new departures as states surrendering some of their 'sovereign rights' and Europe being treated 'as a single whole' have been envisaged. Moreover a subtle and important shift in the purpose for which the war was being fought was evident in the statement (in Paragraph 13): 'we are prepared to cooperate with any state which shows that it genuinely seeks the peace and prosperity of the world by loyally observing its engagements to other states *and by ensuring individual liberty to its own citizens*' (my italics).

This condition arose naturally out of the belief that Hitlerism had to be destroyed, but the link between external aggression and the internal abuse of human rights (as they were later to be called) was now finally made. An inward-looking, conservative autocracy in Germany, such as might have been brought about by the Generals' coup hoped for in 1939, would presumably now not be enough.

By its very boldness, however watered-down and couched in more realistic language than Halifax's first flush of enthusiasm,[78] this kind of statement was bound to create problems and to strain the thin membrane of co-operation between the different political tendencies contained within the Coalition. The personal intimacies, even 'joie de découvrir', of the small Committee were not easily transplanted to the higher levels of Cabinet and party politics. The very nature of the open-ended thinking about the biggest of all possible issues was bound to open Pandora's box of disagreements and philosophical divisions which might otherwise have been left undisturbed, at least for the time being. The problems were compounded when the question arose of making a *public* statement even of general war aims, as this seemed likely to precipitate a storm of reaction and debate like that which Chamberlain's government had ridden out a year before. This time the feedback on a new, much less fundamentally consensual administration, and at a time when there was no military breathing space whatsoever, would be difficult to contain.

The knock-on effects of a further public venture into the war aims morass would be felt in all fields, diplomatic as well as domestic. In early 1941, the Foreign Secretary circulated to the War Aims Committee a document from the Polish Prime Minister-in-exile about the future evolution of Europe, which he envisaged as involving a far more extensive continental commitment for Britain and various boundary changes in the east. In Eden's view,

It would be difficult to subscribe to many of the aims set out in the British memorandum, and, if we were now to discuss them with the Polish Government, we could not avoid discouraging the Poles. This Polish memorandum therefore illustrates the difficulty of laying down our war aims in any detail now, and strengthens the case for confining ourselves to general terms in anything we say in public on this thorny subject.[79]

By the time these words were written certain important changes in the environment of Cabinet policy-making in war aims had taken place. Eden had replaced Halifax as Foreign Secretary and (a not entirely unconnected fact) the Prime Minister was waging an increasingly successful battle against making any public statement at all on war aims. Churchill had begun to realise that the War Aims Committee was releasing a good deal more pent-up intellectual and political energy than he had envisaged at the beginning, and his initial distracted benevolence soon waned. He had always taken the view that at this point it did not do 'to enter into refinements of policy unsuited to the tragic simplicity and grandeur of the times and the issues at stake'[80] and he generally avoided speaking in the parliamentary debates on war aims that left-wing MPs occasionally managed to engineer.[81] Even before he was moved, Halifax had come to think that the War Aims Committee's document would not 'in the last resort ever see light'.[82]

Once Churchill had the War Aims Committee's work in his hands, his lack of concern seems to have turned into positive antipathy. By the end of January 1941 he was telling Harry Hopkins, President Roosevelt's personal emissary 'all this talk about war aims was absurd at the present time: the Cabinet Committee to examine the question had produced a vague paper, four-fifths of which was from the Sermon on the Mount and the remainder an election address'.[83] This scathing dismissal referred undoubtedly to the impact of Halifax's Anglicanism and the Labour Party's domestic preoccupations on the Committee's draft, either of which was probably enough to kill off the idea of a statement in the Prime Minister's eyes, quite apart from the issue of priorities.

It was not so much that Churchill did not think about the need for post-war reform – at least in the international sphere. Indeed, in his first conversation with Hopkins he had had to go swiftly into reverse on hearing that Roosevelt was not interested in war aims, but only in the defeat of Hitler. The Prime Minister had been assuming, with his Cabinet, that the United States wanted to hear 'that we were not devoid of all thoughts of the future'.[84] Churchill also liked to sketch out his own grand plans for post-war Councils and Confederations in Europe, so long as those were confined to the same small hours in which he watched Marx Brothers films or ranged conversationally back and forth over history.⁸⁵

The Prime Minister seems to have been disappointed by the product of the Committee's labours, and this allowed his natural doubts to flourish, encouraged somewhat unexpectedly by Roosevelt and Hopkins. The War Cabinet had a short discussion on war aims on 20 January 1941, precipitated by a Parliamentary Question from the Liberal MP Geoffrey Mander. The impersonal minute suggests a prime-ministerial kiss of death for the Committee's draft statement, which 'it was suggested . . . while admirable in many respects, would not, in its present form, impress public opinion'.[86] Other ministers pointed out that there was 'considerable demand' for a general statement 'of what we were fighting for' but in the end the War Cabinet only invited the Prime Minister to answer Mander's question 'in such a manner as to leave the way open for a statement of our War Aims to be made in general terms on behalf of the Government, but without implying that such a statement was likely to be made in the immediate future'. That Churchill's hand was decisive in imposing a freeze on the draft statement is confirmed by Duff Cooper's caution ten days later in urging Greenwood to consult Churchill – 'as the Prime Minister holds strong views on the subject' – before encouraging the discussion of war aims on the BBC.[87]

Churchill was under various kinds of pressure to go ahead with a statement at this time. He was engaged in a blunt exchange of views with Cecil King of the *Daily Mirror* who was advocating a speech on the question, and tried to distract King by encouraging him to submit a personal memorandum on war aims. Nonetheless, Churchill could not resist repeating what he had said to Mander in the Commons, namely 'that most right-minded people are well aware of what we are fighting for'.[88] It was around the same time that Harold Nicolson committed the *faux pas* which probably cost him his job (and perhaps that of his chief, Duff Cooper, as well), with an article in the New York *Nation* on, *inter alia*, war aims. Churchill was furious: 'It is most improper that an Under-Secretary should attempt to declare the policy of the Government on the gravest matters, especially when I have on several occasions deprecated any attempt to declare war aims.'[89] This was a new policy position, which had emerged more by default and changing prime-ministerial convictions than by any clear-cut process of decision. Thinking about the long term was no longer so acceptable, especially in public. By March it was clear to an occasional visitor like W. P. Crozier of the *Manchester Guardian* that the Prime Minister was firmly against a statement on what Crozier termed 'peace aims',[90] and Churchill himself began to feel under less pressure: 'Agitation here has died down.'[91]

There may have been something of a sub-text to Churchill's growing resistance to following the logic of the Committee which he had agreed to set up the previous August. The relationship between the Prime Minister and his Foreign Secretary, an inherently tense affair, had been given extra edge by the facts that Halifax had had first option on the premiership in May and had opposed Churchill's bravado in June. The evidence suggests that the latter was gradually becoming disillusioned with his most senior colleague, and that Halifax's performance in the van of the War Aims Committee was one significant factor in hastening disenchantment on.

In the first instance, there had been the 'Prytz affair' in June, when R. A. Butler and perhaps Halifax had talked incautiously to the Swedish Minister in London, Björn Prytz, about the possibility of peace.[92] Whatever Butler's guilt in that matter, there is no doubt that the Prime Minister had had the strongest suspicions of a resurgence of appeasement, and that Halifax himself was contaminated by the slur of defeatism after June 1940. The admonition delivered over the Foreign Office's answer to the King of Sweden[93] was an early sign of Churchill's dissatisfaction, and in early October he clashed in Cabinet twice with Halifax, over a Foreign Office statement that it was not in British interests for the USA to become involved in war in the Pacific and then over the question of promising eventual negotiations over Gibraltar so as to buy off Franco.[94] This was the day after Churchill, in a reshuffle, had offered Halifax the choice of staying at the Foreign Office or becoming Lord President of the Council (he chose to stay on).[95] The perpetual undertow in their relations was, however, the knowledge of past and perhaps continuing differences over peace-making. A strange entry in Halifax's diary for late October refers to a Cabinet discussion over prolonging the life of Parliament, 'many people rightly feeling that it was impossible to tie our hands over the matter of an election which might be desirable should any profound difference on war or peace policy emerge'.[96]

Apart from his suspicions of Halifax's attachment to appeasement, however, Churchill was not a natural supporter of the Foreign Office as an institution – as is often the case with Prime Ministers who have themselves never been Foreign Secretary. In October he passed the time on a train journey from Scotland by abusing the Foreign Office in the company of Sir John Dill, the Chief of the Imperial General Staff: 'What is wanted in that department is a substantial application of the boot.'97

Whether Churchill would have been able to disencumber himself of Halifax if Lord Lothian had not died in his post as Ambassador to the United States is a moot point, but his offer to Halifax of a change of office in October, his known desire to have Eden at the Foreign Office and in the War Cabinet and his subsequently critical behaviour once the possibility of a change had occurred are all strong pointers to its likelihood. Yet the move when it came, in December 1940, was opportunistic. Lothian's death was unexpected, and Halifax's name only occurred to Churchill after his first preference, Lloyd George, had turned the post down. Moreover it was a genuinely vital matter that someone of seniority and experience should represent Britain in the United States at a time when it was trying to lure the latter into the war.

These facts did not, however, dispel the gloom which descended on the Foreign Secretary when offered the new appointment, and it is clear that he only accepted out of a sense of duty, putting the final decision in Churchill's hands after making it clear that he did not wish to go.98 One of the Prime Minister's strongest arguments in favour of the change was his powerful political criticism of Halifax as the last of the appeasers, who was now attracting the public odium which had previously focused on Chamberlain, who had died six weeks earlier. The monthly censorship reports (a forerunner of the image-contests by opinion poll which now rule democratic politics) were apparently pointing to Halifax's increasing unpopularity, and with the new spirit of coalition unity abroad (which the Foreign Secretary himself was promoting so keenly in the War Aims Committee), he 'had no future in this country'.99

That Churchill was relieved to have acquired a Foreign Secretary with whom he was in sympathy is evident from his up-beat comment of only two weeks later that 'I think Anthony is putting his hand on the Foreign Office. I see a different touch in the telegrams.'100 What had almost become a contempt for Halifax and the ministers of the Chamberlain Cabinet, at first barely acknowledged by Churchill himself, came out in February in a vituperative note to Halifax over the very issue of war aims. At Churchill's original suggestion, the new Ambassador was planning to give a speech to the Pilgrims' Dinner in

New York largely based on his 'spiritual' paper for the War Aims Committee, and he submitted the speech to Downing Street.[101] Churchill's language was unrestrained:

> I do not understand how the whole world can be compelled to join together to bring the world back to health... All the thought in these few paragraphs suffers from being both hackneyed and loose. There is no truth in it anywhere. I should strongly advise recasting on less ambitious lines. It is a pretty tough job to reshape human society in an after-dinner speech.[102]

The Prime Minister even went on to mock Halifax's predictions about state service being the leitmotif of the western world, in the light of the aristocrat's known preference for fox-hunting on his estate. Thus Churchill poured scorn on his ex-colleague and on the work of the War Aims Committee. The Prime Minister had given the planners the benefit of the doubt in setting up the Committee, but he had finally lost patience and, through a combination of personality and institutional powers, he had won the battle over whether a formal statement should be made by the government. The Committee's draft only ever appeared in the form of Halifax's speech in Washington.[103] Even then, the Prime Minister exerted some influence (asserting, strangely enough, a preference for the general paragraphs on values), and Halifax was cautious enough to leave out the sentence from the draft about nations having to be prepared to surrender some of their sovereign rights. Halifax stood enough of his ground to go ahead with the speech, telling Churchill that 'the peroration of the Gettysburg address might also have been accused of loose thinking', but he had clearly been stung at this careless exercise of prime-ministerial authority.[104]

Churchill was not alone in his growing feeling that a statement on war aims might be a distraction and a snare. Across the party divide, he was supported by Dalton and to a lesser extent Bevin, just as on the other side Halifax and Duff Cooper had joined forces in the Committee with Attlee, Harcourt Johnstone and Toynbee. Dalton believed that 'victory was the first priority' and thus a concern for war aims tended to get in the way. Bevin, despite being a prime mover in the War Aims Committee to get domestic reform on the policy agenda, was also of Churchill's view that not too much intellectual self-indulgence could be afforded.[105] This meant that the Committee, while generally agreed on themes and the need for a statement, was not able to sustain its case in the wider policy-making context, whether inside or outside the Cabinet room. By sitting on the draft and becoming steadily more aggressive in his refusal to make a public statement during the first three months of 1941, the Prime Minister was able to win the short-term phase of what had become a distinctly understated political struggle. Halifax's speech in New York, although made by an ambassador who was still technically a member of the War Cabinet and receiving a good deal of publicity, was not of the same order as Chamberlain's statement to Parliament of 12 October 1939, as both Churchill and his critics in the House of Commons realised only too well.[106] Moreover, of the two prime movers in the War Aims Committee Halifax had been moved overseas and Duff Cooper was soon to go the same way, after becoming discredited as Minister of Information.[107]

FROM WAR AIMS TO RECONSTRUCTION

If a dominant Prime Minister can exert his will even over a united Cabinet Committee, particularly when, as here, it is a matter of avoiding change rather than imposing it, this does not mean that he always wins the longer-term battle. Institutional advantage at the apex of the Cabinet system does not necessarily translate into the control of ideas, agenda and implementation throughout the policy-making process. In this case, for example, although the Labour members of the War Cabinet (whom Churchill could not send abroad on diplomatic duty) did not make an issue of the war aims statement, they were ultimately able to turn it to their advantage. In the first instance Churchill was careful to match the abolition of the War Aims Committee by the creation of a new Reconstruction Problems Committee. Although Attlee did not take on the job of Chairman of the new Committee, his colleague Arthur Greenwood, Minister without Portfolio, was appointed. To a degree this was a subtle way of further down-grading the work of long-term planning, as Greenwood's reputation was being increasingly called into question and he was to be replaced as Committee Chairman in February 1942 by Sir William Jowitt, at that time the Solicitor-General.[108] But the crucial point from Labour's point of view was that the torch had been handed down and not extinguished. Indeed the Prime Minister seemed increasingly willing to hand over consideration of reconstruction issues to Labour, in return for their acquiescence in his dominance in military affairs and in the effective decision not to go ahead with the public debate on war aims which a statement would engender.[109]

This was important to Churchill not only because he could then concentrate on fighting the war but because a damping down of the intellectual side of war aims discussion meant avoiding issues out of which Labour could have made considerable capital, such as collective security and European federalism. Debate on such matters, with the emotional questions of sovereignty and nationalism lurking behind them, would endanger national unity in the short run and raise hares in the long run with the potential to damage the values Churchill stood for at home and abroad.

Thus although this latest round of war aims discussions had begun with a perceived need to counter Hitler's proposals for a new international economic order, it changed character after less than six months to concentrate as much on domestic as foreign policy issues. The very change in nomenclature, from 'war aims' to 'reconstruction', was revealing, the latter being more neutral and noncommittal, as well as implying a focus on the physical problems of rebuilding Britain after the destruction of war.

The seeds of this change can be spotted right back at the beginning of 1940, when references to 'reconstruction' can occasionally be found.[110] Later in the year the very existence of the War Aims Committee naturally stimulated further thoughts on the concept, and there began to be talk of a Reconstruction Ministry, just as there had been calls for a Ministry of Supply the previous year. (The Prime Minister was also actually asked in the House of Commons to set up a Cabinet committee on reconstruction.[111]) The discussion of a secretariat for the War Aims Committee (at that time seen as continuing), by raising the question of what tasks such a staff should take on, meant that reconstruction was on the policy-making agenda.[112] The Foreign Office, aware of the pitfalls of considering new frontiers or regimes, also reasserted the importance of 'the economic aspect of war aims' so as to inspire the countries of Europe once again 'with the will to live as independent entities'.[113]

There seems little doubt that the increasing talk of reconstruction provided the Prime Minister with the opportunity he wanted of diverting attention away from the war aims at the level of high international politics. Equally, a Cabinet committee was a useful device for avoiding the full-scale Ministry of Reconstruction which Churchill thought would be *de trop*[114] (despite its nominal confidentiality, the existence of the Cabinet Committee was common knowledge.)[115] Churchill flattered Greenwood with talk of the importance of chairing a committee on reconstruction (the invitation came just before the turn of the year) and made it clear that 'the general aim will be to obtain a body of practical proposals which will command broadly the support of the main elements in all the political parties'.[116]

The Prime Minister's main concern was to avoid internal strife in the midst of military vulnerability, and to this extent he was constrained by the political context of a Coalition Cabinet. It was a bonus, but essentially a secondary matter, if ways of maintaining consensus could be found which also denied advantage to his domestic political opponents – as sitting on the war aims statement seemed to do. He thus envisaged the advent of the new committee as marking the end of an increasingly inconvenient chapter in policy-making, and the start of a new, more decisive one. Getting rapidly into his stride, Churchill instructed the Cabinet Secretary: 'The Committee on War Aims has largely completed its work in the draft statement which it has drawn up and which should now be circulated to the War Cabinet. In any case war aims is quite a different matter from the reconstruction of this country, which is entrusted to the Minister without Portfolio.'[117]

Greenwood rapidly took up the lead given by his Prime Minister, and personally ensured that the title of the new committee referred to 'reconstruction' rather than 'war aims'.[118] His reply showed that he and Attlee, in Bridges' words, saw 'the working out of our war aims in the foreign and domestic spheres as essentially complementary' because planning a 'better Britain' would be an earnest to the peoples of Europe that a British-inspired order would be worth fighting for.[119] The Committee should deal with 'matters of principle' while the departments and their outside contacts worked out detailed, practical and consensual plans for the future.[120]

Unfortunately this conception of the intellectual division of labour did not wholly mesh with the Prime Minister's view of reconstruction as 'prompt first aid to lightly wounded houses' and the like, which were to have 'marked precedence over attractive plans for the post-war period'.[121] It led to Bridges expressing his own confusion as to whether the Committee was to be a high-level political body working out principles (Greenwood's conception) or 'a working Committee to thrash out schemes' with departmental representatives.

The Cabinet Secretary clearly felt he knew the Minister without Portfolio's interests better than he did himself, for he recommended 'with great respect' and because 'it would really be much more satisfactory to Mr. Greenwood in the long run' the second option, on the grounds that issues of principle would have to come to Cabinet anyway, while senior ministers were too busy to get much involved in reconstruction plans.[122]

Bridges knew his man, and Churchill minuted agreement. Moreover he soon wrote to Greenwood expressing the hope that 'it will not be necessary to come to the Cabinet until after the next few critical months are over, by which time you should have accumulated a considerable volume of material, and surveyed the entire field'.[123] By keeping reconstruction issues away from Cabinet, Churchill was attempting to sideline them, rather than, in the manner of some Prime Ministers with Cabinet committees, reserving them for the attention of his more reliable colleagues. This is evident from the composition of the Reconstruction Problems Committee, which was deliberately altered from that of its predecessor.[124]

It will be seen from Table 9 that three of the eight members of the War Cabinet sat on the Reconstruction Problems Committee, including the two most senior Labour representatives. The Conservatives counted six of the twelve members, including two heavyweights in Kingsley Wood and Viscount Cranborne. Their numerical monopoly of the departments which would be expected to implement reconstruction plans was a check and a balance to Labour's evident ideological leadership of the Committee.

Of the seven members of the old War Aims Committee, four survived onto the new body, namely Attlee, Cranborne, Kingsley Wood and Harcourt Johnstone. Halifax, Duff Cooper and Bevin were not carried over, although Bevin was influential in ensuring that Attlee joined Greenwood on the Committee.[125] It is significant that the Foreign Office was only represented by a Parliamentary Under-Secretary, and one, R. A. Butler, who could not afford another false step after the Prytz affair of 1940.[126] With the Ministry of Information not being represented, the concern for public relations which had helped to give birth to the War Aims Committee was left behind.

Greenwood made a half-hearted attempt to widen the scope of the Committee by asking to bring in Dalton, Amery and the Parliamentary Secretaries to the Board of Education and the Ministry of Ship-

Table 9. *Initial membership of the Reconstruction Problems Committee of the War Cabinet, March 1941*

Arthur Greenwood* (Chairman)	Minister without Portfolio	Labour
Clement Attlee*	Lord Privy Seal	Labour
Lord Reith	Minister of Works and Buildings	
Viscount Cranborne	Secretary of State for the Dominions	Conservative
Sir Kingsley Wood*	Chancellor of the Exchequer	Conservative
R. A. Butler	Parliamentary Under-Secretary at the Foreign Office	Conservative
Robert Hudson	Minister of Agriculture and Fisheries	Conservative
Colonel J. Moore-Brabazon	Minister of Transport	Conservative
Thomas Johnston (only included after protest at his exclusion)	Secretary of State for Scotland	Labour
Ernest Brown	Minister for Health	Liberal National
Harcourt Johnstone	Secretary of the Board of Overseas Trade	Liberal
Charles Waterhouse	Parliamentary Secretary to the President of the Board of Trade	Conservative

* = member of the War Cabinet

ping, but Bridges prompted Churchill to reject this on the grounds that the Committee would then be too big. The case for the offended Secretary of State for Scotland's inclusion proved unanswerable, by contrast, but Bevin was unable to get a place for his own permanent representative. Churchill consoled him by saying that all important material would have to come to Cabinet in any case, and 'you are no more committed to any conclusions reached than I am'.[127] The Prime Minister was keeping the ministers whose help with the war he valued most, such as Bevin, Beaverbrook, Anderson and Eden, away from such distractions. He told Greenwood that a high-level Committee with political balance could not relieve the Cabinet of its ultimate responsibility on questions of principle, while 'It will not be possible for any of the Ministers in charge of Departments mainly concerned with the conduct of the war, to pay real attention to post-war reconstruction.'[128] The Committee should therefore be composed of departments with a practical interest in reconstruction. The small War Cabinet and the Coalition meant that inner Cabinets were not likely to develop, but insofar as the big guns of Churchill's Cabinet in 1941 are identifiable, only Attlee served on the Reconstruction Problems Committee, a mark of its initial status.

The terms of reference of the new Committee showed remarkable continuity with those of its predecessor, with two significant exceptions. The War Aims Committee's brief was inherited *in toto*, but the order in which the two aims were listed was reversed. Thus, where the War Aims Committee had had as its first aim 'suggestions in regard to a post-war European and world system', for the Reconstruction Problems Committee this was relegated to second place behind the domestic goal of perpetuating national unity 'through a social and economic structure designed to secure equality of opportunity and service among all classes of the community'. Moreover, tacked on to the beginning of this domestic section was the requirement of 'the preparation of practical schemes of reconstruction, to which effect can be given in a period of, say, three years after the war'.[129] In one way this reformulation stood as a Churchillian rebuke to the high-flown generalities of Halifax, Toynbee and Duff Cooper, but it also reflected the desire of the Labour Party to set in train plans for social and economic reforms.

Despite the Bridges/Churchill move at the end of January to keep the Committee practical and 'principles' reserved for the Cabinet, Greenwood does not appear to have been diverted. Despite the work already done by the War Aims Committee, and accepting that in the first instance his Committee would concentrate on data-collection, he saw it as giving 'general guidance on policy not meticulous examination of details'.[130] When the Committee met for the first time, on 6 March, Greenwood made a genuflection in the direction of the Prime Minister by saying that 'the major decisions would be for the War Cabinet' and that the Committee would do nothing to distract from the primary task of winning the war, but in the paper he prepared before the meeting he talked of the Committee framing 'a comprehensive reconstruction policy which can be recommended to the War Cabinet' and of many plans necessarily being produced before the end of the war.[131] He saw public opinion as an ally in this high-profile approach.[132]

EPILOGUE

The Greenwood Committee suffered from the political decline of its Chairman and from the Prime Minister's patronising neglect. After the early burst of activity in setting it up, and three meetings before the end of May, it met only once more before the end of the year, and was eventually overtaken by other committees and the gale of publicity anticipating the Beveridge Report. It suffered from interdepartmental sensitivities, and in particular from the lack of interest of Eden's Foreign Office in putting forth schemes on the international side. Greenwood himself did not encourage the Committee to take part in foreign policy discussions, and was probably happy to concentrate on the Labour Party's strongest ground. For fear of stirring up a hornets' nest abroad, he also agreed to an altering of the terms of reference given to the Foreign Research and Press Service (FRPS) of Chatham House (which was to do a considerable amount of work for the Committee) so as to avoid giving publicity to that blunt directive in the terms of reference proper towards 'the problem of adjusting the free life of small countries in a durable international order'.[133]

It is this very caution about upsetting the Prime Minister and the Foreign Secretary which paradoxically reveals the difficulty experienced by a foreign policy executive in the British Cabinet system, particularly under conditions of stress, in controlling all aspects of the foreign policy system. For Greenwood and his like-minded colleagues were thereby buying themselves time and space to develop their own priorities. Churchill had exiled Halifax, and failed to make the expected war aims statement, but he had not been able to prevent his new Ambassador in Washington from using the War Aims Committee's material in his own widely noticed speech. Equally, he deprived the Reconstruction Problems Committee of prominence and Cabinet time, but only at the price of setting in progress a huge mass of research work and contacts with informed outsiders which was eventually to create the new domestic reality in which he had to work.[134] Expectations were aroused among the thousands hungry for ideals and some prospect of real social change by such announcements as that which promised a Ministry of Reconstruction 'when the end of the war can be more clearly foreseen'.[135] Paul Addison's images cannot be bettered. He wrote of the War Aims Committee as the 'first of an unbroken relay of committees, each of which handed over the baton of reconstruction to the next, reaching all the way through to the last meeting of the principal Reconstruction Committee in 1945'. Of the Prime Minister, Addison wrote that reconstruction could not come about through Churchill: 'But gradually it flowed around and past him, like a tide cutting off an island from the shore.'[136]

Perhaps most indicative of this paradox was the speech given by Anthony Eden at the Mansion House on 29 May 1941 (see excerpts from this speech in Appendix 5, below). On the surface it was the product of the Prime Minister's priorities. The speech was largely practical, in that it dealt with economic issues rather than spiritual needs, while plans for the post-war order in Europe were eschewed in favour of the immediate war. Indeed the speech drew only indirectly on the work of the War Aims and Reconstruction Problems Committees.[137] Yet in another important sense this was the war aims speech which Churchill had refused to give. The pressure of steam had finally built up to the point where an outlet was found. Returning to the attack on Hitler's 'New Order' plans which had been the fount of the War Aims Committee in the first place, the Foreign Secretary described (inelegantly, and with what might be thought in the circumstances a degree of dissimulation) how the government had given 'careful thought' to the question of the future of Europe, which would 'depend upon how moral and material construction is brought about throughout the world'; 'social security must be the first object of our domestic policy after the war. And social security will be our policy abroad not less than at home.' Eden went on to talk of the reconstruction of Europe involving a 'peaceful brotherhood of nations' and a new form of international economic system. If in rather a general way, he was thus delivering the positive statement of British objectives for which so many had been calling over the previous year. That Eden was drawing on a slightly different strand of work, that of J. M. Keynes, is of less significance than the fact that the speech was given at all, and thereby encouraged what soon was to become an unstoppable wave of interest in a new post-war order.[138] *The Times* talked of the Foreign Secretary having spoken 'with the full weight of Cabinet authority' and argued that it was vital to plan ahead: 'it is welcome news that the British Government are fully alive to the urgency of the task'.[139] In any case, Keynes had been working for both the Treasury and the Foreign Office in that fluid period around the turn of the year when both war aims and reconstruction had been thought about simultaneously, and his ideas fell on ground already prepared by the Cabinet Committees. Eden played his hand skilfully in obtaining permission from Churchill to publicise this 'economic manifesto' even though in reality his speech contained many of the same kind of grand platitudes which Halifax had been criticised for. Indeed, Lindemann summarised Keynes' paper for the Prime Minister to the effect that 'it does not seem to us that there is any pledge sufficiently clear to be a possible source of embarrassment'.[140]

In all this the War Cabinet had been kept informed, but remained in the background. In such trying times anything with less than urgent priority was bound to be kept away from those most pressed with responsibility. This was also the period when the 'children's hour' for ministers 'below the line' fell into disuse, and there was sufficient talk of prime-ministerial dictatorship to encourage *déracinés* such as Hankey to engage in whispering campaigns against Churchill.[141] Nonetheless, the Cabinet system as a whole still proved capable of coping with the need to consider the longer view, and of preserving an element of genuine collectivity at the apex of government. From his point of view the Prime Minister was right to look with suspicion on the Cabinet Committees dealing with war aims. Although he was able to impose a good deal of discipline on them in the short run, his very concession in setting them up began a process, intellectual and political, which he proved unable in the end to control. Churchill could not focus on all areas of activity with the same intensity, and without his personal chairmanship, or that of a close ally, the War aims and Reconstruction Problems Committees proved both an important outlet for the ideas of Labour and reforming Tory ministers and a catalyst for the progressive ideas latent among the 'attentive public'. They were another important demonstration of the importance of context to the degree of control over government exerted even by strong Prime Ministers.

8. DECISION-MAKING IN CABINET

Between them, the six case-studies in this book have generated a wealth of material on the Cabinet and foreign policy, and each of them could easily have been replicated six times over – such is the level of business conducted by a major power in a period of stress, and the consequent size of the archives available to scholars. The law of diminishing marginal returns, however, means that conclusions become apparent well before every seam has been mined, and this is the basis on which the case-study method is justified. The intention here has been, by focusing on a limited period, to provide a cross-section through the British foreign policy process at its highest level, and from an analytical perspective. It is now possible to summarise the themes which have been emerging in the course of the empirical investigation represented by these cases.

The main focus has been on the nature of Cabinet government in the context of foreign policy, a subject which has so far not attracted detailed attention. The related but rather varied kinds of problem which we have seen the British government tackling between 1938 and 1941 have not produced direct support for either of the two main schools of thought on the operations of the Cabinet in general, which James Barber has called 'the Presidential school' and 'the chairmanship school'.[1] Although any great debate such as this tends to harden into a series of over-simplifications, the argument about whether the Prime Minister dominates or merely orchestrates the Cabinet is still one of the main issues in the study of British politics. But as Barber has recognised, there is room for a middle way: 'both the presidential and chairmanship schools give too fixed a view of the Prime Minister's power and position by failing to recognize many of the variables that affect his position'.[2] The issue remains, however, not only of what those factors might be (and Barber suggests some of the more important, such as the roles of party and of personality), but also of the conditions which affect their variation.

In these years, famous for their associations with the names of Chamberlain and Churchill, it is difficult to get away from the view that there is considerable evidence for the pre-eminence of the Prime Minister. Inevitably modern Prime Ministers do get drawn into the daily business of diplomacy to act as a kind of meta-Foreign Secretary, particularly when the realm is emperilled, as Chamberlain had concluded during September 1938. And there is a great deal of routine executive decision-making, much of it involving important discretionary powers, which together 10 Downing Street and King Charles Street tend to monopolise. Examples outside the strict confines of our six cases are easy to find, such as the decision to visit Mussolini in Rome, which was announced to officials in late October 1938, but not to the Cabinet until 30 November.[3] There was also the recognition of the Franco regime in February 1939, which Chamberlain and Halifax had urged from the start of the year and undertook on their own initiative after getting the Cabinet's broad approval in principle. They had simply by-passed the embryonic opposition in the Foreign Policy Committee from Stanley and Vansittart.[4] Similarly Churchill developed his personal diplomatic relationship with Franklin Roosevelt independently of both his Foreign Secretary and his Cabinet and probably because of the advantage that it gave him in both talking to the United States without having to go through the Foreign Office and representing the American position to his colleagues.[5]

On the other hand, all that the above examples could prove, were they to be multiplied infinitely, is that the executive is often capable of considerable influence over significant decisions, particularly in the realm of implementation.[6] While each illustration gives us important insights into how executive discretion operated in practice, together they are far from enabling us to go beyond this to prove that a narrow circle was structurally predominant in the making of foreign policy (although the logical jump is often made). A list of such examples does not explain why it is that many vital decisions seem to have been subject to a much wider circle of participation, and that equally striking lists can be compiled of these decisions. The Anglo-Soviet negotiations, the crisis of September 1939 and deliberation over war aims in 1939 and 1940 are examples which have been examined in detail here. A contemporary insider was virulent in defence of the Cabinet's reputation:

> It would be the height of ignorance to suppose that foreign policy in matters of this importance [he was referring to the Manchurian affair of 1932] is the personal affair of a particular minister; all important foreign issues, and especially if they have serious implications, are brought before the whole Cabinet at practically every meeting and every Cabinet Minister is supplied with all the dispatches.[7]

On the other hand it would be just as wrong to go to the opposite extreme and assume that the Cabinet was able to set the parameters for all the major decisions, even if the foreign policy executive (Prime Minister and Foreign Secretary) enjoyed certain day-to-day powers. The latter's forcing of the pace in pushing through the Polish Guarantee, together with Churchill's irresistible leadership during the crisis of mid-1940, stand in the way of such a conclusion.

The truth is that in the foreign policy cases under the microscope here policy-making at Cabinet level was too complex to exhibit any simple pattern. Bipolar models which generalise in ascribing ultimate power in the system to Prime Minister or Cabinet do not come near to being adequate explanations. It has been apparent that inside the circle of government there was a variety of ways in which policies were produced, that there was no single source of power and that stable coalitions were not formed.[8]

This is the case even if we disaggregate the period and talk about the separate administrations of Chamberlain and Churchill. Both men, by repute forceful and egocentric leaders, were in fact capable of bowing to the collective wisdom of their colleagues, if at times under duress. Neville Chamberlain may have actually considered resignation over the decision ultimately to go for a Soviet alliance on 24 May 1939, and was forced in the most humiliating fashion on 2 September to do the will of a group of Cabinet rebels – even if to some extent he was here the victim of a misunderstanding. At other times, particularly during the manic activity of late March 1939 but also during some phases of the more measured deliberations of 6–12 October, he was able to take a clear lead and carry colleagues along with him. Thus there was no definite style of Chamberlainite foreign policy-making in Cabinet.

Equally, even the ebullience of Winston Churchill, which so impressed itself on his fellow-ministers (and irritated some of them) from the outset of the war, had to be expressed in the context of a War Cabinet which was small but also ultra-sensitive to its responsibilities for safeguarding the national interest, sometimes from what Cadogan called the Prime Minister's 'rhodomontades'. In the early and most dangerous days of his premiership (from the national if not the personal point of view), Churchill had to face the outright alarm of Halifax and the more cautiously expressed concern of Chamberlain and some other ministers over his assumption that his instinct for fighting on whatever the risks was the only basis on which to make war policy. Later on in our period (although still at a relatively early stage of Churchill's term of office), the Prime Minister found that he was able to frustrate the hopes of those who wanted to raise the war aims issue to the status of major national debate, but unable to stop the inexorable forward momentum of the discussion inside both government and party-political circles. Preoccupied with the war on a daily basis (and unable there always to impose his will on the military), Churchill had the capacity to make the war aims lobby take cover but not to make them give up their campaign.

Strong Prime Ministers, then, may get their way some of the time over foreign policy matters, but they do not succeed on every issue, or even on every aspect of issues where they do score a success. It is inconvenient, and to some extent tedious, to have to conclude, as so often, that the truth is a complicated affair. This does not mean, however, that no patterns are to be found, beyond that of the uniqueness of each event. It will have been evident from the discussion which has gone before that the intention is to construct an argument which accounts for the diversity without resort to procrustean methods.

There are various candidates for the status of underlying explanation. Two of the strongest are the special characteristics of the period under review and the possibility of the powers of Prime Minister or Cabinet having evolved over time, and in a way susceptible to logical explanation. Let us consider these in turn.

The reasons both for choosing the period from Munich to Barbarossa and for regarding it as not wholly untypical of British foreign policy in the twentieth century have been outlined at length in chapter 1. If they are sound, then it follows that the evidence of actual Cabinet behaviour should tell us something about the policy process at the end of the 1930s, and possibly also things which may be applied to other decades. Nonetheless, each period has its own distinctive character, which will always be an important (but not exclusive) determinant of the actions which take place within it. In other words, how much of the variety which was evident between

1938 and 1941 in terms of relations between the Cabinet and its foreign policy executive can be accounted for by the major pressures of those years, and in particular the high salience of foreign policy within them, even by the standards of a country habituated to the great issues of international politics?

It would be foolish to deny that this kind of explanation has a good deal of power. Certainly from 15 March 1939, when the superficial optimism of the previous week suffered such a body-blow, the minds of all ministers were concentrated increasingly on events in central Europe, and the atmosphere of crisis, even violence, grew more palpable by the day. Once war finally broke out, the government acquired an effective operational criterion for distinguishing between its priorities: winning the war meant that certain concerns were mandatory and that others could, with relief, be shelved. In these circumstances, it might be argued (although it has not often been so) that it was not surprising if on some occasions the Cabinet should gratefully accept a decisive lead, while on others ministers should feel impelled to take risks with their posts which they might ordinarily think better of, by standing up against a Prime Minister whose judgement could literally have had fatal consequences. This highlighting of the criterion of the national interest as a motivation for ministers, would, for example, explain the behaviour of a relatively junior minister such as Hore-Belisha, who avoided resigning from Chamberlain's Cabinet as Duff Cooper had done over Munich and therefore accepted various prime-ministerial decisions with which he was unhappy, but also reached certain sticking-points at which he was prepared to display insubordination.

Yet the notion that the period is enough to explain the ups and downs of policy-making in Cabinet, through stimulating interest in struggles over foreign policy questions, also has important limitations. One might expect, for example, that the impact of circumstance would certainly extend to the division that occurs in these years between war and peace, between Cabinet and War Cabinet. Yet there is no strong evidence for such a view. In the first instance the Chamberlain administration ran on until May 1940, with Churchill a loyal (if increasingly obstreperous) member of it. There appears to have been no sharp break in the pattern of relationships between the Prime Minister and his principal colleagues once war had been declared, although of course the majority of the Cabinet proper was now outside the inner circle of the strategic direction of the war, and had to be content with departmental powers, and the weekly 'children's hour' briefing by a member of the War Cabinet. No grand rebellions were staged or major anxieties expressed about what we might now see as the evident unsuitability of Chamberlain for the challenges facing a wartime Prime Minister. On all sides there was something of a determination not to rock the boat unnecessarily, until Churchill could no longer contain his impatience to pull defence policy together, and then to initiate action in Scandinavia – a course which ironically gained him Chamberlain's job, rather than the ignominy of a second Dardanelles, as might so easily have been the case.

Perhaps the dividing-line should more properly be drawn between *de facto* peace and hot war, between the Phoney War and the real conflict of April 1940 onwards, rather than at the formal beginning of 3 September 1939. But this too makes little difference in terms of our understanding of the patterns of Cabinet behaviour. The onset of authentic military crisis did rapidly bring down Chamberlain, but it involved the dislodging of an administration and its outlook by a wholly exceptional parliamentary demonstration. It was not the product of an intra-governmental conflict. Indeed, Sir Samuel Hoare, who had been one of Chamberlain's main opponents over the Soviet Union, was a main target in the newly confident backlash against the appeasers, and had to go into exile as Ambassador in Madrid. Oliver Stanley (Hoare's comrade-in-arms over the USSR) was the other prominent minister to leave the government, while Chamberlain and Simon were demoted.

Furthermore, if anything, the crisis should have made the emergence of strong leadership from the top more likely. This, after all, was why Churchill had been preferred and why Halifax had instinctively felt himself unsuited to be premier. As history knows, Churchill rose to the challenge, but as much in terms of his impact on the British people as in terms of his domination of the War Cabinet. For although, with Chamberlain's evident physical decline, Churchill was by far the strongest personality and the most experienced politician in the government, he was still constrained by the need to sustain the new national Coalition and to avoid alienating Labour leaders. In practice this did not mean diluting the firmness of his positions on matters which he regarded as vital. But it did mean effectively that even in the foreign policy area, which Churchill might have been forgiven in the circumstances for regarding as his *chasse gardée*, compromises were necessary. Thus the Prime Minister was willing to concede the possibility of some future negotiated peace to his critics during the tense days of late May 1940, even if he proved capable over the next few months of eventually putting his stamp on policy and steadily excluding a compromise peace from the realm of the thinkable. Equally, he found it necessary to allow the War Aims Committee of the Cabinet to set under way the process of long-term planning of which he was so profoundly distrustful, and – needing his Minister of Labour's support on the war effort – did not obstruct Bevin's initiatives towards the reform of the Diplomatic Service, made rather prematurely in 1940 and culminating in Eden's White paper of January 1943.[9] Moreover, although Churchill was able by 1941 to cut down the number of War Cabinet meetings a little, he found it much more difficult to restrict the attendance of ministers who were not full members of the War Cabinet, despite several attempts to do so.[10]

War, whether phoney or real, therefore naturally had its impact on the nature of government, but there were not sharp enough differences between the before and after conditions for us to build a theory of Cabinet foreign policy-making on its impact. The same goes for the contrast between Chamberlain's National Government, and Churchill's all-party Coalition. Each had its unique features and bore the stamp of its leader's personality, but each also contained a range of types of ministerial relationship, party traditions and inputs into policy. Thus it seems unlikely that the fact of a shifting time-frame is a sufficient explanation for the varying forms of Cabinet government we have observed. The drama of the years between Munich and the invasion of the USSR undoubtedly made for an electric political atmosphere and sensitised all in Cabinet to the importance of their responsibilities, but it did not in itself determine a particular distribution of power in Cabinet, whether hierarchical or multipolar.

The second possible explanation for the variable pattern evident in the cases under review is what might be termed the learning-curve hypothesis, that is, the possibility that changes took place in relations between the Cabinet and its foreign policy executive over time, but that a new configuration necessarily took time to achieve and to settle down, thus accounting for a certain unpredictability in the events in the Cabinet room. This could work both ways, in that it is plausible to argue that disillusion gradually set in with Neville

Chamberlain as 1939 wore on, producing an initial clash in April and May over the Soviet Union and culminating in the ultimatum on the night of 2 September. Thereafter, the fire went out of the Prime Minister, as much because he was hemmed in by watchful colleagues as because of the psychological defeat of having to declare war. On the other side, it is possible to see Churchill as having also been subject to a learning-curve, in that he entered office in a position of weakness, not even as leader of the Conservative Party, and unable to dispense with the services of the men who had ignored him in 1938–9. Yet, with the passing of time, he was able to assert himself over colleagues from all parties, take over from Chamberlain as leader of the Conservatives and replace Halifax with Eden at the Foreign Office.

Once again, such interpretations have substance, and help to explain such variations over time as can be detected – perhaps indeed more convincingly than the more straightforward distinctions between administrations, or conditions of war and peace, discussed above. Yet they do not amount to a full and satisfying account. For even in the summer of 1939, when Chamberlain had supposedly lost the initiative in his own Cabinet, he was still capable of the active diplomacy of late August to avert the final crisis, and of the blatant disregard of the Cabinet's wishes on 2 September in not announcing an immediate ultimatum. From this personalised diplomacy, which (although not *intended* as further appeasement) could, left to itself and with French connivance, have dragged on for a considerable time, the Prime Minister was only derailed by one of the most determined and self-conscious assertions of Cabinet authority in British history. Even after this humiliation, as we saw in chapter 5, Chamberlain and Halifax continued to keep the Swedish intermediary Dahlerus in play until the end of 1939, despite their evident anxiety that this would break as a political scandal. Thus, although more restricted once war had broken out, with the events of September as a reminder of future possibilities, the executive was not wholly hamstrung in the first months of the conflict, when the Cabinet as a whole was passive and uncertain as to the limits of desirable diplomatic action.

In the second act of this version of the story, while Churchill gained authority through popular acclaim and undoubtedly behaved in an increasingly assertive manner, the passage of time was not the most significant factor in determining his status with his

Cabinet colleagues. It is true that the period looked at here ends after only thirteen months of Churchill's administration, and is not therefore a sufficiently long span on which to generalise about it, but we know that in 1941 there was actually serious talk of some kind of rebellion against Churchill because of his apparent disregard of the Cabinet.[11] This came to nothing in the short term but may have concentrated the minds of Labour leaders at least on the need to reassert their own influence in the government, which they did from 1942 on. In the same way Churchill was almost certainly stimulated to move Halifax on in December 1940 because of the difficulties he had had with him in the Cabinet crisis over fighting on in late May. Rather than a linear progression in one direction, towards either Cabinet control or prime-ministerial dominance, it is more accurate to see events in terms of a dialectical pattern of action and response, with some kind of dynamic equilibrium the desired if not always attained condition. Each political battle in Cabinet left its mark and affected the behaviour of the actors in the next round.

This description suggests that a game-theoretic model might be as helpful as any in promoting understanding of Cabinet interactions, and indeed it would be interesting to observe its application to the cases described here. But the fit with the detailed historical material presented in these case-studies would necessarily be loose. It is more important to take account of the qualitative changes in the environments of policy-making – both operational and psychological – which had perhaps the most decisive impact on British ministers. It is these changes which provide the basis for the explanation of Cabinet behaviour which has been emerging throughout this book.

The hypothesis which ultimately seems to account for most of the variation in the pattern of Cabinet decision-making in the area of foreign policy for this period is built on observations about the interplay between the structure of the problem facing ministers, their perceptions of it and the institutional context of the Cabinet itself.

The basic argument is that decisional procedures emerge in different forms according to the type of issue under consideration. Only thus may we explain the differing degrees of participation from one policy to another, and the fact that the fluctuations in decision-making were not governed by chronology. Thus the degree to which an issue was intrinsically suited to collective deliberation was the crucial variable in determining the style of policy-making. But what specific characteristics of a problem were most significant? Clearly the *importance* of an issue, whether perceived or substantive, was not the decisive factor. While some questions of routine administration were considered insufficiently important for the executive to trouble the Cabinet with, by and large all decisions which might be thought to have structural effects on national interests at some stage went through the Cabinet, giving ministers at least some access for participation. And at this level they were not monopolised by any particular group. All the six cases we have looked at were highly significant for British interests, yet they stimulated very different styles of management:

A more plausible interpretation is that the *urgency* with which a solution was perceived as being required directly affected the number of ministers who could be efficiently involved in its production. *Prima facie*, the need for an immediate response in March 1939 led to executive policy-making – and in the case of the response to the October 1939 peace offer the lack of particular urgency seemed to make for wide ministerial involvement. Unfortunately, this theory again does not fit enough relevant examples. In September 1939 the urgency could not have been greater, but the Cabinet as a whole acted to supervise the implementation of its general will. In April 1939, as the Litvinov proposals demanded a quicker pace in British considerations of the Soviet issue, so more ministers became actively engaged. In May 1940, the perception of a pressing need for some definite decision would actively have worked against executive dominance, since Churchill's attempt to maintain existing British war policy hinged on his ability to delay the resolution of the issue either way.

Urgency, therefore, was not a prerequisite of dominant executive action. More important were *the nature of the options raised by an issue, and their effects upon existing images and comprehensions of the policy environment*. There seems to have been, for example, an inverse relationship between the ability of the foreign policy executive to create policy and the initial clarity of the relevant alternatives. If, when a problem first became salient, the paths of choice were relatively limited and/or clearly defined, then the ability of most ministers to understand, become interested and participate in argument over the issue was significantly increased. Organised discussion was made easier where the problem could be broken down into separate and finite components and dealt with comprehensively. Into this category fall the Anglo-Soviet negotiations and the crisis over the

German invasion of Poland. In each case ministers had from the very beginning a clear idea of the subject under discussion and a choice of distinct strategies. Their understanding fostered confidence in their collective ability to make a decision.[12]

The argument is also sustained by examining the consideration of the 6 October 1939 peace offer. Here the general task was straightforward – to reply to the various points in Hitler's speech – and the conclusions which could be reached were limited by the very motives for which Britain had gone to war, to the task of imposing order on the government's thinking about war aims. The specifying of these attitudes took place in a fairly wide circle of policy-making because by this time most ministers possessed developed general opinions about Germany and the war, and were capable of positive contributions. The difference from the cases of April–May and September 1939 was that there was a more open-ended quality to the deliberations, to the extent that this was seen as an opportunity for thinking through longer-term war aims and the full ramifications of the commitment embarked upon on 3 September. The requirement of ingenuity had worked in favour of executive leadership in March, and it could also have done so here if the diplomatic environment had been fluid, instead of static in the aftershock of the declarations of war, as it was. Chamberlain and Halifax were debilitated and more concerned to avoid further upsets than to take risks with new foreign policy initiatives. Churchill would happily have taken over their executive role in setting the tone for a response, as his personal draft reply indicates, but he was not yet in a position to usurp the powers of the rightful holders of either office.

When options were both cloudy and open-ended, on the other hand, policy-making tended to devolve onto a narrow circle capable of the co-ordinated, imaginative and often intense effort required to produce new programmes, or simply to define the issues in a climate of confusion. The making of the Polish Guarantee, when British policy might have taken a number of different and unpredictable turns, is the best example of what has been termed in this chapter 'creative leadership'. When a problem demanded real originality, it was beyond the function of a collectivity to synthesise varying opinions with sufficient speed to anticipate the executive, who tended automatically to generate responses to what they perceived as new needs. In March 1939 the executive introduced and developed three separate plans for a new British policy within ten days of the emergence of the issue. There was no mechanism by which the Cabinet could equal this, with only four meetings in the same time in which to work out agreed actions.

Churchill's dominating leadership in the crisis of May 1940 flourished on the same inhibitions against a group, however small, forging an agreed strategy when there are no clear proposals laid out from which to choose. Although in essence the problem was simplified down to the choice between war or peace, there were crucial difficulties in perceiving the means by which either strategy might practicably be followed. It was extremely difficult to distinguish a feasible line of action in the gloom of the fall of France. Thus Churchill's strong attempts to make clear a desirable policy fell on the fallow ground of colleagues whose varying opinions increased the natural hesitancy of each individual in advocating a particular course.

The clarity of the options facing ministers in any given problem was itself strongly influenced by perhaps the key circumstance in determining the breadth of participation in policy-making – the extent to which a problem disturbed the settled images of foreign policy held by ministers. The two main examples here of decision-making which was effectively narrowed to a very small area both involved occasions when external events severely ruptured the web of assumptions on which policy had previously been based. These traumatic actions had suddenly broken the continuity of expectations about, respectively, the way in which German expansion would develop during 1939 and the military balance of the war in 1940. Both had created a hiatus of doubt and dispersed consensus. In each the executive fulfilled the function of replacing policies which had suddenly become irrelevant by imaginative and decisive initiatives.

In some of the other cases, even when the overall pattern was different, we can still see flashes of similar processes at work. For example, when in early 1941 it suddenly became clear during Harry Hopkins' visit to Britain that President Roosevelt was not, as had been thought, interested at that stage in adumbrating war aims, Churchill was able to go into reverse and, with all his prejudices reinforced, wage what was – in the short term at least – an effective spoiling campaign against ministerial participation in a public debate on the subject. Later, he did yet another volte-face to complete the full circle on war aims, issuing the 'Atlantic Charter' when considering Roosevelt's surprising suggestions on board the *Prince of Wales*, away from Cabinet control.[13]

In general, the decisions which involved wider ministerial participation confirm this correlation between the effect of an issue on existing stereotypes and the style of its policy-making. They represent the mirror image of the executive's tendency to seize the opportunities for creative initiative. The specification of war aims in October 1939 required the formation of general attitudes, but not, as we have indicated, the reformation of attitudes in a framework of open-ended choice. Hitler's speech introduced no new elements into the frame of assessment: a 'peace offensive' had been anticipated since the outbreak of war. The continuity meant that ministers possessed sufficient information and confidence to be able to participate in the discussion of a response from the beginning. The ideal type of rational discussion consisting of inputs from all participants and the triumph of arguments according to their 'merits' was no more borne out by this than by any other example, but ministers were certainly able to take part extensively in what was essentially a detailed piece of committee drafting. Chamberlain and Halifax were clearly aware that recent events and the nature of the issue made inevitable a multilateral approach to the design of a reply to Hitler.

The same pattern had, moreover, been evident during the evolution of Anglo-Soviet relations from April to August 1939, even though this predated the sense of distrust of the executive which was generated in many ministers by the September crisis. The Soviet question had been raised by the Polish Guarantee and in the eyes of certain key ministers had been left hanging over without resolution. In the increasing tension, the Soviet question was coming to the top of the diplomatic agenda for many British politicians even before the Litvinov proposals, and the debate developed in a Cabinet in which attitudes were steadily crystallising, not dissolving. Between 1 and 3 September, also, it was undoubtedly fundamental for the Cabinet's ultimate control over the decision for war that they held an existing set of attitudes to apply to the Polish crisis when it arose. These were embodied in the formal Guarantee finalised by the bilateral treaty signed on 25 August. There was here no question of crisis descending on unprepared ministers 'like a hawk into a dovecote' as Ted Hughes put it once in another context.

In this crucial lack of confusion the situation was similar to that obtaining during the study of war aims in late 1940. On the latter occasion, although many important particular aspects of the problem were developed anew, the boundaries had already been set in ministers' minds – by a combination of their own attitudes previous to May 1940, Churchill's strong lead in the crisis of that month and the subsequent successful resistance to invasion. The issue of compromise peace was no longer open to debate, while the problem of 'the future world' was general enough for views to be aired without inhibition. That the only urgency in their task related to the tactical consideration of outflanking Hitler's propaganda machine also facilitated the War Aims Committee's task.

It is not suggested that the executive style of policy-making only characterises periods of the greatest political trauma, when agreed preconceptions are suddenly shattered. It is more realistic to suggest the converse, that a broad base of policy-making seems to be encouraged when there is a high continuity between the specific question asked of ministers and their existing set of more general images – that is, the fundamentally linked expectations and attitudes which are sufficiently established to be plotted as a 'cognitive map'.[14] This is especially the case when the available options are distinct and preformulated, requiring choice rather than creativity. Conversely, when there is any need for basic originality, the circle of participation seems to narrow considerably. This may happen at a fairly modest level; although the examples we have developed have been concerned with great events, it seems likely that the executive will also dominate policy-making in relatively undramatic circumstances (such as Hitler's announcement on 28 April 1939 that he no longer accepted the Anglo-German Naval Agreement),[15] so long as they are unexpected and require the positive contribution of a new attitude or position.

Creativity therefore seems to be the distinguishing need fulfilled in situations of executive predominance, but the foreign policy executive also naturally stretches its powers in day-to-day business. Yet the overall nature of the policy process varies according to the range and strength of the inputs involved. Politics is not an exact science precisely because people do not always wish to take advantage of the opportunities which are theoretically open to them, and even on occasions manage to rise above what seem to be insuperable constraints.

Another central characteristic of Cabinet behaviour in this period seems to have been consensus. It is striking that in none of the cases we have looked at has a decision been taken over a dissident minority. On all occasions action was delayed until it was established that almost the whole Cabinet subscribed to the relevant proposal. Even during March 1939, the unhappiness expressed by Hoare and Stanley was about the failure to bring the USSR into the new policy, not about the Polish Guarantee as such. It is true that the rapid execution of the Guarantee showed that in certain circumstances general agreement was reached more by default than full acceptance. In others there was no major conflict, and discussion served the purpose of reconnoitring and perhaps articulating common ground, as with the consideration of war aims at the end of both 1939 and 1940. Here agreement was important but not surprising on fundamentals, and differences tended to be either repressed or merely tactical. Both Churchill and the proponents of a war aims debate made compromises so as not to allow the underlying differences to sharpen beyond a certain point.

Where real disagreement was evident, there were definite attempts to build a consensus and to reconcile divisions before action was initiated. The Cabinet had their own preventive diplomacy. The doubts of Hoare and Stanley about the exclusion of the USSR from policy in March 1939 were overridden but not ignored. Rather, they were accommodated in the compromise agreement to make a later approach – at least to the extent of securing their consent to the Guarantee. Two months later, likewise, although the executive's opposition was overborne in the decision to accept a triple alliance, it was only done by recruiting first Halifax and then Chamberlain to an actual belief in the rightness of the policy. Even the Prime Minister came to accept the principle of alliance on the substantive grounds of the international damage which the breakdown of negotiations would cause. The unity of the government was always a foremost consideration, as the rarity of threats of resignation suggests.

Similarly, in mid-1940 Churchill was very anxious not only to prevent Halifax's initial inclination towards peace from becoming policy, but also to bring round the Foreign Secretary to his own point of view. The Prime Minister felt he could afford no dissent, even if it were in a minority, as his mix of conciliatory and firm remarks to Halifax on 27 May suggests. His later demands for 'confident language from his colleagues, together with his prompt warning to Halifax during the Prytz episode that there should be no repetition

Decision-making in Cabinet 239

of R. A. Butler's 'luke-warmness', were strong pressures on ministers to adhere to a single line of policy.

The Prytz affair was an interesting example of both how easily a Prime Minister's line on policy could be weakened by a colleague (perhaps even unintentionally) and how anxious most ministers were to avoid any accusation of disloyalty – particularly, of course at a time of maximum danger for the state. Butler was reported as having told Björn Prytz (the Swedish Minister in London) that 'common sense and not bravado' would govern British policy towards the war and any possible peace. It is possible, though uncertain, that Halifax himself was briefly a party to the conversation. Certainly the Swedes formed the impression that the Foreign Secretary was at odds with Churchill's implacability. When the Prime Minister got wind of this through a leaked press report, he went on the counter-offensive, not least because he had asserted to the Commons that the government would 'fight on to the death' and that he had taken 'personal responsibility for the resolve of all'. Both ministers protested their innocence strenuously,[16] just as Halifax had opposed Churchill in May with great reluctance, and had not been able to bring himself to demand the formal decision over the peace issue which might have involved complete confrontation. By the time of the July peace offer, the government were united again. In such cases 'collective responsibility' operated less by engineering full agreement before a decision was reached than by avoiding a decision and then securing the subsequent loyalty and silence of the original malcontents.

In the long run, of course, there was scope for a Prime Minister to shift ministers with whom he was not in sympathy. Halifax was undoubtedly moved out of the way by Churchill when appointed against his will Ambassador to the United States in December 1940. But such actions could only take place in the fulness of time, just as Hore-Belisha was offered a demotion by Chamberlain after a long period of dissatisfaction with him (probably on the part of others as much as the Prime Minister).[17] Ministers could not be moved as easily as chess pawns. As with Inskip and Winterton in January 1939, or the grudging appointment of Burgin as Minister of Supply instead of Churchill or Eden, they were usually changed after a period of agonising, and as the result of political compromise. Even strong Prime Ministers act reluctantly over such matters, and rarely as part of grand schemes to manipulate the Cabinet. Churchill had been unable to force the issue when Halifax refused his offer to become

Lord President at the end of September 1940, and was eventually rescued by the opportunity provided by Lothian's death. Moreover, after Halifax had departed to Washington (retaining his War Cabinet status) he stood out against Churchill's insulting comments on his war aims speech to the Pilgrims on 25 March 1941, and went ahead with what was to become a government White Paper. Similarly, when Churchill asked Duff Cooper to leave the Ministry of Information in July 1941 it was only after a long campaign against the Ministry had already done its political damage, and then on the basis that Cooper be compensated with the post of Chancellor of the Duchy of Lancaster, with special responsibility for Singapore. The use of the long knives was largely incompatible with the morale and reputation of the government.

Conversely, a Prime Minister tended to look upon the prospects of outsiders with good credentials for office largely in terms of their effects on the harmony of the government. Chamberlain excluded Churchill in 1939 because he predicted disruptive consequences for the conduct of business while, remarkably, Churchill was willing to consider bringing two men into his Cabinet with 'defeatist' tendencies (Lloyd George and Beaverbrook), probably because he saw them as kindred spirits who might have the effect of slowly and undramatically easing out Chamberlain and Halifax.[18]

That the drive for consensus has figured so prominently points again to the inappropriateness of a model which postulates competitive power-seeking as a first priority within the Cabinet. Conscious exchanges of threats and sanctions were rare even during serious disputes, and a central concern was the dampening down of conflict. Styles of policy-making varied with the type of issue, but ultimately, whatever the particular decisional unit, the outcomes always had to be capable of attracting the overall agreement of the Cabinet, even if on occasions that meant fudging or delaying a decision. This involved an element of 'groupthink', for it meant that even poorly made decisions could escape proper scrutiny as a result of the concern for the unity of the government. Thus when we are trying to account for the evolution of policy we need to analyse the nature of the consensus to which it related. The fact of the varying sources of power in Cabinet government, coupled with a tendency to close ranks, means that the pattern of British policy must be explained by the aggregate preferences of all ministers and not by those of any single individual or sub-group.

Indeed it has been a persistent refrain throughout the various cases studied here that the idea of an 'inner Cabinet' does not stand up against the evidence, at least for foreign policy. The notorious 'big four' of Chamberlain, Halifax, Simon and Hoare is revealed on scrutiny to be an unjustified generalisation from one element of policy-making during the Munich crisis.[19] In 1939 Hoare was in fact the most prominent opponent of Chamberlain's attitudes during discussion of the central issues of the Polish Guarantee and of relations with the Soviet Union. It was he who urged from the outset a close association with the USSR, which goes directly against the usual belief that the 'four' were particularly held together by their sharing of basic values and prejudices. He was also not a member of the drafting committee for the 12 October reply to Hitler. Simon more often held the same opinions as Chamberlain, but did not stand out as a staunch ally. Throughout the foreign policy discussions we have looked at, he was especially reserved and made fewer positive contributions than other supporters of the Prime Minister, such as Morrison. Halifax commented that he was 'a very friendly creature, but a very odd one, with a curious incapacity for exciting affection'.[20] In fact when the final crisis of peacetime developed, Simon was among the leaders of the group of ministers who insisted that Chamberlain procrastinate no longer in making clear Britain's intention to fight. Like Hoare's in April, this was not the action of a close confederate who shared in the making of policy before it came to Cabinet, and closed ranks to ensure its endorsement.[21] Simon was more of a loner, even a trimmer.

The whole notion that major policy was systematically removed from the Cabinet and predetermined by an inner elite is best surrendered. The 'group of four' as such played no significant part in the events we have looked at, and the Foreign Policy Committee was less often a device for mobilising support for Chamberlain than a means of increasing the access of interested ministers to certain types of vital issues. The Prime Minister and the Foreign Secretary would certainly neglect the Foreign Policy Committee if it suited them, probably because of a sense that the Committee enabled ministers to develop the kind of sustained expertise in foreign affairs which would intrinsically reduce their own freedom of manoeuvre – as it promised to do over both the recognition of Franco on 23 January and the Polish Guarantee on 27 March, and finally achieved during the evolution of policy towards the Soviets in April and May.

This may be why the Committee did not meet for seven weeks in February and March. The Foreign Policy Committee was no working inner Cabinet.

The War Cabinet, in both its large initial form and its later streamlined Churchillian model, was in some ways *sui generis*. But it was still attached to the wider group of ministers which made up the full Cabinet, and it had to deal with problems of balance and leadership as much as any normal government. No doubt the War Cabinet represented a form of institutionalised inner Cabinet, and it had the effect of making the ministers outside it often feel marginal to the strategic direction of the war. But as such it could never be a vehicle for prime ministerial government. The figures represented in the War Cabinet were too senior politically, and too aware of their wider responsibilities, not to seek a full role in the making of policy. This was particularly true after May 1940 when they were also representing the major political parties in a new Coalition Government. But party differences had been by no means irrelevant even for its predecessor. Among others, Malcolm MacDonald's Labour origins and the Liberalism of Simon and Hore-Belisha had been significant factors in determining their attitudes to Chamberlain once appeasement began to falter.

For a time Attlee and Greenwood felt the need to play themselves in, and once Churchill had established himself by the end of 1940 he was undoubtedly difficult to control. But, by then with Bevin in their ranks, they soon learned to concentrate on their own priorities, as the early history of war aims and reconstruction discussions shows, and can hardly be thought of as Churchill's camp-followers. As well as contributing to victory, they were concerned to build bridges outwards from the War Cabinet to the Parliamentary Labour Party, the Labour movement and the country at large, so as to prepare the ground for social and political change. The War Cabinet was therefore a forum, hardly a cabal. In March 1941 it was still asserting itself as an entity independent of both Prime Minister and Foreign Secretary, when criticising (on a cross-party basis) Eden's signature in Athens of an agreement with Greece, with Churchill for once caught in the middle.[22]

If there was any real separation between the Cabinet and a small group of its own ministers, then it consisted only in a distinction between the Cabinet and its regular foreign policy executive of Prime Minister and Foreign Secretary. The inevitable co-operation between the two men in the daily administration of foreign relations encouraged them to think together, and often alike, about problems of major policy in advance of consultation with the Cabinet. At times, as we saw over the Polish Guarantee, this led them to capitalise on the opportunities which arise to take dominant initiatives and reduce their colleagues to the role of passive audience. This was even true for Halifax and Churchill on occasions,[23] but here there were also serious disagreements between the two, which meant that the existing uncertainties of policy were dramatically magnified. It is not surprising that Halifax did not last for long as Foreign Secretary once the tensions had become apparent, as Eden had not in his time and George Brown, Francis Pym and Sir Geoffrey Howe were not to do in theirs.

For the most part, however, both Prime Minister and Foreign Secretary saw the advantages of working as a team, and although there were inevitably time-lags as the opinion of one evolved faster than the other, the partnership of first Chamberlain and Halifax[24] and later to a lesser degree that of Churchill and Eden were effectively sustained in the face of adverse conditions for foreign policy-making.[25] Halifax, indeed, ruminated to Dalton on the relationship just before his own departure from office. It was, he said,

> the most delicate of relationships within the Cabinet. If the P.M. is the sort of man who takes an interest in foreign affairs, the Foreign Secretary must be prepared to defer to him on many points. On very high policy, the Foreign Secretary should, if the P.M. resists him and he cannot persuade him, go to the Cabinet. On very small points the P.M. should not interfere at all. On matters of intermediate importance the Foreign Secretary should be prepared to make considerable concessions to the P.M.'s point of view.[26]

Clearly Halifax saw the relationship as potentially problematical but essentially intimate and based on shared involvement in a wide range of foreign policy matters. He went on to describe his work with both Chamberlain and Churchill in these terms, not realising that the latter was evidently not of the same view.

The Halifax–Chamberlain partnership was genuine and based on a measure of mutual respect, even affection. It is difficult to support the view that has been expressed in recent years that Halifax acted as some kind of anti-appeasement conscience inside the government after Munich, gradually stiffening its backbone and leading Chamberlain where he might not otherwise have gone.[27] This is to identify the Foreign Secretary too closely with his advisers, and indeed also to assume that the Foreign Office was of a clearer and more united mind than was, in fast-moving circumstances, the case. In fact, Halifax and Chamberlain were equally responsible for the hand-to-mouth remaking of policy in the second half of March 1939, and were the last two (Halifax admittedly a few days in the lead) to come around to accepting the idea of a Soviet alliance in May. Halifax did not differ from the Prime Minister about delaying the ultimatum on 2 September, and only escaped a share of the odium which then attached to Chamberlain because he had been making the same statement in the House of Lords (see chapter 4, above). Both men had been caught up in diplomacy, and both were responsible for the domestic crisis which ensued.

Halifax was less self-deceiving than Chamberlain,[28] and had less emotional capital vested in past policies. Thus he did tend to be slightly quicker than his Prime Minister, on various occasions, to relinquish the last hopes of negotiation and peace. But he was also out of touch with the Commons, and found it personally difficult to envisage a deal with Communist Russia. Even during the October discussions on a reply to Hitler's speech, Halifax's prolix, somewhat idealistic, draft was nearer to the spirit of Chamberlain's residual optimism about peace than to Churchill's pithy belligerence. He also worked discreetly with Chamberlain until Christmas on the fruitless trails still being laid down by Dahlerus. Certainly the Opposition did not see Halifax as having left appeasement behind. In the May crisis of 1940 the senior Liberal MP Clement Davies reported: 'Attlee & Greenwood are unable to distinguish between the PM and Halifax, and are *not* prepared to serve under the latter.'[29] Three weeks later it was Halifax who asserted the need to consider a compromise peace, and he continued to be far less robust than Churchill throughout 1940.

The main concern of this book has been with the nature of Cabinet government in the context of foreign policy. It has produced the conclusion that the Cabinet does not settle into a rigid pattern of behaviour but produces different styles of policy-making according to the nature of the issue at stake and particularly its capacity to dissolve pre-existing images of the environment in which foreign policy operates. This is a finding which may be restricted to the particular actors and circumstances discussed here, but there is no reason why it should not also constitute a working hypothesis for explaining how the Cabinet works in other periods, other policy-arenas, and even other countries. The political groups which run governments are not always called 'Cabinets' in the British sense but they all have to grapple with the tensions between the individual and the collective, and between initiative and responsibility. Even politburos have not always ossified into admiration societies for General Secretaries, and even modern Italian governments have sometimes produced leadership. Accepting the fact of variation in policy-making styles, without inferring randomness, should bring us nearer to a truthful picture of the politics of foreign policy, namely that it is a dynamic and dialectical process, not to be reduced to static generalisation about where power lies. Foreign policy-making is like other areas of public policy-making, in that it is made up of a set of moving relationships, played out within the limits laid down by institutions, precedents and personalities. But where all policy-makers are subject to an external environment, that of foreign policy is the global system itself, with its vast range of possible inputs, and multiple currents of fast-moving change. Moreover the Prime Minister is likely to become habitually involved with the Foreign Office in a way that will only be replicated with the Treasury. The Prime Minister has not the resources to be part of a health policy executive, or even home policy executive, in the way that he or she is half of the foreign policy executive. The existence of such a partnership may mean that styles of decision-making will tend to oscillate more sharply than those to be found in the narrower confines of 'domestic' policy: foreign policy can sometimes be taken out of Cabinet altogether, but it will also attract high concern and can provoke a strong reaction if ministers feel that they are being excluded on matters of vital national interest. Case-studies in other issue-areas are necessary to explore this hypothesis further.

One of the fundamental assumptions of the decision-making approach which has been in use here is that there is a two-way flow between process and policy; each affects the other. The particular theme of Cabinet government has illustrated the point in that foreign policy decisions have been shown to be subject to internal political argument, just as the pattern of influence within the Cabinet was partly dependent on the *type* of issue at hand. The same process can be seen at work in some other areas which have been touched on in the course of the analysis. Groupthink has already been referred to, and that concept is closely related to the study of behaviour in crises, to which the years 1938–41 are particularly relevant.

Three of the six cases here can be classified as foreign policy crises from the viewpoint of the British government, in that they posed a threat to fundamental values, required a response in a finite time-period and constituted an unavoidable point of choice. These were: the impact of the invasion of Czechoslovakia on 15 March 1939 (although it is arguable as to whether Britain had to come up with a response at all), the invasion of Poland and the imminent defeat of France.

It is interesting that these are the three cases in which the making of British foreign policy was most turbulent, even unstable. It was not just that they produced disagreement – that was also true of the Soviet proposals and of the War Aims Committee's draft statement. What was important was the element of panic to be seen in the rush to judgement over Poland, with a blind eye turned to military advice, in the confrontations at Westminster on the night of 2 September, and in the emotionalism of Churchill's clash with Halifax. The last two of these incidents came close to adding further disasters to already dangerous situations, even if they did not ultimately do so. The Polish Guarantee, however, is difficult to see as anything other than bad policy, badly made.

Thus crisis conditions seem to have imposed extra pressures on the capacity of the Cabinet system to handle foreign policy. Rather than stimulating unity and a self-consciously calm rationality, as occurred to a degree during the American responses to the Berlin blockade and the installation of Soviet missiles in Cuba, British policy in these three crises was made hurriedly, erratically and in two cases in the context of sharp internal conflict. That the problems were then papered over was probably inevitable, but it thus helped to contribute to the perpetuation of such flaws of personnel and procedure as were entrenched (and hidden by group solidarity), until ultimately the system came crashing down in ruins in the case of the Chamberlain administration, and came perilously close to total defeat in the case of Churchill's.

Between Munich and the event which Churchill had prayed for, the entry of the Soviet Union into the war, the British government came face to face with the most elemental of the problems deriving from statehood: how to define its own vital security interests, and then simply how to survive against a savage and apparently irresistible adversary. It is perhaps equally surprising that they did so poorly on the first task, and so well – alone – on the second. As the historians have shown beyond dispute, the lack of co-ordinated preparation for war, and the failure to think through the kind of conflict which might arrive, nearly cost the British people and those who looked to them for help very dearly. It might further be argued that the continuation of such attitudes into wartime, represented by the insistence on thinking about war aims in terms of generality and principles rather than boundaries and regimes, may have contributed to a new round of problems in the peace-making phase at the end of the war, when such hasty dispositions had to be made for Europe.

Many of the reasons for such failures – as indeed for the feat of survival after the fall of France – go deeper than the processes which have been observed in this book. The role of officials *vis-à-vis* ministers, for example, is an important subject which has only been dealt with in passing here. We have seen how the views of the professional military were skirted around or embroidered upon in both March 1939 and May 1940, with the Chiefs of Staff apparently powerless to resist on both occasions. Conversely, the importance of advisers such as Cadogan and Bridges, and of officials turned politicians such as Anderson, Chatfield and Hankey, will have been evident throughout the discussion. The now-burgeoning theories of bureaucratic behaviour can be turned with profit towards the policy processes laid bare in the archives.

But it is the politicians, and at the apex of the system the Prime Minister and the Cabinet, who accept ultimate responsibility for the governing of British democracy, and the way they exercise their powers will be a principal element in determining the success of the country's foreign policy. It is therefore of great importance to know more about the conduct of Cabinet business, especially in the neglected area of foreign policy. Academics quite properly travel the highways and byways of methodology, theory and history in their efforts to explain political action. But it is the elected government and its primary institutions that citizens look to in the first and last instances to secure and improve their lives, and which should be held to account. When political scientists neglect this fact, and their own role in society, they risk aridity. This study has sought to throw light on the British Cabinet in operation, and to capture some of the intense political life which takes place inside it.

APPENDIX 1. THE CHAMBERLAIN CABINET, 31 OCTOBER 1938–3 SEPTEMBER 1939

The starting-date of 31 October 1938 has been chosen because there was a Cabinet reshuffle at the end of October in which a number of lesser posts changed hands. The only other changes before the outbreak of war were (1) on 29 January 1939, involving Morrison (now understudying Chatfield in the Commons), Dorman-Smith, MacDonald, Inskip and Chatfield, and (2) on 21 April, involving Burgin and Wallace (Burgin could not become Minister of Supply proper until legislation had passed through Parliament). Ministers involved in the Cabinet 'mutiny' of the evening of 2 September, at one or other of the meetings with Sir John Simon, are indicated by '(M)'; regular attenders at the Foreign Policy Committee by an asterisk (*).

Prime Minister	Neville Chamberlain*
Lord President of the Council	Viscount Runciman*
Lord Chancellor	Viscount Maugham
Lord Privy Seal	Sir John Anderson (M)
Chancellor of the Exchequer	Sir John Simon (M)*
Foreign Secretary	Viscount Halifax*
Home Secretary	Sir Samuel Hoare*
First Lord of the Admiralty	Earl Stanhope
Minister of Agriculture and Fisheries	W. S. Morrison (to 29.1.39) (M)
	Sir Reginald Dorman-Smith (from 29.1.39) (M)
Secretary of State for Air	Sir Kingsley Wood (M)
Secretary of State for the Colonies	Malcolm MacDonald (M)*
Minister for the Co-ordination of Defence	Sir Thomas Inskip* (to 29.1.39)
	Lord Chatfield* (from 29.1.39)
Secretary of State for the Dominions	Malcolm MacDonald *(to 29.1.39)
	Sir Thomas Inskip* (from 29.1.39)
President of the Board of Education	Earl De La Warr (M)
Minister of Health	Walter Elliot (M)
Secretary of State for India and Burma	Marquess of Zetland
Minister of Labour	Ernest Brown
Chancellor of the Duchy of Lancaster	Earl Winterton (to 29.1.39)
	W. S. Morrison* (from 29.1.39)
Minister without Portfolio	Leslie Burgin* (from 21.4.39) (M)

The Chamberlain Cabinet

Minister of Supply	Leslie Burgin* (from 14.7.39)
Secretary of State for Scotland	John Colville (M)
President of the Board of Trade	Oliver Stanley* (M)
Minister of Transport	Leslie Burgin (to 21.4.39)
	Euan Wallace (from 21.4.39) (M)
Secretary of State for War	Leslie Hore-Belisha (M)

Note:
Of twenty-four ministers, seven sat in the Lords: Runciman, Maugham, Halifax, Stanhope, Chatfield, De La Warr and Zetland. (Earl Winterton was an Irish peer who was an MP.)

Source:
David Butler and Anne Sloman, *British Political Facts, 1900–1979*, 5th edn (London: Macmillan, 1980), pp. 22–5.

APPENDIX 2. ATTENDANCE AT THE FOREIGN POLICY COMMITTEE OF THE CABINET, 14 NOVEMBER 1938– 25 AUGUST 1939

The basis for the calculations made in chapter 3, pp. 70–84, is set out below. Original data is available in Figure 1 and Table 2, pp. 74 and 80), and all figures are corrected to one decimal place.

(1) Attendance of ministers

Average attendance for *Period 1* (FP(36) 32–42, 14 November 1938–11 April 1939, including Anderson, present for one item only at FP(36) 33 = 8.1 Ministers per meeting (89/11).

Average attendance for *Period 2* (FP(36) 43–61, 19 April–25 August 1939, but excluding Meetings 46, 51, 52, 55 and 61, which were not concerned with the Soviet issue) = 9.9 Ministers per meeting (138/14).

Runciman was absent abroad for the period 27 March–19 May 1939 inclusive, i.e. eleven meetings, of which one in the second period was not concerned with the USSR. Five of his absences fall into each period. Adding 5 to the total for each period would alter the averages to 8.5 and 10.2 respectively, a difference of 1.7 rather than 1.8. Runciman therefore cancels out.

Chatfield and Morrison did not join the Committee until 8 February 1939. In order to adjust the figures for the weighting in favour of Period 2 that would otherwise occur we need to add (on the assumption of nearly full attendance for both over 5 missed meetings), say, 9 to the total attendances for Period 1. This leaves an average attendance of 8.9, as compared to 9.9 for Period 2. So the true increase in ministerial attendance from Period 1 to Period 2 is 9.9 − 8.9 = 1.0. This is largely explained by the arrival of Burgin. (If Burgin's net attendances – 11 – are subtracted from the total for Period 2, the average becomes 9.1, or 0.8 lower.)

(2) Rate of absenteeism

Period 1: There were 10 regular attenders (or full members) at the 11 meetings – a total of 110, from which we must deduct 15, since Chatfield, Morrison and Runciman were physically unable to be present at 5 meetings each = 95 possible attendances in total. During this period there were 10 'occasional absences', i.e. a rate of 10.5% absenteeism.

Period 2: There were 11 regular attenders at the 14 meetings – a total of 154, from which we must deduct 8, since 3 of these meetings took place before Burgin was appointed, and for 5 of them Runciman was abroad = 146. During this period there were 9 'occasional absences', i.e. a rate of 6.2% absenteeism.

APPENDIX 3. NEVILLE CHAMBERLAIN'S STATEMENT IN THE HOUSE OF COMMONS, 12 OCTOBER 1939

Source: Hansard, 5th series, *House of Commons Debates*, vol. 352, cols. 563–8.

Last week, in speaking of the announcement about the Russo-German pact, I observed that it contained a suggestion that some peace proposals were likely to be put forward, and I said that, if such proved to be the case, we should examine them in consultation with the Governments of the Dominions and of the French Republic in the light of certain relevant considerations. Since then, the German Chancellor has made his speech, and the consultations I referred to have taken place. I must now state the position of His Majesty's Government. Before, however, I inform the House of the results of our examination of the speech, I must ask hon. Members to recall for a few moments the background against which his proposals appear.

At the end of August His Majesty's Government were actively engaged in correspondence with the German Government on the subject of Poland. It was evident that the situation was dangerous, but we believed that it should be possible to arrive at a peaceful solution if passions were not deliberately stimulated and we felt quite certain that the German Government could, if they desired, influence their friends in Danzig in such a way as to bring about a relaxation of tension and so create conditions favourable to calm and sober negotiation. It will be remembered that in the course of this correspondence the German Chancellor expressed his wish for improved relations between our two countries as soon as the Polish question was settled, to which His Majesty's Government replied that they fully shared the wish, but that everything turned on the nature and method of settlement with Poland. We pointed out that a forcible solution would inevitably involve the fulfilment of our obligations to Poland and we begged the German Chancellor to enter into direct discussions with the Polish Government in which the latter Government had already expressed its willingness to take part.

As everyone knows, these efforts on the part of His Majesty's Government to avoid war and the use of force were in vain. In August last the President of the United States made an appeal to Herr Hitler to settle his differences with Poland by pacific means in order to prevent war breaking out in Europe. At about the same time the King of the Belgians, the Queen of the Netherlands, His Holiness the Pope, and Signor Mussolini all tendered their good offices, but equally in vain. It is evident now that Herr Hitler was determined to make war on Poland, and whatever sincerity there may have been in his wish to come to an understanding with Great Britain it was not strong enough to induce him to postpone an attack upon his neighbour. On 1st September Herr Hitler violated the Polish frontier and invaded Poland, beating down by force of arms and machinery the resistance of the Polish nation and army. As attested by neutral observers, Polish towns and villages were bombed and shelled into ruins; and civilians were slaughtered wholesale, in contravention, at any rate in the later stages, of all the undertakings of which Herr Hitler now speaks with pride as though he had fulfilled them.

It is after this wanton act of aggression which has cost so many Polish and German lives, sacrificed to satisfy his own insistence on the use of force, that the German Chancellor now puts forward his proposals. If there existed any expectation that in these proposals would be included some attempt to make amends for this grievous crime against humanity, following so soon upon the violation on the rights of the Czecho-Slovak nation, it has been doomed to disappointment. The Polish State and its leaders are covered with abuse. What the fate of that part of Poland which Herr Hitler describes as the German sphere of interest is to be does not clearly emerge from his speech, but it is evident that he regards it as a matter for the consideration of Germany alone, to be settled solely in accordance with German interests. The final shaping of this territory and the question of the restoration of a Polish State are, in Herr Hitler's view, problems which cannot be settled by war in the West but exclusively by Russia on the one side and Germany on the other.

We must take it, then, that the proposals which the German Chancellor puts forward for the establishment of what he calls 'the certainty of European security' are to be based on recognition of his conquests and of his right to do what he pleases with the conquered.

It would be impossible for Great Britain to accept any such basis without forfeiting her honour and abandoning her claim that international disputes should be settled by discussion and not by force.

The passages in the speech designed to give fresh assurances to Herr Hitler's neighbours I pass over, since they will know what value should be attached to them by reference to the similar assurances he has given in the past.

It would be easy to quote sentences from his speeches in 1935, 1936 and 1938 stating in the most definite terms his determination not to annex Austria or conclude an Anschluss with her, not to fall upon Czecho-Slovakia and not to make any further territorial claims in Europe after the Sudetenland question had been settled in September, 1938. Nor can we pass over Herr Hitler's radical departure from the long professed principles of his policy and creed, as instanced by the inclusion in the German Reich of many millions of Poles and Czechs, despite his repeated professions to the contrary, and by the pact with the Soviet Union concluded after his repeated and violent denunciations of Bolshevism.

This repeated disregard of his word and these sudden reversals of policy bring me to the fundamental difficulty in dealing with the wider proposals in the German Chancellor's speech. The plain truth is that, after our past experience, it is no longer possible to rely upon the unsupported word of the present German Government.

It is no part of our policy to exclude from her rightful place in Europe a Germany which will live in amity and confidence with other nations. On the contrary, we believe that no effective remedy can be found for the world's ills that does not take account of the just claims and needs of all countries, and whenever the time may come to draw the lines of a new peace settlement, His Majesty's Government would feel that the future would hold little hope unless such a settlement could be reached through the method of negotiation and agreement.

It was not, therefore, with any vindictive purpose that we embarked on war but simply in defence of freedom. It is not alone the freedom of the small nations that is at stake: there is also in jeopardy the peaceful existence of Great Britain, the Dominions, India, the rest of the British Empire, France, and, indeed, of all freedom-loving nations. Whatever may be the issue of the present struggle, and in whatever way it may be brought to a conclusion, the world will not be the same world that we have known before. Looking to the future we can see that deep changes will inevitably leave their mark on every field of men's thought and action, and if humanity is to guide aright the new forces that will be in operation, all nations will have their part to play.

His Majesty's Government know all too well that in modern war between great Powers victor and vanquished must alike suffer cruel loss. But surrender to wrongdoing would spell the extinction of all hope, and the annihilation of all those values of life which have through centuries been at once the mark and the inspiration of human progress.

We seek no material advantage for ourselves; we desire nothing from the German people which should offend their self-respect. We are not aiming only at victory, but rather looking beyond it to the laying of a foundation of a better international system which will mean that war is not to be the inevitable lot of every succeeding generation.

I am certain that all the peoples of Europe, including the people of Germany, long for peace, a peace which will enable them to live their lives without fear, and to devote their energies and their gifts to the development of their culture, the pursuit of their ideals and the improvement of their material prosperity. The peace which we are determined to secure, however, must be a real and settled peace, not an uneasy truce interrupted by constant alarms and repeated threats. What stands in the way of such a peace? It is the German Government, and the German Government alone, for it is they who by repeated acts of aggression have robbed all Europe of tranquillity and implanted in the hearts of all their neighbours an ever-present sense of insecurity and fear.

I am glad to think that there is complete agreement between the views of His Majesty's Government and those of the French Government. Hon. Members will have read the speech which was broadcast by M. Daladier last Tuesday. 'We have', he said, 'taken up arms against aggression; we shall not lay them down until we have sure guarantees of security – a security which cannot be called in question every six months.'

Chamberlain's statement to the Commons

Advantage has also been taken of the presence of the Polish Foreign Minister – whom we have been glad to welcome to this country – to consult with the Polish Government, and I am happy to say that we have found entire identity of view to exist between us.

I would sum up the attitude of His Majesty's Government as follows:

Herr Hitler rejected all suggestions for peace until he had overwhelmed Poland, as he had previously overthrown Czecho-Slovakia. Peace conditions cannot be acceptable which begin by condoning aggression.

The proposals in the German Chancellor's speech are vague and uncertain and contain no suggestion for righting the wrongs done to Czecho-Slovakia and to Poland.

Even if Herr Hitler's proposals were more closely defined and contained suggestions to right these wrongs, it would still be necessary to ask by what practical means the German Government intend to convince the world that aggression will cease and that pledges will be kept. Past experience has shown that no reliance can be placed upon the promises of the present German Government. Accordingly, acts – not words alone – must be forthcoming before we, the British peoples, and France, our gallant and trusted Ally, would be justified in ceasing to wage war to the utmost of our strength. Only when world confidence is restored will it be possible to find – as we would wish to do with the aid of all who show good will – solutions of those questions which disturb the world, which stand in the way of disarmament, retard the restoration of trade and prevent the improvement of the well-being of the peoples.

There is thus a primary condition to be satisfied. Only the German Government can fulfil it. If they will not, there can as yet be no new or better world order of the kind for which all nations yearn.

The issue is, therefore, plain. Either the German Government must give convincing proof of the sincerity of their desire for peace by definite acts and by the provision of effective guarantees of their intention to fulfil their undertakings, or we must persevere in our duty to the end. It is for Germany to make her choice.

APPENDIX 4. LORD HALIFAX'S PAPER FOR THE WAR AIMS COMMITTEE, OCTOBER 1940

Source: CAB 21/1581 in the Public Record Office.

THE SPIRITUAL BASIS OF OUR WAR AIMS

1. Britain, the Dominions and the Allies are fighting not for material goods, but for a way of life, which Hitler is trying by every means in his power to suppress.

2. That way of life flows from the belief that all men are brothers, because they are all children of God, who loves them and wants them to love one another.

3. From this belief there follow certain principles:
   i. the religious principle of the absolute value – for God and therefore for man – of every human soul.
   ii. the moral principle of respect for personality and conscience; and
   iii. the social principle of individual liberty, based on equal opportunity, justice and the rule of law.

4. We value democracy, as we know it, because we believe that it protects these principles. We recognise that it does not yet do so completely; and that other nations, which have other systems of Government, none the less practice [*sic*] the same principles in other ways, and hold the underlying belief in the Fatherhood of God, the Brotherhood of Man, on which these principles are founded.

5. For the Christian, the fundamental truth about the relation of God to man, and man to man, has been most fully revealed in Christianity. There are very many, who are not Christian, but who not less sincerely believe in and act upon the same principles.

6. There is plainly no common ground between those who accept these principles, thereby acknowledging a spiritual Power greater than the State, and Hitler, whose master principle is that the State can claim the whole allegiance of man's body and soul. Where this claim is admitted, truth, conscience, mercy, honour, honesty, justice and decency become offences because, in so far as they have any hold on men's allegiance, they prevent them from being absolutely and unreservedly obedient State slaves.

7. We are fighting to keep ourselves free from this slavery and to liberate our fellow-men who, in the German-occupied territories and in Germany itself,

have fallen under it. This evil cannot be overcome without meeting force by force, but we know that a military victory over it will not dispose of it completely. It will not have been eradicated until the idolatry from which it springs has lost its hold upon Men's minds and hearts.

APPENDIX 5. ANTHONY EDEN'S SPEECH AT THE MANSION HOUSE, 29 MAY 1941 (EXTRACT)

Source: *British Parliamentary Papers, 1940–1941* vol. VIII, Cmd 6829, pp. 4–8.

... So it is that Nazism seeks to pretend to itself that there might be some permanence in the thraldom it imposes. And so it is that Hitler has found it necessary to give some decent covering to the naked policy of terror and robbery on which he has embarked in Europe. He has for this purpose invented what he calls the 'New Order'. Hitler pretends that this New Order is to bring prosperity and happiness to those countries which had been robbed by him of their liberty and their means of livelihood.

But what is the reality behind Hitler's high-sounding announcement? It is not easy to find much which is definite in Germany's New Economic Order, except the plan by which the more important industries are to be mainly concentrated within Germany herself.

Meanwhile, the satellite and tributary nations are to be compelled to confine themselves to agriculture and to other kinds of production which suit German convenience. Currency devices will fix the terms of exchange between Germany's industrial products and the output of the other States, so as to maintain a standard of life in Germany much above that of her neighbours. Meanwhile, all foreign commerce would become a German monopoly. As part of the New Order citizens of tributary states will doubtless be forbidden to learn engineering or any other modern industrial arts. The permanent destruction of all local universities and technical schools will inevitably follow. In this way intellectual darkness must aggravate low physical standards, and the national revivals which Hitler fears so much would be indefinitely postponed.

All this could only be the prelude to an extension of the war, which would carry to other continents the imperialist exploitation which had already devoured Europe. Such is the 'New Order'. It should surely be impossible even for Dr. Goebbels to make attractive to its victims a system of imperialist exploitation verging upon slavery.

Inspired by their theory of the master race, the German plan to be the new aristocracy of the territories under their domination, while the unfortunate inhabitants of non-German origin are to become the mere slaves of their German overlords. This vision of the conqueror's rights and of the treatment to be meted out to the conquered has been long in Hitler's mind. It was clearly laid down in *Mein Kampf*.

The process of national destruction of conquered peoples is in operation wherever the German armies march. *Mein Kampf* shows clearly that it is not merely for the Germans a phase of military operations to be abandoned with the cessation of hostilities. It is much more than this. It is a fixed and deliberate policy of subjugation. The first step in the 'New Order' for Europe is the creating of slaves.

But today it is not my main purpose to expose the hollowness – indeed the wickedness – of Hitler's 'New Order'.

Hitler has destroyed the bases of political and social co-operation throughout Europe and he is destroying her economic structure. The future of Europe will depend upon how moral and material construction is brought about throughout the world.

While all our efforts are concentrated on winning the war, His Majesty's Government have naturally been giving careful thought to this all-important matter, which has been equally in the mind of the President of the United States of America.

We have found in President Roosevelt's message to Congress in January 1941 the keynote of our own purposes. On that occasion the President said: 'In the future days which we seek to make secure we look forward to a world founded upon four essential human freedoms. The first is freedom of speech and expression – everywhere in the world. The second is freedom of every person to worship God in his own way – everywhere in the world. The third is freedom from want, which, translated into world terms, means economic understandings which will secure to every nation a healthy peacetime life for its inhabitants – everywhere in the world. The fourth is freedom from fear, which, translated into world terms, means a world-wide reduction of armaments to such a point and in such a thorough fashion that no nation will be in a position to commit an act of physical aggression against any neighbour – anywhere in the world. That is no vision of a distant millennium. It is a definite basis for a kind of world attainable in our own time and generation. That kind of world is the very antithesis of the so-called "New Order" of tyranny which the dictators seek to create with the crash of a bomb. To that new order we oppose the greater conception – the "moral order".'

On this occasion I will not attempt to elaborate our views about the President's first and second freedoms – freedom of speech and thought, and the freedom to worship God – save to say that we realise that these freedoms are fundamental to human development and to democratic responsibility.

Nor do I today intend to discuss the political questions involved in giving real effect to President Roosevelt's 'freedom from fear'. I will only say that, as I hope to show this afternoon, as His Majesty's Government intend to strive in co-operation with others to relieve the post-war world from the fear of want, so will they seek to ensure that the world is freed from fear.

Today I wish to put before you certain practical ways in which 'freedom from want' may be applied to Europe.

We have declared that social security must be the first object of our domestic policy after the war. And social security will be our policy abroad not less than at home. It will be our wish to work with others to prevent the starvation of the post-armistice period, the currency disorders throughout Europe, and the wide fluctuations of employment, markets and prices which were the cause of so much misery in the twenty years between the two wars. We shall seek to achieve this in ways which will interfere as little as possible with the proper liberty of each country over its own economic fortunes.

The countries of the British Empire and their Allies, with the United States and South America, alone are in a position to carry out such a policy. For, irrespective of the nature of the political settlement, continental Europe will end this war starved and bankrupt of all the foods and raw materials which she was accustomed to obtain from the rest of the world. She will have no means, unaided, of breaking the vicious circle. She can export few goods until she has, first of all, received the necessary raw materials. Wasteful wartime cultivations in many lands will leave agriculture almost as weak as industry. Thus Europe will face the vast problem of general demobilisation with a general lack of the necessary means to put men to work.

Let no one suppose, however, that we for our part intend to return to the chaos of the old world. To do so would bankrupt us no less than others. When peace comes we shall make such relaxations of our war-time financial arrangements as will permit the revival of international trade on the widest possible basis. We shall hope to see the development of a system of international exchange in which the trading of goods and services will be the central feature. I echo Mr. Hull's admirable summing up in his recent declaration, when he said: 'Institutions and arrangements of international finance must be so set up that they lend aid to the essential enterprises and continuous development of all countries and permit payment through processes of trade consonant with the welfare of all countries.'

However, to meet the problems of the immediate post-war period action in other directions will also be required. The liberated countries, and maybe others, too, will require an initial pool of resources to carry them through the transitional period.

To organise the transition to peaceful activities will need the collaboration of the United States, of ourselves, and of all free countries which have not themselves suffered the ravages of war. The Dominions and ourselves can make our contribution to this because the British Empire will actually possess overseas enormous stocks of food and materials, which we are accumulating so as to ease the problems of the overseas producers during the war, and of reconstructed Europe after the war. The Prime Minister has already made clear the importance he attaches to this.

What has Germany to offer on her side? Absolutely nothing. An official of the Reich Economics Ministry, in a moment of hard realism, published last autumn a statement that the present German rationing system must continue for at least one year after the restoration of peace, and perhaps for several. The huge latent demand for food, clothing and other articles of prime necessity which cannot be satisfied under war conditions will, he went on to say, again become active after the signature, but the production of such commodities will not for a long while exceed war-time output.

All this is not only true but obvious. But if peace brings disappointment and such conditions continue beyond the disciplined period of war, social security can hardly survive.

No one can suppose that the economic reorganisation of Europe after the Allied victory will be an easy task. But we shall not shirk our opportunity and our responsibility to bear our share of the burdens. The peaceful brotherhood of nations, with due liberty to each to develop its own balanced economic life and its characteristic culture, will be the common object. But it is the transition to this end which presents the problem. It is the establishment of an international economic system, capable of translating the technical possibilities of production into actual plenty, and maintaining the whole population in a continuous fruitful activity, which is difficult. The world cannot expect to solve the economic riddle easily or completely. But the free nations of America, the Dominions and ourselves alone possess a command of the material means, and, what is perhaps more important, these nations clearly have the will and the intention to evolve a post-war order which seeks no selfish national advantage: an order where each member of the family shall realise its own character and perfect its own gifts in liberty of conscience and person. We have learnt the lesson of the interregnum between the two wars. We know that no escape can be found from the curse which has been lying on Europe except by creating and preserving economic health in every country.

Under a system of free economic co-operation Germany must play a part. But here I draw a firm distinction. We must never forget that Germany is the worst master Europe has yet known. Five times in the last century she has violated the peace. She must never be in a position to play that role again. Our political and military terms of peace will be designed to prevent a repetition of Germany's misdeeds.

We cannot now foresee when the end will come. But it is in the nature of a machine so rigid as the German to break suddenly and with little warning. When it comes, the need of succour to the European peoples will be urgent. Shipping will be short and local organisation in Europe in a state of collapse. It is, therefore, important to begin in good time the discussion of priorities and of allocations. Our friends and Allies now represented in London will tell us what their liberated countries will need most urgently, in order that we may all cooperate and be ready for prompt action.

In speaking of the reconstruction of Europe I do not overlook the fact that its settlement may affect and be affected by developments elsewhere, such as, for example, in the Far East. After the unhappy struggle now in progress between Japan and China, there will obviously be problems of similar magnitude to be faced in that part of the world, in the solution of which all countries concerned will, we hope, play their part.

The right economic outcome after the war requires on our part no exceptional unselfishness, but will require constructive imagination. It is obvious that we have no motive of self-interest prompting us to the economic exploitation either of Germany or of the rest of Europe. This is not what we want nor what we could perform. The lasting settlement and internal peace of the continent as a whole is our only aim. The fact that at the bottom of his heart every combatant knows this is the ultimate source of our strength. To every neutral satellite or conquered country it is obvious that our victory is, for the most fundamental and unalterable reasons, to their plain advantage. But that victory stands also for something greater still. Only our victory can restore, both to Europe and to the world, that freedom which is our heritage from centuries of Christian civilisation, and that security which alone can make possible the betterment of man's lot upon the earth.

In the tasks that lie ahead may there be given to our statesmen the vision to see, the faith to act, and the courage to persevere.

NOTES

1 Cabinets, foreign policies and case-studies

1 Patrick Gordon Walker, *The Cabinet* (London: Fontana/Collins, 1972, revised edn), pp. 138–51.
2 See Ritchie Ovendale (ed.), *The Foreign Policy of the British Labour Governments, 1945–1951* (Leicester: Leicester University Press, 1984) and John W. Young (ed.), *The Foreign Policy of Churchill's Peacetime Administration, 1951–1955* (Leicester: Leicester University Press, 1988).
3 The term 'science' is used here in the European sense of a concern for the systematic accumulation of knowledge, rather than in the American sense of a subject akin to the natural sciences in its predictive capabilities. In *The Limits of Political Science* (Oxford: The Clarendon Press, 1989), Nevil Johnson criticises the profession in Britain for losing its way, torn between Americanisation and 'the naive and descriptive empiricism which is currently predominant' (p. 79).
4 For example, Colin Seymour-Ure, partly in his article 'The "Disintegration" of the Cabinet and the Neglected Question of Cabinet Reform' (*Parliamentary Affairs*, 24: 3 (1971)), and partly in private correspondence with Peter Hennessy, cited in the latter's *Cabinet* (Oxford: Basil Blackwell, 1986), pp. 5–6. See also Brian W. Hogwood, *From Crisis to Complacency: Shaping Public Policy in Britain* (Oxford: Oxford University Press, 1987), especially pp. 81–103.
5 For example, W. Ivor Jennings, *Cabinet Government* (3rd edn, Cambridge: Cambridge University Press, 1959), and H. Daalder, *Cabinet Reform in Britain 1914–63* (Stanford, Calif.: Stanford University Press, 1963).
6 The point of view of Richard Crossman in his Introduction to Walter Bagehot's *The English Constitution* (London: Fontana/Collins, 1963), pp. 48–57. Crossman took his cue from John Mackintosh's *The British Cabinet* (London: Stevens & Sons, 1962; 2nd edn, 1968). The debate has been analysed recently by James Barber, who is also a specialist in British foreign policy. See his 'The Power of the Prime Minister' in R. L. Borthwick and J. E. Spence (eds.), *British Politics in Perspective* (Leicester: Leicester University Press, 1984) and *Who Makes British Foreign Policy?* (Milton Keynes: Open University Press, 1976).
7 The very use of concepts such as threats and sanctions implies that power is consciously sought after, and is more than a mere effect of

policy-making. Further relevant works are: D. N. Chester, 'Who Governs Britain?' (*Parliamentary Affairs*, 15: 4 (Autumn 1962), pp. 519–27); Gordon Walker, *The Cabinet*; A. King (ed.), *The British Prime Minister: A Reader* (London: Macmillan, 1969, and second, much revised edn, 1985); G. W. Jones, 'Development of the Cabinet', in William Thornhill (ed.), *The Modernization of British Government* (London: Pitman, 1975), and G. W. Jones, 'Prime Ministers and Cabinets' (*Political Studies*, 20 (June 1972), pp. 213–22).

8 Confirmed by King, *The British Prime Minister: A Reader*, 2nd edn, pp. 8–9. As an example, Michael Rush's recent textbook barely mentions foreign policy (*The Cabinet and Policy Formation* (London: Longman, 1984)).

9 See, for example, Bernard Donoughue and G. W. Jones, *Herbert Morrison: Portrait of a Politician* (London: Weidenfeld & Nicolson, 1973), Alan Bullock, *The Life and Times of Ernest Bevin*, vol. II: *Foreign Secretary 1945–1951* (London: Heinemann, 1983), and David Dilks, *Neville Chamberlain*, vol. I: *Pioneering and Reform 1869–1929* (Cambridge: Cambridge University Press, 1984).

10 In Michael Brecher, *Decisions in Israel's Foreign Policy* (London: Oxford University Press, 1974), pp. 4–8.

11 Graham Allison, *Essence of Decision* (Boston: Little, Brown, 1971), and Karen Dawisha, *The Kremlin and the Prague Spring* (London and Berkeley: University of California Press, 1985). The term 'structured' refers to the way in which such studies are framed using explicitly theoretical concepts and hypotheses, so that the findings may be tested against other work of a similar nature.

12 For representative works, see Michael Smith, Steve Smith and Brian White (eds.), *British Foreign Policy: Tradition, Change, and Continuity* (London: Unwin Hyman, 1988), and Michael Clarke and Brian White (eds.), *Understanding Foreign Policy: The Foreign Policy Systems Approach* (Aldershot: Edward Elgar, 1989).

13 The first books on the subject were all by foreign writers: Donald Bishop, *The Administration of British Foreign Relations* (Syracuse: Syracuse University Press, 1961), Kenneth N. Waltz, *Foreign Policy and Democratic Politics* (Boston: Little, Brown, 1967), and David Vital, *The Making of British Foreign Policy* (London: George Allen & Unwin, 1968). See also Robert Boardman and A. J. R. Groom (eds.), *The Management of Britain's External Relations* (London: Macmillan, 1973), Joseph Frankel, *British Foreign Policy 1945–73* (London: Oxford University Press, for the Royal Institute of International Affairs, 1975), and William Wallace, *The Foreign Policy Process in Britain* (London: Oxford University Press for the Royal Institute of International Affairs, 1975).

14 Donald G. Bishop, 'The Cabinet and Foreign Policy', in Boardman and Groom (eds.), *Management of Britain's External Relations*; Avi Shlaim, Peter Jones and Keith Sainsbury, *British Foreign Secretaries since 1945* (Newton Abbot: David & Charles, 1977).

15 Ernest May, *'Lessons' of the Past: The Use and Misuse of History in American*

Foreign Policy (New York: Oxford University Press, 1973), and (with Richard Neustadt), *Thinking in Time: The Uses of History for Decision-Makers* (New York: The Free Press, 1986); Irving Janis, *Groupthink* (2nd edn, Boston: Houghton Mifflin, 1982).

16 Avi Shlaim, *The United States and the Berlin Blockade 1948–9: A Study of Crisis Decision-making* (Berkeley: University of California Press, 1983). The exception is more in the fact that Dr Shlaim is based in Britain than in the content of his study, which is largely about the United States.

17 See Dawisha, *The Kremlin and the Prague Spring*, and Shlaim, *The United States and the Berlin Blockade*, and (*inter alia*) Michael Brecher, Jonathan Wilkenfeld and Sheila Moser, *Crises in the Twentieth Century*, vols. I and II (Oxford: Pergamon Press, 1988).

18 Coral Bell, *The Conventions of Crisis* (London: Oxford University Press, 1971); Phil Williams, *Crisis Management* (London: Martin Robertson, 1976); Richard Ned Lebow, *Between Peace and War: The Nature of International Crisis* (Baltimore: Johns Hopkins University Press, 1981).

19 'Post-behaviouralist' because although foreign policy analysis was born out of the behaviouralist revolution in American political science, most of its best work (and all that done in Britain) has come out of an attempt to marry theoretical sensitivity with historical understanding, and a rejection of the notion that general laws of foreign policy behaviour can be discovered.

20 This school is strong on both sides of the Atlantic. See my 'History and International Relations', in Steve Smith (ed.), *International Relations: British and American Perspectives* (Oxford: Basil Blackwell, 1985).

21 Jim Bulpitt, 'Rational Politicians and Conservative Statecraft in the Open Polity', in Peter Byrd (ed.), *British Foreign Policy under Thatcher* (Oxford: Philip Allan, 1988), p. 181.

22 For discussions of the pros and cons of the case-study method, see Alexander L. George, 'Case-Studies and Theory Development: the Method of Structured, Focused, Comparison', in Paul Lauren (ed.), *Diplomacy: New Approaches in History, Theory and Policy* (New York: The Free Press, 1979), pp. 43–68, and J. N. Rosenau, *The Scientific Study of Foreign Policy* (New York: The Free Press, 1971), pp. 25–33, 55–65.

23 For this debate, which lurks behind most analysis of policy-making, see Steven Lukes, *Power: A Radical View* (London: Macmillan, 1974).

24 E. H. Carr, *The Twenty Years Crisis* (London: Macmillan, 1939).

25 On which see the summaries in Esmond Robertson (ed.), *The Origins of the Second World War* (London: Macmillan, 1971), and Wolfgang J. Mommsen and Lothar Kettenacker (eds.), *The Fascist Challenge and the Policy of Appeasement* (London: Allen & Unwin, 1983).

26 The need to look at the last year or so of formal peace in conjunction with the first twenty-one months of war is emphasised in the accounts in Donald Cameron Watt, *Too Serious a Business: European Armed Forces and the Approach to the Second World War* (London: Temple Smith, 1975), and P. M. H. Bell, *The Origins of the Second World War in Europe* (London: Longman, 1986).

27 Alistair Horne, *A Savage War of Peace, Algeria 1954–1962* (London: Macmillan, 1977).
28 Winston S. Churchill, *The Second World War*, vol. III: *The Grand Alliance* (London: Cassell, 1950), p. 24.
29 For an analysis of the role of governmental perceptions of public opinion on foreign policy at this time, see my 'The Decision-making Process in relation to British Foreign Policy, 1938–41' (unpublished D.Phil. thesis, University of Oxford, 1978), pp. 335–82.
30 For a sympathetic, post-revisionist, treatment of Chamberlain along similar lines, see John Charmley, *Chamberlain and the Lost Peace* (London: Hodder & Stoughton, 1989).
31 Of course some crises are intrinsically more likely to lead to war than others, but even in 1939 Chamberlain at times felt normality was almost at hand once more, and he certainly resisted the notion that war was completely inevitable. See Chamberlain Papers, NC 18/1/1087, letter to Ida Chamberlain, 26 February 1939, and NC 18/1/1105, letter to Hilda Chamberlain, 2 July 1939.
32 See, for example, the two most recent accounts of Chamberlain's foreign policy, Donald Cameron Watt's *How War Came* (London: Heinemann, 1989), which illuminates the major issues on the very basis of their changing nature over time, and John Charmley, *Chamberlain and the Lost Peace*, whose relentless story-telling, *per contra*, obscures the argument. The same is true of such earlier works as Keith Middlemas, *Diplomacy of Illusion: The British Government and Germany, 1937–39* (London: Weidenfeld & Nicolson, 1972), Ian Colvin, *The Chamberlain Cabinet* (London: Gollancz, 1971), and Roger Parkinson, *Peace For Our Time* (London: Rupert Hart-Davis, 1971).
33 Still represented by such books as Owen Chadwick, *Britain and the Vatican during the Second World War* (Cambridge: Cambridge University Press, 1986).
34 Ritchie Ovendale, *Appeasement and the English-Speaking World: Britain, the United States, the Dominions and the Policy of Appeasement, 1937–39* (Cardiff: University of Wales Press, 1975); Callum A. MacDonald, *The United States, Britain and Appeasement* (London: Macmillan, 1981); G. C. Peden, *British Rearmament and the Treasury, 1932–39* (Edinburgh: Scottish Academic Press, 1979); Michael Howard, *The Continental Commitment: The Dilemma of British Defence Policy in the Era of Two World Wars* (London: Temple Smith, 1972); Wesley Wark, *The Ultimate Enemy: British Intelligence and Nazi Germany 1933–1939* (Oxford: Oxford University Press, 1986); Franklin Reid Gannon, *The British Press and Germany, 1936–39* (Oxford: The Clarendon Press, 1971).
35 For Donald Cameron Watt's early dissection of the 'British Foreign Policy-making Elite', in which he attempted 'to bridge the gap' between history and political science, see *Personalities and Policies: Studies in the Formulation of British Foreign Policy in the Twentieth Century* (London: Longman, 1965). For a more recent statement of his views on methodology, see 'What about the People? Abstraction and Reality in

History and the Social Sciences', Inaugural Lecture at the London School of Economics and Political Science, published by the latter in 1983. For subsequent, largely American, building on this beginning, see Samuel Williamson, *The Politics of Grand Strategy* (Cambridge, Mass.: Harvard University Press, 1969), and Ernest May and Richard Neustadt, *Thinking in Time*. Interdisciplinary work between history and International Relations has also developed outside the confines of foreign policy analysis. See Robert I. Rotberg and Theodore K. Rabb (eds.), *The Origin and Prevention of Major Wars* (Cambridge: Cambridge University Press, 1989), with contributions from established figures on both sides of the divide.

36 Cameron Watt, for example, in his 1983 inaugural lecture (see n. 35, above), devoted considerable time to defending the study of 'particularity' against the *annalistes* school, and listed four major reasons why the historian should 'distrust' the social scientist (see especially p. 19).

37 J. M. Lee, *The Churchill Coalition 1940–1945* (London: Batsford, 1980).

38 E. H. Carr discusses the determinist viewpoint far more subtly than he has been given credit for. See *What is History?* (Harmondsworth: Penguin, 1964), especially pp. 44–55 and 93–108). For an interesting discussion of another British intellectual bucking the national voluntarist trend, see W. H. McNeill, *Arnold J. Toynbee* (Oxford: Oxford University Press, 1989).

39 Note the distinction between pacifism and pacificism, employed by Martin Ceadel in his *Pacifism in Britain, 1914–45: The Defining of a Faith* (Oxford: The Clarendon Press, 1980).

40 The writers who first took an interest in these issues in foreign policy analysis, and indeed laid down the theoretical framework within which they could be intelligently discussed, were Harold and Margaret Sprout. See in particular their *The Ecological Perspective in Human Affairs* (Princeton: Princeton University Press, 1965).

41 'Counterfactual analysis' is a matter of great controversy among historians (for a deft summary see the entry on p. 142 of Alan Bullock and Oliver Stallybrass, *The Fontana Dictionary of Modern Thought* (London: Fontana/Collins, 1977)). The comments by E. H. Hunt and G. R. Hawke on the work of R. W. Fogel further illuminate the logical and methodological problems raised: 'The New Economic History: Professor Fogel's Study of American Railways', and 'Comment' (*History*, 53: 177 (February, 1968), pp. 3–23).

42 For the first view, see Williamson Murray's assessment of the Chamberlain government's 'lamentable lack of strategic sense', in *The Change in the European Balance of Power, 1938–39* (Princeton: Princeton University Press, 1984), p. 305. For the second, see A. J. P. Taylor, *The Origins of the Second World War* (Harmondsworth: Penguin, 1965), pp. 334–5.

43 Among various difficult pairings, Wilson–Brown and Thatcher–Pym/ late-vintage Howe, stand out in the post-war period, while Chamberlain–Eden and Churchill–Halifax were obviously problem-

atical during the Hitler years. See Shlaim, Jones and Sainsbury, *British Foreign Secretaries*.

44 One of the first and most interesting explanations of how what went on inside the decision-making 'black box' affected the content of policy was Joseph Frankel, *The Making of Foreign Policy* (London: Oxford University Press, 1963).

45 See, for example, the lengthy treatment of the Asquith/Grey administration, in F. H. Hinsley (ed.), *The Foreign Policy of Sir Edward Grey* (Cambridge: Cambridge University Press, 1977). An account of some aspects of foreign policy-making between 1938 and 1941 is provided in my thesis, 'The Decision-making Process'.

46 The term can be justified by the closeness of the two in day-to-day affairs. See Sir Llewellyn Woodward, *British Foreign Policy in the Second World War*, vol. I (London: HMSO, 1970), who points (p. xl) to the contrast with the situation in the United States. In Britain, as a rule, the Foreign Secretary runs the Office itself, but is joined by the Prime Minister when he has to deal with important issues which arise unexpectedly, or which involve direct contact with senior foreign figures.

2 Constructing the Polish guarantee, 15–31 March 1939

1 Prominent in this school of thought is Simon Newman, in his book *March 1939: The British Guarantee to Poland. A Study in the Continuity of British Foreign Policy* (Oxford: The Clarendon Press, 1976).

2 This second line is taken most recently by Anita Prazmowska, who also usefully summarises the debate in the Introduction to her book *Britain, Poland, and the Eastern Front, 1939* (Cambridge: Cambridge University Press, 1987), pp. 1–18.

3 COS 765 (Revise); quoted in David Dilks (ed.), *The Diaries of Sir Alexander Cadogan, 1938–1945* (London: Cassell, 1971), p. 108.

4 *DBFP* III: 3, pp. 252–3, Halifax to Sir E. Phipps, 1 November 1938; Sinclair Papers, B/62, Sir Percy Harris MP to Sinclair, 15 October 1938, reporting a conversation with Halifax: 'In confidence Halifax seemed to think there was every possibility that Czechoslovakia would now be inside the German orbit.' A series of memoranda which illustrate almost isolationist attitudes are brought together in 'Possible future course of British Policy' (FO 371/21659). They are analysed at length by D. Lammers in 'From Whitehall after Munich: The Foreign Office and the Future Course of British Policy' (*The Historical Journal*, 16: 4 (1973), pp. 831–56).

5 Dilks, *Cadogan Diaries*, pp. 152–3, 158. Also *DBFP* III: 4, pp. 160–1, Halifax to Sir R. Lindsay, 27 February 1939. See also Watt, *How War Came*, pp. 146–7 and 164–5, for how such warnings as there were got lost in the 'noise' of conflicting signals and information overload.

6 Expounded in Leon Festinger, *A Theory of Cognitive Dissonance* (Stanford, Calif.: Stanford University Press, 1962).

7 Chamberlain Papers, NC 18/1/1085–6, letter to Ida Chamberlain, 12 February 1939, and letter to Hilda Chamberlain, 19 February 1939. Vansittart was by this time seen as a source of irritation more than support by Chamberlain and (particularly) Cadogan. The optimistic mood produced Hoare's famous gaffe of the 'golden age' speech on 10 March. See Watt, *How War Came*, pp. 162–4.
8 Watt (in *How War Came*, p. 166) says that 'the Secret Intelligence Service (SIS) had given very precise warnings of Hitler's intentions at least a fortnight earlier', but he gives no source for the statement. The same is true of his statements in 'British Intelligence and the Coming of the Second World War in Europe', in Ernest R. May (ed.), *Knowing One's Enemies: Intelligence Assessment between the Two World Wars* (Princeton: Princeton University Press, 1984, p. 249). Cadogan (Dilks, *Cadogan Diaries*, pp. 155–6) refers to such warnings only from 11 March on (with an ambiguous reference to the 9th), and there is no further specification in the official history of intelligence for the period. See F. H. Hinsley, *British Intelligence in the Second World War: Its Influence on Strategy and Operations*, vol. I (London: HMSO, 1979), pp. 58 and 83. Wark's *The Ultimate Enemy* (pp. 116 and 218–19) follows Cadogan on this (as does his 1990 article in *Intelligence and National Security*), and the truth seems likely to be close to Christopher Andrew's version in his *Secret Service: The Making of the British Intelligence Community* (London: Sceptre/ Heinemann, 1986), pp. 584–6. Andrew suggests that warnings were coming from Vansittart's 'private detective agency' (and were therefore discounted by Chamberlain and Cadogan) from late February, but MI5 and the SIS only added their voices from 11 March. Sir John Simon admitted in the Commons on 15 March that the Diplomatic Service had failed to predict the invasion; see Hansard Parliamentary Debates, 5th Series, House of Commons (hereafter *HCD*), vol. 345, cols. 545–6. French intelligence, however, seems accurately to have forecast the blow as far back as 6 March. See Anthony Adamthwaite, *France and the Coming of the Second World War 1936–1939* (London: Frank Cass, 1977), p. 300.
9 Sir John Simon denied to the House of Commons on 15 March that Britain would take on new commitments (*HCD*, vol. 345, cols. 545–59). For the notion of the foreign policy 'executive', see pp. xviii, 7 and 15, above.
10 Hore-Belisha recorded in his diary for 15 March (in the Hore-Belisha Papers) that he had pointed out to the Cabinet that this aggression against non-Germans constituted a new departure and pointed to 'the Drang nach Osten'. (For a description of the composition of the Cabinet at this time, see Appendix 1, pp. 248–9.)
11 CAB 23/98, CM 11(30), 15 March 1939.
12 *DBFP* III: 4, pp. 360–1, 17 March 1939.
13 Blue Book Miscellaneous No. 9 (London: HMSO, 1939): *Documents Concerning German-Polish Relations and the Outbreak of Hostilities Between Great Britain and Germany on September 3 1939*, Cmd 6106, pp. 5–10.
14 The description of the speech as a 'landmark' is taken from the second

Earl of Birkenhead's *Halifax: The Life of Lord Halifax* (London: Hamish Hamilton, 1965), p. 435. Chamberlain himself gives the impression that the speech was his own work (Chamberlain Papers, NC 18/1/1090, letter to Hilda Chamberlain, 19 March 1939), and this is also the view taken by Watt (*How War Came*, pp. 167–9) and Charmley (*Chamberlain and the Lost Peace*, pp. 166–7), although it is clear that the Foreign Office and perhaps the wider political climate were important influences on the Prime Minister. For the impact of the latter see Sidney Aster, *1939: The Making of the Second World War* (London: André Deutsch, 1973), pp. 30–5.

15 John Harvey (ed.), *The Diplomatic Diaries of Oliver Harvey, 1937–40* (London: Collins, 1970), p. 262; Dilks, *Cadogan Diaries*, p. 160 (my italics). 'S. of S.' refers to the Secretary of State (Halifax) and 'O.S.' to Orme Sargent.

16 *Documents on British Foreign Policy* (eds. E. L. Woodward and Rohan Butler) says that Tilea came in the afternoon (*DBFP* III: 4, Halifax to Sir R. Hoare, 17 March 1939, pp. 366–7). Cadogan says the visit was in the evening (Dilks, *Cadogan Diaries*, p. 160). 6 p.m. seems a good compromise, as Tilea had seen the US Ambassador first, who cabled Washington at precisely that time to say that Tilea had just left on his way to the Foreign Office (*Foreign Relations of the United States*, 1939, vol. I, p. 72, Joseph Kennedy to the Secretary of State, 17 March 1939).

17 See Watt, *How War Came*, pp. 169–71.

18 See note 2, above, this chapter. The separate telegram to Moscow left at 9.35 p.m.

19 CAB 23/98, CM 12(39), Saturday 18 March 1939, 5 p.m. In the afternoon before the Cabinet meeting a message had been received from the British Ambassador in Bucharest, requesting the cancellations of the telegrams to 'threatened states', on the grounds that Tilea's scare was false (FO 371/23060; both came in by telephone, the first at 12.30 p.m., and the second at 3.40 p.m.). If the replies were coming in before the Cabinet met, then it is highly likely that Halifax knew that the original telegrams had gone out. He agreed the cancellations, which went out at 1 a.m. the next morning. Cadogan confirms the sequence of events (Dilks, *Cadogan Diaries*, p. 160) and the messages are reproduced in *DBFP* III: 4, p. 369, Sir R. Hoare to Halifax.

20 Harvey, *Diplomatic Diaries*, p. 262.

21 *DBFP* III: 4, p. 367, Halifax to Sir R. Hoare, 17 March 1939.

22 *DBFP* III: 4, p. 365, Halifax to Sir R. Lindsay, 17 March 1939.

23 Dilks, *Cadogan Diaries*, p. 157; Aster (*1939*, pp. 62–4) confirms that the 'bingeing up' – at least insofar as the phrase referred to the question of Roumania – came from Halifax and the Foreign Office (that is, mostly Sargent and Cadogan).

24 Not that Halifax was going as far as some of his officials would have liked. On 17 March Ivone Kirkpatrick, backed by Cadogan and Orme Sargent, wanted the British Army to boycott all contacts with the German officer corps, but the Foreign Secretary refused on the

grounds that he wanted to drive a wedge between the army and the Nazis, not lump them together (FO 371/22994).
25 CAB 23/98, CM 12(39), 18 March (my italics). It is interesting that Ian Colvin, in *The Chamberlain Cabinet* (London: Gollancz, 1971, p. 188), omits the italicised words without acknowledgement.
26 Keith Feiling, *The Life of Neville Chamberlain* (London: Macmillan, 1946), p. 400, and see Aster, *1939*, pp. 30–5.
27 This is insufficiently emphasised by Simon Newman (*March 1939*) in his attempt to emphasise the continuities of British foreign policy between 1938 and 1939.
28 Chamberlain Papers, NC 18/1/1090, letter to Hilda Chamberlain, 19 March 1939. The original plan for the Birmingham speech, to talk about economic and social matters, was completely set aside. See *Documents concerning German-Polish Relations and the Outbreak of Hostilities between Great Britain and Germany on September 3 1939*, Cmd 6106, p. 5.
29 Roger Makins, recorded by Harvey, *Diplomatic Diaries*, p. 266. This phrase in fact referred specifically to the later four-power declaration, but the principle of multilateral consultation was the same.
30 CAB 23/98, CM 12(39), 18 March.
31 This ironically anticipates later arguments by the opponents of a Soviet alliance, to the effect that it would alienate neutrals. Here Elliot clearly means the opposite.
32 Chamberlain and Halifax, plus Stanley and Simon, that is, the executive and one minister from each side of the coming argument about the USSR (FO 371/22967, Minutes of the Meetings of Ministers, 19 March 1939, at 11.30 a.m. and 4.30 p.m.). This is relevant to the 'big four' conception, discussed below in chapter 8.
33 *DBFP* III: 4, pp. 370, 372, 374, 384; Dilks, *Cadogan Diaries*, p. 161.
34 Chamberlain Papers, NC 18/1/1090, letter to Hilda Chamberlain, 19 March 1939. As had been evident with Eden in 1938, Chamberlain could be dismissive of the Foreign Office and its channels. At this time Halifax was still irritated by having to find out from *The Observer* of 12 March what the Prime Minister had said to a Dr Ley of the German Labour Front which had produced the wave of optimism of around 10 March (see FO 371/22967, 27 March 1939). *The Observer* had contained a leader headlined 'Ministers and Peace: The Case for Confidence'. Halifax asked 10 Downing Street for a record of the talks, but was told that no minute had been taken.
35 CAB 23/98, CM 13(39), 20 March 1939.
36 Actually the meeting of ministers had been as concerned for the sensibilities of Holland and Switzerland, an attack on either of which, they had confirmed, would be a casus belli for Britain (FO 371/22967, Meeting of Ministers at 10 Downing Street, 11.30 a.m., 19 March 1939).
37 Stanley's sympathies for the USSR had little effect principally because although Chamberlain and Halifax effectively ignored the Soviet Union, they did not formally close the door on an arrangement with that country (FO 371/22967). See also Aster, *1939*, pp. 80–2, and

Chamberlain Papers, NC 18/1/1091, letter to Ida Chamberlain, 26 March 1939: 'I drafted the formula myself and sent it out.'

38 It is fair to add that Halifax envisaged a later extension of diplomacy to the Balkan states, after the four-power declaration had been achieved as a 'rallying-point' (*DBFP* III: 4, p. 424, Record of Anglo-French Conversations, 21 March, and p. 436, Halifax to Sir H. Kennard, 21 March 1939). And guarantees were given later to Roumania, Greece and Turkey. But these delayed bilateral agreements were a long way from the regional multilateral pact that Ministers seem to have had in mind on 18 March. As Professor Cameron Watt has graphically put it: 'Instead of an interlocking dam against further German expansion in Eastern Europe, its stones well-supported by mutual alliances and guarantees, Britain would be left with a series of stones, each supported only by the strut of unilateral guarantees from the far side of the flood water' (*How War Came*, p. 213).

39 As Secretary for India, Zetland wanted co-operation with Turkey to provide a buffer for the Middle East and ultimately India.

40 CAB 23/98, CM 13(39) 20 March.

41 Dilks' edition of the Cadogan diaries gives the phrase as 'non-intéressement' (p. 161). This makes no sense at all, and must be a calligraphical or typographical error.

42 *DBFP* III: 4, p. 486, note 2, Halifax to Mr Campbell (Paris), 23 March 1939.

43 The final version, as sent off to Paris, Moscow and Warsaw at 11.05 p.m. on 20 March 1939, was slightly tougher and more specific in that it included the promise to consult about the possibilities of joint resistance to aggression (*DBFP* III: 4, pp. 400–1, Halifax to Sir E. Phipps, Sir W. Seeds and Sir H. Kennard, 20 March 1939). However, even this was due to French pressure – see *DBFP* III: 4, p. 473, FO Memorandum, 22 March 1939. Dilks, *Cadogan Diaries*, p. 161, and Aster, *1939*, p. 86.

44 The word in square brackets is not contained in the Dilks text (p. 161), but presumably should be. The italics are Cadogan's.

45 This extraordinary categorisation is to be found in CAB 23/98, CM 13(39), 20 March. See also *DBFP* III: 4, p. 436, Halifax to Kennard, 21 March 1939, where Halifax includes Poland among 'the Great Powers'.

46 The phraseology was Sir William Seeds'. See *DBFP* III: 4, p. 385, Seeds to Halifax, 19 March 1939.

47 *DBFP* III: 4, pp. 385, 392–3, 429–30, 471–2 and 574 contain accounts of Anglo-Soviet diplomacy at this time. The British were clearly taking a different view of conference diplomacy from that current in September 1938. See also FO 371/22967, Meeting of Ministers, 4.30 p.m., 19 March 1939.

48 CAB 23/98, CM 14(39), 22 March.

49 *DBFP* III: 4, pp. 574–5, Seeds to Halifax, 1 April 1939.

50 S. S. Wilson, *The Cabinet Office to 1945* (London: HMSO, 1975), pp. 12–15 and 174, describes the growth of these committees.

51 *DBFP* III: 4, pp. 457–63, Record of Anglo-French Conversations, 22 March 1939.
52 *DBFP* III: 4, pp. 422–7, Record of Anglo-French Conversations, 21 March 1939. Halifax asked Bonnet whether, if they were determined to stop aggression, 'Poland might also be brought to think that it would not be to her interest to see Great Britain and France greatly weakened?' (p. 425).
53 The French concern to bring Poland in was probably an important reinforcement to the British executive's train of thought, *pace* Newman's picture of the initiatives flowing from Halifax (*March 1939*, pp. 135–8).
54 *DBFP* III: 4, pp. 459–50, Anglo-French Conversations, 22 March 1939. One reason for saying this was that if France went to war for Roumania, the Franco-Polish Treaty of 1921 would come into operation.
55 *Ibid.*, p. 461. This 'new procedure' may have involved a certain sleight of hand with the Labour leaders whom Chamberlain met on the next day, 23 March. According to Dalton, he told them that the multilateral declaration was still British policy and (once pressed) that Anglo-Soviet relations were now satisfactory (Dalton Papers, Diary (20), 23 March 1939). But the official record of the meeting – on which Cadogan scribbled at the time 'I think that it is a fair presentation of what passed', as if in anticipation of differing interpretations – says that Chamberlain talked of Poland now being the key and the Soviet conference proposal being impracticable (FO 371/22967, Record of a Meeting with the TUC and the National Executive of the Labour Party, 23 March 1939).
56 Prazmowska (*Britain, Poland and the Eastern Front*, p. 45) makes the point that at this stage British and Polish views of the problem were based on very different preoccupations, even though convergence was increasingly being assumed in London. This process of disjunctive mutual perceptions is common in diplomacy, and was to be particularly evident between Britain and the United States during the Suez and Skybolt affairs, as Richard Neustadt has pointed out in his *Alliance Politics* (New York: Columbia University Press, 1970).
57 One of the first scholars to note this failure to clarify the options available was Robert Manne, in his 'The British Government and the Question of the Soviet Alliance, 15 March–24 August 1939', chapter 1 (unpublished thesis for the B.Phil. in International Relations, University of Oxford, 1972). See also Manne's 'The British Decision for Alliance with Russia, May 1939' (*Journal for Contemporary History*, 9: 3 (1974), pp. 3–26). Clearly Chamberlain and Halifax did not act in a vacuum in coming to their close focus on Poland. They were in continual contact with Cadogan and his senior advisers. But in terms of the internal Cabinet debate there is no evidence that Foreign Office views filtered through at this point in any other way than via the Prime Minister and the Foreign Secretary.
58 *DBFP* III: 4, p. 436, Halifax to Sir H. Kennard, 21 March 1939.
59 This is not to underestimate the strength of Polish hostility to cooperation with the USSR, a phenomenon Dalton also noted after

seeing Raczynski and J. Stanczik, the Polish miners' leader (Dalton Papers, Diary (20), 28 and 30 March 1939).
60 Chamberlain Papers, NC 18/1/1091, letter to Ida Chamberlain, 26 March 1939.
61 *DBFP* III: 4, pp. 500–2, Halifax to Kennard, 24 March 1939.
62 See Prazmowska, *Britain, Poland and the Eastern Front*, especially pp. 47–8.
63 This is confirmed by Anna M. Cienciala, *Poland and the Western Powers 1938–9* (London: Routledge & Kegan Paul, 1968), pp. 216–17.
64 *DBFP* III: 4, p. 20, Halifax to Seeds, 4 April 1939. This document relates the sequence of events in Anglo-Soviet relations, 19–31 March 1939.
65 *DBFP* III: 4, pp. 457–61, Record of an Anglo-French conversation, 22 March.
66 See note 58, above, this chapter.
67 *DBFP* III: 4, pp. 194–7, memoranda on the Red Army and Soviet Air Force, enclosed by Sir W. Seeds in his report to Halifax of 6 March 1939. See also Watt, *How War Came* (pp. 102, 118–20 and 180).
68 *DBFP* III: 4, pp. 530–2, Halifax to Seeds, 28 March 1939, contains an account of Cadogan's meeting with Maisky on the 23rd. The published version of Cadogan's diaries does not contain the remark about 'stalling' Maisky (Dilks, *Cadogan Diaries*, p. 163, compare the manuscript diary in the Cadogan Papers, ACAD 1/8, 23 March 1939). Litvinov and Stalin clearly felt that they had been deceived, to judge by Litvinov's angry interview with Seeds on 1 April (*DBFP* III: 4, pp. 574–5, Seeds to Halifax). See also Watt, *How War Came*, p. 216.
69 Chamberlain Papers, NC 18/1/1091, letter to Ida Chamberlain, 26 March 1939.
70 Dilks, *Cadogan Papers*, p. 163, 25 March 1939.
71 Vansittart, Malkin and Strang were all Foreign Office officials: Vansittart was Chief Diplomatic Adviser, having been succeeded by Cadogan as Permanent Under-Secretary in 1938; Malkin was a Legal Adviser; and Strang was Head of the Central Department, the main part of whose responsibilities was Germany.
72 *Ibid.* See also Harvey, *Diplomatic Diaries*, p. 268, entry of 25 March. Interestingly, Harvey records the same sentiments about the USSR in his entry of 23 March (p. 267), seeing them as one conclusion of the talks with the French over the previous two days.
73 Dilks, *Cadogan Diaries*, pp. 163–4, 26 March 1939. It was on this day that Chamberlain put on paper his famous 'most profound distrust of Russia' views, part and parcel of the concentration on Poland. Cited in Feiling, *Life of Neville Chamberlain*, p. 403. The original is in the Chamberlain Papers, NC 18/1/1091, letter to Ida Chamberlain, 26 March 1939.
74 Dilks, *Cadogan Diaries*, p. 164, 27 March 1939.
75 The power not to call the Cabinet, or to discuss an issue, is of course a limited but definite part of the Prime Ministerial prerogative, discussed in Jennings, *Cabinet Government*, pp. 245–9.

76 CAB 27/624, FP(36), 38th Meeting, 27 March 1939.
77 For contacts between government and press circles, see Hill, 'Decision-making Process', chapter 3, pp. 312–17. Examples of the many inevitable contacts between ministers and politicians outside the government can be found in B. Liddell-Hart, *Memoirs*, vol. II (London: Cassell, 1965), pp. 222–8; Harvey, *Diplomatic Diaries*, p. 270; Nigel Nicolson (ed.), *Harold Nicolson: Diaries and Letters*, vol. I: *1930–9* (London: Collins/Fontana, 1969), p. 386, and in the Dalton Diary (20). Dalton personally saw the Prime Minister, Vansittart, Raczynski and Maisky in these few days, some of whom were more discreet than others.
78 CAB 27/624, FP(36), 38th Meeting, 27 March 1939.
79 Geography, history and ideology all seemed to militate against such an arrangement. But eventually the Poles accepted the idea of Britain pursuing a Soviet alliance. See chapter 3, n. 44, below.
80 The Labour movement had a greater importance than the government's huge parliamentary majority indicated, because of the growing pressure for conscription and increased arms production; see Peter Dennis, *Decision by Default: Peacetime Conscription and British Defence, 1919–1939* (London: Routledge & Kegan Paul, 1972), pp. 184–205. However the Prime Minister was well known for his resistance to criticism. On 4 December 1938 he wrote to his sister Ida: 'The only thing I care about is to be able to carry out the policy I believe, indeed know to be right, and the only distress that criticism or obstruction can cause me is if it prevents my purpose' (Chamberlain Papers, NC 18/1/1078).
81 Referring to Poland's fifty divisions, and a recent appreciation by the British Military Attaché in Berlin that Germany was not yet ready to support a two-front war (CAB 27/624, FP(36), 38th Meeting, 27 March 1939).
82 The psychological obstacles to the criticism of leadership initiatives in the small groups which usually characterise high-level foreign policy-making are entertainingly conveyed by Irving Janis in *Groupthink*.
83 Cadogan Papers, MS Diary, ACAD 1/8, 28 March 1939. See also Dilks, *Cadogan Diaries*, p. 164, for the entry of 27 March which shows surprise at the lack of any protest from Simon. The Simon papers are silent on the matter.
84 CAB 27/624, FP(36), 38th Meeting, 27 March 1939.
85 Hoare's support of an arrangement with the Soviet Union is one of the most surprising single facts to emerge from the public records, particularly in view of the lack of any mention of it in his autobiography, written after he had become Viscount Templewood: *Nine Troubled Years* (London: Collins, 1954). Perhaps writing during the Cold War led him to be prudent about mentioning support for a tie to the Soviets. It was even at odds with his contemporary image. Captain Harry Crookshank, a junior minister who nearly resigned over Munich, wrote on 31 March 1939, 'I am sure that Hoare and Simon are public menaces'

(Crookshank Papers, Ms. Eng. Hist. 359, Diary, vol. 2). His attitude is best understood in terms of his ability to speak Russian, and his firsthand knowledge of Russia, gained during an extensive intelligence mission during 1916–17. See J. Cross, *Sir Samuel Hoare: A Political Biography* (London: Jonathan Cape, 1977), pp. 39–51 and 294–8.

86 There is a relative lack of private papers for the ministers concerned. There are none available for Morrison, while Inskip's and Simon's papers do not cover the period February–March 1939 in any detail.

87 Morrison was no longer performing well enough in the Commons to take exposed positions in Cabinet (Chamberlain Papers, NC 18/1/1088, Chamberlain to Hilda Chamberlain, 5 March 1939).

88 CAB 53/10, COS Meetings, 282–3, 18 March 1939, 11.15 a.m. and 3 p.m.

89 CAB 23/98, CM 12(39), 18 March. None of this, of course, was to stop the announcement of the guarantee to Roumania on 13 April, another example of policy-making by reflex (Dilks, *Cadogan Diaries*, p. 173 and John Charmley, *Lord Lloyd and the Decline of the British Empire* (London: Weidenfeld & Nicolson, 1987), pp. 224–5). It is not surprising, given Chatfield's oscillations, that he later refused to explain even to the 1922 Committee (on grounds of confidentiality) how the guarantees to Poland and Roumania might be implemented (Chatfield Papers, CHT 6/5, speech to the 1922 Committee of 8 May 1939).

90 *DBFP* III: 4, pp. 515–17, Halifax to Kennard and Sir R. Hoare, 27 March 1939, 11.30 p.m.

91 Harvey, *Diplomatic Diaries*, pp. 267–70. Both Harvey and Cadogan record simply that the Foreign Policy Committee 'approved' the telegrams, with little fuss. They make no mention of the Soviet question (Dilks, *Cadogan Diaries*, p. 164).

92 *DBFP* III: 4, pp. 515–17, Halifax to Kennard and Sir R. Hoare, 27 March 1939; CAB 27/624, FP(36), 38th Meeting, 27 March 1939. In Cabinet on 29 March, Halifax said that he had tried to cater for the Home Secretary's views in Paragraph 6 of the telegram. It is this paragraph which contains only the pieties referred to above (CAB 23/98, CM 15(39), 29 March 1939).

93 See above, pp. 38–9.

94 Cadogan was surprised not to find Simon critical of the change in policy, so perhaps the latter's stance was neutral in the FPC (Dilks, *Cadogan Diaries*, p. 164).

95 See chapter 3, pp. 76–8, below.

96 CAB 53/10, COS Meetings 282–3, 18 March 1939, 11.15 a.m. and 3 p.m. This misrepresentation was to be compounded during the Cabinet meetings of 29–30 March, and it has been seen – understandably – as evidence of Chamberlain's willingness to suppress information or advice which went against his own instincts. See Aster, *1939*, pp. 76–106, and also Brian Bond, *British Military Policy between the Two World Wars* (Oxford: The Clarendon Press, 1980), pp. 307–8. There is no direct evidence for the reasons for the sins of omission committed

by the Prime Minister, Foreign Secretary and Minister for the Co-ordination of Defence (only hearsay from Beaverbrook about the non-circulation of the COS memorandum, see Liddell-Hart, *Memoirs*, vol. II (London: Cassell, 1965), p. 221) but Newman, *March 1939* (pp. 119–21, 154–5, 193–8), leans too far towards exculpation in emphasising the priority of political over military considerations. Wark (*The Ultimate Enemy*, pp. 220–1) also sees no anomaly in the sequence of events, but he cannot explain, and indeed barely mentions, the Chiefs of Staff's emphasis on the importance of the USSR.

97 Adamthwaite, *France and the Coming of the Second World War, 1936–1939*, pp. 304–6. Bonnet's and Lebrun's visit to London had been from 21 to 24 March, and Bonnet's remarks about the value of the USSR had been ambiguous, if not clearly hostile. The records of the Anglo-French discussions in London suggest that both sides were skirting the difficult question of what to do about Moscow (*DBFP* III: 4, pp. 422–7, Record of Conversations between British and French Ministers in London, 21 March, 5 p.m., and pp. 457–63, Record of an Anglo-French Conversation, 22 March 1939, 5 p.m.).

98 It is not suggested that Halifax and Chamberlain took a conspiratorial view of the Committee and its management, although they were self-regarding and headstrong during these hectic few weeks. More important is the fact that small groups in general, and British Cabinet Committees in particular, are susceptible to initiatives from the chair *in certain circumstances*.

99 Halifax stressed that 'The essential point was to manage matters so as to secure the support of Poland' (CAB 23/98, CM 15/39, 29 March 1939, a.m.).

100 Bonnet had been impressed by the Red Army in 1934, but by 1939 he had become suspicious of Soviet policy. Nonetheless he had put out some feelers to Moscow after 15 March, and wanted the Soviets in as well as Poland. Halifax may have misperceived the French line, which could never be assumed to be united in any case; see Adamthwaite, *France and the Coming of the Second World War*, pp. 47, 203, 273 and 312–13. Prazmowska further conveys the ambiguity of both French and British positions at this time (*Britain, Poland, and the Eastern Front*, p. 44). France had some concern for the effect of a move towards Moscow on Italy, and a generalised antipathy to 'ideological' divisions in Europe, but it was by no means clear as to whether this ruled out accommodations of interest between a Communist Soviet Union and liberal democratic states. See Halifax to Campbell in Paris, 23 March 1939, in *DBFP* III: 4, pp. 487–90.

101 The telegrams, which had been sent on the 27th with instructions to hold, were released for communication to the Polish and Roumanian governments at 9 p.m. on 29 March (*DBFP* III: 4, p. 451, Halifax to Kennard and Hoare).

102 The present state of documentation in Soviet foreign policy makes it impossible to be more than tentative in such statements. It is possible

that Stalin never had any intention of co-operating with Britain; on the other hand, subsequent Soviet behaviour indicated a clear distrust of British intentions. Sir Samuel Hoare noted: 'The Anglo-Russian negotiations have dragged on, the difficulty being to get the Kremlin to realise that we really are agreed in substance and that their new points are due to quite unnecessary suspicions' (Templewood Papers, X: 4, Hoare to W. W. Astor, 12 June 1939). For the pre-Gorbachev historical consensus on this in the Soviet Union, see Margot Light, 'The Soviet View', in Roy Douglas (ed.), *1939: A Retrospective Forty Years After* (London: Macmillan, 1983), pp. 74–6. For an assessment of the material made available in the last few years, which suggests that the USSR was willing to envisage an agreement on the right terms with Britain and France up to July 1939, see Geoffrey Roberts, 'The War on All Fronts', *Times Higher Educational Supplement*, 18 August 1989. See also Donald Cameron Watt, 'Why Stalin Chose Hitler', *The Independent*, 21 August 1989.
103 See Anne de Courcy, *1939: The Last Season* (London: Thames & Hudson, 1989), pp. 68–74.
104 CAB 23/98, CM 16(39), 30 March 1939. The Guarantee was thus announced earlier than might otherwise have been the case. Some ministers, notably Zetland, Maugham and Kingsley Wood, showed signs of hesitating on the brink. Their unwillingness to provoke a war between Germany and Poland by any declaration of support for the unreliable Beck led to the statement being redrafted along more general lines but did not halt the increasingly rapid progress towards an irrevocable commitment.
105 Aster, *1939*, pp. 100–1, and Charmley, *Lord Lloyd*, p. 222. It is possible that Colvin was being used by anti-Hitler elements in Germany who wanted to push Britain into action, and even that some of his information was correct. See Watt, *How War Came*, pp. 181–4. Whatever his clandestine role, Colvin was surely at twenty-six too young to carry such weight on his own. Christopher Andrew takes the view that Colvin was also used by Cadogan and Halifax 'to force the pace, impress the prime minister and convince the Cabinet'. Andrew does not, however, acknowledge that, as Halifax pointed out the next day, the Cabinet had already decided on the Guarantee in principle. See Andrew's *Secret Service*, p. 588.
106 Newman, *March 1939*, pp. 182–8.
107 On the Territorial Army decision, which caused the military enormous logistical problems, see Bond, *British Military Policy*, pp. 305–6, and Newman, *March 1939*, Appendix, pp. 223–5. The Hore-Belisha Papers (to be read with R. J. Minney, *The Private Papers of Hore-Belisha* (London: Collins, 1960), pp. 187–8) make it clear that the decision was primarily a political one, as 'Halifax was pressing to make a gesture to foreign countries'.
108 CAB 23/98, CM 16(39), 30 March 1939, and note 96 above, this chapter. See also CAB 53/47, Chiefs of Staff Memoranda 870 and 871 of

28 March, and 872 (Revise) of 3 April 1939, all dealing with 'The Military Implications of an Anglo-French Guarantee to Poland and Rumania', and CAB 53/10, Minutes of the 285th Meeting of the COS, on 28 March, which postponed full discussion of the draft paper. The Colvin scare seems then to have overtaken it, and the COS 'aide-mémoire' handed to Chatfield in Cabinet on the 30th at about 12.55 p.m., was to do with the apparent German troop mobilisation on the Silesian frontier, which led to the precipitate announcement of the Guarantee (CAB 53/10, 286th Meeting of COS, 30 March 1939). The failure to circulate the COS paper to Cabinet ministers could conceivably have been justified by the 'five-day rule' that no paper could be discussed in Cabinet unless it had been circulated at least five days previously (CAB 21/1341), but in such a fluid environment this would have been pedantry, and its submergence must either have been due to the fog of quasi-war, or to the manipulation of Colvin, his 'news' and the decision-making process by Chamberlain, Chatfield and others unknown.

109 Chatfield admitted he had not been seeking ministerial office, only a 'stand easy', but was soon 'thoroughly keen on it and only wish to make good'. At his first appearance as Chairman of the Committee of Imperial Defence on 9 February, he had felt 'like Alice in the Looking Glass' (Viscount Norwich Papers, DUFC 2/13, Chatfield to Duff Cooper, 10 February 1939).

110 On followership, see James MacGregor Burns, *Leadership* (New York: Harper & Row, 1978). For Chatfield's volte-face, see chapter 3 below, pp. 64–5.

111 CAB 23/98, CM 17(39), 31 March 1939, 12 noon; at this meeting the Cabinet decided to announce the new policy the same afternoon (*HCD*, vol. 345, cols. 2415–16).

3 The Soviet question, April–August 1939

1 Manne, 'The British Government and the Question of the Soviet Alliance', chapter 1, and Aster, *1939*, pp. 157–87, both contain full accounts.

2 CAB 23/98, CM 15(39), 29 March 1939.

3 *DBFP* III:5, pp. 205–6, Halifax to Seeds, Telegram no. 71, 14 April 1939, 10.20 p.m. (also in CAB 27/627, as having been circulated to the Foreign Policy Committee).

4 CAB 23/98, CM 18(39), 5 April 1939. Halifax agreed with Hudson, to whom he wrote on 4 April: 'Your impressions confirm the conclusions I have drawn from the reports of the Moscow Embassy' (FO 800/322, H/XXXIII/6).

5 The Chiefs of Staff had been distinctly unenthusiastic about the Guarantee, and even the memorandum bearing a ministerial imprint had accepted that 'neither Great Britain nor France could render direct assistance to Poland or Roumania by sea, land, or air, nor could

they supply them with armaments. Assistance from the USSR in this respect is therefore important' (CAB 53/47, COS Paper 872 (Revise), 3 April 1939).

6 Minney, *Private Papers of Hore-Belisha*, p. 189. The problem here is who is meant by 'the Government', and Hore-Belisha's papers themselves do not resolve the matter. On 13 April the guarantees to Greece and Roumania were announced, stimulated this time by Italian aggression. The Prime Minister had made sharp remarks in Cabinet about leaks to the *News Chronicle* on diplomacy towards Italy. Hore-Belisha noted that 'tempers are exacerbated. We are drifting', and that Simon had afterwards described the policy of 'giving guarantees to countries who do not want them' as Micawberish (Hore-Belisha Papers, Diary entry of 13 April 1939).

7 Runciman Papers, R3/32/1–4, C. Hendricks to W. Runciman, 11 April 1939.

8 Dalton Papers, Diary (20), 13 April 1939.

9 This is not to accept Maurice Cowling's picture of Halifax and Chamberlain marching to different drums after Munich (in *The Impact of Hitler: British Politics and British Policy 1939–40* (Cambridge: Cambridge University Press, 1975), pp. 278–83). In March both men had much preferred to concentrate British policy on Poland, and were cool with the USSR. As we shall see below, Halifax was always the more sensitive of the two when it came to spotting the need to shift positions, but it would be wrong to see him as a leader of a hawkish clique in the Cabinet.

10 CAB 23/98, CM 18(39), 5 April.

11 *DBFP* III: 5, pp. 53 and 82, Halifax to Seeds, 5 April and 11 April.

12 *DBFP* III: 5, pp. 209–10, Halifax to Seeds, 14 April, Telegram no. 284 (account of conversation with Maisky).

13 Harvey, *Diplomatic Diaries*, 13 April, p. 279. See also Halifax to Seeds, 14 April 1939: 'I am reluctant to abandon my efforts to secure some measures of co-operation from the Soviet Government' (CAB 27/627 and *DBFP* III: 5, pp. 205–6).

14 CAB 23/98, CM 29(30), 13 April.

15 The text of the proposals is in *DBFP* III: 5, pp. 228–9, Seeds to Halifax, 18 April (received 6.35 a.m.).

16 *DBFP* III: 5, pp. 448–50, Halifax to Seeds, 6 May 1939. The renewed request for a unilateral declaration was softened by assuring the USSR that their support would only be committed to countries whom Britain and France were already obligated.

17 CAB 23/98, CM 21(39), 19 April 1939, 11 a.m.

18 CAB 27/624, FP(36), 43rd meeting, 19 April 1939, 5.30 p.m.

19 After all, Foreign Minister Litvinov had been anxious throughout 1938 to achieve an anti-Nazi front of co-operation with Britain and France over Czechoslovakia. See Adam Ulam, *Expansion and Co-existence: The History of Soviet Foreign Policy, 1917–67* (London: Secker & Warburg, 1968), pp. 253–7.

Notes to pages 53–6   281

20 CAB 27/624, FP(36), 43rd Meeting, 19 April 1939, 5.30 p.m. For a list of the Committee's main attenders, see Appendix 1, below, and also Table 2, on p. 80.
21 Cadogan seems to have been taking the lead at this stage, with Halifax busy (Dilks, *Cadogan Diaries*, pp. 175–6; Harvey, *Diplomatic Diaries*, pp. 281–5).
22 FP(36), 43rd Meeting. Chamberlain, in repeating his view that Russia did not possess a serious offensive capability, cited 'several foreign Prime Ministers... and their opinion had been corroborated by Mr. R. S. Hudson and Sir Percy Loraine'. Hudson (Parliamentary Secretary to the Department of Overseas Trade) had just returned from Moscow; Loraine was between ambassadorial posts in Ankara and Rome.
23 Liddell-Hart, *Memoirs*, vol. II, p. 264. See also the Chatfield Papers, CHT 6/4, which show Churchill sending a memorandum on naval strategy direct to Chamberlain in late March, with only the most cursory nod in the Admiral's direction four days later, prompted by Halifax and unaware that the Prime Minister had passed it straight on in any case. The incident is also dealt with in Martin Gilbert, *Winston S. Churchill*, vol. V: *Companion*, Part 3: *Documents – The Coming of War 1936–1939* (London: Heinemann, 1982), pp. 1413–29.
24 CAB 27/624, FP(36), 43rd Meeting, 19 April 1939.
25 Dilks, *Cadogan Diaries*, p. 175, 19 April.
26 R. A. Butler was Parliamentary Under-Secretary at the Foreign Office, and as such attended two-thirds of the meetings of the Foreign Policy Committee after Munich, although his contributions were minor, as Chamberlain once noted (Chamberlain Papers, NC 18/1/1101, letter to Hilda Chamberlain, 28 May).
27 Dilks, *Cadogan Diaries*, p. 175, 19 April. The Minutes of the Foreign Policy Committee record that a reply was to be drafted along the lines suggested by Chamberlain and Morrison (CAB 27/624, FP(36), 43rd Meeting).
28 CAB 27/624, FP(36), 44th meeting, 25 April. The COS paper is CAB 27/627,FP(36)82, and is also to be found in CAB 53/48 as COS 887.
29 For his general awareness of the Dominions' basic suspicions about a Soviet alliance, see Ovendale, *'Appeasement' and the English-Speaking World*, pp. 267–72. In the Foreign Policy Committee Inskip had pointed out that the South African *aide-mémoire* he had read out setting out Pretoria's misgivings about the Soviet Union was of interest as the first case of a Dominion government offering Britain unsolicited advice on a foreign policy matter.
30 The phrase was Chamberlain's in the Foreign Policy Committee meeting of 25 April (CAB 27/624, FP(36), 44th Meeting). The guarantees given to Greece and Roumania on 13 April were probably still preoccupying the Prime Minister, guarantees which had been hurriedly put together but which owed quite a lot to expressions of concern in Cabinet, notably Hoare's remarks of 8 April, recalled by Halifax at the meeting of 10 April (CAB 23/98, Notes of a Conference of ministers,

Notes to pages 56–8

8 April 1939 (called at short notice over the Albanian crisis, and in Chamberlain's absence) and CM 19(39), 10 April 1939). See also CAB 27/624, FP(36), 42nd Meeting, 11 April 1939.
31 Dilks, *Cadogan Diaries*, pp. 176–7.
32 CAB 23/99, CM 24(39), 26 April 1939.
33 *DBFP* III: 5, pp. 358–9, Halifax to Phipps.
34 See pp. 114–19, below. To some extent the Foreign Policy Committee resembled here the 'partial Cabinet' which Gordon Walker in *The Cabinet* (pp. 87–91) describes as a major vehicle of Cabinet control in the post-war period. G. W. Jones, in a recent overview, argues that '*ad hoc* meetings and cabinet committees do not damage cabinet government: they enhance it' ('Cabinet Government since Bagehot', *LSE Quarterly*, 3:3 (Autumn 1989)).
35 When proposals for implementing conscription were brought to Cabinet on 24 April, doubts were expressed about the sense of bringing an 'Exceptional Powers' bill before Parliament. An *ad hoc* sub-committee, evenly-divided on the issue, was set up, and after its report back the next day, the Prime Minister's original plan was changed. See CAB 23/99, CM 22(39), 24 April 1939, and CM 23(39), 25 April 1939, and also Dennis, *Decision by Default*, pp. 216–18.
36 Even Halifax's last memorandum on 24 May (drafted by Cadogan, and otherwise fair), seemed to find it easier to list at length the cons than the pros of the alliance (CP 124(39), in CAB 21/551 (copy)).
37 Dilks, *Cadogan Diaries*, p. 181.
38 CAB 23/99, CM 30(39), 24 May 1939.
39 *Ibid.*, especially CP 124(39). (Also in CAB 23 and CAB 21/551.) In summary, they wre: concern for the credibility of the guarantees policy; French concern; the vulnerability of Turkey, with whom an agreement had just been announced.
40 The concept of 'policy drift' is described by G. Parry and P. Morriss, in 'When is a Decision not a Decision?', in *The British Political Sociology Yearbook*, vol. I (London: Croom Helm, 1974). Parry and Morriss are interpreting Peter Bachrach's and Morton Baratz's notion of the 'decisionless decision', contained in their *Power and Poverty* (London and New York: Oxford University Press, 1970), pp. 42–3. On the tendency to see the breakdown of negotiations as disastrous even when the goal is not strongly desired, see Fred Iklé, *How Nations Negotiate* (New York: Praeger, 1968), pp. 43–5.
41 CAB 27/625, FP(36), 47th Meeting, 16 May 1939. The change in the Chiefs of Staff's view is difficult to explain unless it is seen as a harking back to their views of the second half of March, when they had preferred the USSR to Poland as an ally (CAB 53/10, COS Meetings 282–3, on the 'Roumanian situation') and which had been so strangely obscured in the panic of 28–31 March (CAB 53/47, COS Papers 871 of 28 March and 872 [Revise] of 3 April 1939; see also Chapter 2, above, notes 96 and 108), *pace* N. H. Gibbs, *Grand Strategy*, vol. I: *Rearmament Policy* (London: HMSO, 1976), p. 727.

Notes to pages 58–60

42 CAB 23/99, CM 30(39), 24 May 1939. Hore-Belisha had privately noted the possibility on 3 May, despite it seeming fantastic (Hore-Belisha Papers, Diary entry of 3 May 1939).
43 For one example, see *DBFP* III: 4, pp. 70–1, Minute by Cadogan, 1 February 1939. The intelligence services do not seem to have been urgently calling attention to this possibility, which is mentioned as a 'very remote' risk in Foreign Office comments read to the Foreign Policy Committee by Cadogan on 19 April (CAB 27/624, CP(36), 43rd Meeting). See also Andrew, *Secret Service*, pp. 593–5 (on the lack of proper central co-ordination of intelligence, see pp. 576–8), and Watt, 'British Intelligence and the Coming of the Second World War in Europe', in May (ed.), *Knowing One's Enemies*, pp. 248–9, and 'An Intelligence Surprise: The Foreign Office Failure to Predict the Nazi-Soviet Pact', *Intelligence and National Security Journal*, 4: 3 (July 1989).
44 *DBFP* III: 5, pp. 636–7, Kennard to Cadogan, 22 May, and pp. 652–3, Sir R. Hoare to Cadogan, 23 May. It is ironic that this conclusion could be elicited after the intractabilities of March. The problem of Soviet troops entering Poland was now dodged, which leads one to suppose that the citation of Polish co-operation was more an *ex post facto* rationalisation than a reason for the change in British policy. By 19 May, when Poland and Roumania were asked for their views, most ministers had been converted to support for an alliance (*DBFP* III: 5, pp. 597–8, Halifax to Kennard and Sir R. Hoare, 19 May 1939).
45 CAB 23/99, CM 30(39), 24 May 1939.
46 Feiling (*Life of Neville Chamberlain*, p. 408) runs together letters of 9 and 29 April 1939. See Chamberlain Papers, NC 18/1/1092–6. It is clear that whatever the merits of Chamberlain's views on the USSR, he had little understanding of Marxism-Leninism.
47 See, for example, Harvey, *Diplomatic Diaries*, p. 290 (20 May 1939), and Chamberlain's letter of 29 April to Hilda, Chamberlain Papers, NC 18/1/1096: Russia was afraid of Germany and Japan and would be delighted to see other people fight them. Disappointment with Soviet reactions to his olive branch in February (see Watt, *How War Came*, pp. 118–19), may have been another factor in his continued antipathy. The tone of the Prime Minister's letters, however, suggests that he was also hardened in his attitude to the Soviets by the very fact that his despised domestic opponents, particularly Lloyd George, were calling for a *rapprochement* (see NC 18/1/1093, letter to Ida Chamberlain, 9 April 1939).
48 CAB 27/625, FP(36), 47th meeting, 16 May 1939.
49 CAB 23/99, CM 26(39), 3 May 1939; Dilks, *Cadogan Diaries*, pp. 181–2.
50 In his letter to Hilda Chamberlain of 29 April, Chamberlain referred specifically to the 'Balkan powers' (NC 18/1/1096).
51 CAB 23/99, CM 26(39), 3 May 1939. On 4 May, Halifax told Lord Camrose that the obstacles to an alliance included the effects on Japan, Roumania, Poland, British Roman Catholics, Spain, Italy and Portugal

(cited in Martin Gilbert, *Winston Churchill*, vol. V: *1922–1939* (London: Heinemann, 1976), p. 1068).
52 CAB 27/625, FP(36), 47th Meeting, 16 May 1939. New Zealand was actually in favour of collaboration with Russia (CAB 21/494, Telegram from Governor-General, 12 May 1939).
53 CAB 23/99, CM 30(39), 24 May 1939.
54 CAB 23/99, CM 26(39), 3 May, and 28(39), 17 May; and see CAB 27/625, FP(36), 47th Meeting, 16 May.
55 CAB 23/99, CM 30(39), 24 May 1939.
56 CAB 27/624, FP(36), 45th Meeting, 5 May; CAB 23/99, CM 27(39), 10 May. The British misread the meaning of Litvinov's removal, which is less surprising than their lack of any apparent concern about the turn of events. See Cameron Watt, *How War Came*, pp. 232–8, and Jonathan Haslam, *The Soviet Union and the Struggle for Collective Security in Europe, 1933–1939* (London: Macmillan, 1984), pp. 212–16.
57 CAB 23/99, CM 26)39), 3 May.
58 As late as 21 May he wrote to his sister that the possibility 'is a pretty sinister commentary on Russian reliability' (Chamberlain Papers, NC 18/1/1100). Chatfield, however, may have become more aware of this dimension after the Chiefs of Staff had warned against it in their paper of 24 April (CAB 27/627, FP(36) 82).
59 CAB 23/99, CM 30(39), 24 May (my italics). The words are Inskip's, interpreting the views of the Dominions.
60 Harvey, *Diplomatic Diaries*, p. 290, 20 May (my italics).
61 Other instances can be found in CAB 27/625, FP(36), 48th Meeting, 19 May (Inskip), and CAB 23/99, CM 30(39), 24 May (Halifax).
62 CAB 27/627, FP(36) 90, and CAB 27/625, 47th Meeting. Only the limited *casus foederis* (Poland and Roumania) and its nomenclature prevented this arrangement from being an alliance proper.
63 Halifax was converted on or around 20 May. See pp. 67–8, below.
64 The growing clamour for an agreement with the Soviet Union is described by Neville Thompson, *The Anti-Appeasers: Conservative Opposition to Appeasement in the 1930s* (Oxford: The Clarendon Press, 1971), pp. 212–15, and John F. Naylor, *Labour's International Policy: The Labour Party in the 1930s* (London: Weidenfeld & Nicolson, 1969), pp. 293–8.
65 France was now pursuing better relations with the Soviet Union more vigorously, but without keeping London fully informed. The two governments were 'out of step', and Molotov did not fail to note the fact, giving Seeds 'a most unpleasant ten minutes'. See Adamthwaite, *France and the Coming of the Second World War*, pp. 311–13, and *DBFP* III: 5, pp. 469–71, Seeds to Halifax, 9 May 1939. This put France in the lead in the new round of diplomacy with the USSR, and therefore exerted pressure on Britain to go further down the road of agreement, but it did not strengthen the image of French reliability in London. Indeed, Seeds wrote to the Foreign Office complaining about not being informed in advance as to whether, with Bonnet's reply to the USSR, he was dealing with 'a gross and deliberate error of tactics or merely . . . the

foolish amateurishness of a politician' (Seeds' private letter to Sir L. Oliphant, 16 May 1939, in *DBFP* III: 5, pp. 571–2). The use of the word 'deliberate' suggests that Seeds felt Britain was being hustled by France, as indeed was probably the case. Robert Young also paints a picture of French initiatives being vitiated by confusions and conservatism, in his *In Command of France: French Foreign Policy and Military Planning, 1933–1940* (Cambridge, Mass.: Harvard University Press, 1978), pp. 221–45.

66 The dependence even of individuals on known reference points as aids to understanding, was classically stated by Herbert Simon in *Administrative Behaviour: A Study of Decision-Making Processes in Administrative Organisation* (3rd edn, New York: The Free Press, 1976), pp. 79–109.

67 CAB 27/624, FP(36), 45th Meeting, 5 May.

68 *Ibid.* This was a considerable commitment, as the argument in the Foreign Policy Committee indicates. The difficulty was recognised in *DBFP* III: 5, pp. 443–4, Halifax to Seeds, 6 May 1939.

69 Military conversations had the prospect of releasing more information about Soviet armed forces. The cautious Chiefs of Staff assessments of the advantages of an arrangement with the USSR had been undermined by the necessarily speculative character of the exercise, enabling sceptics like Chamberlain to cite their own sources as evidence of Soviet weakness (CAB 27/624, FP(36), 43rd Meeting, 19 April 1939).

70 The minutes of the Cabinet meeting of 10 May, and those of the Foreign Policy Committee meetings on 10 and 16 May, as with Cadogan's diary, suggest that these two external developments were not as salient at the time as one might have expected (CAB 23/99, CM 27(39), and CAB 27/625, FP(36), 46th and 47th Meetings). There had been a brief, inconclusive, discussion in the Committee meeting of 5 May immediately after Litvinov's dismissal (see CAB 27/624, FP(36), 45th Meeting, 5 May 1939). Cadogan, remarkably, does not refer to the change (Dilks, *Cadogan Diaries*, pp. 178–80).

71 CAB 23/99, CM 27(39), 10 May 1939; CAB 27/625, FP(36), 47th Meeting, 16 May.

72 *Ibid.*, see also CAB 53/11, COS Meetings 293 and 295 of 9 May and 16 May (11 a.m.) 1939, and CAB 53/49, COS 902, Report on the 'Balance of Strategic Value between Spain as an Enemy and Russia as an Ally', 10 May 1939. Euan Wallace wrote afterwards to Halifax that he had been most struck 'by the very definite change of view expressed by the Chiefs of Staff' (FO 800/322, H/XXXIII/17, 19 May 1939).

73 Simon is not recorded as having spoken. Even Cadogan was not sure of the Chancellor's view. Dilks, *Cadogan Diaries*, p. 181. Simon's memoirs sprint through 1939 in less than five pages (Viscount Simon, *Retrospect: Memoirs* (London: Hutchinson, 1952), pp. 250–4).

74 MacDonald was temporarily absent from this meeting. But he was consistently 'pro-Soviet'.

75 An example can be found in the minutes for the Foreign Policy Committee meeting of 16 May (CAB 27/625, FP(36), 47th Meeting), where the draft version's reference to Russia's whole-hearted assistance being

of 'great value' has been changed by hand to 'appreciable value'. It is not unreasonable to suspect the Prime Minister's influence here.
76 CAB 23/99, CM 28(37), 17 May 1939.
77 CAB 23/99, CM 30(39), 24 May 1939.
78 R. J. Minney, *The Private Papers of Hore-Belisha* (London: Collins, 1960), pp. 196–7. Churchill himself was in favour of close association with Russia in 1939 (Gilbert, *Winston S. Churchill*, vol. V, p. 1067).
79 PREM 1/409, Stanhope to Halifax, 19 May 1939. The Prime Minister had a copy of this letter with him for the decisive Cabinet meeting of 24 May.
80 CAB 23/99, CM 28(39), 17 May 1939. That Chamberlain was to be held to this commitment is indicated by the Minister of Transport's smooth reminder to Halifax on 19 May (FO 800/322, H/XXXIII/17).
81 CAB 27/625, FP(36), 48th Meeting, 19 May 1939; Dilks, *Cadogan Diaries*, p. 181. The Dominions by this time were divided on the question of an alliance, with Australia and New Zealand anxious that negotiations should not break down, South Africa hostile and Canada also unhappy. See the telegrams collected in CAB 21/551, and Ovendale, *'Appeasement' and the English-Speaking World*, pp. 266–74. Thus Inskip's 'collecting of their voices' was bound to be significant.
82 In 1939 W. S. ('Shakes') Morrison's political career had entered a trough from which it was not to emerge (Cowling, *Impact of Hitler*, pp. 318–20).
83 Stanhope to Halifax, 19 May 1939, in CAB 21/551, and PREM 1/409, with a note to the effect that Chamberlain took a copy of this letter with him into the Cabinet meeting of 24 May – clearly to no avail. Stanhope thought that the crucial naval requirement of avoiding conflict with Japan and Spain should only be overridden if Russia and Germany looked like coming to terms, which he deemed unlikely.
84 CAB 27/625, FP(36), 48th Meeting, 19 May 1939.
85 PREM 1/409, Halifax to Chamberlain, 18 May 1939.
86 Harvey, *Diplomatic Diaries*, p. 290.
87 Dilks, *Cadogan Diaries*, pp. 181–2.
88 See *DBFP* III: 5, pp. 569–70, letter from Corbin to Halifax, received 17 May 1939, and pp. 623–5, an account of Halifax's talks in Paris on 20 May about the Russian negotiations (received from Geneva in the Foreign Office at 9.45 a.m. on 22 May, see CAB 24/287, CP 124(39), 'Anglo-Soviet negotiations', Annex I). It is probable that Cadogan had received an earlier summary of these talks by telephone.
89 Nor did the Foreign Office provide him with a very strong steer. Cadogan's full and intelligent memorandum of 22 May, circulated at the Cabinet meeting of 24 May, set out the pros and cons of an alliance in a fair way without taking a final position (*DBFP* III: 5, pp. 639–47), 'Foreign Office Memorandum on the Anglo-Soviet Negotiations', 22 May 1939, which is the published version of CAB 24/287, CP 124(39)).
90 Harvey, *Diplomatic Diaries*, pp. 290–1, 20 and 23 May; Dilks, *Cadogan*

Diaries, pp. 181–2, 19–20 May; CAB 23/99, CM 30(39), 24 May 1939. There is, however, no mention of the possibility of resignation in the Chamberlain letters.
91 See Watt, *How War Came*, pp. 245–6, for a description of these pressures.
92 Dilks, *Cadogan Diaries*, p. 184, 24 May.
93 Chamberlain Papers, NC 18/1/1101, letter to Hilda Chamberlain, 28 May 1939.
94 Gibbs, *Grand Strategy*, vol. I, pp. 737–57, and Haslam, *The Soviet Union*, pp. 217–32, provide an historical account.
95 There were thus twenty-nine meetings in the five phases, plus one more on 25 August before war broke out, a total of thirty since Munich. As the Foreign Policy Committee began its life under Baldwin in April 1936, and met in all sixty-one times, this means that it met thirty-one times in the first two and a half years of its life, or once a month, and on average at least once a fortnight thereafter, as the crisis-slide accelerated. See data in S. S. Wilson, *Cabinet Office to 1945*, Annex II, p. 203.
96 These indicators are not unlike those originally used by Charles Hermann to define crisis (C. F. Hermann, *Crises in Foreign Policy* (Indianapolis: Bobbs-Merrill, 1969), pp. 21–36. Hermann isolates surprise, threat to high priority goals and limited time for response as his key attributes of a crisis. This definition has been superseded since then (particularly in the respect of dropping the condition of 'surprise') following on from Brecher and others. It is not suggested here, however (see chapter 8, below) that crisis as such is the key determinant of the pattern of Cabinet discussion.
97 The attendances at the other four meetings, interspersed through the May–July period were nine, twelve (although Hoare left halfway through this meeting), ten and eleven. This is fully consonant with the general trend in the Foreign Policy Committee at this time, set by the preoccupation with the Soviet question.
98 For the basis of these and other calculations used in this section see Appendix 2, below.
99 Burgin had shown himself concerned to keep the negotiations with the USSR going on 10 May in Cabinet. (This was the day he first attended a Foreign Policy Committee meeting; see CAB 23/99, CM 27(39). The fact of his formal appointment is recorded in the Cabinet Paper CP 125(39), of 25 May 1939, 'The Composition of Cabinet Committees' (in CAB 24/287).) A comparison of this paper with its predecessor of 14 February (CP 41(39) in CAB 24/283) shows that the official membership of the Committee was ten, until Burgin's arrival made it eleven.
100 Leslie Burgin, a National Liberal aged fifty-one, was moved from the Ministry of Transport to the position of Minister without Portfolio when the decision to create a Ministry of Supply was announced on 20 April. He could not take on his new title until 14 July, when the required legislation had passed through Parliament. Burgin had been in Intelligence during the Great War, was 'a brilliant linguist' and an expert in international law. He had been Parliamentary Secretary to the

Board of Trade between 1932–7. See *Keesings Contemporary Archives*, 20 April 1939, p. 3535D, and Cameron Hazlehurst and Christine Woodland (compilers), *A Guide to the Papers of British Cabinet Ministers, 1900–1951* (London: Royal Historical Society, 1974), p. 23.

101 Malkin was Legal Adviser in the Foreign Office. 'Officials' here also includes R. A. Butler (see note 26, above, this chapter) who provided more liaison with both the Foreign Office and the House of Commons. The exact figures of attendance were 2.7 for the period 14 November 1938–11 April 1939, and 3.8 for the meetings of the Soviet negotiations.

102 As late as 8 August, the Cabinet Office and the Prime Minister's adviser were agreeing that Chamberlain would not wish for a full attendance at the Cabinet meeting planned for the 22nd, and therefore that 'a rather discouraging tone' should be employed in any circular (Sir Edward Bridges to Sir Horace Wilson, 8 August 1939, in CAB 21/782).

103 This picture is confirmed by the contemporary impression of Lt Gen. Henry Pownall in the War Office. On 17 July he wrote: 'As soon as our people give way on one point the Russians produce a brand new obstacle which they say is essential or the deal's off. Some six times have they played this trick, and we give way to each in succession' (*Chief of Staff: The Diaries of Lieutenant-General Sir Henry Pownall*, vol. I: *1933–40*, ed. Brian Bond (London: Leo Cooper, 1972), p. 214).

104 This is not to say, with Lord Eustace Percy, that 'no Cabinet, large or small, can ever originate policy' (cited in Mackintosh, *The British Cabinet* (2nd edn), p. 416), merely that ministerial participation was made easier by the negative task required.

105 Allison (*Essence of Decision*, pp. 10–38) demonstrates the ubiquity of such assumptions. See also John Steinbruner's discussion of the 'analytic paradigm' in his *The Cybernetic Theory of Decision* (Princeton: Princeton University Press, 1974).

106 CAB 27/624, FP(36), 43rd Meeting, 19 April 1939.

107 See, for example, Middlemas, *Diplomacy of Illusion*, p. 61.

108 'Regular attenders' were those present at 40 per cent or more of meetings. They are not to be confused with the 'constant attenders' of the meetings after 3 September 1939, who were ministers without formal War Cabinet rank but with access to that body. See chapters 5–7, below.

109 Morrison was appointed to help Chatfield and answer for him in the Commons. He was also 'available to assist with general Parliamentary and other business' (*Keesings Contemporary Archives*, 28 January 1939, p. 3421G). See Appendix 1, below, on Cabinet ministers and their posts.

110 That this was an important consideration is shown by a memorandum sent by Cabinet Secretary Sir Edward Bridges to Chamberlain on 4 July 1939: 'As an after thought, the Chancellor of the Duchy of Lancaster should also be appointed to the Defence of India Committee. It is a sticky business, and most of the members have strong departmental interests to protect' (CAB 21/481).

111 Chatfield had to be on the Foreign Policy Committee, as Minister of

Co-ordination of Defence. Inskip stayed on the Committee as Dominions Secretary, as well as MacDonald, as the latter had previously combined both Dominions and Colonial offices. Inskip had been moved because his position 'in the country' had 'gone back' (see Inskip (Viscount Caldecote) Papers, Diary, vol. II, pp. 4–5, 16 January 1939).

112 Runciman Papers, R3/32/1–4, Reports from Privy Council Office, 3 April–2 May 1939.

113 CAB 27/624–5, FP(36), 33rd, 36th, 51st and 60th Meetings.

114 I am grateful to Mr Donald Simpson of the Library of the Royal Commonwealth Society, and to Dr Joseph Fewster of the University of Durham, for assistance in tracing the movements of Malcolm MacDonald in this period. They are both trustees of the MacDonald Papers, kept at Durham.

115 Figure 2 contains only fifteen ministers; the sixteenth, Anderson, attended for only one item of one meeting.

116 CAB 21/481, Sir Horace Wilson to Sir Edward Bridges, 3 February 1939.

117 See S. S. Wilson, *Cabinet Office*, pp. 13–14 and 57–8, and Captain Stephen Roskill, *Hankey: Man of Secrets*, vol. III, *1931–63* (London: Collins, 1974), p. 373.

118 CAB 21/481, Sir Rupert Howorth to Sir Maurice Hankey, 30 May 1938.

119 It is worth noting that this runs contrary to the tendencies noted by Janis in *Groupthink*. Indeed the risk of groupthink is lessened where there is widespread uncertainty over policy options, and where the composition of a decision-making group owes more to institutional precedent than to personal patronage.

120 Involvement in the Soviet negotiations seems to have educated ministers to make contributions on other issues. Runciman wrote weightily to Chamberlain about both Tientsin and Italy, even threatening resignation on the former (Runciman Papers, R3/38/1–55, Runciman to Chamberlain, 19 June 1939, and R2/42/1–27, Runciman to Halifax and Chamberlain, 29 June 1939).

4 Entry into war, 1–3 September 1939

1 Among whom Cameron Watt's account in *How War Came* (chapter 30, 'Thunder in London') is indispensable.

2 The phrase is that of one of the participants, Sir Reginald Dorman-Smith. See his 'Recollections', in *The Sunday Times*, 6 September 1964, reproduced in Martin Gilbert, *Winston S. Churchill*, vol. V, *Companion*, Part 3, *Documents*, pp. 1607–9.

3 Nicholas Bethell, *The War Hitler Won* (London: Futura, 1976: first published 1972), pp. 1–97, provides a full account of events on the Polish front.

4 Halifax records the delays caused by Mussolini's call for a conference on 31 August (Hickleton Papers, A4.410.3.10, 'A Record of Events Before the War, 1939'; note that Halifax's papers are referred to as

'Hickleton Papers', after his house at Hickleton in the West Riding of Yorkshire).
5 Chamberlain was aware of this as early as April (Chamberlain Papers, NC 18/1/1096, letter to Hilda Chamberlain, 29 April 1939).
6 Avi Shlaim, 'Failures in National Intelligence Estimates: The Case of the Yom Kippur War', *World Politics*, 28: 3 (April 1976), pp. 348–80.
7 Michael Brecher, *Decisions in Crisis: Israel, 1967 and 1973* (Berkeley: University of California Press, 1980), pp. 1–8.
8 Harvey, *Diplomatic Diaries*, p. 298, 19 June 1939.
9 Dilks, *Cadogan Diaries*, p. 195, 12 August 1939.
10 See note 102, chapter 3, above. Only Lord Maugham was absent, out of the total of twenty-three Cabinet ministers. The Prime Minister had told his colleagues to 'have a really good holiday', and had announced his intention to break his own stay in Scotland with a meeting of only those ministers who would be near London on 22 August. In the event he was forced to face the full Cabinet 'in circumstances which could only be described as grave' (CAB 23/100, CM 40(39), 2 August, and CM 41(39), 22 August 1939).
11 Chamberlain Papers, NC 18/1/1115, letter to Hilda Chamberlain, 27 August 1939.
12 CAB 23/100, CM 41 and 43(39), 22 and 26 August also CAB 53/54, COS 966, 25 August.
13 Examples of scepticism can be found in CAB 23/99, CM 26(39), 3 May, CM 38(39), 19 July, and PREM 1/409, 19 May 1939.
14 CAB 23/100, CM 41(39), 22 August 1939. The French were far more badly hit by the news from Moscow. See Watt, *How War Came*, pp. 462–78, chapter 25, 'The Impact of the Nazi-Soviet Pact'.
15 Norman Dixon, *On the Psychology of Military Incompetence* (London: Cape, 1976), pp. 130–44.
16 Space does not permit a full analysis of these images, but there is a wealth of evidence to support the contention made here. Hoare, for example, wrote in May that the situation was slightly improved, but 'one has always to keep in mind the risk that Hitler may change the picture at any moment' (Templewood Papers, X: 4, Hoare to Sir Philip Sassoon, 13 May 1939).
17 CAB 23/100, CM 33(39), 21 June 1939.
18 Chamberlain Papers, NC 18/1/1095 and 1105, letters to his sisters, 23 April and 2 July 1939.
19 Chamberlain Papers, NC 18/1/1101, letter to Hilda Chamberlain, 28 May 1939.
20 Cadogan Papers, MS Diary, ACAD 1/8, 2 September, and Simon Papers, MS Simon 85, Halifax to Simon, 2 September 1939.
21 Keith Robbins, *Munich* (London: Cassell, 1968), and Middlemas, *Diplomacy of Illusion*, pp. 59-66, 308–9.
22 Nigel Nicolson (ed.), *Harold Nicolson: Diaries and Letters 1939–45*, p. 26; A. J. P. Taylor, *Origins*, chapter 11.
23 CAB 23/100, CM 47(39), 1 September 1939 (my italics).

24 *Ibid.*, confirmed in the Hickleton Papers, A4.410.3.10, 'A Record of Events Before the War, 1939'.
25 See S. S. Wilson, *Cabinet Office*, pp. 9–10, and in particular the exchanges among Austen Chamberlain, Balfour and Churchill in 1922 about the propriety of recorded dissent. An unpublished list kindly supplied by the Public Record Office to the author shows that between 1916 and 1943, there were forty-eight recorded cases of dissent not involving resignation in the Cabinet Conclusions. Of these, forty-two fell in the period 1916–1927, and thirty-three in the Coalition Government of 1916–1922. Roughly a third concerned foreign policy questions.
26 Hickleton Papers, A4.410.3.10, 'A Record of Events Before the War', entry of 2 September. Halifax may have been referring to France alone, but this cannot be assumed.
27 *Ibid.*
28 I.e. to withdraw troops from Poland entirely, if Britain was not to fulfil her obligation to Poland. See Cmd 6106 (1939), Blue Book, *British Documents Concerning German-Polish Relations and the Outbreak of Hostilities between Britain and Germany*, p. 168.
29 *DBFP* III: 7, pp. 521–3, Halifax to Sir Nevile Henderson, 2 September 1939, 8 p.m. and 8.20 p.m.
30 See CAB 23/100, 48(39), 2 September 1939, 4.15 p.m. This was the original proposal made by the Prime Minister and Halifax, even before the Cabinet decided on that midnight as the time for the expiry of an ultimatum. It was itself to be subject to an armistice.
31 *Ibid.*
32 *Ibid.* See also Dilks, *Cadogan Diaries*, p. 212, and Minney, *Private Papers of Hore-Belisha*, p. 226. The meaning of 'make up her mind' is slightly unclear, although it seems that this was when an ultimatum was to expire, rather than be delivered, if we follow the leads given in Cadogan's, Hore-Belisha's and Simon's (MS Diary, entry of 2 September) accounts.
33 CAB 23/100, CM 49(39), 2 September 1939, 11.30 p.m.
34 Dilks, *Cadogan Diary*, p. 212, 2 September.
35 *DBFP* III: 7, p. 480, Minutes by Cadogan, 1 September 1939. The interpretation of the word 'immediately' was an obvious difficulty.
36 These conclusions are confirmed by the account in Harvey, *Diplomatic Diaries*, pp. 312–15.
37 Minney, *Private Papers of Hore-Belisha*, pp. 226–7, and Harvey, *Diplomatic Diaries*, p. 315. The statement 'was very badly worded and the obvious inference was vacillation and dirty work' (Crookshank Papers, Diary entry of 2 September 1939). Captain Crookshank was a Junior Minister at the Treasury at the time. Other important sources for the Cabinet rebellion are the Wallace Diary, vol. I, entry of 2 September 1939 (Wallace Papers); the Simon Diary, entry of 2 September 1939 (Simon Papers, MS Simon 11); and Dorman-Smith's 'Recollections', in Gilbert, *Winston S. Churchill*, vol. V, *Companion, 1936–1939*, pp. 1607–9.
38 See Harvey, *Diplomatic Diaries*, p. 315: 'I heard from De La Warr that

there was almost a revolt in the Cabinet after the statement over the failure to put in a definite ultimatum. This was led by John Simon, Morrison, Elliot and De La Warr.'

39 Minney, *Private Papers of Hore-Belisha*, p. 226.
40 S. S. Wilson, (*Cabinet Office*, pp. 1–2, 9–10, 59–63) provides useful information on the working of this doctrine between the wars.
41 Apart from Chamberlain and Halifax, whom we have already examined, the following ministers come into this category, on the criteria of personality and office: Anderson (Lord Privy Seal); Simon (Chancellor of the Exchequer); Hoare (Home Secretary); Kingsley Wood (Secretary for Air); Chatfield (Minister for the Co-ordination of Defence); and Hore-Belisha (Secretary of State for War).
42 I.e. there is none in the diaries of Cadogan, Halifax, Harvey, Hore-Belisha, Inskip or Wallace, and none in the Cabinet Minutes. Nor does Sir John Wheeler-Bennett (*John Anderson* (London: Macmillan, 1962)) provide any information on the point. We know that *after* the debate Anderson saw himself as steadfast, for he wrote to Arthur Greenwood, the Labour leader whose statement after Chamberlain made such an impression, when Greenwood left the War Cabinet in 1942: 'I shall never forget the admiration which your words & bearing in those difficult days at the outbreak of war inspired in me' (Greenwood Papers, Shelf 8, Box marked 'Listed Files 1913–1942', Sir John Anderson to Greenwood, 27 February 1942).
43 Harvey, *Diplomatic Diaries*, p. 314. Simon's Diary (entry of 2 September) confirms his distaste at the 4.15 Cabinet meeting for delay, but although the diary has the ring of veracity, it is typewritten and it is difficult to know how much hindsight had accumulated before it was written up.
44 This view seems strange, given French anxieties about air defences, and allied inactivity once the war began. The probable reason for the military opposing any delay was their nervousness about an imminent German air-attack (the reason for the sirens going off so soon after the ultimatum expired on 3 September) and their desire to give the Luftwaffe as little time to prepare it as possible (Simon Papers, Diary entry of 2 September). However, the two issues of the delay before sending an ultimatum and the time to elapse between an ultimatum's delivery and its expiry have not always been kept distinct either by contemporaries or by historians.
45 CAB 23/100, CM 48(39), 2 September, 4.15 p.m.
46 Minney, *Private Papers of Hore-Belisha*, p. 225.
47 I.e. Brown (Minister of Labour); Burgin (Minister of Supply); Colville (Secretary of State for Scotland); De La Warr (President of the Board of Education); Dorman-Smith (Minister of Agriculture); Elliot (Minister of Health); Inskip (Secretary of State for Dominion Affairs); Macdonald (Secretary of State for the Colonies); Morrison (Chancellor of the Duchy of Lancaster); Runciman (Lord President of the Council); Stanhope (First Lord of the Admiralty); Stanley (President of

the Board of Trade); Wallace (Minister of Transport); and Zetland (Secretary of State for India).

48 Inskip characterised the Cabinet rebels of 2 September as 'the usual people, Oliver Stanley, Walter Elliot, Burgin (not so strong) and Ernest Brown' (Inskip Diary, vol. II, 3 September 1939). Inskip's information (from Kingsley Wood) was not fully accurate, as Brown was not at the rebel conclaves in the evening (see note 56 below, this chapter). See also Cowling, *Impact of Hitler*, pp. 320–6, particularly on De La Warr's and MacDonald's National Labour provenance.

49 Hickleton Papers, A.410.3.10, 'A Record of Events Before the War, 1939', 2 September 1939; CAB 23/100, CM 48(39), 2 September 1939, 4.15 p.m.

50 No source has the other factor, the need to finish evacuation and other defence preparations, as leading to delay after the 4.15 Cabinet meeting, while Anderson, the minister responsible for evacuation, was to be a member of the Simon group that evening. Britain was well ahead of France in this (Wallace Papers, Diary, vol. I, 2 September 1939).

51 This interpretation is now the orthodoxy among modern historians and is supplanting the old anti-appeasement line in the textbooks, for example P. M. H. Bell, *The Origins of the Second World War in Europe* (London: Longman, 1986), p. 108.

52 It is arguable that ministerial determination to declare war if Poland was attacked was such as to have carried the day even if France had pulled out (although the military implications would have been serious). Hoare noted on 28 August: 'No question of not sticking to it. No question of our breaking in The War of Nerves' (Templewood Papers, X: 5; see also Wallace Papers, Diary, vol. I, 31 August).

53 The accounts of both Wallace and Chamberlain confirm this (Wallace Papers, Diary, vol. I, 2 September; Chamberlain Papers, NC 18/1/1116, letter to Ida Chamberlain, 10 September).

54 Simon Papers, Diary, 2 September 1939.

55 Halifax's 'A Record of Events Before the War, 1939', in Hickleton Papers, A4.410.3.10 (also FO 800/317, H/XV/312).

56 *Ibid.*, Chamberlain Papers, NC 18/1/1116, Chamberlain to Ida Chamberlain, 10 September 1939. In fact, by the time the rebels had their second, after-dinner, meeting their number had swollen to thirteen, out of the total of twenty-two Cabinet ministers (excluding the Prime Minister). One of the rebels, De La Warr, sat in the Lords. There were only fifteen Cabinet members (again excluding the Prime Minister) who sat in the Commons. This means that all those in the Cabinet who were also MPs rebelled on the night of 2 September except Hoare, Brown and Inskip (cf. Watt, *How War Came*, p. 581), who totals up only twelve rebels, as he misses out Burgin, mentioned in both Inskip's Diary (3 September, reported by Kingsley Wood) and Hore-Belisha's account (Minney, *Private Papers*, p. 226) as having been present.

57 Dilks, *Cadogan Diaries*, p. 212.

58 Wallace Papers Diary, vol. I, and Simon Papers, Diary, both 2 September 1939.
59 CAB 23/100, CM 49(39), 11.30 p.m., 2 September 1939. The ministers present from the beginning were the rebels, who were at hand. Others, like Hoare and Zetland, were surprised to be raised from their homes and beds (Aster, *1939*, pp. 385–6; see also Templewood Papers, X: 5, Hoare's notes for 2 September 1939). It is not known why Hoare, one of the leading dissidents over the Soviet Union, was so out of things on this occasion. Cross (*Sir Samuel Hoare*, pp. 299–300) speculates that it was because Hoare 'wanted to avoid an embarrassing confrontation with his friend and closest Cabinet colleague', but he says the same of Kingsley Wood, who actually was at the second rebel meeting.
60 Chamberlain said that 'He wanted at once to retrieve the impression he had made in the House' (Minney, *Private Papers of Hore-Belisha*, p. 227).
61 See Keith Wilson, 'The British Cabinet's Decision for War, 2 August 1914', *British Journal of International Studies*, vol. 2 (1975), pp. 148–59, and Zara Steiner, *Britain and the Origins of the First World War* (London: Macmillan, 1977), pp. 215–41.
62 For examples see A. J. P. Taylor, *English History 1914–45* (Oxford: The Clarendon Press, 1965), pp. 190–1 (for Chanak), and Christopher Thorne, *The Limits of Foreign Policy: The West, The League and The Far Eastern Crisis of 1931–3* (London: Macmillan, 1973), pp. 391–403, 412–14.
63 Wallace Papers, Diary, vol. I, 22 August 1939; the document referred to is the Prime Minister's letter to Hitler (*DBFP* III: 7, pp. 125–6, 127–8, nos. 142, 145; Halifax to Henderson, 22 August 1939, 8.40 p.m. and 9.50 p.m.). The significance of Wallace's laconic reference to a draft having been submitted to the Cabinet only halfway through its meeting should not be missed.
64 Martin Gilbert, *Winston S. Churchill*, vol. V: *1922–39*, pp. 1052–115.
65 Zara Steiner, *Britain and the Origins of the First World War*, pp. 233–8, and Samuel Williamson, *The Politics of Grand Strategy*.

5 Reacting to the 'peace offensive', October 1939

1 The term was current in government circles from the last week in September onwards, although speculation about the possibility of a 'peace offer' started almost immediately after the declaration of war. For 'peace offensive' see Lord Hankey's 'War Appreciation' of 29 September 1939 (addendum to that of 12 September, Hankey Papers, 11/1, discussed in Roskill, *Hankey, Man of Secrets*, vol. III: *1931–1963*, pp. 430–1. See also Inskip Papers Diary, 26 September 1939: 'The PM fears a "peace offensive"'. Looking back in 1940, A. V. Alexander thought that 'since the middle of September last the Communist Party of Great Britain, at any rate, had been leaders of a peace offensive' (Alexander Papers, 5/4/31, 28 June–1 July 1940, record of a conversation with Maisky, passed on to Churchill).

2 This was not necessarily true of mass public opinion. Neville Chamberlain told his sister, 'in three days last week I had 2450 letters and 1860 of them were stop the war in one form or another' (Chamberlain Papers, NC 18/1/1124, letter to Ida Chamberlain, 8 October 1939).
3 Hankey Papers, 4/31, Hankey to Smuts, Christmas 1939; Halifax Papers in the Public Record Office, FO 800/324, H/XXXVII/29, Halifax to Lothian, 27 September 1939. This letter is markedly either realistic or pessimistic, according to taste.
4 *The Memoirs of General the Lord Ismay* (London: Heinemann, 1960), p. 101. Brian Bond, in *British Military Policy*, p. 318, discusses the uncertainty in British circles in the months before the war as to how durable Polish resistance would prove.
5 CAB 65/1, WM 9(39), 9 September 1939. See also WM 12(39), 11 September 1939, where the Cabinet noted with interest how the Japanese ambassador had commented on the significance of the announcement of the fact that the British government were planning for a three-year war.
6 Templewood Papers, XI: 3, draft broadcast by Hoare for 22 September at 9.15 p.m.
7 Text in François Bédarida, *La Stratégie secrète de la Drôle de Guerre: le Conseil Suprême Interallié, septembre 1939–avril 1940* (Paris: Presses de la Fondation Nationale des Sciences Politiques, et Editions du CNRS, 1979), p. 90, and note. This is the first of two French versions of the text that are given. The second, from General Gamelin, has Chamberlain saying: 'The war will not inevitably last three years, but we must prepare for it on that basis' (my translation in both cases). The latter is far closer to the official British minute in CAB 99/3, and to what Chamberlain told the War Cabinet on 13 September (CAB 65/1, WM 14(39)), but whether the nuance was appreciated in Paris is unclear.
8 Even Winston Churchill had no desire to fight the Soviets over Poland. Indeed, in a radio broadcast of 1 October, he talked of the Soviet invasion being necessary for Russian safety, and having created both an 'Eastern front... which Nazi Germany does not dare assail' and 'a community of interests' between Britain, France and Russia. See Martin Gilbert, *Finest Hour: Winston S. Churchill 1939–41* (London: Heinemann, 1983), pp. 49–51.
9 Nigel Nicolson, *Harold Nicolson, Diaries and Letters 1939–45*, p. 26.
10 Harvey, *Diplomatic Diaries*, Diary entry of 8 September, p. 317. Harvey was also an Eden supporter, but he and Nicolson do not seem to have been particularly close.
11 Bethell, *The War Hitler Won*, pp. viii and 366–72. It should be noted that Lord Bethell is careful to avoid accusing Chamberlain of actively seeking a sell-out; his criticism is rather of the false assumptions made by the British government about how the war would proceed. Richard Lamb, in his unreliable *The Ghosts of Peace 1935–1945* (Salisbury: Michael Russell, 1987, pp. 131–2) is less inhibited, and argues that Chamberlain and Halifax paid excessive attention to 'anti-war Tory right-wingers' so

as to keep the Tory Party together for the day when he tried to carry Parliament over a negotiated peace.
12 Woodward, *British Foreign Policy*, vol. I, p. 13.
13 Hinsley, *British Intelligence in the Second World War*, vol. I, pp. 56–7. Brief as it is, the account given here of the contacts between the Secret Intelligence Service and German agents purporting to be dissident generals, which culminated in the disastrous meeting at Venlo on 9 November 1939, is of considerable interest. Hinsley argues that those, such as the historian C. A. MacDonald, who have suggested that the Prime Minister was secretly sounding out the possibilities of a compromise peace were wrong, and that the main concern was to encourage a German resistance (see also Dilks, *Cadogan Diaries*, various references to the 'Generals' in this period). Not all documents seen by Hinsley are yet available for public scrutiny. On peace feelers in general, see Bernd Martin's useful *Friedensinitiativen und Machtpolitik in Zweiten Weltkrieg, 1939–1942* (Dusseldorf: Droste, 1974).
14 See K. W. Hancock and M. Gowing, *The British War Economy* (part of the United Kingdom's Cabinet Office *History of the Second World War Civil Series*, revised and confidential edition, London: HMSO, 1975): pages 83–100 contain a pertinent analysis of British reliance on, but also uneasiness about, the notion of the blockade. On expectations of the USA, see David Reynolds, *The Creation of the Anglo-American Alliance 1937–1941: A Study in Competitive Cooperation* (London: Europa, 1981), pp. 75–80.
15 Alexander George, David K. Hall and William E. Simons, *The Limits of Coercive Diplomacy: Laos–Cuba–Vietnam* (Boston: Little, Brown, 1971).
16 The fact that the answers were certainly not self-evident to contemporaries is brought out by A. J. Nicholls and Sir John Wheeler-Bennett in their *The Semblance of Peace* (London: Macmillan, 1972), especially p. 14 and Appendix A, 'Note on the Present Position of the Munich Agreement'.
17 Winston S. Churchill, *The Second World War*, vol. I: *The Gathering Storm*, pp. 317–21. Churchill says that part of the reason for expanding the numbers was his own point that the average age of the original six was too high, at sixty-four. On the Prime Minister's offer to the Liberals of office outside the War Cabinet, see Crookshank's scathing criticism of his own leader (Crookshank Papers, Diary, 29 December 1939).
18 S. S. Wilson, *Cabinet Office*, p. 2. Simon wrote a memorandum on this obviously tricky point at the outset (Simon Papers, memorandum on the 'Position of Leading Ministers outside the War Cabinet' (MS Simon 85), 4 September 1939) in which he talked about the need for a modification of constitutional practice so that the War Cabinet would become an executive body 'entrusted with final decisions ... to which Cabinet Ministers outside the War Cabinet would of course assent'. This would keep the latter's morale up and help in the Commons. Good will and the Prime Minister's 'supremacy' would get over any problems over collective responsibility which might arise.

19 S. S. Wilson, *Cabinet Office*, pp. 88–93. See also CAB 65/1, WM (39)1, 3 September 1939.
20 CAB 21/761, Sir Eric Bridges to E. A. Seal (Admiralty), 15 September 1939, re: Churchill's desire to submit a general political memorandum to the War Cabinet before full consultations had taken place. See also CAB 67/1, WP(G)(39) 1, 'Institution of the War Cabinet: Consequent Changes in the Organisation and Procedure of the Cabinet Offices', 5 September 1939, where it is made clear that although the peacetime 'five-day rule', whereby all papers going before Cabinet have to be circulated at least five days in advance, was to be shelved, this was no reason for not settling as much business as possible without coming to the War Cabinet.
21 Wallace Papers, Diary, 23 October 1939. After this discussion (on the diversion of iron-ore shipping from the east coast) the Cabinet Secretary contacted one of Wallace's group with a draft minute on which he wanted comments, on the ground that discussion had been 'tricky'. But Wallace discovered from the War Cabinet Minutes that evening that his suggestion had not been accepted – due, he thought, to the influence of the Service departments. See also CAB 65/1, WM 57(39), of the same date. 'Gilmour' was Sir John Gilmour, Minister of Shipping since 13 October, and 'Oliver' was Oliver Stanley, President of the Board of Trade.
22 Wallace Papers, Diary, 7 December 1939: 'The Lord Chancellor said how grateful we all were for this new departure and how much we appreciated the Prime Minister taking on an additional burden at this time.' The ministers outside the War Cabinet had been getting restless at having to behave more like permanent under-secretaries than politicians with responsibility for government. According to Wallace's record, these meetings were generally useful and collegial occasions, but ministers who read the circulated documents rarely learnt anything new. From the War Cabinet's perspective they were, therefore, probably more an investment in the solidarity of the administration than a strictly necessary adjunct to decision-making. See pp. 128–29, below, and S. S. Wilson, *Cabinet Office*, p. 98.
23 Bridges to Sir Horace Wilson, 3 September 1939, in CAB 21/777.
24 S. S. Wilson, *Cabinet Office*, pp. 95–109 and 220–39; see also Annex 7b.
25 CAB 21/761: Sir Horace Wilson to Bridges, 4 September 1939; R. J. Harris' comment on letter from Lord Hood, 13 September; and Bridges to Sir Rupert Howorth, 24 September. This no doubt represented Wilson's and Chamberlain's normal instinct of keeping as much of the initiative as possible in the Prime Minister's hands.
26 For a further discussion of cognitive dissonance and related phenomena, see Robert Jervis, *Perception and Misperception in International Politics* (Princeton: Princeton University Press, 1976), pp. 382–406.
27 It is Bethell's view (*The War Hitler Won*, p. 392) that Hitler 'wanted peace, but only just, his inclination was moving more and more towards war with every day that passed'. David Irving (in his *Hitler's War, 1939–*

1942 (London: Macmillan, Papermac, 1983), pp. 35 and 82), describes Hitler's sentimentality towards Britain and the Empire, but does not suggest that he was willing to move very far in order to achieve an accommodation. P. M. H. Bell, in an excellent synthesis (*Origins of the Second World War in Europe*, pp. 81–2 and 275–6) also concludes that Hitler may really have expected to be able to make some general accommodation with Britain at various points up to late 1940, and was baffled not to be able to do so.

28 CAB 65/1, WM 14(39), 13 September 1939.
29 Chamberlain Papers, NC 18/1/1116 and 1122, letters to Ida Chamberlain, 10 and 23 September 1939. The holograph '7' in '17' is not completely clear; the figure could be 19 per cent. I am grateful to Dr Benedikz and his colleagues in the Special Collections section of the University of Birmingham library for their expert assistance with this and other problems relating to the Chamberlain papers.
30 The nature of war aims is an interesting general problem, which has not received the attention accorded to, say, that of how wars end. Individual works of history have made valuable contributions, but there is obvious scope for work relating war aims and their evolution to theories of 'muddling through' and 'non-decision', given the tendency of events in war to overtake the original war aims of states, and indeed often to precipitate quite different objectives as the struggle wears on.
31 'Now there is a relationship of forces which can never be more propitious, but can only deteriorate', speech to the German Commanders-in-Chief, 23 November 1939, in Jeremy Noakes and Geoffrey Pridham (eds.), *Documents on Nazism 1919–1945* (London: Jonathan Cape, 1974), p. 573. Readers will not miss the similarity to the Leninist concept of the 'correlation of forces'.
32 For the public debate on war aims which took place in Britain in the autumn of 1939, and the inherent link to peace diplomacy, see Richard Cockett, *Twilight of Truth: Chamberlain, Appeasement and the Manipulation of the Press* (London: Weidenfeld & Nicolson, 1989), pp. 152–7.
33 Chamberlain Papers, NC 18/1/1116, letter to Ida Chamberlain, 10 September 1939.
34 On 11 September Eden was present at the meeting of the War Cabinet to tell them that the Dominion governments were 'unanimous ... that some further declaration of policy in regard to the War should be made by His Majesty's Government' (CAB 65/1, WM 12(39)). See also WM 29(39), 27 September 1939, which records the demands of the Indian Congress Party for British statement of war aims towards India, and WM 30(39), 28 September, where Eden reported the Dominions' High Commissioners' desire for further consultations on the line to be taken 'in the event of Germany beginning a "peace offensive"'.
35 The interesting paradox of French foot-dragging over Poland and increased militancy (if not literally belligerence) over the prosecution of the war in October, may be explained by internal pulling and hauling. The Foreign Office certainly had a very poor view of Bonnet, whom

they saw as 'défaitiste' and opposed to Daladier, and even considered trying to get him removed. See minutes by Sargent and Cadogan, and Cadogan's letter to Phipps of 6 September 1939, in FO 371/22982. See also Adamthwaite, *France and the Coming of the Second World War, 1936–39*, pp. 108–10 and 335–8.

36 See Harvey, *Diplomatic Diaries*, 9 November 1939, p. 328. There are, however, occasional hints in Chamberlain's letters to his sisters that by this time he might have been considering such an attempt. The events leading up to the Venlo incident, and even the Munich 'outrage' itself, may have been related to British attempts to encourage the German people to get rid of their leader (Chamberlain Papers, NC 18/1/1129 and 1131, letters of 5 and 12 November 1939). Cadogan's diary entries (see pp. 116 and note 65 below, this chapter), can also be read to imply thinking about assassination.

37 Cited in Cockett, *Twilight of Truth*, p. 107.

38 CAB 65/1, WM 21(39), 20 September 1939. For the renewed commitment to the restoration of Poland at the end of the war, see Chamberlain's remarks in Cabinet on 18 September (WM 18(39)).

39 The difficulties of the British position were perfectly summed up by Cadogan in his diary on 23 September: 'H. asked me about "War Aims". I told him I saw awful difficulties. We can no longer say "evacuate Poland" without wanting to go to war with Russia, which we don't want to do! I suppose the cry is "Abolish Hitlerism". What if Hitler hands over to Goering?! Meanwhile what of the course of operations? What if Germany now sits tight? Gamelin doesn't look to me like flinging himself on the Siegfried Line. What do we do? Build up our armaments feverishly? What for? Can we last out the course? "Time is on our side". Is it? What are the Germans doing meanwhile? Must try to think this out...' (Dilks, *Cadogan Diaries*, p. 219).

40 CAB 65/1, WM 24(39), 23 September 1939. According to Martin (*Friedensinitiativen und Machtpolitik*, p. 58), Hitler opened an official German 'peace-campaign' in his speech of 19 September in Danzig, which effectively marked his victory in Poland.

41 The words are Halifax's (CAB 65/1, WM 31(39), 29 September 1939).

42 Wallace Papers, Diary, 29 September 1939.

43 The fact of the meeting, at 6 p.m. on the same day that a minuted Cabinet had met at 11.30 a.m., is recorded in CAB 65/1, but nothing else.

44 Lord Hankey's 'War Appreciation' of 29 September 1939 (Hankey Papers, 11/1; see also note 1, above, this chapter) gives an account of this meeting. He makes it clear that the meeting was devoted to the discussion of the peace offensive and of war aims, 'and virtually came to an unrecorded decision that it would be premature to formulate detailed war aims at this stage of the war'. Britain's general line should be based on a passage from one of Chamberlain's speeches to the effect that: 'our general purpose ... is to redeem Europe from the perpetual and recurring fear of German aggression, and enable the peoples of

Europe to preserve their liberties and their independence. That is the text by which any future peace offer must be judged.' Hankey does not refer to Dahlerus, but it is difficult to imagine why the War Cabinet should have met without officials of any kind, if it were simply a question of discussing general diplomatic strategy (see also Table 5, below, p. 140). On the other hand Hoare's brief diary entry confirms Hankey's statement and goes no further than 'war aims' in describing the content (Templewood Papers, XI: 2, 'Weekly Notes', entry of 26 September 1939).

45 Recorded in a Foreign Office memorandum (C4216/610/G) entitled 'Summary of Principal Peace Feelers September 1939–March 1941', dated 24 February 1941, and clearly used by Churchill, as it is to be found in PREM 4/100/8.
46 CAB 65/3, Confidential Annex to WM 15(39), agenda item no. 4 on air policy and international law, 14 September 1939. Three days before, however, Kingsley Wood had argued against bombing on the grounds that keeping Britain's air force intact would make it much easier to refuse any peace offers when they came (*ibid.*, WM 12(39), item 6).
47 Military intelligence had broadly predicted the sequence of events, with a defeat of Poland followed by peace offers, as early as 4 September. See F. H. Hinsley, *British Intelligence*, vol. I, p. 113.
48 CAB 65/1, WM 33(39) and WM 34(39), 1 and 2 October 1939.
49 *Keesings Contemporary Archives*, 23–30 September 1939, pp. 3729C–3750. The German press then itself began to talk of a 'peace offensive' (p. 3756D).
50 CAB 65/3, Confidential Annexes of WMs 34(39), item 13, and 36(39), item 8, 2 and 4 October 1939. See also Bethell, *The War Hitler Won*, pp. 366–9, and the account in FO memorandum C4216/610/G, of 24 February 1941, in PREM 4/100/8, pp. 3–4.
51 Dilks, *Cadogan Diaries*, p. 220.
52 Chamberlain Papers, NC 18/1/1123, letter to Hilda Chamberlain, 1 October 1939.
53 CAB 65/3, Confidential Annex to WM 38(39), item 8, 5 October 1939.
54 Harvey, *Diplomatic Diaries*, entry of 5 October, p. 324. The speech, however, did not make a sufficient impact on Harold Nicolson to rate a mention in his lengthy diary for 3 October, which is largely about caballing to replace Chamberlain with Churchill (Nigel Nicolson, *Harold Nicolson: Diaries and Letters 1939–45*, pp. 34–5). Moreover Harvey's interpretation is not strictly justified by what Chamberlain is recorded as having said (*HCD*, vol. 351, cols. 1855–61). The Prime Minister committed himself to the war for the principle that 'the word of governments, once pledged, must be kept', and also said that if any peace proposal was on its way it would be examined and tested in the light of this principle. But he did not specify who could or could not be a negotiating partner. Perhaps, as so often, however, it was the perception of what had been said rather than the reality, which was important.

Notes to pages 112–15 301

55 CAB 65/3, Confidential Annex to WM 38(39), 5 October 1939; the words are Halifax's.
56 CAB 65/1, WM 35(39), 3 October 1939. Awareness of what was to occur did not mean that any public relations contingency plans had been made by the Ministry of Information. The Cabinet, via Sir Samuel Hoare and the Home Policy Committee, only discovered this fact on the day of the speech itself (CAB 65/1, WM 39(39), 6 October 1939). See also pp. 115–16, below.
57 The Dominions' High Commissioners wanted to talk to the War Cabinet about how to respond to the 'peace offensive', see CAB 65/1, WM 30(39), 28 September 1939. For the anxious speculation about the neutrals, the Vatican and Italy, see WMs 33, 34, 35(39), 1, 2 and 3 October 1939. The failure of the Ministry of Information to keep the foreign press happy and the pessimism of the American Ambassador in London, Joseph Kennedy, were further sources of concern (WM 19(39), 19 September 1939). See also Ian McLaine, *Ministry of Morale: Home Front Morale and the Ministry of Information in World War II* (London: George Allen & Unwin, 1979), pp. 34–42. Lloyd George spoke in the House of Commons on 3 October and called for 'very careful consideration' of anything Hitler might offer, on the grounds that if non-belligerents were brought into any negotiations they would force Hitler to be moderate (*HCD*, vol. 351, vols. 1870–80, 3 October 1939). See also Paul Addison, 'Lloyd George and Compromise Peace in the Second World War', in A. J. P. Taylor (ed.), *Lloyd George: Twelve Essays* (London: Hamish Hamilton, 1971), pp. 361–84.
58 Both in CAB 65/1, WM 39(39), 6 October 1939. The starting-point for these remarks was Chamberlain's belief that the USSR could be drawn into accepting a British treaty with Turkey, thereby exposing the hollowness of the German-Soviet relationship. Chamberlain had been briefed in some detail (presumably immediately after the speech, made in the afternoon) by Sir Horace Wilson; see Wilson to Chamberlain, 6 October 1939, in PREM 1/395.
59 A translation of Hitler's speech is contained in somewhat shortened form in *Keesing's Contemporary Archives*, 30 September–7 October 1939, pp. 3756D–3758. The full Reuters translation, together with Chamberlain's personal summary, is in PREM 1/395. For background see Bethell, *The War Hitler Won*, pp. 385–6.
60 See Brecher, *Decisions in Crisis*, and Lebow, *Between Peace and War*, pp. 7–12. These authors tend to prefer the probability of the onset of military action as their third defining characteristic of crisis (finite time and threat to basic values being the others), but as crisis can occur in non-war environments, I prefer to substitute the notion of an unavoidable choice, or turning-point, in the stream of events facing decision-makers, to complete the definition.
61 'I have always been more afraid of a peace offer than of an air-raid' (Chamberlain Papers, NC 18/1/1124, letter to Ida Chamberlain, 8 October).

62 CAB 65/1, WM 40(39), 7 October 1939, and see note 118 below, this chapter.
63 CAB 65/1, WM 39(39), 6 October 1939, and see note 54 above, this chapter.
64 *Keesing's Contemporary Archives*, 30 September–7 October 1939, 3578A.
65 This was the only Cabinet meeting of the five which Cadogan attended, and he thought it 'not a v. useful discussion'. Getting rid of Hitler was his aim as much as Halifax's, but some members of Cabinet, he thought, would also object to this '*war* aim – not peace aim' (Dilks, *Cadogan Diaries*, p. 221, entry of 7 October, Cadogan's own emphasis).
66 CAB 65/1, WM 40(39), 7 October 1939.
67 Dilks, *Cadogan Diaries*, pp. 222–3, and Cadogan's report of 8 October to Halifax and Chamberlain on the Corbin talks, in PREM 1/395. Corbin and Daladier thought that Britain was making 'too much of Herr Hitler's speech', and feared that they were only making it seem more important in the public mind.
68 Dilks, *Cadogan Diaries*, p. 223, entry of 8 October.
69 For Churchill's draft, his letter to Halifax of 8 October and his letter to Chamberlain of 9 October, see PREM 1/395. Halifax had apparently invited Churchill to write something, 'in the friendliest manner'.
70 PREM 1/395. It should be noted that Churchill had spent the day at Chartwell, lunching alone with Victor Cazalet, who had found him 'absolutely loyal to PM'. Presumably he came up to London in the evening, as he often did. See Robert Rhodes James, *Victor Cazalet: A Portrait* (London: Hamish Hamilton, 1976), p. 219, Cazalet's journal entry of 11 October 1939.
71 Chamberlain Papers, NC 18/1/1124, letter to Ida Chamberlain, 8 October 1939.
72 This would certainly be in line with the predictions of groupthink theory, which sees leaders as seeking often to secure agreement by conceding at least the appearance of participation. See Janis, *Groupthink*.
73 As with other drafts and letters cited here, this comes from the PREM 1/395 file. But those drafts which eventually became formal War Cabinet memoranda, starting with Halifax's reworking of Cadogan's draft, are also to be found in CAB 66/2, WPs 77, 79 and 81(39).
74 Vansittart's minute of 8 October, PREM 1/395.
75 Halifax to Chamberlain, 8 October 1939, with marginalia by Wilson, PREM 1/395. Halifax ended Vansittart's minute with the carefully phrased advice that it was 'worth just looking at'.
76 *Ibid.* This draft became, as WP 77(39), the first to be considered by the War Cabinet, on 9 October.
77 Churchill's draft of 8 October 1939, in PREM 1/395, never received the formal status of a War Cabinet memorandum, and does not seem to have come before the War Cabinet. Nor are there any formal minutes of the drafting committee.
78 Chamberlain Papers, NC 18/1/1124, letter to Ida Chamberlain, 8 October 1939 (emphasis in the original). This sense of a harmonious

atmosphere is broadly supported by other sources (see Lothian Papers, Victor Cazalet to Lothian, 16 October 1939). Cazalet had seen Churchill, Eden and Halifax often. They were agreed that 'there is not the slightest dissension of any kind between them and the PM'. See also Simon Papers, Diary, entry for 7 October 1939, and Roskill, *Hankey: Man of Secrets*, vol. III, pp. 427–8. By November, however, Caldecote was recording that Hoare had told him that Churchill was being 'difficult in the Cabinet, but the PM handles him v. well' (Inskip Diary, vol. II, 21 November 1939, p. 84, abbreviation in the original).

79 See below, pp. 39-42. The phrase probably originated in the Cabinet Office itself. See S. S. Wilson, *Cabinet Office*, paras 904 and 911–12 (pp. 89 and 91).
80 Thus echoing Churchill's letter to him of that day (PREM 1/395, and see pp. 137–41, below).
81 All references to the discussion of 9 October are taken from CAB 65/1, WM 42(39), unless otherwise stated.
82 Although Cadogan had noted on 7 October that some ministers would object to any attempt 'to get rid of Hitler', together with the French – no doubt less because of squeamishness than because of scepticism about the policies of the likely replacements (Dilks, *Cadogan Diaries*, p. 221).
83 Dilks, *Cadogan Diaries*, p. 223.
84 Cadogan Papers, MS Diary, ACAD 1/8, 10 October 1939 (not in Dilks); see also the Simon Papers: (i) Diary entry of 13 October 1939, which confirms that he and Churchill had been 'specially told off to settle the document with the Prime Minister and Foreign Secretary', and (ii) MS Simon 34 (Simon's appointment diary for 1939).
85 Chamberlain Papers, NC 18/1/1125, letter to Hilda Chamberlain, 15 October 1939.
86 Wallace Papers, Diary entry of 11 October 1939.
87 The Simon Papers contain many letters paying tribute to Simon's 'masterly intellect', as Neville Chamberlain phrased it in a deathbed tribute (Chamberlain to Simon, 6 October 1940, in the Simon Papers, MS 87).
88 The two versions to compare are WP 79(39) of 9 October, and WP 81(39) of 10 October, both to be found in CAB 66/2. More details are available in PREM 1/395, which contains a first draft of WP 79(39), with Chamberlain's handwritten alterations.
89 It is interesting that at about this time Sir Thomas Inskip could write of Chamberlain: 'The PM is sometimes v. child-like in his naiveté' – the Prime Minister had thought it was 'to the credit of Hitler' that he had not been associated with investment scandals – while for his part Chamberlain was observing of Churchill, 'Winston is in some respects such a child that he neither knows his own motives or [sic] sees where his actions are carrying him.' See Inskip Diary, vol. II, 26 September 1939, and Chamberlain Papers, NC 18/1/1124, letter to Ida Chamberlain, 8 October 1939.

90 PREM 1/395. Marginal comments on the various drafts, particularly by Horace Wilson, substantiate these claims. See the copies in this file of WP 79(39) and WP 81(39).
91 Such figures are obtained by measuring the length of Cabinet minutes in terms of pages or parts of pages, and are, of course, only to be regarded as rough measures.
92 CAB 65/3, Confidential Annex of WM 43(39), 10 October 1939. In fact Dahlerus did return for various talks in December 1939. See Table 5, below, p. 140.
93 As with all quotations from this meeting, unless otherwise stated, this is from CAB 65/1, WM 43(39), 10 October 1939.
94 It is interesting how French reluctance to fight was the excuse for the Cabinet meeting on 2 September, while by October it was France's apparent belligerence which was the cause of the problems.
95 On the general relationship between the Dominions and British foreign policy and its making up to the start of the war, see Ovendale, *'Appeasement' and the English-Speaking World*. See also D. C. Watt, 'The Influence of the Commonwealth on British Foreign Policy: The Case of the Munich Crisis', in his *Personalities and Policies*, and for a study of the wartime conflict over decision-making at the highest level, David Day, *Menzies and Churchill at War: A Controversial New Account of the 1941 Struggle for Power* (North Ryde: Angus & Robertson, 1986).
96 The main items of correspondence between the British government and the Dominion governments in this period are contained in CAB 21/952, 'Anglo-German hostilities: peace proposals'. For the Canadian suggestion mentioned here, see in particular the telegram from Mackenzie King to Chamberlain of 8 October, together with the cable of 9 October from the British High Commissioner in Ottawa, reporting his own conversation with the Canadian Prime Minister. That this had become general Dominion policy was reported (too late) by Eden to the War Cabinet on 12 October, after a meeting with their High Commissioners in London (CAB 65/1, WM 45(39), 12 October 1939).
97 CAB 65/1, WM 43(39), 10 October 1939. The earlier draft referred to is WP 77(39). Ministers also agreed at this point to substitute the phrase 'the German government' throughout for 'Germany' or 'the German people'.
98 PREM 1/395, comment on the first effort of the drafting committee, WP 79(39).
99 Compare Menzies to the British government, no. 133 of 11 October 1939, in CAB 21/952, with the statement in *HCD*, vol. 352, cols. 563–8, 12 October 1939.
100 CAB 65/1, WM 44(39), 11 October 1939.
101 CAB 65/1, WM 45(39), 12 October 1939. Cadogan recorded that Smuts, the South African Prime Minister, was the main factor in leading him to attempt further redrafts on that morning, but nothing came of it (Dilks, *Cadogan Diaries*, p. 223). R. A. Butler, Parliamentary Under-Secretary at the Foreign Office, also tried his hand at redrafting the con-

clusions on 10 October, and came up with a rhetorical discussion of what an alternative to Versailles might look like, but he too insisted on guarantees against further German aggression as preconditions. See PREM 1/395.
102 See Appendix 3, below, for the text of the statement. Halifax claimed a sore throat, although he stayed for the whole proceedings, and made a short further statement at the end. This was non-committal in the extreme: every word of the original statement had, he said, been 'most carefully weighed' and 'I should be very unwilling to add words that were not equally carefully considered' (*House of Lords Debates*, vol. 114, cols. 1389–1416, 12 October 1939). Similarly, Chamberlain thought it would be best to postpone his planned radio broadcast: to depart from the language of the agreed statement 'would have been dangerous' (CAB 65/1, WM 46(39), 13 October 1939). Both men were clearly nervous of extemporising and possibly incurring Cabinet wrath at going beyond collective positions.
103 *HCD*, vol. 352, col. 568, 12 October 1939. The only dissent came in a powerful speech by the pacifist George Lansbury. The debate lasted nearly six hours, and some MPs commented on their surprise at being able to agree with the Prime Minister. 'Former critics of Appeasement called it the strongest and clearest statement he had ever made', according to *News Review*, 8: 16 (19 October 1939) (a lively news magazine from the Odhams stable; copy in the Greenwood papers, Shelf 8, file on 'Miscellaneous, 1940–45' in box marked 'Labour Party Correspondence 1948–54'). Chamberlain himself thought it had gone better than he had anticipated, thanks to help from Halifax and Churchill, who had originally thought the speech 'not sharp enough' (Chamberlain Papers, NC 18/1/1125, letter to Hilda Chamberlain, 15 October 1939). The senior intelligence officer Rear-Admiral Godfrey, noted that the statement 'was received with relief because it gave no signs of appeasement' (Godfrey to Gladwyn Jebb, in FO 371/22946; and see note 167, below, this chapter).
104 CAB 65/1, WM 46(39), 13 October 1939.
105 *DGFP*, vol. VIII, no. 246. See also Irving, *Hitler's War*, p. 35, and *Ciano's Diary, 1939–43*, ed. Malcolm Muggeridge (London: Heinemann, 1947), p. 167.
106 CAB 65/1, WM 40(39), 7 October 1939, and WM 49(39), 16 October 1939.
107 On 22 October 1939, Chamberlain wrote to Ida (Chamberlain Papers, NC 18/1/1126), that 'there are a terrible lot of people who never think clearly or continuously and often therefore forget what we are fighting for'. For optimism about Hitler, see NC 18/1/1129, letter to Ida Chamberlain, 5 November 1939.
108 For the problems of implementation, see Allison, *Essence of Decision*, and Steve Smith and Michael Clarke (eds.), *Foreign Policy Implementation* (London: Allen & Unwin, 1985).
109 We still lack a full historical account of these issues, but Reynolds, *The Creation of the Anglo-American Alliance 1937–1941*, is good on the Welles

mission of February–March 1940, while Cowling, (*Impact of Hitler*, pp. 355–65) has some material on the domestic political dimension of the peace problem. See also the Foreign Office memorandum 'Summary of Principal Peace Feelers September 1939–March 1941', CC4216/610/G, in PREM 4/100/8.
110 See pp. 104–7 above.
111 Wallace Papers, Diary, 9 May 1940. Inskip referred to this group more neutrally as 'the second XI of would-be Cabinet Ministers' (Inskip Diary, vol. II, 12 January 1940). But see also note 22, above, this chapter.
112 The Crookshank diary gives an interesting impression of the humdrum work-life of a junior minister, waiting for the occasional pronouncements of the Cabinet oracle on his specialised area, and only meeting the occasional senior figure, whether minister or official. On the other hand, Crookshank was driven by dislike of the Minister of War, Hore-Belisha and with his contacts in the Guards, may have been involved in some intrigues against him. The latter was forced out, for reasons still not fully understood, in early January 1940 (see p. 239, below).
113 Inskip Diary, vol. II, 20 September 1939.
114 *Ibid.*, 9 October 1939. The abbreviations are Caldecote's, 'H.', of course, referring to Hitler. Other entries bear out the general point: on 21 November there is a wistful and isolated reference to Hoare having told him that Churchill is 'difficult in the Cabinet, but the PM handles him very well'; on 4 December we learn that 'the War Cabinet maintains complete secrecy about anything planned for the future'.
115 Crookshank Papers, Diary, 13 September 1939. Wallace also noted that ministers 'above the line' were 'to work as a sort of Home Defence Committee under Hoare to submit matters to the War Cabinet, rather on the lines of the C.I.D.' (Wallace Papers, Diary, 5 September 1939).
116 Wallace Papers, Diary, 6 October 1939.
117 See pp. 115–16, above.
118 Crookshank Papers, Diary, 6 October 1939. The full reference to the discussion reads: 'Hitler peace speech. All blah.' It is possible that the reference is to Hitler, rather than the Committee. See also the official record, CAB 75/1, HPC(39), 7th Meeting, and also conveniently contained in CAB 21/952. This reads in part: 'It was agreed that this was a matter of fundamental importance which could not be left to the discretion of the BBC and which should be undertaken by the experts of the Foreign Office and Ministry of Information...'.
119 See p. 115, above.
120 CAB 21/1324, Sir Edward Bridges to Sir Horace Wilson, 30 October 1939. This complaint arose out of the flood of unpopular domestic regulation produced by the War Cabinet but handled by the Home Policy Committee.
121 The Prime Minister formed three groups for the Sunday rota: (i) himself, Halifax and Chatfield; (ii) Simon, Churchill and Kingsley Wood; and (iii) Hoare, Hore-Belisha and Hankey (CAB 65/1, WM 8(39), 8

September 1939). It was accepted that normally these meetings would 'not include memoranda and statements on matters of first importance' (CAB 65/1, WM 7(39), 7 September 1939).

122 This is not quite true of Anderson who (particularly at first) did not always attend for every item. Originally Anderson had only asked to be present for Item 1 on the agenda, that is the developments in the war, and the Prime Minister had agreed that he should leave thereafter unless an item relevant to his department came up (CAB 21/761, Sir Horace Wilson to Sir Edward Bridges, 4 September 1939). But practice overcame theory, and soon Anderson was running a very close second to the almost ever-present Eden.

123 CAB 65/1, WM 1(39), 3 September 1939. By contrast, the Empire was more taken for granted in that neither MacDonald (Secretary of State for the Colonies) nor Zetland (India) were granted permanent membership. The latter appeared rather more often as an irregular attender.

124 The Earl of Avon, *The Eden Memoirs: The Reckoning* (London: Cassell, 1965), pp. 62–3 and 90–1.

125 Churchill, *The Gathering Storm*, p. 328. There were, of course, also officials present, notably Sir Horace Wilson and the three Chiefs of Staff, making a total of fiteeen. The Cabinet Office compared this to the 1916–1919 experience, concluding on the basis of a limited sample that there was an average of 15.75 ministers and officials present at meetings during the Great War, although only an average of 7.45 was present throughout the whole meeting. In this last respect Chamberlain's War Cabinet were certainly more assiduous (CAB 21/1324).

126 Avon, *The Reckoning*, p. 91.

127 The Cabinet memorandum WP(G)(39) 1, 'Institution of the War Cabinet: Consequent Changes in the Organisation and Procedure of the Cabinet Offices', required that the Cabinet Minutes be restricted to mere Conclusions unless the Prime Minister directed otherwise.

128 CAB 21/1324, minute by W. D. Wilkinson, 25 October 1939, commenting on the remark by his colleague Lawrence Burgis that 'what the eye does not see etc.'.

129 It is revealing that in a handwritten alteration to the draft reply, he changed 'something more solid than pacts . . . are wanted now to give back to the world the confidence it has lost', by substituting 'the confidence which has been shattered' for the last part of the sentence. See 'First Drafting Committee draft', in PREM 1/395.

130 Watt, *How War Came*, for example p. 578.

131 See pp. 115–16, above. Also the remarks of the two men in the Cabinet of 6 October (see p. 113, above), can be interpreted as subtly different.

132 Dilks, *Cadogan Diaries*, p. 221. Cadogan's own emphasis.

133 Unless we make the assumption that Halifax deliberately encouraged Churchill to submit what he doubtless knew would be a strongly antipeace draft, so as to stiffen Chamberlain's resolve. But this, as we have seen (pp. 117–18, above) is only one of several possible interpretations.

134 Chamberlain Papers, NC 18/1/1124, letter to Ida Chamberlain, 8 October 1939.
135 Although he expected his own talents to come back fully into their own at such a time (Chamberlain Papers, NC 18/1/1116, letter to Ida Chamberlain, 10 September 1939). This letter shows how feelings were liable to rapid change at such times as the start of war, for here Chamberlain wrote that the discussion of peace terms might be a 'long way off'.
136 CAB 65/1, WM 42(39), 9 October 1939. Halifax returned to the charge with Hoare and Chatfield the next day (WM 43(39), 10 October 1939), and partially succeeded, but the Prime Minister continued to stick to his view of the previous day that 'we should avoid any precise statement of our war aims'.
137 Chamberlain Papers, NC 18/1/1116, letter to Ida Chamberlain, 10 September 1939; Hankey Diary, 23 August 1939, entry printed in Roskill, *Hankey, Man of Secrets*, vol. III, pp. 412–13.
138 On Simon's caution, see Grigg Papers, 2/29, Sir John Simon to Sir P. J. Grigg, 10 February 1940, about policy towards India: 'It is difficult to say these things in Cabinet without seeming to be unduly critical'.
139 Hore-Belisha Papers: the note, suggesting a joint Anglo-French declaration, was drafted on 11 September and sent to Hoare (with a copy to Chatfield) 'as a suggestion for the PM'. That it was a shot across Chamberlain's bows seems clear from the marginal comment: 'NB it seems very important not to include in the formula such a reference to "settlement by negotiation" as gives a handle to Ciano and the Peace Offer.'
140 Hoare's own memoirs (as Viscount Templewood), *Nine Troubled Years*, came too early to benefit from revisionist approaches to appeasement (London: Collins, 1954), but they contain a number of revealing chapters on such subjects as 'Chamberlain's Mind'. The more recent biography by J. A. Cross (*Sir Samuel Hoare: A Political Biography* (London: Jonathan Cape, 1977)) is a balanced account which redresses a good deal of the earlier, prejudicial, comment.
141 R. A. Butler, in a preface to J. A. Cross' biography (*Sir Samuel Hoare*, p. x), called Churchill Hoare's 'great enemy'.
142 Templewood Papers, XI: 2, 'Weekly Notes', 2 October 1939.
143 Templewood Papers, I: 2, 'Weekly Notes', entries of 7 October and 6–8 October. The omissions in this citation are largely the numbers Hoare used to tabulate his points.

Runciman had left the Cabinet in apparent relief on the outbreak of war, and was thus free to think about the broader issues, while Lord Londonderry was a habitual 'dabbler in foreign affairs' and member of the 'Watching Committee' which Lord Salisbury and other sceptics had newly set up to make sure that the government's performance was closely monitored. See Simon Papers, MS Simon 85, Runciman to Simon, 19 September 1939; Martin Gilbert, *The Roots of Appeasement* (London: Weidenfeld & Nicolson, 1966), p. 186; and Cowling, *Impact of Hitler*, p. 378.

144 P. 117, above.
145 Hore-Belisha, to judge from the evidence of his private papers, does not seem to have been very much involved in the issue. Those with responsibility for the war (apart from the ubiquitous Churchill) had plenty on their plates.
146 See pp. 117–20, above.
147 Gilbert, *Finest Hour*, p. 60. 'Edward' is, of course, Halifax. It may be, however, that Churchill had shown his piece around his contacts in the Secret Intelligence Service (SIS) as the use of the term 'secret circle' seems to have referred to SIS rather than any inner Cabinet. See the tribute to SIS paid by Churchill cited as the frontispiece to Anthony Cave Brown's *The Secret Servant: The Life of Sir Stewart Menzies, Churchill's Spymaster* (London: Michael Joseph, 1988). Churchill said to Menzies in 1945: 'Will you, within the secret circle, convey to all possible my compliments and gratitude'. Alex Danchev, in '"Dilly-Dally", or Having the Last Word: Field-Marshal Sir John Dill and Prime Minister Winston Churchill' (*Journal of Contemporary History*, 22: 1 (January 1987), p. 29 and nn. 25–7) is perhaps ingenuous in seeing 'the secret circle' as referring merely to Churchill's intimates and spear-carriers.
148 Gilbert, *Finest Hour*, p. 56. In the Churchill Papers, still not yet open to researchers, the reference is 19/2, 'A Note on the German Peace Suggestions', 8 October 1939.
149 Gilbert, *Finest Hour*, p. 56; for Churchill's vitriolic view of Chatfield's appeasing outlook, see p. 1122. See also Rhodes James, *Victor Cazalet*, p. 219, Cazalet's diary entry of 11 October 1939. As for Hore-Belisha, relations with him deteriorated badly once Churchill had become Prime Minister. Churchill certainly did not attempt to rescue him from dismissal in January 1940, and may even have been instrumental behind the scenes in encouraging his removal.
150 The *Mirror* newspaper was, as early as 1 October, calling for Churchill's installation as Premier. See Cockett, *Twilight of Truth*, p. 158. See also the front page of the *Sunday Pictorial* for 1 October (reproduced in Paul Addison, *The Road to 1945: British Politics and the Second World War* (London: Jonathan Cape, 1975), by p. 64). The headline 'Hitler Plans New "Peace" Trap' is accompanied by a large photo of Churchill and the by-line 'This Is The Man He Fears – "Churchill Will Be Our Next Premier" – See Page 9'. The quotation about the September leak is from Hankey to Lady Hankey, 3 September 1939, reproduced in Roskill, *Hankey: Man of Secrets*, vol. III, pp. 419–20.
151 Chatfield Papers, CHT 6/4, correspondence between Churchill and Chatfield, December 1939 and January 1940.
152 On Venlo, see note 13 above, this chapter, and also Andrew, *Secret Service*, pp. 608–16. An account is also given by Anthony Cave Brown in *The Secret Servant* (pp. 208–23), although basic errors do not inspire confidence in its reliability. When Chamberlain and Halifax, who had authorised the risky contacts with Germany, finally disclosed the course of events to the War Cabinet, before its dénouement, they were shaken by their hostile reception: 'PM frightened by the Cabinet!' (Cadogan

on 1 November, in Dilks, *Cadogan Diaries*, p. 228; see also CAB 65/2, WM 67(39), item 15, 1 November 1939). According to Hinsley (*British Intelligence*, p. 57) this is a Confidential Annex, but there is no trace of it in the relevant file, CAB 65/4. There was undoubtedly a real squall in Cabinet, but the ban on release of intelligence materials may have led to the suppression even of reference numbers. Simon may have been one of the critics; he was sceptical of the view that Hitlerism would be brought down from within (Simon Papers, Diary entry of 13 October 1939).

153 It will be seen from Table 5 that Dahlerus still had access to Cadogan in London as late as 28 December 1939, although by then he had begun to turn his attention to Scandinavia more than direct Anglo-German contacts. Unfortunately Dahlerus' own detailed record of his activities, and the commentaries on it made by Halifax, Sir Llewellyn Woodward, and various Foreign Office professionals close to the story, such as Frank Roberts, stop at the outset of the war. See Hickleton Papers, A4.410.3.10. See also Birger Dahlerus, *The Last Attempt*, translated by Alexandra Dick and with an Introduction by Sir Norman Birkett (London, Hutchinson, 1947).
154 CAB 65/3, WM 38(39), 5 October 1939. See pp. 112–13, above.
155 CAB 65/1, WM 40(39), 7 October 1939.
156 Despite the view of the contemporary *News Review* on 19 October that during Chamberlain's statement Churchill 'was like an author in the front row of the stalls, listening to the unfolding of his play. For many of the phrases were his.'
157 CAB 65/1, WM 42(39), 9 October 1939.
158 Hankey Papers, 11/1. See also note 1, this chapter.
159 This was the *Daily Mirror*'s phrase on 5 June 1940, after the 'we will fight on the beaches' speech; see also Churchill's completely authoritative tone to Halifax, only a week after entering the government: 'it would make no difference to our action if Poland were forced into a defeated peace ... we intend to see the war through to a victorious conclusion, whatever happens to Poland' (cited in Colvin, *The Chamberlain Cabinet*, p. 22, reference given as 'FO800').
160 The reference to a 'grim struggle' comes from Hoare's plain-spoken broadcast on the BBC's Home Service on 22 September; see pp. 101–2, above. The longer quotation is from Hoare's letter to Lord Lothian in Washington of 7 October 1939 (Templewood Papers, XI:5, and also reproduced in Templewood's *Nine Troubled Years*, pp. 405–6).
161 Sir John Anderson to Sir Horace Wilson, 11 October 1939, PREM 1/395. Wilson initialled, and said that the PM had seen, the letter, a copy of which had also been sent to Hoare.
162 See pp. 119–20, above.
163 Cazalet to Lothian, 16 October 1939 (Lothian Papers, vol. 399).
164 Bethell, *The War Hitler Won*, p. 386.
165 Minute of 3 August 1940, PREM 4/100/3. 'Chips' Channon recorded that the Prime Minister read 'his famous statement which many have

read and had a finger in' (Robert Rhodes James (ed.), *Chips: the Diaries of Sir Henry Channon* (London: Weidenfeld & Nicolson, 1967), p. 224.
166 Simon Papers, Diary entry of 13 October 1939.
167 For the way in which the 12 October statement became the authorised version of government policy see PREM 1/442, in which Sir C. Stuart, writing to A. N. Rucker on 18 February 1940, refers to the speech among 'such authoritative statements of British war aims as have been made'. On doubts about public opinion in the early part of the war, see a report on home morale sent by Rear-Admiral Godfrey (of the Naval Intelligence Staff, and Churchill's candidate for Head of the Secret Intelligence Service, according to Cave Brown, *The Secret Servant*), to Gladwyn Jebb in the Foreign Office (C17694, in FO 371/22946), which talked of much depression being caused by lack of leadership and 'the everlasting silence' from Government, particularly on war aims. This was sent on approvingly by Cadogan to Halifax on 19 October 1939 (presumably the opinions it reported were formed before the statement of 12 October could have had much effect) and Halifax minuted that he would think 'whether we can go any way to meeting what he suggests'.

6 To continue alone? May–July 1940

1 In the period 3 September 1939–22 June 1941 (659 days), the War Cabinet met 496 times, or on three out of every four days. Between 1 May and 31 July 1940 (92 days) it met 108 times, or 6 times in every 5 days (CAB 65/1, 2, 5, 6, 7, 8, 9, 17 and 18). Given how often the War Cabinet met, this increase in frequency – of about 50 per cent – is probably significant. Events were critical, but this did not mean that the War Cabinet was pushed to the sidelines.
2 Anthony Storr argues that Churchill found in the dangers of 1940 a release with elation from the 'black dog' of depression. Other temperaments, like Sir Samuel Hoare's, seem to have been completely disorientated (A. Storr, 'The Man', in A. J. P. Taylor *et al.*, *Churchill: Four Faces and the Man* (Harmondsworth: Pelican, 1973), pp. 205–46; on Hoare, see Dilks, *Cadogan Diaries*, pp. 286–8; and FO 800/323, Hoare to Halifax, 1 June 1940.
3 See Winston S. Churchill, *The Second World War*, vol. II: *Their Finest Hour* (London: Cassell, 1949), pp. 21–2. Churchill says that he sent Roosevelt 950 messages throughout the war, and received 800. See also Joseph P. Lash, *Roosevelt and Churchill, 1939–41: The Partnership that Saved the World* (New York: W. W. Norton, 1976), pp. 21–4 and 62; F. L. Loewenheim, H. D. Langley, M. Jonas (eds.), *Roosevelt and Churchill: Their Secret War-time Correspondence* (London: Barrie & Jenkins, 1975), pp. 94–7; and James Leutze, 'The Secret of the Churchill–Roosevelt Correspondence, September 1939–May 1940', *Journal of Contemporary History*, 10: 3 (July 1975), pp. 465–92. The telegrams were usually sent via the US Ambassador in London, by-passing the Foreign Office (PREM 4/27/3).

4 Churchill, *Their Finest Hour*, p. 21; CAB 65/7, WM 130(40), 19 May 1940.
5 Churchill, *Their Finest Hour*, pp. 22–3 and 49–50.
6 See Williamson, *The Politics of Grand Strategy*, pp. 367–72.
7 Certainly since the scares about an attack on the Low Countries in early 1939 (CAB 23/97, CM 3(39) and 6(39), 1 and 8 February 1939); Gibbs, *Grand Strategy*, vol. I, pp. 657–63.
8 CAB 65/7, WM (40) 122, 14 May, 7.00 p.m. The following account of the military events of May–June 1940 is based primarily on J. R. M. Butler, *Grand Strategy*, vol. II, *Official History of the Second World War* (London: HMSO, 1957), pp. 195–246; Bond, *Chief of Staff*, pp. 306–69; Peter Calvocoressi and Guy Wint, *Total War: Causes and Courses of the Second World War* (London: Allen Lane, The Penguin Press, 1972), pp. 118–31; General Andre Beaufré, *1940: The Fall of France*, trans. Desmond Flower (London: Cassell, 1967), pp. 179–215; and Eleanor M. Gates, *End of the Affair: The Collapse of the Anglo-French Alliance, 1939–40* (Berkeley: University of California Press, 1981), pp. 71–142.
9 CAB 65/7, WM 123(40), 15 May 1940, and Confidential Annex, CAB 65/13, WM 123(40), item 2.
10 CAB 65/7, WM 124(40), 16 May 1940, 11.30 a.m.; and Confidential Annex, CAB 65/13, WM 124(40), item 1.
11 CAB 65/7, WM 125(40), 16 May 1940, 11 p.m.
12 Gilbert, *Finest Hour*, pp. 352–3.
13 CAB 65/7, WM 127(40), 18 May 1940, 11.30 a.m. By contrast, the BEF the day before had been under such pressure that at one stage it was feared that German divisions were moving in on Calais (Bond, *Chief of Staff*, pp. 318–20).
14 CAB 65/13, Confidential Annex, WM 139(40), 26 May; Butler, *Grand Strategy*, vol. II, p. 191. Gort had in fact already begun to retreat, on his own decision.
15 CAB 65/7, WM 132(40), 21 May 1940, 11.30 a.m.
16 CAB 65/13, Confidential Annex, WM 134(40), item 1, 22 May, 10.30 a.m. As early as the 19th Pownall was thinking of arrangements for a possible withdrawal from France and on the 20th was writing of the 'folly' of Churchill's orders (Bond, *Chief of Staff*, pp. 322–3).
17 Parkinson, *Peace for our Time*, pp. 360–1. In the meantime there was a serious breakdown in communications between both the Cabinet and the front, and the British and French military commanders. General Weygand was under the impression that Churchill was encouraging a general British retreat on the 23rd (J. Weygand, *The Role of General Weygand: Conversations with His Son*, trans. J. H. F. McEwen (London: Eyre and Spottiswoode, 1948), pp. 66–71).
18 See above, and also J. R. Colville, *Man of Valour: The Life of Field Marshall the Viscount Gort* (London: Collins, 1972), pp. 185–226, and Bond, *Chief of Staff*, p. 347.
19 These images were remarkably undeveloped, but the government had been broadly aiming for victory through defensive strength. See

Chamberlain Papers, NC 18/1/1122, letter to Ida Chamberlain, 23 September 1939: 'I do not believe that holocausts are required to gain us the victory', and NC 18/1/1124, letter to Ida, 8 October 1939: 'keep up the economic pressure ... take no offensive unless Hitler begins it. I reckon that if we are allowed to carry out this policy we shall have won the war by the Spring'. See also Chatfield Papers, CHT 6/2, Chatfield to Lothian, 26 September 1939: 'an effective blockade, as in the last war, will have to be our chief method'.
20 Invasion of the UK itself now became a realistic possibility, as the Chiefs of Staff pointed out on 22 May (COS 376(40) in CAB 80/11).
21 In his first broadcast as Prime Minister on 19 May Churchill romanticised, 'It is better for us to perish in battle than to look at the outrage of our nation and our altar.' But this was belief as much as rhetoric ('Memoir by Sir John Martin', in *Action This Day: Working with Churchill*, ed. Sir John Wheeler-Bennett (London: Macmillan, 1968), pp. 153–6).
22 Churchill, *Their Finest Hour*, p. 48.
23 CAB 65/13, Confidential Annex, WM 128(40), item 1 (my italics). The Committee which accepted this brief consisted of Chamberlain, Halifax, Anderson, Attlee and Hankey.
24 Chamberlain Papers, NC 2/24A, Diary entry of 19 May 1940.
25 CAB 65/7, WM 133(40), 22 May 1940. The full findings of Chamberlain's Committee on emergency powers are contained in CAB 66/6, WP 162(40), 20 May.
26 Churchill, *Their Finest Hour*, pp. 78–9; CAB 65/7, WM 139(40), 26 May, 9.00 a.m., and Confidential Annex, CAB 65/13, WM 139(40), item 1; COS 394(40) in CAB 80/11 (my italics).
27 The actual phrasing of the Chiefs of Staff's conclusion was cautious. Churchill, *Their Finest Hour*, pp. 78–9; CAB 66/7, WP 169(40), 26 May 1940, and see p. 180, below.
28 CAB 65/7, WM 141(40), 27 May 1940, 11.30 a.m., and Confidential Annex, CAB 65/13, WM 141(40), item 9.
29 CAB 65/13, WM 139(40), item 1, Confidential Annex, 26 May, 9.00 a.m. This was not wholly at odds with the view that Halifax had been coming to during the previous October, namely that 'his chief war aim was the elimination of Herr Hitler' (CAB 65/1, WM 40(39), 7 October 1939). Moreover, by February he had been willing to discuss privately with Hankey 'the possibility of making a preliminary peace to be followed by a more considered and wider peace later' (Hickleton Papers, A7.8.3, Diary entry of 19 February 1940).
30 CAB 65/13, WM 139(40), item 1; and Dilks, *Cadogan Diaries*, pp. 289–90. This approach was made despite Mussolini's discouraging reply to a message from Churchill on 16 May (Woodward, *British Foreign Policy*, vol. I, pp. 229–37).
31 The first Chiefs of Staff draft is COS 390(40), WP 168(40) in CAB 66/7, 25 May 1940. Churchill himself had been receiving relatively optimistic projections about the trend of air power from his personal adviser, Prof. F. A. Lindemann, who had written on 26 April: 'The combined

Metropolitan air strength of England and France is at present about 2/3 of that of Germany, and on the 1st July it will be nearly 3/4.' The fall of France prevented Lindemann or Churchill from producing new figures on air power until August 1940 (Cherwell Papers, OFF 1: 1, January–May, and May–September 1940, Minutes to PM; PREM 4/94/4, Lindemann to Churchill, 10 August 1940).

32 At the second meeting that day it was decided that Sir Archibald Sinclair, the Secretary for Air and Leader of the Liberal Party, should be present when the question of Italian mediation was next discussed (CAB 65/13, WM 140(40), Confidential Annex).

33 Labour ministers Attlee and Greenwood were certainly anti-fascist. This did not commit them, however, to a full-hearted support of the British Empire's world role (see Naylor, *Labour's International Policy*, pp. 215–17, and Attlee's pamphlets 'Your Constituencies in War-time', and 'Labour's Peace Aims', Winter 1939–40, Attlee Papers (Oxford), Box 8).

34 In this Churchill the historian saw British experience repeating itself. See his speech on the surrender of Belgium (*HCD*, vol. 361, cols. 421–2, 28 May 1940). (My italics in text.)

35 For the detailed chronology, see Gilbert, *Finest Hour*, pp. 402–680.

36 Woodward, *British Foreign Policy*, vol. I, pp. 229–45.

37 On 26 May, Reynaud suggested going beyond the existing general feelers to Mussolini, hoping to keep Italy out of the war, to explore the possibility of Italian mediation in an overall settlement (CAB 65/13, Confidential Annex, WM 140(40), 26 May, 2 p.m.; CAB 66/7, WP 170(40)). See also Gates, *End of the Affair*, pp. 142–52.

38 CAB 65/13, Confidential Annex, WM 140(40), 26 May, 2 p.m.; Churchill had initially seen Reynaud without Halifax, and had not encouraged him to develop the proposal.

39 *Ibid.*; Record of Conversation between Halifax and the Italian Ambassador (attached also as telegram to Sir Percy Loraine, 25 May, no. 413); Halifax's memory had faded by 1942, when he denied having wished to broaden the approach to Mussolini (Hickleton Papers, A4.410.4.17, Halifax to Sargent, 12 October 1942).

40 Hickleton Papers, A7.8.3, Diary entry of 27 May 1940. See also Birkenhead, *Halifax*, p. 458.

41 Hickleton Papers, A7.8.4, Diary entry of 26 May 1940.

42 Chamberlain Papers, NC 2/24A, Diary entry of 26 May 1940.

43 CAB 65/13, Confidential Annex, WM 142(40), 27 May 1940, 4.30 p.m.

44 See, for example, Hickleton Papers, A7.8.3, Diary entry of 30 May 1940: 'I have never seen so disorderly a mind. I am coming to the conclusion that his process of thought is one that has to operate through speech. As this is exactly the reverse of my own it is irritating.'

45 Both without departmental responsibilities: Attlee as Lord Privy Seal, Greenwood as Minister without Portfolio.

46 CAB 65/13, Confidential Annex, WM 140(40), 26 May 1940, 2.00 p.m.

47 CAB 65/13, Confidential Annex, WM 142(40), 27 May 1940, 4.30 p.m.

These crucial discussions about peace were confined to meetings attended only by full members of the War Cabinet, plus Sinclair.
48 *Ibid.*; the same day Attlee reassured a bullish Dalton: 'There is no shake among politicians here ... we shall fight it out, and are confident that with the resources behind us, we shall win' (Dalton Papers, 17, Dalton to Attlee, 27 May 1940; Diary (22), entry of 27 May).
49 Especially as German peace feelers had been made at regular intervals even after Hitler's offer of October 1939 (documented in a Foreign Office minute (C4216/610/G, in PREM 4/100/8).
50 Hickleton Papers, A7.8.3, Diary entry of 27 May 1940, and Birkenhead, *Halifax*, p. 458.
51 Dilks, *Cadogan Diaries*, pp. 290–1. Halifax had already decided that in Cabinet 'certainly there is no comparison between Winston and Neville as Chairman' (Hickleton Papers, A7.8.4, Diary entry of 13 May 1940). For his part, Churchill does not mention the dispute (*Their Finest Hour*, pp. 108–11).
52 Birkenhead, *Halifax*, pp. 282 and 328–9.
53 Dilks, *Cadogan Diaries*, p. 291. See also Jonathan Knight, 'Churchill and the Approach to Mussolini and Hitler in May 1940: A Reply to David Carlton', *British Journal of International Studies*, 3: 1 (April, 1977), pp. 92–6.
54 CAB 65/13, Confidential Annex, WM 145(40), 28 May 1940, 4.00 p.m. At this time the War Cabinet was meeting twice a day.
55 *Ibid.* The echo of Munich must have been painfully evident to Chamberlain, sitting at the same table.
56 CAB 65/13, Confidential Annex, WM 140(40), 26 May 1940, 2.00 p.m.
57 CAB 65/13, WM 142(40), 27 May, 4.30 p.m. This statement clearly exasperated Halifax: 'he could not recognise any resemblance between the action he proposed, and the suggestion that we were sueing for terms which would lead us to disaster'.
58 Churchill had tried to set a lead when First Lord, but his role had confined the impact of his personality. The Prime Minister had found his barrage of letters annoying (Chamberlain Papers, NC 18/1/1124, letter to Ida Chamberlain, 8 October 1939).
59 CAB 65/13, Confidential Annex, WM 145(40), 28 May 1940, 4.00 p.m. (my italics).
60 On 25 May Halifax seems to have drafted a letter to Roosevelt (never sent) asking the USA to use its influence on Hitler to ensure that any terms 'that were intended to destroy the independence of Great Britain or France' were not insisted on, but recognising that Hitler had the right to offer terms favourable to himself and unfavourable to the defeated. This was a significantly different perspective from that of Churchill (Hickleton Papers, A4.410.4.1, Draft (by Halifax) of message from the Prime Minister to the President, 25 May 1940).
61 In this, however, Churchill was still being necessarily optimistic about British financial and industrial resources. Correlli Barnett has pointed out that military advice was to fight a long war, whereas the Treasury

thought Britain could only afford a short one (Correlli Barnett, *The Audit of War: The Illusion and Reality of Britain as a Great Nation* (London: Macmillan Papermac, 1987), p. 144; see also Paul Kennedy, 'Strategy versus Finance in Twentieth Century Britain', in his *Strategy and Diplomacy 1870–1945* (London: Fontana, 1984, pp. 101–2). Lend-Lease was to square that circle, but its scale could hardly have been counted on in mid-1940. In 1939–40 Britain was caught between open-ended commitments and very limited resources. The only option, as G. C. Peden has pointed out (*British Rearmament and the Treasury*, pp. 149–50), was to hope that by concentrating resources on air defence Britain would be able to hold out until the putative assets of the Empire and American assistance eventually came into play.

62 CAB 65/13, Confidential Annex, WM 140(40), 26 May 1940. Churchill was not alone in this view (Hankey Papers, 4/32, Hankey to Hoare, 19 July 1940).
63 Dilks, *Cadogan Diaries*, pp. 290 and 293.
64 In part this is reminiscent of the irresistible optimism (also well founded) of General Douglas MacArthur before the Inchon landings in Korea. It is also another example of the effects of cognitive dissonance (see Joseph De Rivera, *The Psychological Dimension of Foreign Policy* (Columbus, Ohio: C. E. Merrill, 1968), pp. 175–81).
65 See CAB 23/100, CM 36(39), 5 July 1939, 5.30 p.m.; CAB 65/5, WMs 15 and 21(40), 16 and 23 January 1960. See also the papers of the Cabinet's Defence Preparedness Committee, CAB 27/662, DM 21(39), 1 September 1939.
66 CAB 65/13, Confidential Annex, WM 123(40), item 2, 15 May 1940.
67 The Marquess of Lothian was Ambassador in Washington between 22 August 1939 and 12 December 1940. Hoare had considerable private correspondence with him (Templewood Papers, XI, 1, 3 and 5). Chatfield had also corresponded with Lothian during the Phoney War, if less frequently than Hoare (Chatfield Papers, CHt 6/2).
68 CAB 65/7, WM 131(40), 20 May 1940.
69 CAB 65/13, Confidential Annex, WM 145(40), item 1, 28 May 1940 4.00 p.m. and CAB 65/7, WM 145(40).
70 CAB 65/7, WM 159(40), 9 June 1940. From the perspective of crisis decision-making, which sometimes breeds optimism as a way of coping with a deterioration in circumstances, it is worth noting the contrast of Smuts' outlook here with his letter of 26 January 1940 to Hankey, which the latter had rightly described as 'rather a depressed view of the situation' and had passed on to Chamberlain, Churchill, Eden, Halifax and Simon (Hankey Papers, 4/32, and Simon Papers, MS Simon 86).
71 CAB 65/13, WM 163(40), 12 June 1940, 5.00 p.m. At nearly the same time Lothian was saying circumspectly that the US could not do more for Britain without entering the war, a prospect bedevilled by 'the natural instinct of every democracy to avoid war if it possibly can' (Lothian Papers, vol. 399, Lothian to Victor Cazalet, 1 July 1940).
72 David Reynolds has analysed sharply the circularities and rationalis-

ations of British future policy at this time. He also suggests that the private Churchill shared far more doubts with his colleagues than he allowed them to realise. See 'Churchill and the British "Decision" to Fight On in 1940: Right Policy, Wrong Reasons', in Richard Langhorne (ed.), *Diplomacy and Intelligence in the Second World War: Essays in Honour of F. H. Hinsley* (Cambridge: Cambridge University Press, 1985), pp. 147–67.

73 If Roosevelt were successful in the November election (CAB 65/13, Confidential Annex, WM 165(40), 13 June 1940, 10.15 p.m.). Yet very soon Churchill was to be 'terribly disappointed', in Joseph Kennedy's phrase, at Roosevelt's refusal of his request to publish the message for fear of upsetting the Congress (*FRUS*, 1940, vol. I: *General*, pp. 248–51, correspondence between Kennedy and Cordell Hull, 13–14 June 1940). See also Gilbert, *Finest Hour*, pp. 539–42.

74 CAB 65/13, WM 165(40), 13 June 1940; Beaverbrook did not become a full member of the War Cabinet until 2 August 1940, and was attending here as Minister of Aircraft Production because of the last crisis over France. He was also on good terms with Roosevelt (see A. J. P. Taylor, *Beaverbrook* (Harmondsworth: Penguin, 1974), pp. 514–16).

75 See Chamberlain Papers, NC 2/24A, Diary entry of 12 June 1940, which interprets the report given by the Prime Minister to the Cabinet as 'a most gloomy prospect', with no prospect of substantial American help 'for many months'. Chamberlain thought that the First Sea Lord and the Chief of the Imperial General Staff were markedly less confident than was Churchill.

76 Given that by the end of the 1930s the general stereotype of American foreign policy being hamstrung by domestic politics had become firmly established (see Watt, *Personalities and Policies*, pp. 42–3), it is a little surprising – in rationalist terms – that more scepticism was not shown about Churchill's claims.

77 CAB 65/7, and CAB 65/13, Confidential Annex, WM 165(40), 13 June 1940, 10.15 p.m. It was out of this Cabinet meeting that the notion of Anglo-French union arose, in Churchill's telegram to Reynaud (Churchill, *Their Finest Hour*, pp. 162–7).

78 CAB 65/13, Confidential Annex, WM 165(40), 13 June 1940, 10.15 p.m. See also P. M. H. Bell, *A Certain Eventuality: Britain and the Fall of France* (Farnborough: Saxon House, 1974), pp. 64–7.

79 On non-decisions, see Lukes, *Power: A Radical View*, e.g. pp. 42–5.

80 CAB 65/13, Confidential Annex, WM 140(40), 26 May, 2.00 p.m. The day before, Chamberlain had noted that 'there are indications that the internal position in Germany is uneasy' (Chamberlain papers, NC 2/24A, Diary entry of 25 May 1940). The image of a Germany teetering on the edge of internal upheaval was a long time dying. Just over two weeks later Halifax noted a secret report from a military attaché in Berlin painting a picture of 'considerable depression, in spite of the victories', with anxiety about a long war. Halifax thought this 'solid ground for encouragement' (Hickleton Papers, A7.8.4, Diary entry of

11 June 1940). Even then, let alone before Dunkirk, this was clutching at straws and an example of the wild swings in outlook which tend to be induced by high levels of stress.
81. Confirmed by the account in Woodward, *British Foreign Policy*, vol. I, pp. 197–204.
82. CAB 65/13, Confidential Annex, WM 142(40), 27 May 1940, 4.30 p.m. See also Chamberlain Papers, NC 2/24A, Diary entry of 26 May 1940, which records Churchill as having said that 'if we could get out of this jam by giving up Malta & Gibraltar & some African colonies, he would jump at it. But the only safe way was to convince Hitler that he couldn't beat us.' Reynolds ('Churchill and the British "Decision" to Fight On in 1940', p. 153) links Churchill's relative moderation over the October 1939 peace offer to the occasional signs of doubt about ultimate victory evident in mid-1940, so as to suggest that he might have shared a willingness to accept some kind of negotiated peace. In my view this both underestimates Churchill's political nous and willingness to stall so as to fight another day and makes too much of minor hesitations in conditions of chaos.
83. CAB 65/13, Confidential Annex, WM 145(40), 28 May 1940, 4.00 p.m.
84. *Ibid.*; less coolly, Churchill also thought that 'the nations which went down fighting rose again, but those which surrendered tamely were finished'.
85. But a number of Labour politicians (including Attlee) had preferred Halifax to Churchill in the succession crisis of early May (Dalton Papers, Diary (22), 9 May 1940, and Addison, *Road to 1945*, pp. 99–102).
86. CAB 65/13, Confidential Annex, WM 140(40), 26 May 1940, 2.00 p.m.; WM 145(40), 28 May, 4.00 p.m. (my italics).
87. CAB 65/13, Confidential Annex, WM 141 (40), 27 May 1940, 11.30 a.m. Churchill issued the injunction two days later. See n. 91, below.
88. CAB 65/13, Confidential Annex, WM 145(40), 28 May 1940, 4–6.15 p.m. and 7 p.m. onwards. Six non-War Cabinet ministers had been present at the morning meeting (WM 144(40), 11.30 a.m.), but their long agenda had not included this issue.
89. Dalton Papers, Diary (22), 28 May 1940. The vociferous trio were all newcomers to the government, and all 'anti-appeasers'.
90. Churchill was quite capable of exploiting his own strong feelings for effect. As Donald Cameron Watt has said of his deliberate flattery of Roosevelt, 'romanticism was, however, merely the palette from which he painted' (*Succeeding John Bull: America in Britain's Place 1900–1975* (Cambridge: Cambridge University Press, 1984), p. 90.
91. Churchill's general minute of 29 May 1940 (Simon Papers, MS Simon 86). The minute went to all ministers, including those outside the War Cabinet, to forty-six 'high officials' and to the six Dominion representatives. It is reproduced in Gilbert, *Finest Hour*, p. 428.
92. Churchill's lifelong zest for battle and command is powerfully conveyed by Basil Liddell-Hart's 'The Military Strategist' in A. J. P. Taylor *et al.*, *Churchill: Four Faces and the Man*.

Notes to pages 173–7

93 CAB 65/13, Confidential Annex, WM 141(40), item 1, 27 May 1940, 1.30 a.m. (my italics).
94 *Ibid.*; the three Service ministers, plus Anderson, Caldecote (formerly Inskip) and Duff Cooper were also present at this meeting. This record is consistent with the resigned views expressed privately by Chamberlain on 26 May, when he described the position as 'the most terrible in our history', and thought that although Hitler might make an offer, 'it looks as though it would be best for us to fight on in the hope of maintaining sufficient air strength to keep the Germans at bay till other forces can be mobilised, perhaps in USA' (Chamberlain Papers, NC 2/24A, Diary entry of 26 May 1940).
95 Even Eden recalls having seen 'nothing to quarrel about' in Maisky's contemporary judgement that 'though he believed we could withstand all Hitler's attacks, he did not see how we could win the war' (Avon, *The Reckoning*, p. 121).
96 CAB 65/13, Confidential Annex, WM 145(40), 28 May, 4.00 p.m. Italics mine (see text below). The statements are in sequence, but were made at different stages of the discussion.
97 Peter Howard, Michael Foot and Frank Owen were writing *Guilty Men* at precisely this time; see Addison, *Road to 1945*, pp. 110–11.
98 Dalton Papers, Diary (22), 28 May 1940; 'The Old Umbrella' must be Chamberlain.
99 Halifax's first impression of his new colleagues in Cabinet had led him to believe that they would not contribute much (Hickleton Papers, A7.8.4, Diary entry of 13 May 1940).
100 CAB 65/13, Confidential Annex, WM 140(40), 26 May; WM 142(40), 27 May; WM 145(40), 28 May; J. Weygand (*Role of General Weygand*, p. 91) described Attlee as showing 'approval' of Churchill's optimism at the Supreme War Council of 3 May; and see n. 48 above, this chapter.
101 Chamberlain Papers, NC 2/24A, Diary entry of 26 May 1940.
102 *Ibid.*
103 CAB 65/13, Confidential Annex, WM 145(40), 28 May, and WM 140(40), 26 May. See also Halifax's diary entry of 27 May, printed in Birkenhead, *Halifax*, p. 458.
104 *Ibid.*; Sinclair thought that 'some exhortation on the lines suggested by the Prime Minister' should be added to the reply to Reynaud (turning down a direct appeal to Mussolini). A contemporary observer also noted the War Cabinet's halfway position: 'text of telegram (which) seems to envisage possibility of Musso mediating at a later date. It looks as if Halifax may have evolved some scheme for mediation by Italy on an offer of terms to Hitler. Incredible though it sounds, I cannot put it past him' (John Harvey (ed.), *The Diplomatic Diaries of Oliver Harvey, 1937–40* (London: Collins, 1970), p. 372, 29 May 1940).
105 Chamberlain Papers, NC 2/24A, Diary entry of 28 May 1940. The diary gives rather more space on that day to the possibility of Chamberlain's enemy Lloyd George joining the Cabinet than to ministerial discussions. Psychologically, Chamberlain was turning inwards.

106 As Roy Douglas says about the meeting of 28 May, 'the language of that Cabinet was not the language of men who were not prepared to consider any sort of negotiated peace with the enemy on any terms' (*New Alliances 1940–41* (London: Macmillan, 1982), p. 27).
107 The two Labour leaders were not yet personally equipped to take a lead in Cabinet (Addison, *Road to 1945*, pp. 112–13, and Hankey to Chamberlain, 9 May 1940, quoted in Roskill, *Hankey: Man of Secrets*, vol. III, p. 463).
108 This picture, which would have seemed outrageous to many of the war generation itself, is now near to being the orthodoxy among those who have been able to use the public records. See for example Reynolds, *Creation of the Anglo-American Alliance*, pp. 95–120, chapter 4: 'Britain Alone', and Gilbert, *Finest Hour*, pp. 402–36.
109 For example O. Holsti, 'Cognitive Dynamics and Images of the Enemy', and R. North, 'Perception and Action in the 1914 Crisis', both in J. C. Farrell and A. P. Smith (eds.), *Image and Reality in World Politics* (New York: Columbia University Press, 1968). See also Brecher, *Decisions in Crisis*, pp. 342–7, which qualifies Holsti's findings by showing that decision-makers can resist 'cognitive closure' up to a point. The onus is, however, on them.
110 The last time on which a possible peace move had come before the Cabinet had been in March 1940, on the occasion of American Under-Secretary of State Sumner Welles' visit to Germany and Italy (CAB 65/6. WMs 167(40) and 169(40), 3 and 5 March 1940).
111 Documented in Lawrence Pratt, *East of Malta, West of Suez: Britain's Mediterranean Crisis, 1936–1939* (Cambridge: Cambridge University Press, 1975).
112 This involved not attacking Britain, so as to achieve 'a working arrangement' with the British Empire (see FO memorandum C4216/619/G, pp. 8–9, in PREM 4/100/8).
113 *FRUS*, 1940, vol. I: *General*, p. 233, Ambassador Kennedy to Secretary of State (Cordell Hull), 27 May 1940, sent at 9 p.m. Kennedy's cack-handed use of English does not obscure the sense. He also admitted that he did not know whether the 'English people' (*sic*) would follow 'the do or die' group, 'or the group that wants a settlement'. He provides no evidence as to the make-up of the would-be negotiators.
114 For Joseph Kennedy's defeatism, see Nigel Nicolson, *Harold Nicolson: Diaries and Letters 1939–45*, entry of 29 February 1940, and John Colville, *The Fringes of Power, Downing Street Diaries 1939–1955* (London: Hodder & Stoughton, 1985), entry of 29 November 1939.
115 It seems clear that complacency – about both the end of the war and Britain's likely response to peace feelers through Sweden – was the main reason for Hitler's delaying a formal offer until 19 July; see Irving, *Hitler's War*, pp. 125–39.
116 The importance of 'feedback' and the form it takes is discussed in theoretical terms by Karl Deutsch, in *The Nerves of Government: Models of*

Political Communication and Control (New York: The Free Press, 1963), chapter 11.
117 He thought that the brief 'left freedom to the Chiefs of Staff to express their view, whatever it might be'. On the other hand, 'I knew beforehand that they were absolutely determined; but it is wise to have written records of such decisions' (*Their Finest Hour*, p. 78).
118 Gates, *End of the Affair*, p. 145. The first Chiefs of Staff report on 'British Strategy in a Certain Eventuality' (i.e. the fall of France and loss of much of the BEF) was very downbeat and notably avoided a conclusion on the general question of whether Britain could hold out. They would only say that the blockade would be 'our only hope of bringing about the downfall of Germany'. On the question of resistance to an aerial onslaught the Chiefs of Staff could not assess the various factors with any certainty: 'it is impossible to say whether or not the United Kingdom could hold out in all circumstances' (CAB 66/7, WP 168(40), 25 May 1940). The response to Churchill's revised brief was WP 169(40), 'British Strategy in the near Future', of 26 May 1940, reproduced in Churchill, *Their Finest Hour*, pp. 78–9. Gilbert's account in his *Finest hour*, pp. 407–9, is useful but wrongly dates Churchill's request for a revised paper to 27 rather than 26 May.
119 CAB 66/7, WP 169(40), 26 May 1940 (also COS 397(40), in CAB 80/11). A note at the end of this document says that the Chiefs of Staff 'have not had a chance to see this Report in its final form and reserve to themselves the right to suggest such modifications as they may wish to put forward'. This was not unusual in the pressured circumstances of 1939–40. More curiously, however, the Confidential Annexes to the COS Minutes from 2 May 1940 to 19 April 1941, together with those from 3 September 1939 to 7 February 1940, have been missing from the Public Records since at least 1949.
120 Churchill, *Finest Hour*, p. 78.
121 But Dunkirk was still 'as great a military disaster as history can show', a major blow to the chances of victory (Bond, *Chief of Staff*, p. 360, Pownall Diary, June 1940).
122 Chamberlain Papers, NC 2/24A, e.g. Diary entry of 28 May: 'it is unlikely that we shall save more than 30 or 40,000 out of 200,000' (of the BEF), and compare that for 2 June: 'a result that no-one could have anticipated a week ago'.
123 CAB 65/7, WM 161(40), 11 June 1940, 2.30 p.m.
124 CAB 65/13, Confidential Annex, WM 162(40), item 9, 12 June 1940; in response to COS Report WP 201(40).
125 What evidence there is as to the actual impact of Dunkirk on popular morale suggests that an initial wave of cheerfulness soon gave way to apprehension (but not defeatism) (Mass Observation Files 75, 79, 81, 83 and 96, June 1940).
126 See, for the renewed consensus on ultimate victory, CAB 65/14, Confidential Annex, WM 222(40), item 4 (telegram to Dominions), and WM 222(40), item 9 (reply to King of Sweden's peace feeler), 8 August

1940; CAB 65/15, Confidential Annex, WM 244(40), item 1 (prospects for a strategic air offensive in 1941), 6 September 1940.
127 An interpretation also to be found in Patrick Cosgrave, *Churchill at War*, vol. I: *Alone, 1939–40* (London: Collins, 1974), p. 221.
128 CAB 65/7, WM 163(40), 12 June 1940, 5.00 p.m.
129 CAB 65/13, Confidential Annex, WM 165(40), item 1, 13 June 1940, 10.15 p.m.
130 CAB 66/7, WP 168(40) (COS 390(40)), 25 May 1940. See also CAB 66/8, WP 201(40), along the same lines, discussed at the Cabinet meeting of 12 June (CAB 65/13, Confidential Annex, WM 162(40), item 9).
131 CAB 65/13, Confidential Annex, WM 168(40), item 1, 16 June, 10.15 a.m.
132 CAB 65/7, WM 165(40), 13 June 1940, 10.15 p.m.
133 CAB 65/13, Confidential Annex, WM 168(40), item 1, 16 June 1940, 10.15 a.m. This was after Churchill's burst of optimism after Roosevelt's message to Reynaud on 13 June. By November Halifax had left thoughts of peace well behind him. He wrote to the Archbishop of York of 'perfectly groundless hopes' that a Christmas truce 'might speedily be developed into something more permanent. This might well be dangerous' (letter of 27 November 1940, FO 371/24362).
134 Baron von Weizsäcker in the German Foreign Ministry observed on 23 July that 'Churchill's resistance is not logical but psychological in origin' (cited in Irving, *Hitler's War*, note to p. 143). The Nazis, of all people, should have realised that most great gambles involve defying logic.
135 CAB 65/7, WM 177(40), 23 June 1940.
136 CAB 65/7, WM 176(40), 22 June 1940, 9.30 p.m.
137 CAB 65/8, WMs 189(40) and 192(40), 1 July, 11.30 a.m., and 3 July 1940, 11.30 a.m. In fact the RAF had been more damaged by the war in France than it was to be in the coming Battle of Britain. See R. J. Overy, *The Air War, 1939–45* (London: Europa, 1980), pp. 30–7.
138 Dilks, *Cadogan Diaries*, p. 309, Diary entry of 2 July 1940.
139 Churchill, *Their Finest Hour*, p. 152. In August Churchill sent a similar minute to Halifax to ensure 'a firm reply' to the King of Sweden. The Government, he said, 'would all rather perish in the common ruin than fail or falter in their duty'; there is no record of Halifax's reaction (PREM 4/100/3, Churchill's minute of 3 August 1940).
140 See chapter 8, below, pp. 238–9 on the Prytz affair.
141 CAB 65/8, WM 199(40), 10 July 1940.
142 For some of the background to German diplomacy at this time, see James Graham-Murray, *The Sword and the Umbrella* (London: Times Press and Anthony Gibbs & Phillips, 1964), chapter 8; *Documents on German Foreign Policy*, Series D, vol. X, pp. 49–50, 87–9, 245–8 and 287; and Irving, *Hitler's War*, pp. 139–45.
143 *DGFP*, vol. X, pp. 249–50 and 318–19; *The Times*, Saturday, 20 July 1940.
144 CAB 65/8, WM 209(40), 22 July 1940; Churchill, *Their Finest Hour*, p. 229. In the light of Halifax's subsequent removal, discussed in chap-

ter 7, below, it is worth noting the slightly contemptuous innuendo about Halifax's frequent absences from the Foreign Office. By the standards of a modern Foreign Secretary, of course, and particularly in 1940, Halifax was hardly ever out of town on business, and was, therefore, much more in his Prime Minister's way. As it happened, Halifax dined at Chequers on Sunday 21 July, where Churchill improved the language of the broadcast his colleague was to make on the next evening, and in which, *inter alia*, Hitler's speech was given short shrift (Hickleton Papers, A7.8.5, Diary entries of 19–22 July 1940).

145 A transcript of the broadcast can be found in *The Times*, Tuesday, 23 July 1940.

146 For a counter-example, of 'his incredible energy and imagination, his rich mixture of egoism and idealism, romanticism and realism' proving a handicap in its divisive effects on the Cabinet, see John Young, 'Churchill's Bid for Peace with Moscow, 1954', in *History*, 73: 239 (October, 1988), pp. 425–8.

147 Denis Kavanagh, *Crisis, Charisma and British Political Leadership: Winston Churchill as the Outsider* (London: Sage Professional Paper in Contemporary Political Sociology, vol. 1, no. 06–001, 1974), puts this finding in the wider context of British politics and society.

7 The longer term: War Aims and other committees, October 1940– June 1941

1 Cherwell Papers, 12A, Churchill to Lindemann, 20 April 1947, enclosing a draft section of his book. The reference was actually to the invention of a parachute mine which was then never used.

2 This was common and virtually interchangeable usage. For a rare distinction between the two, made on the grounds that war aims meant grand strategy, and peace aims objectives for the post-war period, see Hankey Papers, 11/3, 'The Second German War. The Beginning of the Second Year. An Appreciation', para. 18, 3 September 1940.

3 There is as yet little written about this, but see chapter 5, above, and for an example of press campaigning, the major article 'The Allied War Aims: A Plan for European Peace' in the *News Chronicle* of 2 November 1939, in which Sir Walter Layton, the paper's chairman, set out what he thought the government should say in the fuller statement for which they were being pressed. A copy of this is to be found in the Stafford Cripps Papers, 800/522, together with various pacifist documents. Cripps told a Mrs Cardigan on 19 October 1939: 'I certainly think we all ought to express more clearly what are our War Aims with a view to terminating hostilities at the earliest possible moment.'

4 Crookshank Papers, MS Eng. Hist. 598, fo. 111. Crookshank made these remarks at the start of a speech in Chelsea on 11 March 1940, specifically about the question: 'Why is it that we are at war, and how and when are we going to bring it to a victorious end?' He went on to talk about the moral character of the war.

5 See chapter 6, above, and CAB 65/8, WM 209(40), 22 July 1940.

6 Keynes, of course, had been the author of the most famous and scathing critique of Versailles, *The Economic Consequences of the Peace* (London: Macmillan, 1919). See also pp. 222–3, below.
7 Curtis to Halifax, 14 May 1940, in FO 371/24300. Curtis had submitted a long paper to Halifax on 'Anglo-French post-war collaboration', which was probably very influential in the eventual desperate proposal for an Anglo-French union.
8 This is a quotation from the Prime Minister's speech in Birmingham on 24 February 1940, contained in FO 371/24364. For a list of government statements on war aims compiled at the Royal Institute of International Affairs in collaboration with the Foreign Office, see FO 371/24362, June 1940.
9 *Ibid.*, Halifax to Corbin, 22 December 1939. Chamberlain's speech at the Mansion House on 9 January 1940 marked this new departure, which was soon noted by the 'Nazi propagandists'. See also (1) Cadogan to Halifax, 25 July 1940, in FO 371/25207, and largely reproduced in Dilks, *Cadogan Diaries*, pp. 316–17, from the copy in FO 800/322; (2) unsigned memorandum on 'peace aims' of 7 August 1940, in INF 1/862, which states that Churchill had not modified the British position since the fall of France, and takes Chamberlain's speech of 24 February as the authoritative statement; (3) Gates, *End of the Affair*, pp. 61–8.
10 Minute by Ivone Kirkpatrick, 10 January 1940, referring to Sir Ronald Campbell's telegram of 30 December 1939 on French views of war aims, in FO 371/24362. Kirkpatrick regarded much of the material being sent in by outside bodies like Political and Economic Planning as 'tripe', as is evidenced by his comment on Rex Leeper's minute of 22 December 1939.
11 Minute by Cadogan, 24 January 1940, commenting on a letter on war aims from Professor John Wheeler-Bennett, in FO 371/24363.
12 Lothian's speech, to the Chicago Council of Foreign Relations, 4 January 1940, in the Lothian Papers, vol. 399. Lothian saw economic reform as involving a higher general standard of living, and very low unemployment.
13 Circular telegram D, no. 145 to Canada, Australia, New Zealand and South Africa, 22 April 1940, in PREM 4/43A–11. Also WP(G) (40) 95 in CAB 67/5. The Dominion Prime Ministers were not yet ready for a meeting, which was in any case aborted through events. At this time also Toynbee and Hankey were pressing for new 'peace handbooks', and the FO agreed at least to let the Royal Institute of International Affairs and the Political Intelligence Department loose on some subjects (FO 371/24370).
14 FO 371/24364, note of 3 May 1940, and FO 371/24363, Halifax's note of 29 March 1940, in which he recorded having told Lytton that 'it was no good running too far ahead of public opinion', but also that Lytton's view that some alternatives were needed, if war was to be ruled out as a method of settled disputes, was 'perfectly fair'.
15 E. L. Woodward to W. Strang, 26 June 1940, in FO 371/25207. Wood-

ward had been seconded from All Souls College, Oxford and was always listened to very seriously in the Foreign Office.
16 On 27 June Woodward wrote to Leeper about this, and he responded that 'our blockade of Europe is a necessary instrument of war, but politically it can be represented as purely negative', while R. A. Butler also saw the latter and suggested that the Foreign Office and RIIA prepare a draft reply to Hitler's likely proposal (FO 371/24370). On 9 July Woodward sent in a further memorandum with Leeper's acknowledged full agreement (FO 371/26207).
17 Sargent's minute of 1 July 1940, FO 371/25207.
18 *Ibid.*, comments by Cadogan and Halifax on Sargent's minute, which was also initialled by Butler and Vansittart.
19 Leeper to Harold Nicolson, 11 July 1940. Nicolson was the junior minister in the Ministry of Information.
20 CAB 66/10, WP 275(40), 20 July 1940, 'Propaganda for the Future'.
21 Memorandum by T. N. Whitehead, agreeing with Ronald, 29 July 1940, in FO 371/25207.
22 CAB 65/8, WM 213(40), 26 July 1940. For Halifax's account of this meeting, and Cadogan's briefing to him, see FO 371/25207, minutes of 25 and 26 July 1940. Cadogan in particular believed that 'the removal of Hitler, if that could by one means or another be brought about, must have a profound effect', and placed some reliance on stirring up the German people against their leader.
23 All of the above paragraph refers to Duff Cooper's letter to Halifax of 29 July 1940, contained in FO 371/25207. See also INF 1/862.
24 CAB 65/8, WM 219(40), 5 August 1940. A form of agreement was found, which ministers thought would enable them to square the circle. They did not, however, fool de Gaulle. See Woodward, *British Foreign Policy*, pp. 407–8.
25 Halifax to Duff Cooper, 9 August 1940, in FO 371/25207. The reference to the paper being written is to Duff Cooper's second memorandum, WP 322(40), in CAB 66/11.
26 Duff Cooper to Halifax, 12 August 1940, in FO 371/25207. Cooper had previously pointed out how 'there is no doubt that the minds of a great many people whom you would not expect to agree are now moving in the same direction' (Duff Cooper to Halifax, 2 August 1940, in INF 1/862).
27 CAB 66/11, WP 322(40), 19 August 1940, on 'Post-war Policy'.
28 CAB 66/11, WP 332(40), 22 August 1940, on 'Post-War Policy'.
29 These and other references to the discussion of 23 August 1940 are taken from CAB 65/8, WM 233(40).
30 For Cooper's original suggestions, see Duff Cooper to Halifax, 12 August 1940, and for Halifax's account of the meeting with non-War Cabinet ministers, Halifax to Duff Cooper, of 30 July 1940, both in FO 371/25207.
31 Actually taking over on 7 October, and thus missing the first meeting of the Committee on 4 October; see CAB 21/1582.

32 Halifax's minute of 15 August 1940, on the memorandum by Professor Julian Huxley's 'Post-War Reconstruction Group', in association with Political and Economic Planning (an intellectual pressure group, founded in 1931, aiming to encourage industrial and social reform), is in FO 371/25207. Cranborne sent in a formal comment to Ronald on 10 September.
33 *Ibid.*, minutes by Sargent (28 August) and Halifax (30 August). R. A. Butler also asked to be kept informed 'as you know I am very interested and involved in the "brave new world"'. Halifax added: 'of course'.
34 See Gilbert, *Finest Hour*, pp. 800 and 817.
35 *Ibid.*, pp. 205–6 and 740, note 4.
36 WA 4(40), 15 October 1940, on the terms of reference of the Committee, in CAB 87/90.
37 Halifax to Duff Cooper, 10 September 1940, in CAB 21/1582.
38 *Ibid*. Cranborne was formally appointed on 7 October, Wood on 13 October. The Prime Minister wanted Kingsley Wood to be a member 'in view of the bearing of finance, currency, and economics, upon these problems'. Attlee agreed (PREM 4/100–4).
39 PREM 4/100–4, especially Amery's letter to Churchill of 24 August 1940 and subsequent comments. Amery eventually submitted a memorandum to the Committee (CAB 87/90, WA (40), item 7, 29 October 1940).
40 All the official papers of the War Aims Committee are to be found in CAB 87/90, although copies and correspondence are also to be found in CAB 21/1581, 1582 and 1584.
41 See Addison, *Road to 1945*, chapter 5, and Tom Harrisson, *Living through the Blitz* (London: Collins, 1976), pp. 314–16. See also the evidence of the Mass Observation files 511, 'political awareness in wartime' (1 December 1940), and 688, on 'the ends of the war' (6 May 1941), which suggest that while people's political feelings were gradually becoming further aroused, they were still confused and pessimistic about what might be expected in post-war Britain.
42 Perhaps encouraged by his friend and colleague at the Foreign Office, R. A. Butler, who wrote retrospectively of this period, 'the challenge of the times provided a stimulus for the rethinking of the purposes of the social system' (*The Art of the Possible* (London: Hamish Hamilton, 1971), p. 92).
43 Halifax to Duff Cooper, 30 July 1940, in FO 371/25207. Halifax had been very struck by the point, evidently made by Bevin, that 'We spend 9 millions a day in war without asking for financial return, but if in peace someone wants 100 millions to recondition life for Durham miners everybody asks whether it will pay 4%' (Hickleton Papers, A7.8.5, Diary entry of 29 July 1940).
44 *Ibid.*, Halifax to Duff Cooper, 9 August 1940.
45 See below, pp. 204–5, and for Llewellyn Woodward, p. 192, above. This involvement was despite the contemporary fiction, sustained up to the present, that Cabinet committees were secret, and their existence (like

that of MI6) not officially acknowledged. See James Callaghan's personal minute of 1978, continuing the tradition of secrecy, printed in Hennessy, *Cabinet* (pp. 89–90).

46 For instance, it was the influential figure of Jan Smuts who suggested in July that 'brain trusts' be set up to work out the democratic alternatives to Hitler's plans for Europe. The Foreign Office did not want to encourage this, and so continued to stall Smuts, despite Caldecote's intercession; see FO 371/25207. Equally, when Australian Prime Minister Robert Menzies suggested a Dominions Heads of Government summit in London, the War Cabinet decided to buy him off by simply issuing a personal invitation (CAB 65/9, WM 282(40), 4 November 1940).

47 See pp. 193–4 and 195–6, above.

48 CAB 65/9, WM 268(40), 9 October 1940. See also the principle enunciated on 25 November, in WM 295(40). It is not clear whether the foot-dragging was more the fault of the departments concerned or of the Cabinet Office for not chasing them.

49 CAB 65/9, WM 293(40), 21 November 1940.

50 CAB 66/13, WP 444(40), 15 November 1940, 'Propaganda Policy'.

51 CAB 65/10, WM 292(40), 2 November 1940.

52 Ben Pimlott (ed.), *The Second World War Diary of Hugh Dalton, 1940–1945* (London: Jonathan Cape, in association with the London School of Economics and Political Science, 1986 – hereafter Pimlott, *Dalton's War Diary*), entry of 20 November 1940, pp. 105–6. Dalton records that the Prime Minister intended to wait and see what was put up to him, and that he did not want to pronounce 'unctuous platitudes'.

53 Apart from the minutes of the meeting in CAB 87/90, a fuller record, probably that used as the basis of the minutes, is to be found in CAB 21/1582.

54 CAB 87/90, meeting of 4 October 1940.

55 *Ibid.* The material about no 'detailed' statement comes from the record in CAB 21/1582.

56 *Ibid.* See also Attlee to Toynbee, 9 October 1940, in CAB 21/1581.

57 Hickleton Papers, A7.8.6, Diary entries of 4 and 17 October.

58 Nigel Nicolson, *Harold Nicolson: Diaries and Letters, 1939–45*, diary entry of 26 October 1940.

59 CAB 87/90. Even Duff Cooper's paper, WA (40), item 2, was written after consultation with Toynbee.

60 Hickleton Papers, A7.8.6, Diary entry of 31 October: 'Bevin behaved in a fashion mixed between a spoilt child and a bear with a sore head. We had to be politely rude to him to [*sic*] any sort of order.' But see note 105, below, this chapter.

61 A notion described in Henry Butterfield Ryan, *The Vision of Anglo-America: the US-UK Alliance and the Emerging Cold War, 1943–46* (Cambridge: Cambridge University Press, 1987).

62 This is WA (40), no. 8, in CAB 87/90, entitled 'A note on the essential points for a declaration on war aims', 1 November 1940.

63 In, for example, WA (40), no. 2, 'Proposed terms of reference', 7 October 1940, point 1; CAB 87/90.
64 CAB 21/1581, Memorandum of 31 October 1940, entitled 'Planning of reconstruction' by an unknown civil servant (the initials are virtually indecipherable, but could be those of either G. N. Flemming or Sir George Chrystal, both of the War Cabinet Secretariat).
65 CAB 87/90, WA (40), no. 9, Attlee's 'Note on a War Aims Secretariat', 22 November 1940. See also CAB 21/1584.
66 CAB 21/1581, memorandum of 31 October 1940. Halifax himself had exhorted Toynbee to 'make the professors as little intellectual as possible' (Hickleton Papers, A7.8.5, Diary entry of 27 August 1940).
67 CAB 87/90, WA (40), 3rd Meeting, 26 November 1940. Halifax was warming to the subject. He was burning the midnight oil in writing his paper, and thought the meeting 'less barren than usual' (Hickleton Papers, A7.8.6, Diary entries of 8 and 26 November and 2 and 5 December 1940).
68 Halifax's memorandum of 25 November, discussed here, is WA (40), no. 10, in CAB 87/90.
69 CAB 87/90, WA (40), 4th Meeting, 11 December 1940. The memoranda considered by the Committee included that by Halifax (see n. 68, above), its revised version (WA (40), no. 11) and Toynbee's syntheses (WA (40), no. 12), and further, unnumbered, version, trying to pull together all the others). It is not wholly clear if the actual text of Harcourt Johnstone's paper (WA (40), 13, first dated 13 December) was before the Committee.
70 Duff Cooper to Attlee, 4 December 1940, in INF 1/863. Toynbee's draft is referred to here as that of 23 November. This must be an unnumbered later version of WA (40), no. 6, of 22 October (CAB 87/90).
71 INF 1/863, Duff Cooper to Attlee, 4 December 1940. Duff Cooper was anxious that Churchill should not make a speech without showing the text to a few colleagues, to 'avoid many dangers'. The significance of 4 January was probably the expectation of a major speech which Roosevelt was to make – actually delivered on 6 January 1941, on the 'four freedoms' which needed defending.
72 Hickleton Papers, A8.7.6, Diary entry of 11 December 1940.
73 CAB 87/90, WA (40), 4th Meeting, 11 December 1940, and see chapter 5, above, pp. 123–6.
74 Leslie H. Gelb with Richard K. Betts, *The Irony of Vietnam: The System Worked* (Washington DC: The Brookings Institution, 1979); 'careful' because Gelb's and Betts' argument hinges on the need to distinguish between an efficient *process* and a desirable outcome.
75 Meaning WA (40), no. 14, 13 December 1940 (in CAB 87/90), circulated by Halifax.
76 Halifax had attempted to cast his 'spiritual' remarks in a way that would appeal to all religions, and had enlisted Toynbee's help in so doing (Hickleton Papers, A7.8.6, Diary entry of 23 October 1940), but still failed to avoid the trap of what would now be called 'ethnocentrism'.

77 The philosophy of economic 'interdependence' is clearly beginning to emerge in the documents of the War Aims Committee, and Toynbee even uses the term in WA (40), no. 6, on 22 October 1940 (Para. 14). Interestingly, Conservative revisionists have begun to see this phase as a crucial intellectual surrender to 'collectivism' (see Maurice Cowling, 'Why We Should not have Gone to War', *Sunday Telegraph*, 20 August 1989). Certainly the facts about the life of the poor revealed by enlistment and evacuation soon impressed themselves on the highest in the Conservative Party. Chamberlain said he felt 'ashamed' of his own ignorance and decided to 'make amends by helping such people to lead cleaner and healthier lives', while Halifax talked at length to Hoare about the fact that Britain could no longer be called 'a Christian country' in this respect: 'truly we are living off our capital' (Chamberlain Papers, NC 18/1/1121, letter to Hilda Chamberlain, 17 September 1939, and Hickleton Papers, A7.8.3, Diary entry of 5 March 1940).

78 In the last stages of formulation, Cadogan, Butler and Vansittart started to work with Halifax and the Chatham House intellectuals on the draft (Cadogan Papers, MS Diary (ACAD 1/8) entries of 29 November, and 5 and 10 December 1940; also Dilks, *Cadogan Diaries*, p. 338, entry of 4 December 1940).

79 CAB 87/90, WA (41), no. 2, memorandum by the Secretary of State for Foreign Affairs, 22 January 1941.

80 PREM 4/100–3, Churchill to Halifax, 3 August 1940, criticising as 'too clever' a Foreign Office reply to the King of Sweden's peace feeler.

81 See, for example, PREM 4/100–8, the Prime Minister's minute to the effect that he would not speak to an Independent Labour Party motion on war aims on 7 December 1940. In fact the occasion seems to have been a question from the Communist MP William Gallacher (see *HCD*, vol. 367, cols. 784–5). At the same time Churchill's Private Secretary was noting Churchill's opposition to a 'declaration of peace aims' (Colville, *Fringes of Power*, diary entry of 3 December 1940, p. 305).

82 Nigel Nicolson, *Harold Nicolson: Diaries and Letters, 1939–45*, diary entry of 3 December 1940. Cadogan also noted at the Cabinet meeting of 18 November 'Winston discursing on difficulty of formulating peace aims' (Cadogan Papers, MS Diary, ACAD 1/9, 18 November 1940).

83 Cadogan Papers, MS Diary entry of 26 January 1941, p. 346.

84 Cadogan Papers, MS Diary entry of 11 January 1941, p. 334. See also Martin Gilbert, *Finest Hour*, pp. 985–6.

85 Colville, *Fringes of Power*, pp. 310 and 312–13, diary entries of 12 and 13 December 1940: 'all this was a thing of the still distant future . . . at present he could utter no such ideals when every cottage in Europe was calling for German blood . . . '

86 CAB 65/17, WM 8(41), 20 January 1941.

87 CAB 117/208, Duff Cooper to Arthur Greenwood, 30 January 1941.

88 PREM 4/66–2, particularly Churchill to Cecil King, 5 February 1941. For his reply to Mander, who clearly knew that the draft statement was

being sat upon, see *HCD*, vol. 368, cols. 22–3, 21 January 1941. Churchill said that the government was 'always on the look-out for any opportunity of making a statement that would be helpful to our victory', but refused to add anything at that time. Further pressure was exerted on the government in the Commons throughout the next six months.

89 Churchill to Duff Cooper, 10 February 1941, in PREM 4/100/8. See also Nigel Nicolson, *Harold Nicolson: Diaries and Letters, 1939–45*, entries of 11 February and 18 July 1941, Nicolson was unlucky in that the article had actually been written in the previous September and published in the December, when the War Aims Committee had been in favour of such expositions. Churchill accepted the proferred apologies, but seems not to have forgotten the incident. Nicolson was removed on 18 July and Duff Cooper moved at the same time to Singapore, albeit retaining ministerial rank as Chancellor of the Duchy of Lancaster.

90 A. J. P. Taylor (ed.), *W. P. Crozier: Off the Record: Political Interviews 1933–1943* (London: Hutchinson, 1973), p. 212.

91 PREM 4/100/8, Telegram 1049, Churchill to Halifax, 25 February 1941. A few back-benchers kept up the pressure for a statement in the Commons, not being satisfied with Halifax's speech of 25 March 1941 in New York, but ministers closed ranks. See remarks by Attlee (*HCD*, vol. 368, cols. 1486–8, 12 February 1941), Duff Cooper (*HCD*, vol. 370, cols. 1529–32, 8 April 1941) and Butler (*HCD*, vol. 371, cols. 2108–10, 29 May 1941).

92 See chapter 8, below, pp. 238–9.

93 See note 80, above, this chapter.

94 CAB 65/9, WM 264(40), 2 October 1940. See also Pimlott, *Dalton War Diary*, entry of 2 October 1940 (p. 87), on Gibraltar: 'Halifax, therefore, was unanimously over-ruled, a thing I have seen happen before.' The Cabinet Minutes are silent on the matter, agendum 7 being 'not open to inspection'.

95 Colville, *Fringes of Power*, p. 254, entry of 1 October 1940.

96 Hickleton Papers, A7.8.6, Diary entry of 22 October 1940. The entry for 19 August also displays an attitude towards a compromise peace still very different from that of Churchill. For supporting evidence of Halifax's 'pacifist' moods, see Dilks, *Cadogan Diaries*, p. 249 and 309, diary entries of 24 January and 2 July 1940.

97 Colville, *Fringes of Power*, p. 275, entry of 24 October 1940. Dill himself was to feel the impact of this boot in November 1941.

98 *Ibid.*, p. 318. See also Hickleton Papers: (i) microfilm, A4.410: 4: 11, (ii) Halifax Diary, A7.8.7, entries of 12–23 December 1940; Birkenhead, *Halifax*, pp. 467–70; and Simon Papers, MS. Simon 87, Halifax to Simon, 31 December 1940: 'I am not at all sure that I am cut out for the job, but in these times one can only do what those in authority think most useful.'

99 Colville, *Fringes of Power*, p. 321, entry of 20 December 1940.

100 *Ibid.*, p. 330, entry of 6 January 1941.

101 Churchill had suggested that Halifax use the draft in America, perhaps

as a diversionary tactic. The two men then agreed in February to postpone the speech because of the delicacy of Congressional politics over the Lend-Lease bill, and it was eventually made on 25 March (PREM 4/100–8, Halifax's telegram no. 742 of 17 February).
102 Gilbert, *Finest Hour*, p. 995, and Churchill's telegram to Washington of 1 March 1941, in Churchill Papers. The whole correspondence is in PREM 4/100–8: Churchill's telegrams 1049 and 1143 of 25 February and 1 March, and Halifax's replies of 26 February and 3 March (telegrams 889 and 976).
103 The speech was later printed as Cmnd 6264 (see *British Parliamentary Papers, 1940–41*, vol. VIII). It drew heavily on paras. 11–15 and 23 of WA (40) no. 14, and Churchill, announcing his approval, took the opportunity to say that no detailed planning would be possible, and he would not be producing 'a catalogue of war and peace aims himself'. See *HCD*, vol. 370, cols. 858–9, 1 April 1941, and *The Times*, 12 April 1941.
104 Hickleton Papers, A7.8.8, Diary entry of 2 March 1941: 'I have no doubt that his real mind is that he doesn't really want anything said except about the war.'
105 Dalton Papers, Diary (23), 23 August (the day the War Aims Committee was set up). In the Bevin Papers, there is a document headed 'War aims' of uncertain date, but probably of the War Aims Committee period, in Box 13: 1. The papers from Bevin's visit to Lancashire on October 1940 (Box 1: 5) reveal a single-minded preoccupation with winning the war, not worrying about its purpose.
106 The Labour MP Richard Stokes, for example, continued to call for a statement in April, saying in reference to Halifax that 'surely the right place for stating our peace aims is in this House' (*HCD*, vol. 370, cols. 1523–8, 8 April 1941).
107 See Nigel Nicolson, *Harold Nicolson: Diaries and Letters, 1939–45*, diary entries of 3 and 11 August 1940; McLaine, *Ministry of Morale*, chapter 8, pp. 217–39; and John Charmley, *Duff Cooper: The Authorized Biography* (London: Weidenfeld & Nicolson, 1986).
108 Pimlott, *Dalton War Diary*, p. 372, and Lee, *Churchill Coalition*, p. 32.
109 For example, in late September the Prime Minister referred Labour's demand for an abolition of the means test to a sub-committee of Attlee, Bevin, Greenwood, Halifax and Kingsley Wood. Kingsley Wood complained to Chamberlain that 'this was a very unjudicial body. Halifax knew nothing of the subjects and he would be left alone to face the three' (Chamberlain Papers, NC 2/24A, Diary entry for 30 September 1940).
110 See, for example, Lord Lothian's address to the Chicago Council of Foreign Relations of 4 January 1940 (text in Lothian Papers, vol. 399), and the British government's circular telegram to the Dominions of 22 April, referring to the opportunity which a meeting of heads of government might provide for 'the preliminary consideration of the problems of post-war reconstruction' (Telegram D. 145, in PREM 4/43A–11).

111 *HCD*, vol. 365, col. 1198, 5 November 1940. The questioner was Mander, and the answer given: 'it is too soon to think of this'.
112 See Norman Brook to Arthur Greenwood, 30 December 1940, in CAB 21/1583, where the new secretariat was envisaged as enabling the ideas of outsiders to be channelled into practical proposals. Practicality was to be the guiding star of the Reconstruction Committee's work.
113 Minute by Orme Sargent, 10 December 1940, W11253 in FO 371/25208.
114 Churchill's general minute, sent to Greenwood, of 30 December 1940, in PREM 4/88–1, where he describes a ministry as 'grandiose' and unnecessary.
115 See, for example, Greenwood's replies in the House of Commons, on 18 February 1941 (*HCD*, vol. 369, vols. 45ff.) and 9 April 1941 (*HCD*, vol. 370, cols. 1562–3), which refer to the Committee.
116 Churchill to Greenwood, and general minute of the same date, 30 December 1940, in PREM 4/88–1 and CAB 67/8, WP(G) 338(40), 'Note by Prime Minister'.
117 Churchill to Sir Edward Bridges, 4 January 1941, in CAB 21/1583. The Minister without Portfolio was, of course, Greenwood. Churchill added the familiar warning that 'we must be careful not to allow these post-war problems to absorb energy which is required, maybe for several years, for the prosecution of the war'.
118 According to a note by Bridges to be found in CAB 21/1584, and borne out by Greenwood's memorandum of 6 January 1941 in CAB 21/1583.
119 Bridges to Churchill, 9 January 1941, in PREM 4/11/1 and CAB 21/1583.
120 Greenwood to Churchill, 6 January 1941, enclosing a short memorandum setting out Greenwood's ideas, in PREM 4/88/1. Some of this correspondence is also in CAB 117/1.
121 Churchill to Greenwood, 13 January 1941, PREM 4/88/1.
122 Bridges to Churchill, 29 January 1941, in PREM 4/88/1.
123 Churchill to Greenwood, 1 February 1941, in PREM 4/88/1.
124 Churchill's minute of 4 January 1941 (PREM 4/88/1, also in CAB 21/1583) included the (for once rough-hewn) sentence: 'I do not consider that the kind of Committee for Post-war Reconstruction is at all filled by the personnel of the Committee on War Aims.'
125 CAB 21/1583, Bevin to Churchill, 11 December 1940. Bevin thought that a paper by Reith on post-war problems 'with a strong political flavour' meant that the Prime Minister's first view, that only one of Greenwood or Attlee should be on the Committee, was mistaken. Churchill agreed to Attlee's inclusion, if that was what the latter wanted.
126 He was also not even close to his own Secretary of State. See Colville, *Fringes of Power*, p. 367, diary entry of 27 March 1941. Butler was promoted to the Board of Education, where he was to make such a mark, in July 1941. For more about the Prytz affair, see below, chapter 8.
127 PREM 4/88/1, correspondence of April 1941 between Bevin, Greenwood and Churchill.

128 Churchill to Greenwood, 1 February 1941, in CAB 21/1583. The Prime Minister went on to 'reluctantly' exclude himself, 'though I shall be very glad to hear from time to time how you are progressing'.
129 The terms of reference of the War Aims Committee are to be found in WA (40), no. 4, of 15 October 1940, in CAB 87/90. Those of the Reconstruction Problems Committee are in RP (41), no. 1, in CAB 87/1. Churchill and Bridges explicitly suggested to Greenwood that he have the Committee's terms of reference 'amended as shown on the annexed sheet to give rather greater prominence to the domestic side of the work' (Churchill to Greenwood, 1 February 1941, in CAB 21/1583).
130 A note, probably by Greenwood in advance of a discussion with the Prime Minister in January 1941, in CAB 21/1583.
131 CAB 87/1, Minutes of the first meeting of the Reconstruction Problems Committee, 6 March 1941, and the Minister without Portfolio's preparatory note, RP (41), no. 2, of 27 February 1941.
132 See CAB 87/1, RP (41), no. 4, a further paper by Greenwood of 27 February, which noted the already considerable volume of correspondence on reconstruction, and thought that the Committee should encourage its upward trend. Greenwood's (uncatalogued) private papers contain duplicates of the Committee's minutes and memoranda, and a good deal of material on health, housing, and other domestic matters (see various boxes marked 'War Cabinet, 1940/42' and 'Reconstruction').
133 For the sensitivities of the Ministry of Economic Warfare and of the Foreign Office, see CAB 117/77, e.g. Sir Frederick Leith-Ross to Sir George Chrystal, 3 April 1941, and Frank Ashton-Gwatkin to Toynbee, 2 May 1941. For the Foreign Office's reticence, see the correspondence between Butler and Greenwood of April 1941 (note also the absence of references to reconstruction in Cadogan's diary of the period, in Dilks, *Cadogan Diaries*), and for an example of Greenwood's willing acquiescence, CAB 117/85, where he and Butler agree not to bother the Committee with Trygve Lie's radical plans for Norway's post-war departure from isolationism. The adaptation of the terms of reference for the FRPS, again agreed between Greenwood and Butler, can be found in the minutes of the first meeting of the Reconstruction Problems Committee (CAB 87/1, 6 March 1941).
134 See for example Greenwood to Churchill, 21 July 1941, in the Greenwood Papers, Box marked 'Arthur Greenwood, listed files 1913–42', where Greenwood reports on the Committee's work, and lists his range of departmental contacts on all domestic and international topics, excluding only the conduct of the war itself. The seeds of reconstruction thinking were being quietly but extensively scattered.
135 Official announcement of Greenwood's role in chairing a group of ministers working on reconstruction problems, *The Times*, 7 January 1941. See also Churchill in the Commons, 22 January 1941 (*HCD*, vol. 368, cols. 264–5).

136 Addison, *Road to 1945*, pp. 123 and 126.
137 The speech is to be found in *The Times*, 30 May 1941. It was eventually published, after requests in the Commons, as Cmd 6289 (see *British Parliamentary Papers 1940–41*, vol. VIII).
138 Reynolds (*Creation of the Anglo-American Alliance*, pp. 256–7) discusses the influence of Treasury and Foreign Office advice on the speech. Reynolds also points out (pp. 256–61) how in August Churchill had to change his line on war aims, yet again under American pressure, as the Atlantic Charter became a sudden possibility.
139 *The Times*, first leader, 30 May 1941. In fact, although the speech had not come before the Cabinet, they had been informed of it at an early stage of Keynes' work (CAB 65/17, WM 8(41), 20 January 1941). The staff of *The Times*, their natural sense of authority reinforced by Robin Barrington-Ward's reforming zeal, had submitted their own memorandum on war aims to the Reconstruction Committee in February 1941 (see CAB 87/1).
140 For the consultations between Eden and Churchill over Keynes's memorandum and Lindemann's one-page summary of 21 May, see PREM 4/100/5.
141 For Dalton's report on the War Cabinet that 'one of its members says it is hardly worth belonging to any more', see Pimlott, *Dalton War Diaries*, p. 165, diary entry of 24 February 1941. For Hankey's alarms and intrigues, see Hankey Papers, e.g. 5/4, correspondence with Halifax, and 5/6, correspondence with Salisbury, as well as Roskill, *Hankey: Man of Secrets*, vol. III, pp. 497–519. Hankey was to be demoted further in July, suggesting that Churchill had become aware of his activity.

8 Decision-making in Cabinet

1 James Barber, 'The Power of the Prime Minister', in Borthwick and Spence, *British Politics in Perspective*, p. 73.
2 *Ibid.*, p. 100.
3 See Paul Stafford, 'The Chamberlain–Halifax' Visit to Rome: A Reappraisal', *English Historical Review*, 98: 386, pp. 61–100.
4 Recognition was announced on 27 February, after Halifax's paper on the situation in Spain of 13 February, for the Cabinet meeting of 15 February (CAB 23/97, CM 7(39), and CAB 24/283, CP 46(39)). Opposition had been expressed in the Foreign Policy Committee on 23 January, at the 3 p.m. meeting (CAB 27/624, FP (36), 35th Meeting), but not again at its next two meetings on 26 January and 8 February. The Committee then did not meet again until 27 March. Discontent about the freedom enjoyed by Chamberlain and Halifax from Cabinet control then surfaced in the House of Commons in speeches by Attlee and Sinclair on 28 February (*HCD*, vol. 344, cols. 1099–1222, 28 February 1939). Cadogan, at least, was enthusiastic about the defeat of the Republic; see Cadogan Papers, MS Diary, ACAD 1/8, entry of 28 March 1939.
5 See pp. 147–9, above.

6 On the opportunities for discretionary action which the implementation phase of decision-making gives actors at various levels, see Smith and Clarke, *Foreign Policy Implementation*.
7 Simon Papers, MS Simon 87, Simon to Lord Davies, 4 April 1941.
8 Recent writers are beginning to gravitate towards this position, 'that inevitably, the empirical pattern is going to be patchy'. See A. G. Jordan and J. J. Richardson, *British Politics and the Policy Process: An Arena Approach* (London: Unwin Hyman, 1987), pp. 160–1. Jordan and Richardson also observe that 'there is no such thing as a debate on prime ministerial government – in the sense that both sides are remarkably close in their positions once they have qualified, reserved and glossed their starting points'. Comparative studies, while important, cannot by definition investigate one angle in depth. See Thomas T. Mackie and Brian Hogwood, 'Decision Arenas in executive Decision Making: Cabinet Committees in Comparative Perspective', *British Journal of Political Science*, 14 (July 1984), pp. 285–312.
9 See Bevin Papers, Box 21: 1, memorandum marked 'Nov. or Dec. 1940', and referring to discussions held with R. A. Butler and Sir Alexander Cadogan about Bevin's feelings that the Foreign Office was 'out of touch with the growing forces of labour, Trade Unionism and the socialist organisations in the world'. The memorandum is fourteen pages long, and consists of wide-ranging analysis, together with proposals for change. See also Alan Bullock, *The Life and Times of Ernest Bevin*, vol. II: *Minister of Labour* (London: Heinemann, 1967), pp. 199–202, and *Foreign Secretary* (London: Heinemann, 1983), pp. 72–4.
10 See CAB 21/1324, including WP(G)(40) 164, in which Churchill said on 27 June 1940 that the Service Ministers, Chiefs of Staff, Home Secretary, Dominions Secretary, Minister of Information *et al.* should attend the War Cabinet only on Mondays and Thursdays unless for a special purpose. A minute by Bridges of 11 December recounted how this arrangement soon broke down, and the Prime Minister ordered it to be resuscitated on 22 December. The attendance records of subsequent Cabinets show that in this attempt he was hardly more successful.
11 See p. 223, above.
12 Perceived clarity can cut both ways, leading to the formation of stereotypes, as with Sir Robert Vansittart's view of Germany. Jervis, *Perception and Misperception*, pp. 72–181.
13 Dilks, *Cadogan Diaries*, pp. 397–402, and Reynolds, *Creation of the Anglo-American Alliance*, pp. 258–60.
14 Robert Axelrod has shown how we can analyse overall belief-systems, particularly in a political context, by using the formal device of the cognitive map, or causal chart (Robert Axelrod (ed.), *Structure of Decision: The Cognitive Maps of Political Elites* (Princeton: Princeton University Press, 1976)).
15 Halifax and Chamberlain played down the significance of Hitler's breach of the Agreement (CAB 23/99, CM 26(39), 3 May 1939).
16 Churchill to Halifax, 26 June 1940, *et seq.* (FO 800/322,

H/XXXIII/38–9; FO 371/24859; *The Times*, correspondence of 9–16 September 1965). Churchill's letter to Halifax, and Butler's letter of explanation to Halifax, also on 26 June, are reproduced in Lamb's otherwise not wholly reliable *Ghosts of Peace* (pp. 143–6). See also Wilhelm Carlgren, *Svensk Utrikespolitik 1939–1945* (Stockholm: Allmanna Forlaget, 1973), pp. 193–5. I am most grateful to Mr Trevor Gunn for translating these pages from the Swedish for me. The two extant versions of Prytz's report do not clear up the issue of Halifax's involvement at the time of Butler's talk with Prytz. Butler's letter makes no mention of the Foreign Secretary being at hand, but this may have been the same kind of exculpatory exercise that Hoare had performed for the whole government in 1935. In his memoirs, Butler is careful not to say that he did not say what he was reported as having said – only that he did not 'recall' having given any grounds for suspicions of defeatism (Butler, *Art of the Possible*, pp. 80–2). The Germans certainly picked up on the possibility of 'differences of opinion . . . in the British Cabinet' – see the Naval Intelligence report of 22 June 1940 reproduced in David Irving (ed.), *Breach of Security: The German Intelligence File on Events Leading to the Second World War* (London: Kimber, 1968), pp. 170–1.

17 Chamberlain Papers, NC 18/1/1137; Gilbert, *Finest Hour*, pp. 120–1; Crozier, *Off the Record*, pp. 127–33; Colville, *Fringes of Power*, pp. 66–71; see also Churchill, *Gathering Storm*, pp. 436–7 (a most guarded account which is circumstantial evidence for the latter's involvement in the affair), and A. Trythall, 'The Downfall of Leslie Hore-Belisha', *Journal of Contemporary History*, 16: 3 (July 1981), pp. 391–412.

18 It is true that, as David Dilks points out in 'The Twilight War and the Fall of France: Chamberlain and Churchill in 1940' (*Transactions of the Royal Historical Society*, 5th ser., 28 (1978), pp. 61–86), Churchill came to have respect for his predecessor, and behaved well during the latter's difficult last months. Nonetheless he also put considerable pressure on Chamberlain to accept his bitter enemy, Lloyd George, as a Cabinet colleague (pressure which was successful, although Lloyd George eventually turned down the offer; Chamberlain Papers, NC 2/24A, Diary entries between 28 May and 7 June 1940). For his part Beaverbrook had been encouraging the anti-war Independent Labour Party in April 1940, and continued his political intrigues inside the government as he had done outside it. See PREM 4/100/6; A. J. P. Taylor, *Beaverbrook*, pp. 524–7; and Dalton Papers, Diary (23 and 24), 11 December 1940 and 18 and 25 June 1941. Lady Halifax thought that Beaverbrook had had a hand in her husband's downfall (Hickleton Papers, A7.8.7, Diary entry of 20 December 1940). Halifax barely noticed; Chamberlain described him as 'Edward who is innocent and doesn't read the papers' (Chamberlain Papers, NC 2/24A, Diary entry of 5 June 1940).

19 For the conventional generalisation, see Andrew Boyle, *Poor, Dear Brendan: The Quest for Brendan Bracken* (London: Hutchinson, 1974), p. 225. For the meetings of the inner group in September 1938, see CAB 27/646, and Middlemas, *Diplomacy of Illusion*, p. 65 and *passim*.

20 Hickleton Papers, A8.7.8.3, Diary entry of 2 February 1940.
21 Simon was in any case a National Liberal, not a Conservative like Chamberlain and Halifax. Nor, to judge by the virulence of his protest over the Anglo-French union proposal in 1940, was he a sycophant of Chamberlain's (Simon to Chamberlain, 17 June 1940; copy in the Hankey Papers, 4/32 (cf. Middlemas, *Diplomacy of Illusion*, p. 65 and *passim*).
22 Dilks, *Cadogan Diaries*, pp. 360–2, diary entries of 1–7 March.
23 See, for example, Hickleton Papers, A7.8.5, Diary entry of 14 August 1940 on the issue of American destroyers: 'Winston, who had been difficult last week, had now come round entirely to my view as to how to handle it and carried the Cabinet without difficulty.'
24 As Chamberlain wrote to Cadogan on 2 January 1940, 'The relations between the PM and the FO are bound to be delicate especially in days when foreign affairs are so much in the limelight but under the present regime I at any rate, am never conscious of any difficulty' (Cadogan Papers, ACAD 4/1).
25 There are different views on the quality of the Churchill–Eden relationship in office between 1940 and 1945, although it was clearly better in the first year than at various points thereafter. Elizabeth Barker is positive, saying that Churchill believed in a harmonious relationship between the two office-holders, and 'if the Prime Minister's relations with his colleagues were all in some degree unequal, those with his Foreign Secretary were less unequal than others' (Elizabeth Barker, *Churchill and Eden at War* (London: Macmillan, 1978), pp. 15–28). David Carlton, however, is more sceptical, seeing Eden as the only minister to influence Churchill in the international sphere, but still being driven near to resignation by the Prime Minister's interference and unreliability (David Carlton, *Anthony Eden: A Biography* (London: Allen Lane, 1981), pp. 199–221).
26 Pimlott, *Dalton's War Diary*, p. 125, 18 December 1940.
27 Cowling, *Impact of Hitler*, pp. 294 and 303; Watt, *How War Came*, pp. 99–108, chapter 6, 'Lord Halifax is Alarmed', and pp. 615–17.
28 This is not to say very much. When Churchill was manoeuvering him out of office in December 1940, Halifax's wife, Lady Dorothy, saw clearly what was happening, but the Foreign Secretary himself was naive enough to allow the Prime Minister to make the decision for him, assuming that the latter would act as an impartial judge (Hickleton Papers, A7.8.7, Diary entries of 19 and 20 December 1940).
29 Robert Boothby to Churchill, 9 May 1940 (Churchill Papers, 2/392, cited in Gilbert, *Finest Hour*, p. 303; Boothby's italics).

BIBLIOGRAPHY

I Primary sources

(i) *The Public Records* (London)

CAB 21	Cabinet Office Registered Files
CAB 23	Cabinet Minutes and Conclusions, 1938–9
CAB 24	Memoranda for Cabinet Meetings, 1938–9
CAB 27	Minutes and Papers of the Foreign Policy Committee of the Cabinet, 1938–9
CAB 53	Chiefs of Staff Committee of the Committee of Imperial Defence, Minutes and Papers, 1938–9
CAB 65	War Cabinet Minutes, Conclusions and Confidential Annexes, 1939–41
CAB 66	War Cabinet Memoranda, 1939–41
CAB 67	War Cabinet Memoranda (WP (G) series), 1939–41
CAB 75	War Cabinet: Home Policy Committee
CAB 79	War Cabinet Chiefs of Staff Committee, Minutes 1939–41
CAB 80	War Cabinet Chiefs of Staff Committee, Memoranda 1939–41
CAB 87	War Cabinet Committees on Reconstruction, 1940–1
CAB 99/3	Records of Supreme War Council
CAB 117	Reconstruction Secretariat Files, 1940–1
PREM 1	Prime Minister's Office Files (Chamberlain)
PREM 4	Prime Minister's Office Files (Churchill)
FO 371	Foreign Office, Political Correspondence; selected files for 1938, 1939, 1940, 1941
FO 800	Papers of Lord Halifax
INF 1	Correspondence Files of the Ministry of Information, 1939–41

(ii) *Private collections*

A. V. Alexander Papers (Churchill College, Cambridge)
Clement Attlee Papers (Churchill College, Cambridge and University College, Oxford)
Ernest Bevin Papers (Churchill College, Cambridge)
Sir Alexander Cadogan Papers (Churchill College, Cambridge)

Bibliography 339

Viscount Caldecote (Sir Thomas Inskip) Diary (Churchill College, Cambridge)
Neville Chamberlain Papers (University of Birmingham Library)
Admiral Lord Chatfield Papers (National Maritime Museum)
Viscount Cherwell Papers (Nuffield College, Oxford)
Sir Stafford Cripps Papers (Nuffield College, Oxford)
Viscount Crookshank Papers (Bodleian Library, Oxford, MS Eng. Hist. 359)
Hugh Dalton Papers (British Library of Political and Economic Science, London)
Geoffrey Dawson Papers (Archive of *The Times* newspaper)
Arthur Greenwood Papers (Bodleian Library, Oxford)
P. J. Grigg Papers (Churchill College, Cambridge)
Lord Hankey Papers (Churchill College, Cambridge)
Hickleton (Lord Halifax) Papers (Churchill College, Cambridge, on microfilm, and the Borthwick Historical Institute, York (for Halifax's Diary))
Leslie Hore-Belisha Papers (Churchill College, Cambridge, HOBE 1/5)
Marquess of Lothian Papers (Scottish Public Record Office, Edinburgh)
David Margesson Papers (Churchill College, Cambridge)
Mass Observation Archive (Library of the University of Sussex, Brighton)
Viscount Norwich (Alfred Duff Cooper) Papers (Churchill College, Cambridge)
Viscount Runciman Papers (Library of the University of Newcastle)
Viscount Simon Papers (Bodleian Library, Oxford: Simon's diary is MS Simon 11)
Sir Archibald Sinclair Papers (Churchill College, Cambridge)
Templewood (Sir Samuel Hoare) Papers (Cambridge University Library)
Sir Robert Vansittart Papers (Churchill College, Cambridge)
Euan Wallace Papers (Bodleian Library, Oxford, MS Eng. Hist. 495–8)
Marquess of Zetland Papers (North Riding County Record Office, Northallerton)

(iii) *Published sources*

(a) *Parliamentary papers*
Cmd 6106: *Documents concerning German-Polish Relations and the Outbreak of Hostilities between Great Britain and Germany on September 3 1939*; Blue Book, Miscellaneous no. 9 (London; HMSO, 1939)
Cmnd 6264: 'Speech of Lord Halifax, British Ambassador to the United States, to the Pilgrims, New York, 25 March 1941', in *British Parliamentary Papers 1940–41*, vol. VIII
Cmnd 6289: 'Speech given by the Foreign Secretary, Mr Anthony Eden, at the Mansion House, 29 May 1941', in *British Parliamentary Papers 1940–41*, vol. VIII
Hansard: *Parliamentary Debates (Commons)* (cited throughout as *HCD*), 5th Series, 1938–41, vols. 343–72
Parliamentary Debates (Lords), 5th Series, 1938–41, vols. 111–19

(b) *Collected documents*
Churchill, Winston S., *Secret Session Speeches*, compiled by Charles Eade (London: Cassell, 1946)
War Speeches 1939–45, vol. I, compiled by Charles Eade (London: Cassell, 1951)
Documents on British Foreign Policy, 1919–39, 3rd Series (cited throughout as *DBFP* III), vols. 3–10, ed. E. L. Woodward and Rohan Butler (London: HMSO, 1950–61)
Documents on German Foreign Policy 1918–45, Series D, vols. IV–XII (Washington: US Government, 1953–62) (cited throughout as *DGFP*)
Foreign Relations of the United States: 1939, vols. I and II; 1940, vols. I–III; 1941, vols. I–III (Washington: Department of State, 1956–9) (cited throughout as *FRUS*)
Le Livre jaune français: documents diplomatiques 1938–9 (Paris: Ministère des Affaires Etrangères, 1939)
Noakes, Jeremy, and Geoffrey Pridham (eds.), *Documents on Nazism 1919–1945* (London: Jonathan Cape, 1974)

(c) *Edited diaries, letters etc.*
Bond, Brian (ed.), *Chief of Staff: The Diaries of Lieutenant-General Sir Henry Pownall*. Vol. I: *1933–40*. London: Leo Cooper, 1972
Colville, Sir John, *The Fringes of Power: Downing Street Diaries 1939–1955*. London: Hodder & Stoughton, 1985
Dilks, David (ed.), *The Diaries of Sir Alexander Cadogan*. London: Cassell, 1971
Harvey, John (ed.), *The Diplomatic Diaries of Oliver Harvey, 1937–40*. London: Collins, 1970
King, C., *With Malice Towards None: A War Diary*. London: Sidgwick & Jackson, 1970
Loewenheim, F. L., H. D. Langley and M. Jonas (eds.), *Roosevelt and Churchill: Their Secret War-time Correspondence*. London: Barrie & Jenkins, 1975
Muggeridge, Malcolm (ed.), *Ciano's Diary, 1939–43*. London: Heinemann, 1947
Nicolson, Nigel (ed.), *Harold Nicolson: Diaries and Letters*, 2 vols., *1930–9* and *1939–45*. London: Fontana/Collins, 1969–70
Pimlott, Ben (ed.), *The Second World War Diary of Hugh Dalton, 1940–45*. London: Jonathan Cape, in association with the London School of Economics and Political Science, 1986
Rhodes James, Robert (ed.), *Chips: The Diaries of Sir Henry Channon*. London: Weidenfeld & Nicolson, 1967
Taylor, A. J. P. (ed.), *W. P. Crozier: Off the Record: Political Interviews 1933–1943*. London: Hutchinson, 1973

(d) *Newspapers, polls etc.*
Cantril, H. (ed.), *Public Opinion 1935–46* (collected Gallup Poll data). Princeton: Princeton University Press, 1951
Mass Observation Bulletin, 1940–1

Press cuttings, 1939–41, in the Library of the Royal Institute of International Affairs, Chatham House, London
The Times, selected issues, 1938–41

(e) *Reference books*

Aster, Sidney, *British Foreign Policy, 1918–54: A Guide to Research and Research Materials*. Tunbridge Wells: T. J. Costello, 1984
Burke, J. (ed.), *Loose-leaf War Legislation*, 2 vols. London: Hamish Hamilton, 1939–40
Butler, David and Anne Sloman, *British Political Facts 1900–79*, 5th edn. London: Macmillan, 1980
Cook, Chris, *et al.*, *Sources in British Political History 1900–51*, vol. I: *A Guide to the Archives of Selected Organisations and Societies*. London: Macmillan, 1975
Hazlehurst, Cameron and Christine Woodland (compilers), *A Guide to the Papers of British Cabinet Ministers, 1900–51*. London: Royal Historical Society, 1974
Keesings Contemporary Archives. Bristol, 1939–41
The Second World War: A Guide to Documents in the Public Record Office, Public Record Office Handbook no. 15. London: HMSO, 1972
Swann Brenda, and Maureen Turnbull, *Records of Interest to Social Scientists 1919–39*, Public Record Office Handbook no. 14. London: HMSO, 1971
Wilson, S. S., *The Cabinet Office to 1945*, Public Record Office Handbook no. 17. London: HMSO, 1975

II Secondary sources

This section has been divided into two parts, one covering the historical period 1938–41, and the other those books which have been of help in adopting an analytical approach. The second section therefore contains theoretical works as well as those which deal with Cabinet government and other institutions of government, together with empirical works relating to other periods.

(i) *British Foreign Policy, 1938–41*

Adamthwaite, Anthony, *France and the Coming of the Second World War 1936–1939*. London: Frank Cass, 1977
Addison, Paul, *The Road to 1945: British Politics and the Second World War*. London: Jonathan Cape, 1975
Andrew, Christopher, *Secret Service: The Making of the British Intelligence Community*. London: Sceptre/Heinemann, 1986
Aster, Sidney, *1939: The Making of the Second World War*. London: André Deutsch, 1973
Avon, the Earl of, *The Eden Memoirs: The Reckoning*. London: Cassell, 1965

Ayerst, D., *Guardian: Biography of a Newspaper*. London: Collins, 1971
Barker, Elizabeth, *Churchill and Eden at War*. London: Macmillan, 1978
Barnett, Correlli, *The Audit of War: The Illusion and Reality of Britain as a Great Nation*. London: Macmillan Papermac, 1987
Beaufré, General André, *1940: The Fall of France*, trans. Desmond Flower. London: Cassell, 1967
Bédarida, François, *La Stratégie secrète de la Drôle de Guerre: le Conseil Suprême Interallié, septembre 1939–avril 1940*. Paris: Presses de la Fondation Nationale des Sciences Politiques, et Editions du CNRS, 1979
Bell, P. M. H., *A Certain Eventuality: Britain and the Fall of France*. Farnborough: Saxon House, 1974
  The Origins of the Second World War in Europe. London: Longman, 1986
Bethell, Nicholas, *The War Hitler Won*. London: Futura, 1976
Birkenhead, Lord, *Halifax: The Life of Lord Halifax*. London: Hamish Hamilton, 1965
Bond, Brian, *British Military Policy between the Two World Wars*. Oxford: The Clarendon Press, 1980
Boyle, Andrew, *Poor, Dear Brendan: The Quest for Brendan Bracken*. London: Hutchinson, 1974
Bullock, A., *The Life and Times of Ernest Bevin*, vol. II: *Minister of Labour 1940–51*, and *Foreign Secretary 1945–1951*. London: Heinemann, 1967, 1983
Butler, J. R. M., *Grand Strategy*, vol. II: *Official History of the Second World War*. London: HMSO, 1957
Butler, R. A. (Lord), *The Art of the Possible*. London: Hamish Hamilton, 1971
Calder, Angus, *The People's War: Britain 1939–45*, 2nd edn. London: Panther, 1971
Calvocoressi, Peter and Guy Wint, *Total War: Causes and Courses of the Second World War*. London: Allen Lane, The Penguin Press, 1972
Cameron Watt, Donald, *see* Watt, Donald Cameron
Carlgren, Wilhelm, *Svensk Utrikespolitik 1939–1945*. Stockholm: Allmanna Forlaget, 1973
Carlton, David, *Anthony Eden: A Biography*. London: Allen Lane, 1981
Carr, E. H., *The Twenty Years Crisis*. London: Macmillan, 1939
Cave Brown, Anthony, *The Secret Servant: The Life of Sir Stewart Menzies, Churchill's Spymaster*. London: Michael Joseph, 1988
Chadwick, Owen, *Britain and the Vatican during the Second World War*. Cambridge: Cambridge University Press, 1986
Charmley, John, *Duff Cooper: The Authorized Biography*. London: Weidenfeld & Nicolson, 1986
  Lord Lloyd and the Decline of the British Empire. London: Weidenfeld & Nicolson, 1987
  Chamberlain and the Lost Peace. London: Hodder & Stoughton, 1989
Churchill, Winston S., *The Second World War*, vol. I: *The Gathering Storm*, vol. II: *Their Finest Hour*, vol. III: *The Grand Alliance*. London: Cassell, 1948, 1949, 1950
Cienciala, Anna M., *Poland and the Western Powers 1938–39: A Study in the Inter-

dependence of Eastern and Western Europe. London: Routledge & Kegan Paul, 1968

Cockett, Richard, *Twilight of Truth: Chamberlain, Appeasement, and the Manipulation of the Press*. London: Weidenfeld & Nicolson, 1989

Colville, J. R., *Man of Valour: The Life of Field Marshal the Viscount Gort*. London: Collins, 1972

Colvin, Ian, *Vansittart in Office: An Historical Survey of the Origins of the Second World War based on the Papers of Sir Robert Vansittart*. London: Gollancz, 1965

The Chamberlain Cabinet. London: Gollancz, 1971

Cosgrave, Patrick, *Churchill at War*, vol. I: *Alone, 1939–40*. London: Collins, 1974

Courcy, Anne de, *1939: The Last Season*. London: Thames & Hudson, 1989

Cowling, Maurice, *The Impact of Hitler: British Politics and British Policy 1939–40*. Cambridge: Cambridge University Press, 1975

Cross, J. A., *Sir Samuel Hoare: A Political Biography*. London: Jonathan Cape, 1977

Dahlerus, Birger, *The Last Attempt*, trans. Alexandra Dick, with an Introduction by Sir Norman Birkett. London: Hutchinson, 1947

Danchev, Alex, '"Dilly-Dally", or Having the Last Word: Field-Marshall Sir John Dill and Prime Minister Winston Churchill'. *Journal of Contemporary History*, 22: 1 (January 1987), pp. 21–44

Day, David, *Menzies and Churchill at War: A Controversial New Account of the 1941 Struggle for Power*. North Ryde: Angus & Robertson, 1986

Dennis, Peter, *Decision by Default: Peacetime Conscription and British Defence, 1919–39*. London: Routledge & Kegan Paul, 1972

Dilks, David, 'The Twilight War and the Fall of France: Chamberlain and Churchill in 1940', *Transactions of the Royal Historical Society*, 5th series, 28 (1978), pp. 61–86

Neville Chamberlain, vol. 1: *Pioneering and Reform 1869–1929*. Cambridge: Cambridge University Press, 1984

Donoughue, B. and G. W. Jones, *Herbert Morrison: Portrait of a Politician*. London: Weidenfeld & Nicolson, 1973

Douglas, Roy, *New Alliances 1940–41*. London: Macmillan, 1982

(ed.), *1939: A Retrospective Forty Years After*. London: Macmillan, 1983

Douglas-Hamilton, J., *Motive for a Mission*. London: Macmillan, 1971

Feiling, Keith, *The Life of Neville Chamberlain*. London: Macmillan, 1946

Gannon, Franklin Reid, *The British Press and Germany 1936–39*. Oxford: The Clarendon Press, 1971

Gates, Eleanor M., *End of the Affair: The Collapse of the Anglo-French Alliance, 1939–40*. Berkeley: University of California Press, 1981

Gibbs, N. H., *Grand Strategy*, vol. I: *Rearmament Policy*. London: HMSO, 1976

Gilbert, Martin, *The Roots of Appeasement*. London: Weidenfeld & Nicolson, 1966

Winston S. Churchill, vol. V: *1922–1939*. London: Heinemann, 1976

Finest Hour: Winston S. Churchill 1939–41. London: Heinemann, 1983 (ed.), *Winston S. Churchill*, vol. V: *Companion*, Part 3: *Documents: The Coming of War 1936–1939*. London: Heinemann, 1982

Graham-Murray, James, *The Sword and the Umbrella*. London: Times Press and Anthony Gibbs & Phillips, 1964

Hancock, K. W. and M. Gowing, *The British War Economy* (part of the United Kingdom's Cabinet Office *History of the Second World War Civil Series*), revised and confidential edition. London: HMSO, 1975

Harrisson, Tom, *Living Through the Blitz*. London: Collins, 1976

Haslam, Jonathan, *The Soviet Union and the Struggle for Collective Security in Europe, 1933–1939*. London: Macmillan, 1984

Hill, Christopher, 'The Decision-making Process in Relation to British Foreign Policy, 1938–41'. Unpublished D.Phil. thesis, University of Oxford, 1978

Hinsley, F. H., *British Intelligence in the Second World War: Its Influence on Strategy and Operations*, vol. I. London: HMSO, 1979

Howard, Michael, *The Continental Commitment: the Dilemma of British Defence Policy in the Era of Two World Wars*. London: Temple Smith, 1972

Irving, David, *Hitler's War, 1939–1942*, vol. I. London: Macmillan Papermac, 1983 (first published 1977)

(ed.), *Breach of Security: The German Intelligence File on Events Leading to the Second World War*. London: Kimber, 1968

Ismay, General the Lord, *The Memoirs of General the Lord Ismay*. London: Heinemann, 1960

Kavanagh, Denis, *Crisis, Charisma and British Political Leadership: Winston Churchill as the Outsider*, Sage Professional Papers in Contemporary Political Sociology, 1, no. 06–001. London: Sage, 1974

Knight, Jonathan, 'Churchill and the Approach to Mussolini and Hitler in May 1940: A Reply to David Carlton'. *British Journal of International Studies*, 3: 1 (April, 1977), pp. 92–6

Lamb, Richard, *The Ghosts of Peace 1935–1945*. Salisbury: Michael Russell, 1987

Lammers, D., 'From Whitehall after Munich: The Foreign Office and the Future Course of British Policy'. *The Historical Journal*, 16: 4 (1973), pp. 831–56

Langhorne, Richard (ed.), *Diplomacy and Intelligence in the Second World War: Essays in Honour of F. H. Hinsley*. Cambridge: Cambridge University Press, 1985

Lash, Joseph P., *Roosevelt and Churchill, 1939–41: The Partnership that Saved the West*. New York: W. W. Norton, 1976

Lee, J. M. *The Churchill Coalition 1940–1945*. London: Batsford, 1980

Leutze, James, 'The Secret of the Churchill–Roosevelt Correspondence, September 1939–May 1940'. *Journal of Contemporary History*, 10: 3 (July, 1975), pp. 465–92

Liddell-Hart, Captain B., *Memoirs*, vol. II. London: Cassell, 1965

MacDonald, Callum A., 'Economic Appeasement and the German "Moderates" 1937–39: An Introductory Essay'. *Past and Present*, 56 (August, 1972), pp. 105–35

The United States, Britain and Appeasement. London: Macmillan, 1981

Madge, C. and T. Harrison, *Britain by Mass Observation.* London: Penguin Special, 1939

Manne, Robert, 'The British Government and the Question of the Soviet Alliance, 15 March–24 August 1939'. Unpublished thesis for the B.Phil. in International Relations, University of Oxford, 1972

'The British Decision for Alliance with Russia, May 1939'. *Journal for Contemporary History*, 9: 3 (1974), pp. 3–26

Martin, Bernd, *Friedensinitiativen und Machtpolitik in Zweiten Weltkrieg, 1939–1942.* Dusseldorf: Droste, 1974

May, Ernest R. (ed.), *Knowing One's Enemies: Intelligence Assessment between the Two World Wars.* Princeton: Princeton University Press, 1984

McLaine, Ian, *Ministry of Morale: Home Front Morale and the Ministry of Information in World War II.* London: George Allen & Unwin, 1979

McNeill, W. H., *Arnold J. Toynbee.* Oxford: Oxford University Press, 1989

Medlicott, W. N., *British Foreign Policy since Versailles, 1919–1963*, 2nd edn. London: Methuen, 1968

Middlemas, Keith, *Diplomacy of Illusion: The British Government and Germany, 1937–39.* London: Weidenfeld & Nicolson, 1972

Minney, R. J., *The Private Papers of Hore-Belisha.* London: Collins, 1960

Mommsen, Wolfgang J. and Lothar Kettenacker (eds.), *The Fascist Challenge and the Policy of Appeasement.* London: Allen & Unwin, 1983

Murray, Williamson, *The Change in the European Balance of Power, 1938–39.* Princeton: Princeton University Press, 1984

Naylor, John F., *Labour's International Policy: The Labour Party in the 1930s.* London: Weidenfeld & Nicolson, 1969

Newman, Simon, *March 1939: The British Guarantee to Poland. A Study in the Continuity of British Foreign Policy.* Oxford: The Clarendon Press, 1976

Nicholls, A. J. and Sir John Wheeler-Bennett, *The Semblance of Peace.* London: Macmillan, 1972

Northedge, F. S., *Freedom and Necessity in British Foreign Policy*, an inaugural lecture delivered on 14 October 1971 at the London School of Economics and Political Science. London: Weidenfeld & Nicolson, 1972

Ovendale, Ritchie, *'Appeasement' and the English Speaking World: Britain, the United States, the Dominions and the Policy of 'Appeasement', 1937–39.* Cardiff: University of Wales Press, 1975

(ed.), *The Foreign Policy of the British Labour Government, 1945–1951.* Leicester: Leicester University Press, 1984

Overy, R. J., *The Air War, 1939–1945.* London: Europa, 1980

Parker, R. A. C., 'The Pound Sterling, the American Treasury and British Preparations for War, 1938–1939'. *English Historical Review*, 98: 387 (April, 1983), pp. 261–79

Parkinson, Roger, *Peace for our Time.* London: Rupert Hart-Davis, 1971

Blood, Toil, Tears and Sweat. The War History from Dunkirk to Alamein. London: Hart-Davis MacGibbon, 1973

Peden, G. C., *British Rearmament and the Treasury, 1932–39*. Edinburgh: Scottish Academic Press, 1979
  'The Burden of Imperial Defence and the Continental Commitment Reconsidered'. *The Historical Journal*, 27: 2 (June, 1984). pp. 405–23
Pelling, Henry, *Britain and the Second World War*. London: Fontana/Collins, 1970
Pratt, Lawrence, *East of Malta, West of Suez: Britain's Mediterranean Crisis, 1936–1939*. Cambridge: Cambridge University Press, 1975
Prazmowska, Anita, *Britain, Poland, and the Eastern Front, 1939*. Cambridge: Cambridge University Press, 1987
Rankin, W., 'What Dunkirk Spirit?' *New Society*, 15 November 1975, pp. 368–9
Rasmussen, J. S., 'Government and Intra-Party Opposition: Dissent within the Conservative Parliamentary Party in the 1930s'. *Political Studies*, 19: 2 (June, 1971), pp. 172–83
Reynolds, David, *The Creation of the Anglo-American Alliance 1937–1941: A Study in Competitive Cooperation*. London: Europa, 1981
  'Churchill and the British "Decision" to Fight On in 1940: Right Policy, Wrong Reasons', in Richard Langhorne (ed.), *Diplomacy and Intelligence in the Second World War: Essays in Honour of F. H. Hinsley*. Cambridge: Cambridge University Press, 1985
Rhodes James, Robert, *Victor Cazalet: A Portrait*. London: Hamish Hamilton, 1976
Robbins, Keith, *Munich*. London: Cassell, 1968
  'Appeasement: New Tasks for the Historian' (review article). *International Affairs*, 48: 4 (October, 1972), pp. 625–30
Roberts, Geoffrey, 'The War on All Fronts', *Times Higher Education Supplement*, 18 August 1989
Robertson, Esmond (ed.), *The Origins of the Second World War*. London: Macmillan, 1971
Roskill, Stephen, *Hankey: Man of Secrets*, vol. III, *1931–63*. London: Collins, 1974
Ryan, Henry Butterfield, *The Vision of Anglo-America: The US–UK Alliance and the Emerging Cold War, 1943–46*. Cambridge: Cambridge University Press, 1987
Schmidt, Gustav, *The Politics and Economics of Appeasement: British Foreign Policy in the 1930s*, translated from the German by Jackie Bennet-Ruete. Leamington Spa: Berg, 1986
Simon, Viscount, *Retrospect: Memoirs*. London: Hutchinson, 1952
Stafford, Paul, 'Political Autobiography and the Art of the Plausible: R. A. Butler at the Foreign Office 1938–1939'. *The Historical Journal*, 28: 4 (December, 1985), pp. 901–22
  'The Chamberlain–Halifax Visit to Rome: A Reappraisal'. *English Historical Review*, 108: 386 (January 1983), pp. 61–100
Taylor, A. J. P., *The Origins of the Second World War*. Harmondsworth: Penguin, 1965 (first published 1961)
  Beaverbrook. Harmondsworth: Penguin, 1974
  Lloyd George: Twelve Essays. London: Hamish Hamilton, 1971

Taylor, A. J. P. et al., *Churchill: Four Faces and the Man*. Harmondsworth: Pelican, 1973

Taylor, Philip M., *The Projection of Britain: British Overseas Publicity and Propaganda 1919–1939*. Cambridge: Cambridge University Press, 1981

Templewood, Viscount (Sir Samuel Hoare), *Nine Troubled Years*. London: Collins, 1954

Thompson, Neville, *The Anti-Appeasers: Conservative Opposition to Appeasement in the 1930s*. Oxford: The Clarendon Press, 1971

Thorne, Christopher, *The Approach of War, 1938–39*. London: Macmillan, 1968

'Chatham House, Whitehall, and Far Eastern Issues, 1941–5'. *International Affairs*, 54: 1 (January, 1978), pp. 1–29

Trythall, A., 'The Downfall of Leslie Hore-Belisha'. *Journal of Contemporary History*, 16: 3 (July, 1981), pp. 391–412

Ulam, Adam, *Expansion and Co-existence: The History of Soviet Foreign Policy, 1917–67*. London: Secker & Warburg, 1968

Waley, Daniel, *British Public Opinion and the Abyssinian War 1935–36*. London: Temple Smith/LSE, 1975

Wark, Wesley, *The Ultimate Enemy: British Intelligence and Nazi Germany 1933–1939*. Oxford: Oxford University Press, 1986

'Something Very Stern: British Political Intelligence, Moralism and Strategy in 1939'. *Intelligence and National Security*, 5: 1 (January, 1990), pp. 150–70

Watt, Donald Cameron, 'Appeasement: The Rise of a Revisionist School?'. *Political Quarterly*, 36: 2 (April–June, 1965), pp. 191–213

Personalities and Policies: Studies in the Formulation of British Foreign Policy in the Twentieth Century. London: Longman, 1965

Too Serious a Business: European Armed Forces and the Approach to the Second World War. London: Temple Smith, 1975

'The Historiography of Appeasement', in Chris Cook and Alan Sked (eds.), *Crisis and Controversy: Essays in Honour of A. J. P. Taylor*. London: Macmillan, 1976

'What about the People? Abstraction and Reality in History and the Social Sciences', inaugural lecture at the London School of Economics and Political Science. London: LSE, 1983

Succeeding John Bull: America in Britain's Place 1900–1975. Cambridge: Cambridge University Press, 1984

How War Came: The Immediate Origins of The Second World War, 1938–1939. London: Heinemann, 1989

'An Intelligence Surprise: The Foreign Office Failure to Predict the Nazi-Soviet Pact'. *Intelligence and National Security Journal*, 4: 3 (July, 1989), pp. 512–34

Weygand, J., *The Role of General Weygand: Conversations with his Son*, trans. J. H. F. McEwan. London: Eyre & Spottiswoode, 1948

Wheeler-Bennett, Sir John, *John Anderson, Viscount Waverly*. London: Macmillan, 1962

(ed.), *Action This Day: Working with Churchill*. London: Macmillan, 1968

Woodward, Sir Llewellyn, *British Foreign Policy in the Second World War*, vol. I. London: HMSO, 1970
Young, John W. (ed.), *The Foreign Policy of Churchill's Peacetime Administration, 1951–1955*. Leicester: Leicester University Press, 1988
Young, Robert J., *In Command of France: French Foreign Policy and Military Planning, 1933–1940*. Cambridge, Mass.: Harvard University Press, 1978

(ii) *Cabinet government and foreign policy analysis*

Allison, Graham, *Essence of Decision*. Boston: Little, Brown, 1971
Anderson, T. E., *Public Policy-Making*. London: Nelson, 1975
Axelrod, Robert (ed.), *Structure of Decision: The Cognitive Maps of Political Elites*. Princeton: Princeton University Press, 1976
Bachrach, Peter and Morton Baratz, *Power and Poverty* (Part 1). London and New York: Oxford University Press, 1970
Barber, James, *Who Makes British Foreign Policy?* Milton Keynes: Open University Press, 1976
Bell, Coral, *The Conventions of Crisis*. London: Oxford University Press, 1971
Beloff, M., *Foreign Policy and the Democratic Process*. Baltimore: Johns Hopkins University Press, 1955
Birch, A. H., *Representation*. London: Macmillan, 1972
Bishop, Donald G., *The Administration of British Foreign Relations*. Syracuse, N.Y.: Syracuse University Press, 1961
Boardman, Robert and A. J. R. Groom (eds.), *The Management of Britain's External Relations*. London: Macmillan, 1973
Borthwick, R. L. and J. E. Spence (eds.), *British Politics in Perspective*. Leicester: Leicester University Press, 1984
Boulding, K., *The Image*. Ann Arbor: University of Michigan Press, 1965
Boyce, D. G., 'Public Opinion and Historians', *History*, 63: 208 (June, 1978), pp. 214–28
Brecher, Michael, *The Foreign Policy System of Israel*. London: Oxford University Press, 1972
 Decisions in Israel's Foreign Policy. London: Oxford University Press, 1974
 Decisions in Crisis: Israel, 1967 and 1973. Berkeley: University of California Press, 1980
Brecher, Michael, Jonathan Wilkenfeld and Sheila Moser, *Crises in the Twentieth Century*, vols. I and II. Oxford: Pergamon Press, 1988
Bulpitt, Jim, 'Rational Politicians and Conservative Statecraft in the Open Polity', in Peter Byrd (ed.), *British Foreign Policy under Thatcher*. Oxford: Philip Allan, 1988
Carr, E. H., *What is History?* Harmondsworth: Penguin, 1964
Ceadel, Martin, *Pacifism in Britain, 1914–45: The Defining of a Faith*. Oxford: The Clarendon Press, 1980
Chester, D. N., 'Who Governs Britain?'. *Parliamentary Affairs*, 15: 4 (Autumn, 1962), pp. 519–27

Clarke, Michael and Brian White (eds.), *Understanding Foreign Policy: The Foreign Policy Systems Approach*. Aldershot: Edward Elgar, 1989

Cohen, B. C., *The Public's Impact on Foreign Policy*. Boston: Little, Brown, 1973

Crossman, R. H., Introduction to his edition of Walter Bagehot's *The English Constitution*. London: Fontana/Collins, 1963

Daalder, H., *Cabinet Reform in Britain, 1914–63*. Stanford, Calif.: Stanford University Press, 1963

Dahl, Robert, *Who Governs? Democracy and Power in an American City*. London: Yale University Press, 1961

Dawisha, Karen, *The Kremlin and the Prague Spring*. London and Berkeley: University of California Press, 1985

De Rivera, Joseph, *The Psychological Dimension of Foreign Policy*. Columbus, Ohio: C. E. Merrill, 1968

Deutsch, Karl, *The Nerves of Government: Models of Political Communication and Control*. New York: The Free Press, 1963

Dixon, N. F., *On the Psychology of Military Incompetence*. London: Jonathan Cape, 1976

Ehrmann, J., *Cabinet Government and War, 1890–1940*. Cambridge: Cambridge University Press, 1958

Farrell, J. C. and A. P. Smith (eds.), *Image and Reality in World Politics*. New York: Columbia University Press, 1968

Festinger, Leon, *A Theory of Cognitive Dissonance*. Stanford, Calif.: Stanford University Press, 1962

Franck, T. M. and E. Weisband (eds.), *Secrecy and Foreign Policy*. New York and London: Oxford University Press, 1963

Frankel, Joseph, *The Making of Foreign Policy, An Analysis of Decision Making*. London: Oxford University Press, 1963, 2nd edn, 1967

Gelb, Leslie H., with Richard K. Betts, *The Irony of Vietnam: The System Worked*. Washington DC: The Brookings Institution, 1979

George, Alexander, David K. Hall and William E. Simons, *The Limits of Coercive Diplomacy: Laos–Cuba–Vietnam*. Boston: Little, Brown, 1971

Gordon Walker, Patrick, *The Cabinet*, revised edn. London: Fontana/Collins, 1972

Heasman, D. J., 'The Prime Minister and the Cabinet'. *Parliamentary Affairs*, 15: 4 (Autumn, 1962), pp. 150–70

Hennessy, Peter, *Cabinet*. Oxford: Basil Blackwell, 1986

Hermann, C. F., *Crises in Foreign Policy*. Indianapolis: Bobbs-Merrill, 1969

Hill, Christopher, 'History and International Relations', in Steve Smith (ed.), *International Relations: British and American Perspectives*. Oxford: Basil Blackwell, 1985

Hinsley, F. H. (ed.), *The Foreign Policy of Sir Edward Grey*. Cambridge: Cambridge University Press, 1977

Hogwood, Brian W., *From Crisis to Complacency: Shaping Public Policy in Britain*. Oxford: Oxford University Press, 1987

Hunt, E. H. and G. R. Hawke, 'The New Economic History: Professor Fogel's

Study of American Railways', and 'Comment'. *History*, 53: 177 (February, 1968), pp. 3–23
Iklé, Fred, *How Nations Negotiate*. New York: Praeger, 1968
Janis, Irving, *Groupthink*, 2nd edn. Boston: Houghton Mifflin, 1982
Janis, Irving, and Leon Mann, *Decision-Making: A Psychological Analysis of Conflict, Choice, and Commitment*. New York: The Free Press, 1977
Jennings, W. Ivor, *Cabinet Government*, 3rd edn. Cambridge: Cambridge University Press, 1959
Jervis, R., *The Logic of Images in International Relations*. Princeton: Princeton University Press, 1970
  Perception and Misperception in International Politics. Princeton: Princeton University Press, 1976
Johnson, Nevil, *The Limits of Political Science*. Oxford: The Clarendon Press, 1989
Jones, G. W., 'Prime Ministers and Cabinets'. *Political Studies*, 20 (June, 1972), pp. 213–22
  'Development of the Cabinet', in William Thornhill (ed.), *The Modernization of British Government*. London: Pitman, 1975
  'Cabinet Government since Bagehot'. *LSE Quarterly*, 3: 3 (Autumn, 1989), pp. 236–54
Jordan, A. G. and J. J. Richardson, *British Politics and the Policy Process: An Arena Approach*. London: Unwin Hyman, 1987
Kennedy, Paul, *Strategy and Diplomacy 1870–1945*. London: Fontana, 1984
King, Anthony (ed.), *The British Prime Minister: A Reader*. London: Macmillan, 1969; 2nd much revised edn, 1985
Kissinger, H., 'Domestic Structure and Foreign Policy' (first published in 1966, but most easily available in *International Politics and Foreign Policy* (2nd edn), ed. J. Rosenau, pp. 261–75. New York: The Free Press, 1969)
Lauren, Paul (ed.), *Diplomacy: New Approaches in History, Theory and Policy*. New York: The Free Press, 1979
Lebow, Richard Ned, *Between Peace and War: The Nature of International Crisis*. Baltimore: Johns Hopkins University Press, 1981
Lindblom, C. E., *The Policy-Making Process*. Englewood Cliffs, N.J.: Prentice Hall, 1968
Lukes, S., *Power: A Radical View*. London: Macmillan, 1974
Mackie, Thomas T. and Brian Hogwood, 'Decision Arenas in Executive Decision Making: Cabinet Committees in Comparative Perspective'. *British Journal of Political Science*, 14 (July, 1984), pp. 285–312
Mackintosh, J., *The British Cabinet*, 2nd edn. London: Stevens & Sons, 1968 (first published 1962)
May, Ernest, *'Lessons' of the Past: The Use and Misuse of History in American Foreign Policy*. New York: Oxford University Press, 1973
  (with Richard Neustadt), *Thinking in Time: The Uses of History for Decision-Makers*. New York: The Free Press, 1986
Neustadt, Richard, *Alliance Politics*. New York: Columbia University Press, 1970

Paige, G., *The Korean Decision*. New York: The Free Press, 1968
Parry, G. and P. Morriss, 'When is a Decision not a Decision?', in *The British Political Sociology Yearbook*, vol. I. London: Croom Helm, 1974
Reynolds, P., *An Introduction to International Relations*. London: Longman, 1971
Richards, P. G., *Parliament and Foreign Policy*. London: Allen & Unwin, 1967
Rosenau, J. N., *The Scientific Study of Foreign Policy*. New York: The Free Press, 1971
  (ed.), *International Politics and Foreign Policy*, 2nd edn. New York: The Free Press, 1969
  (ed.), *Comparing Foreign Policies: Theories, Findings, Methods*. New York: Sage Publications, 1974
Rotberg, Robert I. and Theodore K. Rabb (eds.), *The Origin and Prevention of Major Wars*. Cambridge: Cambridge University Press, 1989
Rush, Michael, *The Cabinet and Policy Formation*. London: Longman, 1984
Seymour-Ure, Colin, 'The "Disintegration" of the Cabinet and the Neglected Question of Cabinet Reform'. *Parliamentary Affairs*, 24: 3 (1971), pp. 196–207
Shlaim, Avi, 'Failures in National Intelligence Estimates: The Case of the Yom Kippur War'. *World Politics*, 28: 3 (April, 1976), pp. 348–80
  The United States and the Berlin Blockade 1948–9: A Study of Crisis Decision-making. Berkeley: University of California Press, 1983
Shlaim, Avi, Peter Jones and Keith Sainsbury, *British Foreign Secretaries since 1945*. Newton Abbot: David & Charles, 1977
Simon, H. A., *Administrative Behaviour: A Study of Decision-Making Processes in Administrative Organisation*, 3rd edn. New York: The Free Press, 1976
Smith, Michael, Steve Smith and Brian White (eds.), *British Foreign Policy: Tradition, Change and Continuity*. London: Unwin Hyman, 1988
Smith Steve and Michael Clarke (eds.), *Foreign Policy Implementation*. London: Allen & Unwin, 1985
Snyder, R., M. Bruck and B. Sapin, *Foreign Policy Decision Making*, 3rd edn. New York: The Free Press, 1976
Sprout, Harold and Margaret, *The Ecological Perspective in Human Affairs*. Princeton: Princeton University Press, 1965
Steinbruner, J., *The Cybernetic Theory of Decision*. Princeton: Princeton University Press, 1974
Steiner, Zara, *The Foreign Office and Foreign Policy, 1898–1914*. Cambridge: Cambridge University Press, 1969
  Britain and the Origins of the First World War. London: Macmillan, 1977
Thorne, Christopher, *The Limits of Foreign Policy: The West, the League and the Far Eastern Crisis of 1931–33*. London: Macmillan, 1973
Verba, S., 'Assumptions of Rationality and Non-Rationality in Models of the International System', in H. K. Jacobson and W. Zimmerman (eds.), *The Shaping of Foreign Policy*. New York: Atherton Press, 1969
Vital, David, *The Making of British Foreign Policy*. London: George Allen & Unwin, 1968

Wallace, William, *The Foreign Policy Process in Britain*. London: Oxford University Press for the Royal Institute of International Affairs, 1975

Waltz, Kenneth N., *Foreign Policy and Democratic Politics*. Boston: Little, Brown, 1967

Williams, Phil, *Crisis Management*. London: Martin Robertson, 1976

Williamson, Samuel R., *The Politics of Grand Strategy*. Cambridge, Mass.: Harvard University Press, 1969

Wilson, Keith, 'The British Cabinet's Decision for War, 2 August 1914', *British Journal of International Studies*, 1: 2 (July, 1975), pp. 148–59

Wolfers, A. *Discord and Collaboration*. Baltimore: Johns Hopkins University Press, 1962

INDEX

academics, inputs into policy, 191–2, 194, 196, 200, 206, 247
Addison, Paul, 221
Albania, 49, 71
Allison, Graham, 3
Amery, Leopold, 172, 197, 205, 218
Anderson, Sir John, 81–2, 92–3, 96, 120, 130–1, 137, 143, 219, 247
'appeasement', policy of, 89, 94, 100, 102–3, 108, 134, 154, 163, 170, 175, 243–4
army, British, *see* military, the British
Asquith, Herbert, 97–8, 148
Atlantic Charter, 235–6
Attlee, Clement, 127, 152, 156–7, 161, 165, 173, 175–7, 179, 182, 195–8, 203–6, 214, 217–18, 220, 242, 244
Australia, and reply to Hitler, Oct. 1939, 125–6; *see also* Dominions
Austria, 104, 109, 253

Bagehot, Walter, 2
Baldwin, Stanley, 165
Barber, James, 224
Bastianini, Giuseppe, 156, 159
Battle of Britain, 179, 182
BBC (British Broadcasting Corporation), 211
Beaverbrook, Lord, 138, 168, 219, 240
Beck, Josef, 33, 51, 59, 88
Belgium, 152,. 252
Bell, Coral, 4
Beneš, Eduard, 110
Bethell, Nicholas, 103, 144
Betts, Richard K., 208
Beveridge Report, 221
Bevin, Ernest, 196–8, 202, 205–6, 214, 218–19, 230, 242
Bishop, Donald, 4

Bonnet, Georges, 31–3, 44, 68, 91, 298n35
Bracken, Brendan, 138
Brecher, Michael, 3, 4, 86
Bridges, Sir Edward, 106, 134, 175, 203 (Table 8, n1), 217–18, 220, 247; *see also* Cabinet Office; Cabinet Papers
Britain, capacity to win the war, 87, 101, 103–4, 108, 114, 142–3, 149, 152–3, 158, 171, 174, 180–1, 183–5, 202, 315n61; evacuation of children from, 185; morale in war-time, 173, 180–1, 185, 190, 192–3, 203; possibility of making peace with Germany in 1940, 147; *see also* British foreign policy
British Expeditionary Force (BEF), *see* military, the British
British foreign policy, 14, 18, 95, 97; Anglo-French military conversations 1905–14, 98, 148; in inter-war period, 8, 170; in wake of Hitler's attack on Czechoslovakia, 18–47; in response to Hitler's attack on Poland, 85–99; reply to Hitler's peace offer, October 1939, 100–45; subjects discussed in Cabinet Committee 1938–9, 70–1; *see also* crisis; Soviet Union, possible British alliance with; war aims, British
Brown, Ernest, 81, 130
Brown, George, 243
Bruce, Stanley M., 171, 173, 204–8
Bulpitt, Jim, 5
Burckhardt, Dr Carl, 186
bureaucracy, behaviour of, 201; *see also* Foreign Office; officials; policy-making, implementation phase
Burgin, Leslie, 50, 64–5, 73, 81, 92, 105, 130, 239, 287n100

353

354 *Index*

Burns, John, 93
Butler, R. A., 36, 54, 69, 212, 218, 239

Cabinet and cabinet government:
  committees, 206, 219, 236 (*see also various entries under* Committee *as well as* Foreign Policy Committee *and* Home Policy Committee); consensus, 238–40; dissent in cabinet, 291n25; inner groups, 26, 27, 28–9, 115, 121–3, 136–7, 193, 220, 241–2; rebellions, 85–99, 135, 226–7, 231–2; vacation break 1939, 76, 86; *see also* Cabinet Papers; Cabinet Office; collective responsibility; Foreign Policy Committee; foreign policy executive; Home Policy Committee; Committee on Reconstruction Problems; Committee on War Aims; War Cabinet
Cabinet Office, 82–3, 111, 130–1; *see also* Bridges, Sir Edward
Cabinet Papers, 111, 128–9, 147, 226; confidential annexes to, 105, 107; memoranda, 107; minutes of the Foreign Policy Committee, 66; minutes (also known as Conclusions), 28, 90, 93, 105, 106–7, 120, 131, 139, 176–7, 201
Cadogan, Sir Alexander, 11, 21, 22–3, 29, 33–5, 36, 53, 54–5, 56, 58, 67–9, 78, 86, 88, 91, 97, 111, 117–19, 121, 134, 140, 162, 167, 185, 191–3, 247
Caldecote, Viscount, *see* Inskip, Sir Thomas (Viscount Caldecote)
Cameron Watt, Donald, 9, 134
Canada, and draft reply to Hitler, 121, 124, 143; *see also* Dominions
case-study approach to the study of foreign policy, 5–6, 13–14
Cazalet, Victor, 143
Chamberlain, Neville, 1–187 *passim*, 224–47 *passim*; and crisis over France 1940, 153–4, 157, 173–9, 181–2; at Munich, 116; attitude to Churchill, 117–18; attitude to Foreign Office, 27; Birmingham speech, 17 March 1939, 21–3; death, 213; first Chairman of War Aims Committee, 196–7; optimism over an end to the war, 127, 135; personality, 96, 109, 173, 244; relationship with Halifax, 134–5; statement of 12 October 1939, 144, 252–5; style of governing, 106–7, 120; threat of resignation, 68–70; *see also* 'appeasement', policy of, foreign policy executive
Chatfield, Admiral of the Fleet Lord, 25–6, 28–9, 40–1, 46, 53–5, 58, 60, 64–6, 73, 79, 81, 93, 106, 111, 121, 123, 125, 136, 137, 138, 141, 143, 167, 247
Chatham House, *see* Royal Institute of International Affairs
Chiefs of Staff, 19, 41, 43, 46, 53–5, 56, 58, 64–6, 129, 202, 247, 278n108, 321n119; views on Britain's capacity to fight on alone, 154–5, 157, 180–1, 183
China, 202, 261
Churchill, Winston Spencer, 98, 106, 112–13, 131, 135–7, 142–4, 224–47; and war aims discussions 1940–1, 188–223; explains leak of Cabinet paper, 138; leadership during May–June 1940, 146–87; relations with Roosevelt, 147–9, 167; style of government, 106–7; takes initiative in replying to Hitler, 117–24, 137–41
Ciano, Count Galeazzo, 90–1, 159–60
civil defence, 90
Clausewitz, Karl von, 7, 100
coalition government 1940–5, 200–1, 220, 229, 242
cognitive dissonance, theory of, 19, 107, 139, 166n64
cognitive maps, 237
collective responsibility, Cabinet doctrine of, 12, 93, 105, 145, 239
Colville, John, 92
Colvin, Ian, 45, 278n105
Committee on Post-war Internal Economic Problems (of the War Cabinet), 203 (Table 1, n2)
Committee on Reconstruction (of the War Cabinet), 203 (Table 8, n2)
Committee on Reconstruction Priorities (of the War Cabinet), 203 (Table 1, n2)
Committee on Reconstruction Problems (of the War Cabinet), 203 (Table 8, n2), 215–23
Committee on War Aims (of the War Cabinet), 188–223, 230
Conservative Party, 147, 199, 208, 218, 223, 231

Cooper, Alfred Duff, *see* Duff Cooper, Alfred
Corbin, Charles, 31, 68, 117
counter-factual approaches, 11
Cranborne, Viscount, 196, 203, 206, 218
crisis: impact of on decision-making, xix, 7, 17, 114, 162–3, 165, 168, 173, 178, 187, 228–9, 236–7, 246–7, 316n70; definitions of, 86; Summer 1914, 97–8; September 1938, 63; 15–31 March 1939, 18–47; 1–3 September 1939, 8, 85–99; May 1940, 123, 146–87; 1940–1, 188, 192, 198–9; Berlin 1948, 246; Cuba 1962, 246; October 1973, 86
Crookshank, Captain Harry, 128–9, 189, 306n112
Crozier, W. P., 212
Curtis, Lionel, 190
Czechoslovakia, 18–20, 104, 109–10, 116, 119–20, 125, 253, 255; warnings of German attack on, 19, 70–1

Dahlerus, Birger, 89, 91, 110–13, 123, 140, 141 (note to Table 5), 231, 244
Daily Mirror, 138, 211
Daladier, Edouard, 68, 85, 91, 102, 108, 124, 254
Dalton, Hugh, 50, 172, 175, 197, 202, 214, 218, 243
Danzig, Polish-German dispute over, 32–3, 43, 71, 86, 91
Davies, Clement, 244
Dawisha, Karen, 3
decision-making, theories of, 10–11, 169n79; and question of war aims, 298n30; non-decisions, 177–8, 179; *see also* policy-making
De Gaulle, Charles, 194
De La Warr, 9th Earl, 82, 92, 94
determinism, theories of, 10
De Valera, Eamon, 201
Dill, General Sir John, 213
disarmament, 116, 119
Dominions, 9, 60, 108, 113, 117, 121, 123–7, 129, 130–1, 136, 139, 143, 173–4, 191, 200–2, 207, 252, 254, 256, 260; Dominions Office, 167; *see also* Australia, Canada, South Africa
Dorman-Smith, Sir Reginald, 92
Dowding, Air Marshal Hugh, 150
Duff Cooper, Alfred, 228; and War Aims Committee, 193–8, 200, 203, 204, 207–8, 211, 214–15, 218, 220, 240
Dunkirk, 179, 180–1, 184

Economic Warfare, Ministry of, 183
Eden, Anthony, 106, 113, 120–1, 123, 126, 134, 136–7, 197, 209–10, 213, 219, 221–3, 230, 239, 242–3; 'Eden group', 102; position in Chamberlain's War Cabinet, 130–1; relations with Churchill, 337n25; speech 29 May 1941, 258–62
Eire, 201
election, possibility of in October 1940, 212
Elliot, Walter, 26, 44, 92, 94
executive, foreign policy, *see* foreign policy executive
external environment, inputs from, 61, 76–7, 108, 161, 166, 177, 190, 199, 245

federalism in Europe, in relation to post-war situation, 193, 195–6, 206, 210, 216
Feiling, Keith, 23
Finland, 38, 114
Foreign Office, 9–10, 52, 61, 68, 111, 135, 138, 144, 167, 192, 194, 199–200, 212–13, 216, 221, 230, 244–5; Political Intelligence Department, 192; *see also* Cadogan, Sir Alexander; Kirkpatrick, Ivone; Malkin, Sir William; Sargent, Sir Orme; Strang, William; Vansittart, Sir Robert
foreign policy, nature of, 177–8, 245; domestic sources of, 15, 62, 244–5
foreign policy analysis, 3–4, 16–17, 265n19
Foreign Policy Committee (of the Cabinet), 21, 30, 34, 36–43, 52–84, 225, 241–2; attendance at, 73–5, 78–83, 250–1; frequency of meetings, 70–1, 75–6, 82
foreign policy executive (of the Cabinet), xviii, 7, 15, 225–7, 230–1, 233–47; possible divisions within, 134–5, 169–73, 212–15, 243; under Chamberlain, 28, 42–3, 47, 51, 55, 59–60, 62, 64–5, 67, 77, 83, 98, 112–13, 115, 118, 129, 134–6; under Churchill, 147, 160, 221, 337n25
France, 27, 29, 30–1, 35, 43, 55, 56, 59, 60, 62, 64, 69, 90–2, 95, 98, 101,

France (cont.)
109–10, 117, 118, 121, 123–5, 142, 191, 252, 254–5, 277n100, 284n65; fall of, 146–87; Free French, 194; see also war aims, French
Franco, General Francisco, 212, 225, 241

Gamelin, General Maurice, 90, 150
Gates, Eleanor M., 180
Gelb, Leslie H., 208
George, Alexander, 104
Georges, General Joseph, 150
Germany, 18–19, 35, 48, 55, 58, 70–1, 84, 85–7, 89, 95, 98, 111, 125, 154–5, 156–9; defeat of France, 146–52; 'New Order' proposals, 258–61; possible peace offer from, 101, 170, 178–9, 182, 185–6; possibility of German agreement with Soviet Union, see Soviet Union; British ultimatum to, 89–91, 94–5; see also Hitler, Adolf; 'peace offensive' by Germany; public opinion, images of

Gibraltar, 175, 212
Gilbert, Martin, 138
Gilmour, Sir John, 106, 130
Goebbels, Dr Joseph, 258
Göring, Reichsmarshall Hermann, 91, 110–12, 140
Gordon Walter, Patrick, 1
Gort, General Lord, 151–2
Greece, 23, 25, 27, 28, 41, 71, 114, 242
Greenwood, Arthur, 46, 152, 157, 161–2, 173, 175–7, 182, 211, 215, 217–21, 242, 244
Grey, Sir Edward, 97–8, 148
groupthink, theory of, 17, 240, 245–6, 289n119
guarantees, to Greece, Roumania and Turkey, 71; to Poland, 13, 18–47, 48–50, 56, 71, 85–90, 94–5, 97, 101–2, 144, 234
Guderian, General Heinz, 149

Haldane, Viscount, 148
Halifax, Viscount: and Committee on War Aims, 190–223, 256–7; becomes Ambassador in Washington, 213–15, 239–40; breaches Cabinet decision, 115, 129; converted to Soviet alliance, 61, 67–8; drafts reply to Hitler, October 1939, 117–20; feelings about Churchill, 160, 162–3, 212–14, 227, 239; offer of premiership to, May 1940, 11, 229; personality and beliefs, 119, 141, 160, 199, 204, 244; prefers long-term planning, 123, 135; relationship with Chamberlain, 134–5; see also foreign policy executive
Hankey, Sir Maurice (later Lord), 82, 101, 106, 123, 135–8, 142, 144, 223, 247
Harvey, Oliver, 21, 22, 35, 41, 51, 102, 109, 112
Henderson, Sir Nevile, 19
Hendricks, C., 50
Hinsley, F. H., 103
history, academic subject of, 4–6, 9, 17, 247, 266n35
Hitler, Adolf, 91, 98, 100, 108, 110, 127, 140, 168, 192, 208, 222; attack on Czechoslovakia, 15 March 1935, 19; attack on Poland, 1 September 1939, 85–6; attitudes towards Britain, 107; British images of, 103, 109, 112, 116, 119, 162, 166, 169, 184, 256, 258–9; Chamberlain's reply to, October 1939, 252–5; denounces Anglo-German naval agreement, 237; possible elimination of, 88, 109, 116; Reichstag speech 6 October 1939, 102–4, 111, 114; Reichstag speech 19 July 1940, 158, 186, 189; see also Germany; 'peace offensive' by Germany
Hoare, Sir Samuel, 39–40, 42–4, 50, 52, 53–4, 56, 62–7, 79, 81–2, 93–4, 101–2, 112, 117, 121, 123, 125–6, 129–31, 136–8, 143, 167, 229, 241; special knowledge of Russia, 137, 275n85
Home Policy Committee (of the War Cabinet), 129–30
Hopkins, Harry, 210–11, 235
Hore-Belisha, Leslie, 20, 25–6, 37, 50, 60, 61, 65, 92–3, 105 (note to Table 3), 123, 130, 136, 138, 228, 239, 242
Howe, Sir Geoffrey, 243
Howorth, Sir Rupert, 82
Hudson, Robert S., 49
Hull, Cordell, 260
Hungary, 20
Huxley, Professor Julian, 196, 204

India, 113, 163, 202, 254

Index 357

Information, Ministry of, 115–16, 117, 129, 134, 192–4, 199, 218, 240
Inskip, Sir Thomas (Viscount Caldecote), 25, 40, 42, 54, 55, 65–7, 81, 94, 128, 239
intelligence, British, 9, 19; and warnings of attack on Czechoslovakia, 269n8
interdependence, concept of, 328n77
inter-disciplinary work in social science, 1–5
international relations, academic subject of, 3–4, 6
Ironside, General Sir Edmund, 150–1
Italy, 28, 35, 38, 58, 60, 113, 175, 178–9; and fall of France, 156–9, 161; *see also* Mussolini, Benito

Janis, Irving, 4
Japan, 55, 60, 65, 67, 87, 202, 261
Johnstone, Harcourt, 197, 206–7, 214, 128
Jowitt, Sir William, 215

Kennedy, Joseph, 22, 179
Keynes, John Maynard, 190, 222–3
King, Cecil, 211
Kirkpatrick, Ivone, 118, 140, 191

Labour movement, British, 38, 168, 242, 275n80
Labour Party, 199–200, 208, 210, 215, 218, 220-1, 223, 229, 232, 242, 273n55
Lansbury, George, 305n103
League of Nations Union, 191
Lebow, Richard Ned, 4
Lee, J. M., 10
Leeper, Rex, 192
Liberal Party, 105
Liddell-Hart, Captain Basil, 37
Lindemann, Professor F. A. (Viscount Cherwell), 223
Litvinov, Maxim, 30, 60, 64; proposals of 17 April 1939, 51–3, 56, 78, 233
Lloyd, Lord, 172
Lloyd George, David, 113, 115, 213, 240
Londonderry, 7th Marquess of, 137
Lothian, 11th Marquess of, 167, 186, 191–2, 213, 240
Lytton, Lord, 191

Macdonald, Malcolm, 24, 54–5, 61, 62–3, 64–5, 81, 92, 94, 242

McDougall, Frank, 204
Macmillan, Lord, 106
Maisky, Ivan, 30, 33–4, 37, 50–1
Malkin, Sir William, 35, 75
Malta, 175
Manchester Guardian, 212
Manchurian affair, 226
Mander, Geoffrey, 211
Mason-MacFarlane, Colonel F. N., 45
Maugham, Lord, 26, 93, 106
May, Ernest, 4, 9
Mein Kampf, 258–9; *see also* Hitler, Adolf
Memel, German absorption of, 45
Menzies, Sir Robert, 126
military, the British, 9, 149–52, 181, 184, 270n24; *see also* Chiefs of Staff; Royal Air Force; Royal Navy
Minney, R. J., 50
Molotov, Vyacheslav, 60, 64
Monson, Sir Edmund, 110
morale, *see* Britain, morale in war-time
Morley, John, 93
Morrison, Herbert, 172
Morrison, W. S., 25, 26, 40, 54, 59, 65, 67, 73, 79, 81–2, 92, 106, 130, 241
Mussolini, Benito, 102, 104, 157–9, 161–3, 169, 176, 179, 225; offers mediation, 85, 252

Nation (New York publication), 211
Nazi-Soviet Pact, 86–7, 101, 114; *see also* Soviet Union, possible German alliance with
Netherlands, 252
'neutrals', concern for, 113, 115, 121, 125–6, 135, 166, 190, 193
Newall, Air Chief Marshall Sir Cyril, 150
Newman, Simon, 45
Nicolson, Harold, 102, 204, 211

officials, role of in policy-making, 15, 106, 110, 193, 247; *see also* Bridges, Sir Edward; Cabinet Office; Cadogan, Sir Alexander; Economic Warfare, Ministry of; Foreign Office; Information, Ministry of; Treasury; Wilson, Sir Horace
Ogilvie-Forbes, Sir George, 89, 140
Operation Sealion (German plan for the invasion of Britain), 182

Papacy, offer of mediation by, 185
Papen, Franz van, 111–12, 114

358 Index

Parliament, British, 180, 186, 201, 207, 210–12, 215; House of Commons, 24, 46, 69, 89–92, 112, 115, 117, 126, 129, 216, 244; House of Lords, 106, 244, 249 (note to Appendix 1)
peace aims, 189; *see also* war aims, British
'peace offensive', by Germany, 100–45, 179, 191, 193; *see also* Germany; Hitler, Adolf
peace offers, *see* Germany, possible peace offer from
Peden, George, 9
Phelan, Mr, 204
Phipps, Sir Eric, 56
Phoney War ('sitzkrieg'), 103, 127, 189, 229
Poland, 23, 25–7, 29, 31–3, 35, 58–9, 64, 85–99, 101–2, 104, 109, 114, 116, 252–3; future of, after defeat, 120, 125, 209–10; *see also* Danzig, Polish-German dispute over; guarantees, to Poland
Polish Guarantee, *see* guarantees, to Poland
policy-making, 208, 215, 232–8, 240, 244–7; delays in, 143–4; formulation phase, 63, 77, 144–5, 165, 173, 179–80; implementation phase, 88, 92, 101, 113, 114, 115, 127, 201; policy drift, 58, 280n6; slippage, 129, 151–2, 166; *see also* crisis; decision-making, theories of; foreign policy executive; rationality, as applied to the policy-making process
political science, 2–3, 9–10, 16, 237, 247
Portugal, 38, 60
press, the, 9, 115, 189; see also *Daily Mirror*; *Manchester Guardian*; *Sunday Express*; *Times, The*
pressure-groups, 191, 200
Prime Minister, powers of, 28, 171, 173, 183, 215, 225, 245
propaganda, British, 129, 190, 192–5, 201–2
Prytz, Björn (and the 'Prytz affair'), 186, 212, 218, 238–9
public opinion, images of: in Britain, 93, 108, 115, 116–17, 121, 124, 127, 129, 143, 171, 193, 196, 199, 203, 211–13, 220, 223, 295n2; in Europe, 60, 117, 199; in Germany, 115, 142; in the United States, 199; world opinion, 142, 204

Public Record Office, archives of, 5, 321n119
Pym, Francis, 243

Raczynski, Count Edward, 32–3
rationality, as applied to the policy-making process, 57, 77, 236, 246
reconstruction, 191, 199, 215–23
Reconstruction Committee, *see* Committee on Reconstruction
Reconstruction Problems Committee, *see* Committee on Reconstruction Problems
Reith, Sir John, 197
Reynaud, Paul, 149–51, 163, 168, 176–7, 181, 183
Ronald, Nigel, 193
Roosevelt, Franklin Delano, 147–9, 167–8, 192, 202, 210–11, 225, 235–6, 259
Roumania, 20, 21, 24–5, 27, 31–2, 35, 38–9, 41–2, 44–5, 58–9, 64, 114
Royal Air Force, 181
Royal Institute of International Affairs (Chatham House), 200, 206; Foreign Research and Press Service of, 221
Royal Navy, 201
Runciman, Lord, 50, 73, 79, 81, 94, 106, 137, 250
Russia, *see* Soviet Union

Sandys, Duncan, 138
Sargent, Sir Orme, 20, 35, 192, 196
Scandinavia, military crisis over, 229
Second World War, 6–7, 8 and *passim*
Seeds, Sir William, 64
Simon, Sir John, 24, 27, 29, 39, 40, 42, 54, 65, 67, 79, 81, 88, 92–6, 117, 121–2, 136–8, 144, 229, 241–2
Sinclair, Sir Archibald, 161, 175–7, 196
Singapore, 87, 240
Smuts, General Jan, 167
sources, scholarly, 15, 16, 28, 321n119
South Africa, 55; *see also* Dominions
Soviet Union, 26, 27, 29, 31, 32–3, 35, 37–44, 46, 111, 121, 142, 233–4, 253; attack on Poland, 101–2, 104; possible British alliance with, 24, 46, 48–84, 87; possible German alliance with, 55, 58–9, 60–1, 66, 84; *see also* Litvinov, Maxim; Nazi-Soviet Pact
Spain, 38, 64–5, 67, 87
Stanhope, 7th Earl, 25, 65, 67, 127

Stanley, Oliver, 20, 25, 27, 29, 40, 42, 44, 50, 52, 54, 62–7, 79, 81, 92, 94, 105–6, 130, 225, 229
Strang William, 35
Sunday Express, 138
Sweden, King of, 212

Temple, Archbishop William, 204
Territorial Army, decision to increase size of, 45
Tientsin incident, 71
Tilea, Virgil, 20–2
Times, The, 110, 131, 222
Topham, A. M. R., 203 (Table 8, n1)
Toynbee, Arnold, 200, 203–5, 207–8, 214, 220
Treasury, 9, 222, 245
Turkey, 20, 23, 25, 27, 28, 41, 60, 71

United States of America, 9, 113, 121, 147–9, 154, 167–8, 183–4, 190, 192, 205, 212–14, 225, 252, 259–61; Congress of, 168–9; *see also* public opinion, images of, in the United States
USSR, *see* Soviet Union

Vansittart, Sir Robert, 11, 19, 35, 118, 225
Vatican, the, 113, 252
Venlo incident, 139, 296n13
Versailles, Treaty of, 114
voluntarism, theories of, 10

Wallace, Captain Euan, 92, 97–8, 122
Wallace, William, 3
war aims, British, 13, 72, 87, 101–2, 104, 108–10, 114, 129, 156, 170, 187–223, 253–5, 258–62; and Christianity, 204–5, 207, 211, 256–7, 259, 262; linkage between domestic and foreign, 202–3, 208–9, 216–17, 259–60; question of statement on, 120–1, 126, 209–11, 214–16; towards Germany, 121–3, 254; *see also* peace aims; reconstruction; Committee on War Aims
war aims, French, 104
War Aims Committee, *see* Committee on War Aims
War Cabinet, 104–7, 160, 242; attendance at, 130–3, 148 (Table 6); frequency of meetings, 106, 146; internal dynamics, 136–44; party issues, 201; relations with full Cabinet, 105–6, 115, 128–33, 148 (Table 6), 172–3, 223, 228–9; *see also* Committee on War Aims
Wark, Wesley, 9
Weygand, General Maxime, 151
Whitehead, T. North, 193
Williams, Phil, 4
Williamson, Samuel, 9
Wilson, Sir Horace, 82, 119, 121, 126
Winterton, 6th Earl, 82, 239
Wood, Sir Kingsley, 26, 65, 92–3, 112, 117, 123, 138, 197, 203, 206, 218
Woodward, Llewellyn, 192
Woolf, Leonard, 204
world opinion, *see* public opinion

Yugoslavia, 25, 27, 38

Zetland, Marquess of, 25, 28, 60, 65, 79, 84, 130

LSE MONOGRAPHS IN INTERNATIONAL STUDIES

Titles out of print

KIN WAH CHIN
The defence of Malaysia and Singapore
The transformation of a security system 1957–1971
RICHARD TAYLOR
The politics of the Soviet cinema 1917–1929
ANN TROTTER
Britain and East Asia 1933–1937
J. H. KALICKI
The pattern of Sino-American crises
Political military interactions in the 1950s
ARYEH L. UNGER
The totalitarian party
Party and people in Nazi Germany
ALABA OGUNSANWO
China's policy in Africa 1958–1971
MARTIN L. VAN CREVELD
Hitler's strategy 1940–1941
The Balkan clue
EUGEN STEINER
The Slovak dilemma
LUCJAN BLIT
The origins of Polish socialism
The history and ideas of the first Polish socialist party 1878–1886